Richenda Miers

SCOTLAND'S
HIGHLANDS & ISLANDS

'Golden eagles gliding over bleak moorland...
stark mountains streaked with snow-filled
corries, dramatic against incandescent
skies... an island-fringed west coast,
bordered by shell-sand beaches and sheer
cliffs eroded into stacks and arches.'

D0094220

CADOGANguides

1 The lighthouse at Ardnamurchan Point, the
most westerly point on Britain's mainland
2 Autumnal leaves on a Highland hillside

3 Waterfalls amid the classic post-glacial
  scenery of Glencoe
4 Highland deer grazing in the wild

5 Standing stones on Machrie Moor, part of
a spectacular concentration of prehistoric
monuments on Arran

6 Urquhart Castle, the Loch Ness stronghold
captured by Robert I in 1308

7 Exposed to the elements: a ruined church on Skye
8 High Victoriana at Inverness: the iron suspension
  footbridge over the Ness
9 Colour-washed houses along the shore at Tobermory, Mull

Dogs on Leads Please
Sheep/Cattle on Hill

8

9

10 Mountains plunging to the sea along the
   coast of Skye

11 Loch Ness, one of three lochs in the Great
Glen, a rift valley across the Highlands

12 Scots pines in silhouette by the Firth of Tay

About the author

Richenda Miers is a novelist, freelance journalist and travel writer. Directly and legitimately descended from Mary Queen of Scots, she lives on the Black Isle with her husband who served in a highland regiment. Of her four children, one was born in Inverness, two went to school in Aberdeen, two went to Scottish universities and two own houses in Scotland.

About the updater

James Alexander has worked on a range of guidebooks for Cadogan, as both contributor and editor. He is also author of Cadogan's upcoming guide to Malaysia, Brunei & Singapore. When not on the move, he lives with his wife and two young children in Hastings.

Contents

Cadogan Guides
2nd Floor, 233 High Holborn,
London WC1V 7DN
info@cadoganguides.co.uk
www.cadoganguides.com

The Globe Pequot Press
246 Goose Lane, PO Box 480, Guilford,
Connecticut 06437–0480

Cover photographs: © Arch White / Alamy,
© John Morgan / Alamy
Photo essay: © OLIVIA
Maps drawn by Maidenhead Cartographic
Services Ltd. Based on Ordnance Survey
material and reproduced by permission of
Ordnance Survey on behalf of HMSO
© Crown copyright 2006. All rights
reserved. Licence number 100037865

Art director: Sarah Gardner
Managing Editor: Natalie Pomier
Editor: Tim Locke
Editorial Assistant: Nicola Jessop
Proofreader: Elspeth Anderson
Indexing: Isobel McLean

Printed in Italy by Legoprint
A catalogue record for this book is available
from the British Library
ISBN 10: 1-86011-340-0
ISBN 13: 978-1-86011-340-6

The author and publishers have made every
effort to ensure the accuracy of the
information in this book at the time of
going to press. However, they cannot
accept any responsibility for any loss, injury
or inconvenience resulting from the use of
information contained in this guide.

Please help us to keep this guide up to date.
We have done our best to ensure that the
information in this guide is correct at the
time of going to press. But places and
facilities are constantly changing, and
standards and prices in hotels and restaurants fluctuate. We would be delighted to
receive any comments concerning existing
entries or omissions. Authors of the best
letters will receive a copy of the Cadogan
Guide of their choice.

Introduction

01

*To the southern inhabitants of Scotland, the state of the mountains and the islands
is equally known with that of Borneo and Sumatra: of both they have only heard
a little, and guess the rest.*
    Dr Samuel Johnson, 1773

The further you go from the main hubs of activity, the more you discover the
Highlands proper: golden eagles gliding over bleak moorland inhabited mostly by
sheep; stark mountains streaked with snow-filled corries, dramatic against
incandescent skies; turbulent rivers and waterfalls swirling through steep-sided
glens to feed peat-dark, trout-filled lochs; an island-fringed west coast, bordered by
shell-sand beaches and sheer cliffs eroded into stacks and arches, undermined by
caves, where the raucous cries of sea birds blend with the boom of thunderous waves.

The enigma of the 'Highland Line' is explained by a geological fault running
diagonally and curvaceously across Scotland from around Helensburgh, on the Clyde
estuary, to the Moray Firth, near Nairn. In this book, the Highlands lie west and north
of this line, a capricious division that excludes mountainous Grampian but includes
flat Caithness and all the islands.

Tourism is one of the main industries in the Highlands today, and is expanding fast.
Around the chief tourist centres there are myriad attractions catering for almost
every taste: historic buildings, museums, leisure and craft centres, gardens, nature
reserves, theme parks and much else.

A superficial grasp of the history of the Highlands and Islands, a place often
darkened by violence, tragedy and treachery, and illuminated by heroism and
romance, greatly enhances appreciation of this mystical land. The gaunt ruin of a
once-mighty fortress, blown up by government soldiers, peopled by the ghosts of
persecuted Jacobites, holds far more fascination than mere remains on a lonely
hillside; a scattering of tumbled stones in a remote glen makes little impact unless
one knows that a thriving community lived here until it was evicted to make way for
thousands of lucrative sheep. This book tries to bridge some of these gaps.

Until relatively recently, the Highlands and Islands were so isolated that few
outsiders ventured into them. Hostile mountain ranges and numerous lochs, rivers
and bogs made intercommunication arduous, and it was not until after the first
Jacobite rising in 1715 that travel became easier.

General Wade, Commander in Chief of North Britain in 1724, built 240 miles of
military roads and 40 bridges in the Highlands, to try to control rebellious Highlanders,
allowing travellers such as Johnson and Boswell to explore this untapped source of
purple prose. These formed the nucleus from which today's network of roads evolved.
Main roads are excellent now, though not always dual carriageway, and it is sometimes
necessary to drive many extra miles to circumnavigate lochs and mountains when
the linear distance is a mere stone's throw. The loveliest areas are often
unapproachable except along single-track roads, on foot or by boat. This inaccessibility
has helped to preserve rare species of land birds, flora and fauna in some of the last
wildernesses in Europe, and to harbour vast colonies of sea birds, unknown on more
populous coasts. Of the 790 islands that fringe the northern and western shores, only
about 130 are inhabited – and not all of these are served by public transport.

Chapter Divisions

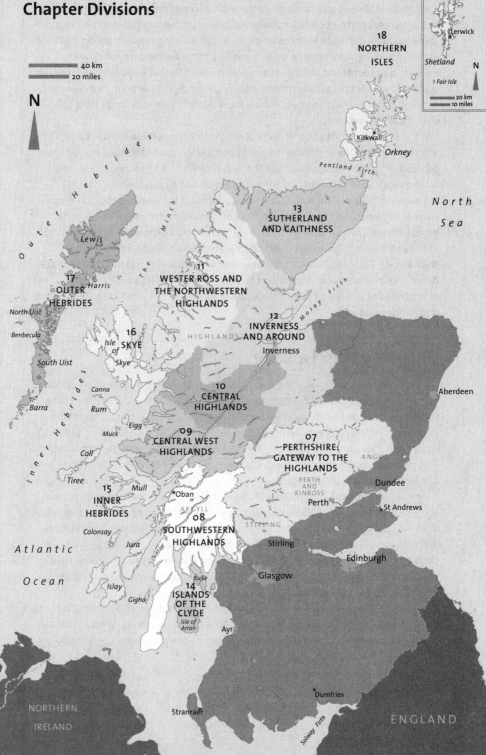

40 km
20 miles

N

18 NORTHERN ISLES

Foula

•Lerwick

Shetland

N

◦ Fair Isle

20 km
10 miles

Outer   Hebrides

•Kirkwall

Orkney

Pentland Firth

North

Sea

Lewis

13 SUTHERLAND AND CAITHNESS

The Minch

11 WESTER ROSS AND THE NORTHWESTERN HIGHLANDS

17 OUTER HEBRIDES *Harris*

North Uist

Benbecula

South Uist

Moray Firth

16 SKYE

Isle of Skye

HIGHLANDS

12 INVERNESS AND AROUND

Inverness

Inner   Hebrides

Canna

Rum

10 CENTRAL HIGHLANDS

Aberdeen

Barra

Eigg

Muck

09 CENTRAL WEST HIGHLANDS

07 PERTHSHIRE: GATEWAY TO THE HIGHLANDS

ANGU

Coll

PERTH AND KINROSS

Tiree

Mull

Dundee

15 INNER HEBRIDES

•Oban

Perth

•St Andrews

ARGYLL

STIRLING

08 SOUTHWESTERN HIGHLANDS

Colonsay

Stirling

Atlantic

Jura

Bute

Glasgow

Edinburgh

Ocean

Islay

Gigha

14 ISLANDS OF THE CLYDE

Isle of Arran

Ayr

•Dumfries

NORTHERN

Stranraer

Solway Firth

ENGLAND

IRELAND

Agriculture, fishing and tourism are the main occupations of today's Highlanders. In the remoter parts, not much has altered in the last century. Television brought some changes, particularly to community life, but a strong sense of national pride remains, and Highland hospitality is unrivalled. There are modern hotels with en-suite bathrooms and thick pile carpets, but round the back you may find a dozen discarded vehicles peacefully rusting away; and the detritus of crumpled beer cans, tattered polythene and empty bottles is more likely to be left by locals than by ecologically aware tourists.

In the western Highlands, and particularly in the Islands, there are still bards and storytellers who sing and recite the songs and folklore that have been passed down by word of mouth over generations. The best fiddlers and pipers have their roots in areas that were untouched by the Reformation and by the Calvinists' stern suppression of gaiety. Highland Games are popular in the summer, those in remoter parts being less showy and more spontaneous than smarter gatherings around Royal Deeside. The games originated in early times, when competitions for strength, speed and dexterity gave clan chiefs an opportunity to talent-spot men fit for their armies. Such dangerous encouragement of martial arts was quashed with the Act of Proscription, but was revived in its present form when Sir Walter Scott masterminded a romantic tartan renaissance, keenly perpetuated by Queen Victoria and her descendants.

Choosing Your Holiday

Except for guaranteed sunshine, holiday-makers can find every type of attraction in the Highlands and Islands. International climbers train in the Cuillins; the skiing can be excellent, although you have to be tough; hill-walkers are spoilt for choice; windsurfers flock to Tiree; fishermen cross the world for Scottish salmon and trout; sailors and divers find endless scope off the west coast; naturalists and ornithologists find many species of rare bird, insect and plant in the blanket bog of the Flow Country and in other remote parts of the country.

Local ingredients enhance gourmet food, and distilleries look after the inner man. An enthusiastic revival of Gaelic culture is manifest in public ceilidhs, but even better, if you are lucky, you can sit in a croft-house kitchen, pungent with acrid peat smoke, and listen to Gaelic songs and stories from the past. In the north, in the right conditions, you can witness that elusive stunt, the *Aurora Borealis* (Northern Lights), when shafts of coloured lights, mostly green and red, flash across the sky like an unearthly pageant of searchlights.

Let yourself be guided by the philosophy of the Highlander: *ùine gu lèoir* is Gaelic for 'time enough', and *uisge beatha*, 'water of life', has given us 'whisky'. With all that the Highlands and Islands have to offer, what more could anyone want?

History

02

From the Ice Age to Christianity

The Ice Age eradicated evidence of any previous habitation in Scotland. **Stone Age** settlers, at least 7,000 years ago, were the first to leave clues to their existence. Burial sites and middens (rubbish heaps) from those times have thrown up enough to tantalize archaeologists, but not enough to leave more than a shadow of their identity. They came from Asia and Europe, through England and Ireland, wave after wave of them, creeping up the coast in dug-out canoes, settling for long enough to leave traces of their culture and way of life, before vanishing into obscurity. They lived off deer and wild boar, fish and crustaceans. Some only stayed a short time, living in caves. An excavated house in Grampian, a round stone building about 25ft (8m) across, dates from 7000 BC. Later, farmers came from the Continent and introduced agriculture. People settled for longer periods, burning forests and enriching the land with potash.

After the hunters and gatherers came the **Beaker People**, who laid beakers in the tombs of their dead. They were skilful engineers, and historians puzzle over their mysterious stone circles and monoliths, and over the true purpose of their **brochs** (massive stone towers built near the sea in the far north, about 2,000 years ago). Metal was introduced about 1,000 years before Christ, and with it the sword and shield. Scotland, on the trade route between Ireland and Scandinavia, was able to barter food and hides for bronze and copper. During this millennium the Celtic-speaking Britons arrived, a sturdy, fair-haired race, combative and quick to attack in order to acquire precious land. The local people built defensive forts, with ditches and ramparts, such as on Barry Hill and Finavon, and skirmishing became part of life.

The **Romans** arrived in AD 82 and with them came the first record of Scottish history, written by the historian Tacitus. Tacitus describes how his father-in-law, Agricola, defeated an army of tall, red-haired men on an unidentified hillside in the northeast, in the Battle of Mons Graupius. The exact location of this battle is debatable, but it was somewhere in today's Grampian, so called from a misprint of 'Graupius' by a 16th-century chronicler. Roman remains were found as far north as the Moray Firth and Tacitus recorded that they 'discovered and subdued' Orkney.

The Romans called their victims *picti*, the painted ones, from which the name **Picts** is thought to derive, and failed to subdue them. Highly trained legionnaires could not compete with hostile tribes who faded into the mountains, forests and marshes, refusing to fight army-to-army, preferring to lay cunning ambushes for their aggressors. The Romans fell back having, it has long been believed, lost the entire Ninth Legion in a savage massacre. In fact, evidence of their having been merely posted elsewhere was unearthed recently when traces of their later existence were found around the Danube.

Four races dominated Scotland, then called Alba or Alban, in the years after the Romans withdrew. The Celtic Picts were the most powerful, occupying the land from Caithness to the Forth; the Teutonic Angles, or Anglo-Saxons, occupied Bernicia, south of the Forth; the Britons, another Celtic race, occupied the western lands south of the Clyde. Finally there were the **Scots**: Celts who had come over from Ireland during the

3rd and 4th centuries and settled north of the Clyde, establishing the Kingdom of Dalriada and eventually giving their name to all Scotland.

St Ninian founded the first Christian centre at Whithorn, near the Solway Firth, in 397, and started the daunting task of converting the pagans. Then came **Columba**, a clever man of royal birth, who was exiled from Ireland and arrived in Scotland in 563. He established himself on the island of Iona, continuing St Ninian's work, and sent missionaries to the mainland and to the other islands. They penetrated further and further into Pictland. Columba's influence was political as well as religious and he did much to consolidate the strength of the Scots. By the end of the 7th century, the four kingdoms of Alban were nominally converted to a Celtic Christianity, not yet in line with that dictated by Rome.

The Birth of Scotland

At the end of the 8th century, Norsemen began to attack from the north, conquering Orkney and Shetland, the Western Isles, Caithness and Sutherland, while the four kingdoms continued to fight amongst themselves, weakening their resistance to outside attack.

In 843 **Kenneth Macalpine**, King of the Scots, achieved some sort of union between Scots and Picts, making himself king over all the territory north of the Forth and Clyde, which then became Scotia. The Picts, who had been dominant for more than 1,000 years, vanished forever. They remain an enigmatic people whose history is unrecorded and unknown; an elusive ghost-race who will perhaps never be fully understood. It was not until 1018, however, that **Malcolm II** defeated the Angles and brought Bernicia, or Lothian, into the kingdom. He was succeeded in 1034 by his grandson **Duncan I** who already ruled the Britons, and so the four kingdoms were finally united into one Scotland, except for those parts occupied by the Norsemen. The country was divided into seven main kingdoms, of which Fife was the strongest, plus a few smaller ones, each ruled by a *mormaer*. The *Ard Righ* or High King was their overlord – King of the Scots, but not of Scotland, for each *mormaer* owned his land. In those days, under a remarkable clan system in which no one was subservient and each played an important part, Scotland was truly democratic. Duncan I was killed in 1040 by **Macbeth**, whose portrayal by Shakespeare should not be taken too literally. He was the last Celtic king and his 17-year reign was chronicled as a time of plenty. He was killed by Duncan's son, **Malcolm Canmore**, with the help of the English, in 1057. *Ceann Mor* is Gaelic for 'big head', referring to Malcolm III's status rather than any anatomical defect or conceit.

Malcolm Canmore's second wife, **Margaret**, was a refugee from the Norman conquest of England. She imported English clergy and established an English court, transforming Scotland into a kingdom similar to Norman England. The Lowland clans gave up their democracy: *mormaers* became earls and established a feudal system, while the Highlands and Islands retained the old, patriarchal clans. **David I**, ninth son of Malcolm Canmore, inherited the throne in 1124. He had been brought up in England and gave away large Scottish estates to his Anglo-Norman friends. The Highlanders took little notice of these southern interlopers.

The Stone of Destiny

Traditionally, the **Stone of Destiny** was the pillow on which Jacob laid his head when he dreamt about the ladder of angels reaching from earth to heaven. Its subsequent history is shadowy. It floated round the world carrying mystical powers of sovereignty until it arrived in Ireland, whence it was brought to Dunadd by early missionaries and used as a throne in the coronation of Scottish kings.

In those days *mormaers* owned their kingdoms and the High King was their overlord, King of the Scots but not of Scotland. At the coronation each *mormaer* filled a shoe with earth from his kingdom and poured a little into a footprint carved into a rock. The king sat on the Stone of Destiny and put his foot over this cocktail of Scottish soil.

From here the Stone was moved to Dunstaffnage. In the 9th century Kenneth Macalpine took it to Scone where it continued to be a coronation throne for the united Scots and Picts. Edward I, believing firmly in its mystical powers, pinched what he thought to be the Stone of Destiny during one of his ravages of the north and whisked it off to become part of the Coronation Chair in Westminster Abbey. There it remained, apart from a brief hiatus in 1950 when some daring students from Glasgow University kidnapped it on Christmas morning. They carted it north, dodging roadblocks and border patrols (via a pub in Glasgow where they placed it on the bar while having a quick pint), and hid it for a couple

Malcolm IV was 13 when he inherited the throne from his grandfather, David I. Known as Malcolm the Maiden, he was nevertheless a brave young man, whose courage inspired many of his followers. Gentle and religious, he ruled for only 12 years before he died, to be succeeded by his brother, **William the Lion**, who launched an ill-conceived expedition into Northumberland in 1174. It failed, William was captured, and he was forced to sign the humiliating Treaty of Falaise, placing Scotland under feudal subjection to England.

Alexander II succeeded to the throne in 1214 and directed his attention to the Western Isles, whose lords gave their allegiance to Norway. It was his son, **Alexander III**, however, who managed to expel the Norsemen from the Hebrides by defeating old King Haakon IV of Norway in the **Battle of Largs** in 1263. The Hebrides became part of the Kingdom of Scotland again, though the Lords of the Isles continued to pay little heed to any authority but their own.

When **Edward I** of England declared himself to be overlord of Scotland, there were several claimants to the throne, the strongest being **John Balliol**, son of the regent, and **Robert the Bruce**. Edward insisted that Scotland should contribute to English defence costs and join with them in an invasion of France. Rather than do this, the Scots instead formed an alliance with France in October 1295. The **Auld Alliance**, as it became known, was between two independent kingdoms, rather than being forced by a stronger state on a weaker one, as England had sought to do to Scotland. Edward saw it as practically a declaration of war. In 1296 Edward's army progressed through Scotland, compelling nobles and lairds to sign the **Ragman Roll** acknowledging him as of weeks in Arbroath Abbey. In 1996, thanks to John Major, the then Prime Minister who had the vision to see a way to appease Scottish antagonism towards their 'oppressors' in Westminster, the Stone was ceremoniously returned and installed in Edinburgh Castle.

However, as is well known, the Scots were far too canny to allow King Edward to walk off with one of their most sacred possessions. The stolen stone was almost certainly substituted for the real, intricately carved Stone of Destiny, which is safely hidden in a secret cavern, possibly on the Isle of Iona. It will be brought out by its hereditary guardians when the time is right, its whereabouts having been passed down orally from father to son over the centuries.

O Flower of Scotland when will we see your like again
That fought and died for your wee bit hill and glen
And stood against him proud Edward's army
And sent him homeward tae think again.

The hills are bare now and autumn leaves lie thick and still
O'er land that is lost now which those so dearly held.
Those days are past now and in the past they must remain
But we can still rise now and be the nation again.
                         – Flower of Scotland by The Corries

their king. He then returned to England, taking with him what he thought to be the Stone of Destiny, brought from Ireland seven centuries earlier and believed to embody special powers of sovereignty. It had always been used in the coronation of Scottish kings (*see* box above). Edward was convinced he had finally conquered Scotland.

Robert the Bruce, grandson of John Balliol's rival, became Guardian of Scotland, alongside Balliol's nephew, Red John Comyn. Bruce resigned the guardianship in 1302 and went over to Edward's side. In 1306 Bruce and Comyn met at Greyfriars Kirk, in Dumfries, but they quarrelled and Bruce killed Comyn, possibly because of his refusal to help Bruce in a campaign for the Scottish throne. Seizing the initiative, Bruce went to Scone and had himself crowned King of Scotland in March 1306, but Edward hurried north and defeated Bruce a month later at Methven. Outlawed, his friends and allies dead, Bruce went into hiding but, like a persistent spider, he returned to reclaim his crown in 1307. He overcame all other claimants to the throne and defeated Edward I's successor, **Edward II**, at **Bannockburn** in 1314.

Bruce was succeeded by his young son, **David II**, with **Thomas Randolph, Earl of Moray**, as regent. The 42 years of David's reign were troubled times for Scotland. He was captured by the English at the **Battle of Neville's Cross** in 1346 and spent the next 11 years in England as a captive. Following his ransom and release in 1357, David was offered easier terms for the ransom's repayment if he would name Edward III or one of his sons as his successor. Not surprisingly, the Scottish Parliament rejected this notion. David reigned until his death in 1371, to be succeeded by his nephew and steward, Robert.

The Stewarts

The Stewarts were a family of incoming Normans named FitzAlan who became hereditary High Stewards to the kings of Scotland, and changed their name accordingly. **Robert**, the first Stewart king, was a better regent than monarch. Anarchy, rebellion and internal squabbles disturbed the peace he strove for. **Robert II** died in 1390 and was succeeded by his son, **Robert III**. Crippled by a kick from a horse, Robert was in poor health and much of the responsibility of government passed to his brother, the Duke of Albany. The ailing Robert III sent his son and heir, **James I**, to France in 1406, fearing Albany had plans to remove him from the succession, but the young prince was captured by pirates and handed over to the English. Robert died a month later, leaving Albany in full power for 18 years while James was held hostage. Powerful nobles seized the opportunity to consolidate their strength. They expanded their estates and built up private armies, many of them becoming as powerful as kings. Most notable among them was the **Douglas** family, whose lands and subjects rivalled those of the king. Meanwhile, in the northwest, the Lords of the Isles allied themselves with the English and continued to live their own lives with little regard for central government.

James I returned to his throne in 1424, aged 29, to find his country in turmoil. His first step was the execution of the Albany family in 1425 and the seizure of their considerable estates. In 1427 he summoned the Highland chiefs and arrested 40; Alexander of the Isles retaliated by burning Inverness. Further rebellion from the west was subdued and James redressed the balance of power in the Lowlands by annexing many of the earldoms that threatened his supremacy. His policies earned him many enemies, and in 1437 three of them stabbed him to death, leaving his six-year-old son **James II** as his heir. James II came to the throne in 1449 at the age of 19. He continued the reforms so dear to his father, but was threatened by an alliance between the Douglases, Crawfords and John of the Isles. James was killed in 1460 when a cannon exploded during the siege of Roxburghe.

James III was nine when his father died and, until his accession at the age of 19, Scotland was once more ruled by regents. He married the King of Norway's daughter, whose dowry included Orkney and Shetland. James was an intellectual, better fitted for academic life than a crown. He survived one attempt to dethrone him, but six years later his son led a successful coup against him, becoming James IV in his place. James III was killed in mysterious circumstances at the decisive Battle of Sauchieburn, a parliamentary inquiry recording simply that the King 'happinit to be slane'.

James IV, most popular of the Stewart kings, was 15 when he came to the throne. He was clever and charming, a good leader, pious and energetic, generous, flamboyant and sensual. The arts and education blossomed and James led the way. He authorized the building of palaces and churches. His court was elegant and cultured and the country was peaceful and prosperous. But the peace was not absolute: on the doorstep the Lords of the Isles continued to live as they always had: fiercely patriarchal, their loyalties rooted in their clans and chieftains. James, who had learnt Gaelic, decided to visit the Western Highlands and Islands, hoping to win the friendship of the clans. His attempts were viewed with suspicion, so he desisted and appointed overlords to rule them. This resulted in an uprising of the Macdonalds and Macleans, who stormed and burned Inverness in 1503.

In that same year, James married 12-year-old Margaret Tudor and signed a Treaty of Perpetual Peace with England, but in 1511 his brother-in-law, Henry VIII of England, joined the Pope, the King of Spain and the Doge of Venice in a Holy League against France. James passionately desired a united Europe and, determined to maintain a balance of power, renewed the Auld Alliance with France and tried, in vain, to mediate. In 1513, threatened from all directions, France appealed to Scotland for help. James in turn appealed to Henry, who replied with insults.

Against advice, in August 1513, James led a Scottish army across the Tweed, to **Flodden Field**, where they were massacred by the superior forces of the English. The king, his nobles and most of Scotland's best men were killed in a battle as pointless as it was valiant: it was perhaps Scotland's greatest tragedy. The country was left leaderless, its army slain, its new king, **James V**, a toddler and its regent, Margaret Tudor, with divided loyalties.

There followed a period of more turmoil until the king was old enough to take office and try to restore order. His second wife, **Marie de Guise-Lorraine**, bore him two sons, both of whom died, and a daughter, **Mary, Queen of Scots**, only a few days old when her father died after his army was defeated by Henry VIII at Solway Moss in 1542.

Henry VIII, determined to absorb Scotland, proposed a marriage between Mary and his delicate son, Edward, but the Scottish Parliament rejected such a proposal and renewed instead the Auld Alliance with France. Mary, aged five, was sent to France for safety, where she stayed for 15 years, marrying the French Dauphin. While she was away, Protestantism was gaining power in Scotland. In 1554 Marie de Guise-Lorraine, the dowager Queen Mother, replaced the Earl of Arran as Regent. The presence of many French officials in the Regent's government greatly upset the Scottish nobility. Several of them, calling themselves 'The Lords of the Congregation', declared their support for the Protestant religion. In 1559 **John Knox**, a powerful Reformer, delivered a fiery sermon in Perth, denouncing the Church of Rome.

Mary's French husband died at the end of 1560 and she returned to her country as queen in 1561 – no longer Mary Stewart, but Mary Stuart, the French form of her name which was adopted in England. A devout Catholic, she had no desire to tangle with the Protestants and merely wished to be allowed to practise her own religion in peace. This horrified John Knox and his followers, who found her light-hearted ways obnoxious. In 1567 an ill-advised marriage to the Earl of Bothwell sparked off an inferno of protest from both Catholics and Protestants. Mary was imprisoned and Bothwell forced into exile. Humiliated, Mary was forced to abdicate in favour of her baby son, **James VI**. Her half-brother, James Stewart, Earl of Moray, bastard son of James V, was proclaimed Regent. Mary fled to England and threw herself on the mercy of her cousin, Elizabeth I. Elizabeth, without an heir, could not forget Mary's claims to the English throne, and imprisoned her for 20 years before ordering her execution.

James VI proclaimed himself king in 1585 and found himself head of a country divided between Catholics and Protestants. He aspired to impartiality, incurring the animosity of both factions. A Protestant in name, if not belief, James had no wish to antagonize his Protestant cousin Elizabeth of England and spoil his chances of inheriting her throne. He concluded an alliance with England and made no more than a formal protest when Elizabeth agreed to the execution of his mother in 1587.

The Protestant religion in Scotland now presented problems. It was divided between the extreme Presbyterians, who wanted a religion of the purest simplicity with equality of ministers and no bishops or elaborate ritual, and James' English form of Protestantism, with bishops appointed by the Crown and a formal liturgy. He tried to impose his will on the Kirk, but failed. In 1603 Elizabeth I died, appointing James her heir. Thus he became James VI of Scotland and I of England. He hurried to London and only returned to Scotland once, preferring the magnificence of the English court, and the ritual of the Church of England. But he still tried to foist Episcopacy on his northern subjects and reinstate formal worship. He died in 1625 and his son, **Charles I**, succeeded him.

Charles had no love for the Kirk. When he went north for his Scottish coronation, his subjects were scandalized by the 'popish' practices he brought with him. Thousands flocked to Greyfriars Kirk in Edinburgh in February 1638 to sign the National Covenant, condemning all Catholic doctrines and upholding the 'True Religion'. The Covenant, however, was somewhat ambivalent: its signatories swore, not only to uphold the True Religion, but also to be loyal to a king who demanded the Episcopacy they shunned. Loyal subjects of the Crown thus found themselves torn between obedience to the king and obedience to their new religion.

When civil war broke out in England, the Covenanting Scots agreed to help the English Parliamentarians. In 1649 Charles I was defeated by Cromwell and executed. The Scots grasped this opportunity to advance their quest for stability and invited his exiled son, **Charles II**, to Scotland as king, on condition that he supported the Covenant. Furious, Cromwell invaded Scotland. Charles went back into exile and Cromwell ruled both countries until he died in 1658. The Restoration in 1660 brought Charles II to the throne. He ignored the promises he had made and sought to reintroduce Episcopacy, rekindling the fervour of the Covenanters, who fled to the hills and worshipped in secret 'Conventicles'. In 1670 these conventicles were declared treasonable, and there followed the **Killing Times**, when thousands of Covenanters were slaughtered.

Charles II died of apoplexy in 1685 and was succeeded by his brother, **James VII/II**, Scotland's first Catholic sovereign for 120 years, who tried unsuccessfully to introduce tolerance for all religions. He was deposed in 1688 by his Protestant daughter, Mary, and her Dutch husband, William of Orange, and fled to France. Some Scots, mostly Highlanders, remained true to James. The **Jacobites**, as they were called, rose under Graham of Claverhouse and almost annihilated William's army in a savage battle at Killiecrankie in 1689. But Claverhouse was killed, leaving them leaderless, and they lost heart and returned to their Highlands.

The government, uneasy about the rebellious Highlanders, issued a proclamation ordering all clans to take an oath of allegiance to the Crown by the first day of 1692. Circumstances prevented **Alasdair Maclain of Clan Donald** from taking the oath until after the deadline. This provided the government with a chance to intimidate the Highland clans. A company of Campbell soldiers, commanded by a relation of Maclain's, Captain Robert Campbell of Glenlyon, billeted themselves on the MacDonalds in Glencoe. They rose at dawn and slaughtered their hosts. The barbarity of the Massacre of Glencoe produced public outcry, not so much because of the number killed – 38 out of about 150 – but because of the abuse of hospitality. The king denied all foreknowledge: as a gesture, he sacked his Secretary of State, Sir John Dalrymple the Master of Stair, who had instigated the deed.

Union and Enlightenment

Between 1698 and 1700, Scotland's economy was shattered by an unsuccessful attempt to colonize the Darien coast on the isthmus of Panama. Scotland, bankrupt and plunged into political crisis, was forced to accept the Treaty of Union in 1707, uniting the parliaments of England and Scotland. This carefully worded document brought advantage to both countries, giving Scotland a badly needed boost to her economy and the right to Presbyterianism, and removed the threat of further war between the two countries.

The signing of the Treaty of Union forced the Scots to accept a Hanoverian succession, but Jacobite loyalties still prevailed in the Highlands. **James Edward Stuart**, son of the deposed James VII/II, was regarded by many as Scotland's true king. The Old Pretender, as he was called by the Hanoverians, made three unsuccessful attempts to regain his throne. (Pretender is from the French *prétendre* – to claim, not from the English word for make-believe.) His expedition from France in 1708 only got as far as the Firth of Forth. In 1715 the Earl of Mar, upset by his treatment at the hands of the Hanoverian George I, raised the Pretender's banner and proclaimed James king. The rising looked promising but, after an inconclusive battle at **Sheriffmuir**, support for it dwindled. The Old Pretender put in a brief appearance in Scotland but soon returned to France. In 1719 a final attempt was made, backed by the Spanish, but the supporting fleet was lost in a storm and the Highlanders dispersed.

Stringent measures were taken to quell the clans. Between 1726 and 1737 General Wade built military roads, bridges and forts, linking strategic strong points at Fort William, Fort Augustus and Fort George and opening up the Highlands. He raised a regiment of clansmen loyal to the Whig Government, the Black Watch, whose duty was to keep order among the resentful clans.

George I, an unattractive German, disliked the British as much as they disliked him. When he died, his son **George II**, equally Germanic and unsuitable to rule over Highlanders, gave them excuse enough to cling to their Jacobite dreams. Exiled in Rome, the Old Pretender's son, **Prince Charles Edward Stuart**, was a brave young man with charisma and magnetism. He pawned his mother's rubies, set sail for Scotland and landed in Eriskay on 23 July 1745, determined to win the crown for his father.

At first his reception was daunting: Macdonald of Boisdale told him to go home. 'I am come home', he retorted. MacLeod and Macdonald of Sleat refused to help, but Macdonald of Clanranald stood by him. Cameron of Lochiel was reluctant to encourage what he believed to be romantic folly, but he was won over and on 19 August the standard was raised in **Glenfinnan**, the Old Pretender proclaimed King James VIII/III, and Prince Charles his regent. Subsequent events are well known. The prince attracted support as he advanced on Edinburgh, but his army probably never exceeded 8,000 men. Capturing Perth on the way, he held glorious court at Holyrood, defeated General Cope's soldiers at **Prestonpans** and inflamed Jacobite hearts with optimism.

On 1 November Prince Charles led his motley army south with the intention of taking London, hoping to woo more Jacobites on the way. Meeting little resistance, but picking up disappointingly few recruits, they reached Derby on 4 December, only 127 miles from their target. At this point Charles' prudent advisers insisted that to go further was madness. On 6 December he agreed reluctantly and the Highlanders turned round to march in an orderly retreat back to Scotland. On 17 January 1746 the Jacobites won their last battle, defeating Cope's successor, General Hawley, at Falkirk. Hearing news of the advance of the Duke of Cumberland's army from England, the Prince took his army back into the Highlands, capturing Inverness on 21 February. On 16 April Cumberland marched towards Inverness, his forces meeting the Jacobite army on Drummossie Moor, south of **Culloden**. Outnumbered and outgunned, the Jacobites were soon defeated. Defeat turned into a rout in which Cumberland's men showed no mercy to their opponents. The Prince escaped, with a price of £30,000 on his head, and spent the next five months in hiding in the Western Highlands and Islands. Aided by brave **Flora Macdonald**, he escaped eventually to Europe where he lived in squalid exile for the rest of his life, dying in Rome in 1788.

The English and the Lowland Scots were determined to squash the rebellious Highlanders forever. They enforced the **Act of Proscription** in 1747, banning the wearing of tartan and Highland dress and the bearing of arms, with later measures to abolish the hereditary jurisdiction of the chiefs. Jacobites who had not died at Culloden were either executed or transported. The old way of life was dead. The act was repealed in 1782, largely thanks to the intervention of the Highland Society of London, but by this time it was no longer relevant: the **Highland Clearances** had begun.

Between 1780 and 1860, thousands of crofters were evicted from their homes in the Highlands and Islands to make way for sheep. Many others emigrated voluntarily, to escape persecution, to Canada, America, New Zealand and Australia. In the mid-19th century Ireland's potato famine reached the Highlands, resulting in appalling hardship and causing further emigration. By the end of the 19th century, the rural Highlands and Islands were almost deserted.

A flourishing cotton industry collapsed in the 1860s when the American Civil War cut off supplies of raw cotton, and heavy industry developed instead. Glasgow, once the biggest tobacco importer in Britain, led the world in shipbuilding. Expanding industries meant expanding labour forces; there were concentrations of population in industrial areas, fed by refugee Highlanders and Irish. Shipbuilding and engineering developed rapidly from the mid-19th century until, by the beginning of the 20th century, some 100,000 jobs were related to Clydeside shipbuilding alone. The Steel Company of Scotland, founded in 1871, replaced iron, and the entire economy of west and mid Scotland depended on Glasgow's heavy industry. The First World War took its toll of Scottish manhood, but it needed a constant supply of arms and ships and machinery and there was more than enough work for those left behind.

It was the Great Depression in the 1920s and 1930s that dealt Scotland a mortal blow. After the Wall Street Crash in 1929 the global wave of economic disaster washed over Clydeside, and by 1936 the output from the shipyards had fallen from three-quarters of a million tons to less than 60,000, with at least two-thirds of the workforce unemployed. In order to try to increase efficiency and generate more trade, firms merged and pruned their labour forces still further, resulting in more job losses. Not surprisingly, socialism flourished, passionately fuelled by leaders like **James Maxton** and **Emmanuel Shinwell**. Public opinion favoured the plight of the workers, and by the end of the 1930s things were beginning to look up. The Second World War brought with it a fresh demand for armaments and ships: Clydeside boomed and Scotland grew prosperous again. But after the war competition from abroad began to steal trade. Shipyards, steelworks and factories closed; less coal was needed, so coal mines closed. The oil boom in the 1970s brought new prosperity for a while but this was short-lived.

A new generation of enterprising minds, particularly from Glasgow, turned the tide of apathy. Diversification spread a rash of light industry throughout the country, and workers are now more inclined to negotiate for rights than to cripple their livelihood with strikes. Politically, Scotland leans to the left and juggles with nationalism. Those in favour of autonomy hold that they are the poor relations of politicians at Westminster, whose survival-of-the-fittest policies make no allowance for Scotland's circumstances. In 1979, when they were first invited to vote for devolution, over 36 per cent didn't bother to vote and the Nationalists lost through the nation's apathy.

There were further stirrings of nationalist feeling prior to the general election of 1992, when it seemed likely that the Conservative Party's 13-year grip on government would be loosened. The opposition parties were united in offering greater or lesser degrees of autonomy to the Scottish people, but these promises came to nothing when the Conservatives, although winning a mere 11 of Scotland's 72 seats in parliament, were once again returned to power in the south.

In the 1997 general election, New Labour led by **Tony Blair** won a landslide victory in Britain, wiping out all Tory constituencies north of the border. Most of Scotland's most able MPs won seats in England, leaving no obvious national leader. A referendum was held in September 1997 and the Scots voted by 74 per cent for a Scottish Parliament and by 63.5 per cent for that parliament to have tax-raising powers. The outcome was greeted with widespread jubilation and celebration, but there remained a number of questions to be answered before 1999 when the first **Edinburgh Parliament** assembled, among them the 'West Lothian Question': why should Scottish MPs continue to vote on English matters at Westminster, while English MPs are denied reciprocal rights in Edinburgh? As yet there are no answers. The Scottish Parliament is still in its relative infancy. Time alone will uncover its strengths and weaknesses, its successes and failures. It has already had its teething problems: the first First Minister **Donald Dewar** died of heart failure, in office; his successor was forced to resign after allegations of misuse of public funds. There have been squabbles in the governing Liberal/Labour coalition over university fees, and a huge dispute over the New Scottish Parliament buildings at Holyrood. The winning design was submitted by a Spaniard, over the heads of many excellent Scottish designers. The spiralling cost of this extraordinary edifice has resulted in drastic pruning: no bars for the MSPs to relax and refuel in; no £3m ceremonial entrance. For the full scandalous story, read *All the First Minister's Men* by David Black.

Scottish Nationalists continue to hail devolution as the first step on the road to independence. They believe that an alliance with Europe would be better than union with England, whose rulers seem sometimes aloof. Either way, Scotland's economic forecast looks rosy. In addition to record visitor numbers and abundant resources of oil and natural gas, the nation teeters towards independence as one of Europe's leading centres for high-tech industry and finance. Meanwhile, in a secret cavern somewhere in the Scottish hills, the true Stone of Destiny gathers dust...waiting.

Topics

03

Clans and Tartans

The Scottish clan system was once an integral part of the Highlands and Islands. Every member of the clan bore the name of the chief, whether related by blood or by allegiance, and each was an equal member of the clan family (Mac means 'son of'). The chief was the father, ruler and judge, and the strength of the clan lay in his justice, kindness and wisdom, and in the loyalty of the members of the clan, to him and to one another. Rents were mostly paid in kind or man-rent and, in return for his patronage and protection, the chief could call on his people at any time to form an army and fight for him.

It is known that Highlanders wore some sort of brightly coloured, striped and checked material as far back as the 13th century, though whether the designs, or 'setts', were related to clans or to territories is not known for certain. The Suppression of the Highlands after Culloden in 1746 broke up clans, forbade tartan and Highland dress to all civilians, and led to the death of the clan system. During the 36 years Highland dress was banned, many of the old setts were lost or forgotten.

However, the Highland regiments were exempt from the ban, and it is through them that the kilt survived. The early regiments all wore the Government, or Black Watch, tartan, sometimes introducing coloured overstripes to differentiate one regiment from another. It was not until Hanoverian George IV appeared at Holyrood in 1822 in an astonishing Highland outfit that the fashion for tartan was revived: in a wave of enthusiasm a large number of tartans were hastily designed, and adopted by Highlanders, and even by Lowlanders whose ancestors would have died rather than be seen in Highland dress. It is these relatively modern patterns that make up most of today's enormous range of tartans, which can be seen all over the world, in cloth and adorning luggage, footwear and a staggering range of souvenirs. On the whole kilts are kept for ceremonial or formal occasions, or for 'Sunday best', and many Scotsmen don't even own one.

Clan feelings still run strong, but the clan name is now no more than an umbrella for clan societies, museums, annual gatherings and ceremonial, with the chief as a figurehead, in his tartan costume. The mystique that has grown up round clan tartans is put into perspective by the apocryphal story of the irate chieftain, towering over one of a coach party visiting his ancestral castle: 'By what right are you wearing my tartan, my man?'; and the response: 'By the ri' o' purrchis, at fifteen pounds a yard, my lord.' *See also* 'Clans and Families', pp.301–7.

Fishing

With thanks to Michael Wigan.

In the first half of the 19th century, southern fishermen began making the stagecoach trek to Scotland to ply for salmon with rod and line. The Industrial Revolution had begun to pollute England's great salmon rivers, and was to wipe the salmon out in many of them by the turn of the 20th century. The Scottish lairds had been accustomed to sending forth their *sealgairs* (hunters) to procure fish and game for them, frequently disdaining such activities themselves. They were delighted to be paid by these newcomers for the right to dangle their baits in the water.

Much has changed since Scotland made its name as the world's best fishing venue. The night-time revellers who hunted spawning salmon in their breeding places with lamps and pronged spears have been replaced by fishermen and women throwing out hi-tech fishing lines with rods made of supremely light, flexible and strong new materials. Whereas once the huge bulk of Scottish salmon was caught by estuary nets, now salmon nets (challenged by the low price of farmed salmon) are becoming uneconomic; many have fallen into disuse, or been bought up and laid to rest by the rod angling fraternity. The silver king of the river is chiefly valuable as a game fish, and the value of fishing rentals to Scotland, apart from the benefits fishing brings to many sideline economies, is enormous. The capital value of salmon fishing in Scotland has been calculated at close to £1 billion.

It is no exaggeration to say that in the valleys of some of the great rivers like the Spey and Tay, the way of life is chiefly determined by the fishery. Fishing hotels and lodges occupy strategic positions above the precious waters, and ghillies' and water bailiffs' houses are never far from the fish that sustain their livelihood. In many villages on rivers the focal point is the tackle shop, trading not only in fishing paraphernalia, but also in gossip about pools in which fish have been caught and the flies that have caught them. The news of big hauls is particularly influential with trout fishermen, and round any loch in which someone has struck lucky, large concentrations of anglers are to be observed days later, trying in vain to repeat an individual's one-off glory.

The joy of a river is that its course connects contrasting parts of the country. The sources of many of Scotland's great rivers are swampy spring-fed patches in hanging valleys high in the mountains, or even springs in the floors of lochs. Many Scottish rivers can be fished from the mountain burns near the headwaters right through to the wide, sleepy stretches flowing through farmland nearer the coast. In some places fishermen use rod and line to spin for migratory fish in the sea off the river mouths, usually for sea trout.

Sea trout are the members of the native brown trout family which choose to migrate to sea, but – unlike the Atlantic salmon which forage as far as the Greenland shelf to feed – sea trout winter offshore, generally returning in spring and early summer. In seeking enjoyment from duping fish, many methods have been devised to balance the challenge of a catch with applications of physical strength and manual skill. Fishing is an outwitting art, and man delights in playing the deceiver.

Salmon fishing in Scotland is classically associated with the wet fly, a contraption of feathers and other titbits which need bear no resemblance to any known insect or creature, but for certain well-tested reasons rouses fishes' aggressive urge. On the bigger rivers spinning is practised in slow, wide pools; but fly-fishing is in the ascendancy, and spinning increasingly frowned on. The ancient practice of worming, which is suited to deep pools where the worms twirl enticingly in the current, is discouraged even more.

Dapping is a technique developed for catching sea trout and brown trout in windy conditions on lochs. By deploying a loose silky cord from a pole-like rod, the fly can be made to dance over the surface like an insect blown from land and trying unsuccessfully to rise. Nymph fishing employs a wingless body in imitation of the fly at larval stage. When a trout takes a nymph it is capitalizing on the momentary opportunity offered by a fly as it rises from the river bed prior to hatching on the surface. Dry fly, like nymph, is imitative, and although in most Scottish salmon rivers the water is too cold for dry fly to be successful, trout fishermen use it on warm evenings on the lochs, when the puffed-up wings of the dry fly keep it popped up on the surface.

The water surface to all fishermen is a hypnotic thing, always moving, always changing with the shifting light in the sky. Cunliffe Pearce has written evocatively of 'the top of the water, that magic looking-glass through which trout and man mysteriously make acquaintance with each other'. In Scotland there is the extra factor of supreme scenery. The Highland lochs – Loch Lomond, Loch Awe – are famed for beauty, yet also loved in a different way by connoisseurs for the fishing they offer. Some of the far north rivers – Helmsdale, Brora, Naver, Dionard – open out through heather moorland, and become faster as they drop through rocky passages before entering the sea. The Outer Isles have magnificent salmon and sea trout fishing, and it is on the magical Grimersta, where running fish can stream by in a seemingly endless flow, that the British record catch by one man in a day was recorded – 52 salmon. Some of the most exciting trout lochs are those gem-like bodies of water in the far north, famous for being dour and unco-operative in one mood, then exploding into action the next. A hundred fish in a day to two rods is not unimaginable.

Scottish salmon fishing is not, as is sometimes said, the preserve of rich tenants on famous water. There are thousands of miles of fishing in Scotland, and many opportunities for those who seek them out. The game fishing magazines, *Trout and Salmon* and *Salmon Trout and Seatrout*, advertise plenty of rentable fishing and, once embarked on the salmon fishing circuit, chances spring up for keen fishermen through contacts made along the way. Some local councils own water, and many rivers are open to day-ticket fishermen either through angling associations, fishing hotels, local river boards, or private riparian owners. Salmon fishing permits start at around £10 per day. Trout fishing is available in great supply, particularly in the far north and west of Scotland, and some of the famous fishing hotels have access to numerous remote lochs which never see a fisherman year-round. A boat on a loch costs around £10 a day, bank fishing about £8. Tourist information centres give fishing and accommodation information. More expensive salmon-fishing possibilities are marketed through the main sporting agencies, and are often sold in exclusive packages based in neighbouring fishing lodges (also see p.42).

The Highland Clearances

'The Clearances' is an emotive subject, and it has to be remembered that the first emigration ship sailed out of Fort William as early as 1773. There were several reasons for the depopulation of the Highlands after Culloden. Some Jacobites who had escaped execution found it expedient to go abroad for a few years; others were transported. Many Catholics, unable to practise their religion publicly at home, sought the liberty to do so across the ocean. The Proscription Act of 1747 suppressed the Highlands and broke up the clan system, depriving chiefs of their hereditary status as patriarchs. Many drifted south to become London Scots.

Away from the womb of the clan and the benefits of feudality, however, they felt the pinch financially. Vast, infertile estates in the north, overpopulated by impoverished peasants, brought in little or no revenue. Rents paid in kind were no use to those trying to keep up with society in fashionable assembly rooms or pay off gambling debts in gentlemen's clubs. Sheep farmers from the south offered good rent for sheep-runs in the north, but they wanted land free of people. Highland landowners, desperate for money, began to evict their tenants. Some built resettlement towns and villages for them and established new livelihoods such as fishing; some merely served eviction notices and employed agents to enforce them; some offered to assist with fares to new countries. Hundreds of crofting communities – those which relied entirely on their smallholdings for a living – broke up and scattered. Those who didn't emigrate flocked to the cities in the hope of finding work, or to settlements, mainly on the coast, where the land was unsuitable for sheep.

Meanwhile, in the Islands, landlords basked in a false prosperity from the kelp industry. Seaweed, of which there was an apparently inexhaustible supply, was collected after each tide, burned in kilns, processed into valuable fertilizer and exported. All that was needed was a huge labour force to cut, carry and burn it. Island proprietors with an eye to the main chance offered tiny plots of land to dispossessed crofters from the mainland. They charged high rent and ensured each tenant had not enough land for self-sufficiency, forcing them to work at the kelp. By 1812 the Islands were crammed with people entirely dependent on kelp for their living.

After the Napoleonic Wars, import duty was abolished and cheap foreign kelp flooded the market: prices plummeted; people starved. Proprietors and politicians, faced with the problem of destitute multitudes, offered inducements to encourage emigration, and many people went.

The final blow came in 1846. The potato famine had already decimated Ireland; now wind-borne spores drifted across the sea and descended on Scotland, half of whose population lived on potatoes. For the already starving Highlanders and Islanders, the effect was catastrophic. Many of those who had managed to stay on, often surviving several evictions, were forced to join their compatriots in Canada, America, Australia and New Zealand. By the end of the 19th century, the rural Highlands and Islands were almost completely deserted.

The Islands

Scotland's islands add greatly to its charm; each one has its own character, 'entire of itself': a native of Eriskay feels homesick living a mile away across the water in South Uist. About 130 of these 790 islands are inhabited. Until recently, almost untouched by the distractions of an increasingly materialistic world, islanders tended to build their lives around God and the Church – a church that varies, depending on the island, from staunch Roman Catholic to extreme Presbyterian. With improved communications, younger generations are more in tune with the modern world and less prepared to subscribe to the old values which made their ancestors a 'race apart'.

The Islands can be divided into four main groups: the islands of the Clyde, the Inner Hebrides, the Outer Hebrides – all lying to the west – and the Northern Isles. First known to be populated around 3800 BC, many of the islands are rich in archaeological sites, many of which have yet to be dug. Mesolithic man gave way to Neolithic, who came in boats made of animal hide, bringing skills and culture and leaving burial cairns as evidence of his existence. Gaelic immigrants from Europe arrived with Celtic arts; building brochs and stone circles, practising a Druid religion and worshipping nature gods, until the first Christian missionaries from Ireland landed early in the 6th century. Norsemen took a number of the islands over at the end of the 8th century and remained until the defeat of King Haakon by Alexander III at Largs in 1263. Haakon's son, Magnus VI, realized that the Viking era in the Western Isles was over, and he signed the Treaty of Perth in 1266, ceding them to the Scottish Crown in return for an annual fee.

Stronger than the authority of the Crown was the Lordship of the Isles: chiefs who were as powerful as kings, paying no heed to a government which ruled from the lowlands of mainland Scotland. A succession of Stewart kings tried to whip in the arrogant clans of the Western Isles, but they clung to their traditions and loyalties. A patriarchal clan system existed, with every member of the clan family independent and equal in status, looking to their chief for guidance and justice but not for oppressive authority. This proud independence endures in the Hebrides today; a classless pride that has survived even the suppression of the clans after Culloden and, in the 19th century, the appalling depopulation caused by the Highland Clearances.

The outer islands to the south of Benbecula, following the inclination of their chiefs, rejected the Reformation, their faith kept alive by Gaelic-speaking monks who came over from Ireland. These islands remain almost entirely Catholic, while the rest of the Western Isles embraced the Reformed Church with such enthusiasm that visitors today must be careful not to offend their Sabbatarianism.

People who go to the islands for holidays enjoy outdoor life: walking, climbing, bird-watching, wild flowers, boating, fishing and shooting. Whatever the weather – and it is often good – each day is an adventure. Walk five miles to an isolated beach, collect driftwood and make a fire using dried heather twigs as kindling. Cook sausages or fresh-caught mackerel and wash them down with peat-coloured water from a burn. Collect mussels from rocks below the high tide and rake cockles out of the white sand; pick wild mushrooms from the grassy hillsides. You can even have a quick swim – diving into deep icy water as clear as glass.

Although Skye and Mull, being more accessible, have a much more modern culture than the outer islands, only in Portree, and Stornoway in Lewis, will you find many shops, and these are mainly general stores and Co-op supermarkets which stock most things from boots to butter. There are a few craft/souvenir/postcard shops, weavers, and a post office here and there, but people for whom 'shopping' is an integral part of a holiday tend to stay on the mainland. Because of deeply held religious beliefs, most businesses are closed on Sundays and there is no scheduled public transport on Harris and Lewis. On the Presbyterian islands, hotel bars, pubs and restaurants also close, though some hotels are open to non-residents for meals. A few B&B landladies and self-catering proprietors prefer guests not to arrive or depart on Sundays, so it is worth checking to avoid giving offence (*see* 'Religious Differences', pp.26–7).

For public entertainment, there may be a local ceilidh in a village hall to mark a particular occasion, or spontaneously erupting in a hotel bar; and there are Highland Games in the summer on the larger islands. Otherwise, evenings are spent in front of a peat fire with a book, or the television if there is one, or, if you are lucky, in the pub listening to the tales of local people who can still tell much of the old folk-lore, and who will often make music for you. For a truly balanced, modern-day view of the Western Isles, read *Isles of the West* by Ian Mitchell (Canongate – 1999). Mitchell sails from his home in Islay north through the islands to Harris and back via the Shiants Summer Isles, Skye and Mull. On the way, he examines all the contemporary problems that beset the modern crofter, whose traditional way of life is more and more influenced by all the different bodies of conservationists with their various acronyms. For more information about the Western Isles, visit *www.visithebrides.com*.

Crofting

Most island families have their own croft, or smallholding, their tenancy carefully controlled by the Crofters' Commission, enacted in 1886 as a result of public indignation after the Clearances. A croft is a smallholding, with a few acres, as many sheep as the land will support, and sometimes cows and poultry. If there is arable land it will be tilled. In the old days, *feannagan* (inappropriately named 'lazy beds'), were dug for potatoes, involving much hard work, deep digging and the carting of heavy creels of seaweed for fertilizer. Some of the work on the croft is still done communally – sheep-dipping and shearing for instance, and cutting the peat and haymaking. Peat is still used as fuel in some areas. Composed of partially rotted vegetation, compressed in waterlogged conditions in temperate or cold climates, it takes a year to form 5mm, so peat bogs are running out. In the spring it is cut into oblong slabs, using a special spade, and stacked *in situ* on end like miniature wigwams until dry. Sometimes machines are used for cutting, but this device has not yet been perfected and the resulting sausages of peat are too small, don't store well and there is a lot of wastage. In a wet summer the peat can still be lying late into the year. Once dry, it is built into neat beehives. As recently as the 1970s, hay was cut with scythes, and is still sometimes turned with pitchforks until dry.

The family dwelling is the croft-house – often mistakenly called the croft. Less than 50 years ago, many Highlanders still lived in a *tigh dubh* or black house, now almost extinct except as a folk museum or byre. It had thick, double walls, about 6ft (1.8m) high, made of local stone and packed with earth and rubble. Unlined on the inside, it had rounded corners, no gables, and a reed- or heather-thatched roof anchored by boulders tied to ropes of plaited heather. Inside, the furniture was functional and, in the Outer Isles where there were no trees, often made of driftwood: a dresser, box beds, a bench, stools, rat-proof meal chests, coffers and a spinning wheel. A peat fire was laid on a stone slab on the earthen floor in the middle of the room, the smoke escaping out of a hole in the thatch or left to seep out through cracks. The accumulation of this smoke gave the black houses their name. In earlier times, light came from a *crùisgean* – a lamp fuelled with fish-liver oil burning on a wick of plaited rushes. Even during the 20th century, in some island communities the beasts shared the family house, penned at one end with the floor sloping down towards them and the effluent running out through holes in the wall.

Open rebellion by some communities (*see* 'The Battle of the Braes and the Glendale Martyrs', p.239) against draconian landlords at the climax of the Clearances, attracted the attention of the contemporary 'media' over rights of crofters, the owners or tenants of the croft. Unwelcome publicity, coupled with unrest over the demand for Irish Home Rule, forced Gladstone's government to set up a Royal Commission of Inquiry in 1883, with Lord Napier in the chair. The Commission comprised two landowners who were sympathetic to the crofters' problems, two Gaelic scholars and an MP who was also a member of the Highland Land Law Reform Association. These men toured the Highlands and Islands during 1883 and 1884 (once being shipwrecked off Stornoway), collecting overwhelming evidence in favour of reform.

With the extension of the parliamentary franchise in 1885, entitling crofters to vote, the crofter question became a dominant issue in the general elections of 1885 and 1886, with a new political party emerging. As always, Scottish affairs seldom received priority at Westminster, but public opinion was by now so strong that the Crofters' Holdings (Scotland) Act was passed, in which crofters were granted security of tenure and a Crofters' Commission was appointed to fix fair rents. There were teething problems, but by the end of the century crofters' rights were secure and peace prevailed.

These days most crofters have a subsidiary job as well: fishing, building or public works. Recent legislation has made it possible for crofters to buy their crofts. This has not been an attractive proposition for many, except in a few cases such as Assynt where a community 'buy out' has taken place aided by government funding. In theory, communities in crofting areas can now buy fishing and mineral rights, but the complications and ramifications are endless and stretch into the future across a morass of invective.

Ceilidh

Céilidh (pronounced 'kayly') is a Gaelic word meaning visit. During the long winters, when darkness fell, crofters gathered in one of the houses and packed in around the central fire. An older member, often a bard or musician, acted as the master of ceremonies, and everyone was expected to contribute to the entertainment. The women knitted or spun, men repaired fishing nets or whittled wood; everyone listened. Stories, songs, poems, proverbs and legends were recited, passing history, folklore and tradition from one generation to the next. Their music stirred the soul: mouth-music, straight from the heart; Gaelic songs; pipe, harp and fiddle music.

Children grew up steeped in the past and could tell you who their great-great-great-grand-uncle was and whose sweetheart he had run off with. The practice is dying now, thanks to television, and ceilidhs tend to be commercial shows, staged in halls and hotels. Attempts have been made to capture some of this ancient folklore and put it down on paper, but this isn't the same: it was a living thing, passed on orally through generations, embroidered and altered year by year.

Gaelic

Gaelic, which is much older than English, stems from the Goidelic branch of Celtic languages, which were an offshoot from the earlier Indo-European language. Scottish Gaelic became a distinct dialect separate from Irish around the 13th century, but there are still many similarities. Gaelic is still the first language in the Outer Hebrides, but even there, with an influx of non-Gaelic speakers and television, the children are growing up speaking English among themselves. Elsewhere it is no longer a living language, though many people are trying to revive it and there are many great Gaelic scholars. **Sabhal Mor Ostaig**, in Skye, is a popular and very successful Gaelic college; television and radio have a lot of Gaelic slots. It is taught in schools and in adult classes and there are a large number of Gaelic publications. It is an almost impossible language to 'pick up' by ear and eye because the spoken word bears little resemblance to the written. More and more notices are appearing in the Highlands and Islands, proclaiming place names in Gaelic. They must have cost a fortune; local people don't need them, and visitors can neither understand, nor pronounce them.

With the revival of Gaelic has come a revival of Gaelic culture. Groups like Runrig and Capercaillie, who perform modern-style Gaelic music, are enormously popular and an important part of the Scottish music scene.

Piping

With thanks to David Murray.

Two kinds of bagpipes are played in Scotland these days, the 'warm wind' and the 'cold wind'. The Highland bagpipe, being mouth blown, is 'warm wind'; the Lowland or Border bagpipe is blown by a bellows operated by the piper's right elbow, hence the 'cold wind pipes'. The Highland bagpipe is designed to be played out of doors; the Lowland is essentially an indoor instrument. Recent improvements in the manufacture of the Highland bagpipe, along with the higher standards now being demanded by audiences, have altered the tone of the instrument until it can be listened to with pleasure indoors, where the most prestigious piping events are held. The Highland bagpipe no longer 'skirls'. The 'Small Music' of the Highland bagpipe includes marches and dance tunes in differing tempi; the *ceòl mor*, the 'Great Music' (usually anglicized as 'pibroch' from *pìobaireachd*, meaning piping) comprises tunes constructed on a theme followed by up to ten variations.

Pibroch pieces date from the late 15th century and their names commemorate great events in Highland history. Pibroch is listened to in silence. It is unwise for the visitor to interrupt, even by a whisper. The Lowland pipes are intended to accompany social events indoors and fit in well with the folk music groups now popular in Scotland and beyond. Their tone is sweet and mellow and the repertoire includes the ancient Border ballads from the days of the cross-border raids and feuds, as well as a wide range of dance music and song airs. Both instruments are taken seriously in Scotland, for their own sake as well as for their traditional connotations. Derogatory comment is not appreciated, especially if voiced in the accents of southern Britain. The pipes were never specifically proscribed by the Disarming Act of 1747, but it would have been a brave piper who played within earshot of a government post. The oldest thesis on pipe music was written during the Proscription, and several pibroch pieces were composed while the Act was still in force.

Religious Differences

In the Highlands and Islands, where communities tend to be slow to change, there are predominantly Catholic areas, where they rejected the Reformation and reconverted, and other areas which, following the laird, became Protestant. On the whole, Catholics and Protestants live together happily with few of the sectarian problems experienced in Northern Ireland. Sometimes, however, there is a conflict between the strict Sabbatarian beliefs and practices of a few Presbyterians and the more liberal Catholics, and invariably the media manage to stir up an 'incident'.

In the Outer Hebrides, South Uist, Eriskay and Barra are almost entirely Catholic. In their belief, God belongs to every day and Sunday is for celebration. North Uist, Harris and Lewis are Presbyterian and the most rigid Protestants in Britain. Their interpretation of the Fourth Commandment is enforced by the Lord's Day Observance Society, who exert moral, social and political pressure. Sunday is for long sermons in church, full of the threat of damnation; for reading the Bible and holy tracts; for dark clothes and solemn faces. No work must be done, not even cooking; washing must come in off the line; fishing boats must lie at anchor. In some places, they say, the swings are padlocked and cocks are separated from hens. Not so long ago, no ferries ran to the islands on Sundays. When Caledonian MacBrayne announced a changed schedule including some Sunday sailings, the uproar was clamorous with threats of barricades.

Running in tandem with this dispute, was friction over a new £12 million school, built at taxpayers' expense, on the island of Benbecula, midway between the Catholic south and Protestant north and serving both. The predominantly Protestant Western Isles Council would not employ supervisory staff on Sundays, so no one could use the school's leisure facilities. Catholics protested that their beliefs allowed them to have fun on Sundays and they saw no reason why Sabbatarian rules should prevent them from doing so. The situation was satisfactorily resolved in the end, but not without damage to the hitherto dignified, laissez-faire attitudes that enabled such extreme creeds to live side by side in harmony.

The majority of Scots church-goers belong to the Established Church of Scotland, or Presbyterian Church, and its many breakaway sects. The Episcopal Church, with its bishops, is the equivalent of the Church of England. The Free Presbyterian Church of Scotland (Wee Frees) is a tiny, fundamentalist sect whose members believe that the Pope is 'Antichrist' and the Mass 'the most blasphemous form of religious worship that Satan ever invented; an offence unto God and destructive of the souls of men.' In 1989 Britain's Lord Chancellor, Lord Mackay of Clashfern, a member of this strict sect, was castigated by fellow members of his congregation because he attended Requiem Masses for two of his Catholic friends. The Free Church Synod suspended him from his position as a senior Elder of the Kirk, and from Communion. Lord Mackay, who once said his Church gave 'the most tender love that has ever been described', was forced to resign from it.

Seers, Sorcerers and Superstition

The second sight, *taibhsearachd* in Gaelic, goes hand in hand with sorcery. Among the many seers who emerged from the Celtic mists was the **Brahan Seer**, Còinneach Odhar, an enigmatic figure of unauthenticated provenance, known for his uncannily accurate prophecies about the Highlands, some of which are still to be fulfilled. He fell asleep, so it is said, on an enchanted hillside, and awoke clutching a stone with a hole in it, through which he could see the truth and the future. He foretold the de-population of the Highlands, the demise of crofting, the arrival of rich landowners, and the making of the Caledonian Canal, and said that when it was possible to cross the River Ness in Inverness dryshod in five places, a terrible disaster would strike the world. A fifth bridge was erected over the Ness to replace one that was about to be demolished. It was opened at the end of August 1939: on 1 September Hitler marched into Poland.

The Brahan Seer met his death by antagonizing his patroness, the Countess of Seaforth. The Earl had visited France soon after the Restoration of Charles II in 1660, and had not yet returned. The Countess sent for the Brahan Seer and asked of her husband. After much pressure, he revealed the Earl was in a sumptuous gilded room, decked out in velvet, silk and cloth of gold, with a voluptuous lady on his lap. The furious Countess accused him of malice and ordered him burnt in a barrel of tar at Fortrose. Before he died he predicted the downfall of the Seaforth Mackenzies, whose line came to an end precisely following the prophecy, in 1815.

Communities also lived in terror of Devil-worshippers and sorcerers, whom they believed could control the elements and cause plague, famine, drought, miscarriages and crop failure. In the Middle Ages, fertile Celtic minds were fed by inherited paganism, folklore, ignorance and religion. This was particularly so in Galloway and the Highlands, where remote communities were separated by vast tracts of moor, hill and loch, far from urban influence, schools and the steely eye of the Church. Every act from pre-birth to death was vulnerable, and the power of evil had to be propitiated. Offerings of food, herbal potions, benisons, gestures, talismans and rites were employed in the hope of warding off supernatural ills. Curiously shaped stones had magic properties, and certain lakes and wells were thought to be especially efficacious. Pilgrims brought their sick and their petitions and tied votive offerings to trees and bushes. People still go to some of these Clootie Wells as they are called. At Culloden, coachloads of people arrive on or around May Day, the Celtic Beltane, and throw money into the well. Superstition or not, when the Highland Division was being pounded on the beaches of St Valery-en-Caux, in the summer of 1940, the Culloden Clootie Well attracted throngs of petitioners. Another, on a back road in Ross-shire, is so festooned with squalid old rags, it looks like a tinkers' tip, yet even today no one removes them for fear of reprisals from the god of the well.

It was by no means just ignorant peasants who believed in sorcery. Macbeth's encounter with the three witches was not a figment of Shakespeare's rich imagination. His source for the story was Holinshed, the 16th-century chronicler, who describes 'three women in strange and wild apparel, resembling creatures of eldritch world', who 'vanished immediatlie' having delivered their prophecies. The last execution for witchcraft in Scotland was believed to be in Dornoch in 1727, when a mother was found guilty of riding upon her daughter, who had been transformed into a pony and was about to be shod by the Devil. She was placed in a barrel of pitch having first warmed her cold feet at the fire that was to consume her.

Food and Drink

04

National Dishes

Fair fa' your honest, sonsie face,
Great chieftain o'the puddin'-race!
Aboon them a' ye tak your place,
Painch, tripe, or thairm:
Weel are ye wordy of a grace,
As lang's my arm.

from 'Address to a Haggis', by Robert Burns

Everyone should try **haggis** – if only once. It is made of the heart, liver and lungs of a sheep, mixed with suet, oatmeal and onion, highly seasoned and sewn into the sheep's stomach. Traditionally it is eaten with 'bashed neeps' (mashed turnip; turnip, in Scotland, is what the English call swede) and washed down with neat whisky. Try black pudding, too: its unusual flavour is strangely addictive.

Scotland has an unmatched reputation for **salmon**, both fresh and smoked. The development of fish farming has increased the availability, but it has to be said that 'wild' salmon is usually nicer than the farmed variety. Apart from salmon, national dishes include trout, sea fish, shellfish, game, beef, lamb and venison. Almost without exception you should go for these served simply in the traditional ways. Poached salmon with mayonnaise, new potatoes and cucumber; a freshly caught **mackerel**, fried so that its skin is crisp and curling, with wedges of lemon and watercress; an **Aberdeen Angus fillet steak**, medium-rare, an inch thick, with a green salad of lettuce, chives and a hint of garlic; well-hung roast **grouse** with game chips, fresh petits pois, fried breadcrumbs, bread sauce, and gravy. These will linger on the taste buds as well as in the memory long after any dish wrapped up in an exotic sauce and given a pretentious name.

Arbroath smokies are fresh haddock, dry-salted and smoked in pairs; a delicate, mild flavour makes them particularly delicious and the best way to eat them is cold, with brown wholemeal bread and butter, a generous squeeze of lemon juice and plenty of freshly ground black pepper.

Porridge is no longer a national habit, but you can usually get it in hotels. The popular myth that Scotsmen eat their porridge with salt, standing up or walking about, is quickly disproved when you discover how many of them sit down and tuck into it heaped with sugar and cream, and sometimes even syrup.

Scottish **cheeses** are worth pursuing. Crowdie is unique to Scotland, a creamed cottage cheese made from skimmed milk. Dunlop cheese, originally made in an Ayrshire village of the same name, is now also made in Orkney, Arran and Islay. Caboc is a rich double-cream cheese rolled in pinhead oatmeal. Galic and Hramsa are both soft cream cheeses flavoured with wild garlic and herbs.

Oatcakes are unsweetened biscuits made with oatmeal, best eaten with cheese, honey or marmalade. Brand-named oatcakes can be somewhat dull compared with delicious local and home-made varieties that crumble and melt in the mouth.

Shortbread originated in Scotland and is known all over the world. You will find many local variations.

Soups include Cock-a-leekie, made with chicken and leeks; Scotch broth, made with mutton stock and barley; Cullen skink – delicious – made with smoked haddock; and partan bree, made with crab.

Scotch pies are to be found all over the country: small round pies made of hot-water pastry filled with minced meat, eaten hot. **Bridies** are pies made with a round of pastry folded over, filled with meat, sometimes padded with potatoes and vegetables.

Cranachan, if properly made, is memorable: double cream, and sometimes crowdie, is mixed with toasted oatmeal, sweetened and eaten with fresh soft fruit, preferably **raspberries** – another of Scotland's specialities.

Visit Scotland has a food grading symbol (**Eat Scotland**), consisting of a crosssed knife and fork on a dark blue rectangle, mimicking the St Andrew's flag.

Drink

Inspiring, bold John Barleycorn!
What dangers thou canst make us scorn!
Wi' tippenny [ale], we fear nae evil;
Wi' usquabae [whisky], we'll face the devil!
                    from 'Tam o' Shanter', by Robert Burns

Among the myths that need to be taken with a pinch of salt is the **whisky** myth. The average canny Scot will go for the two bottles of cut-price blended whisky that he can get from the supermarket, for the price of one bottle of vintage malt. On the whole, except among the rich, malt whisky is kept for special occasions, bought as presents for other people – or exported. There are over a hundred malts and every connoisseur will swear to the unquestionable superiority of his particular fancy. However, experiments involving the transfer of a 'favourite' malt into a bottle with a rival label will often prove that it is the eye rather than the taste buds that dictate preference. Most of the distilleries are on Speyside, northeast of Aviemore, in the north, or on the islands of Islay and Jura, and a large number of them run guided tours lasting about an hour, complete with a free dram, showing the process of whisky making. The **Malt Whisky Trail**, on Speyside, is a 70-mile voyage of discovery, taking in eight distilleries. Tourist information centres will provide details.

Traditionally malt whisky should be drunk neat or with a little water. Purists will tell you that any other additions spoil the flavour. No other country in the world has the essential ingredients for that unique taste that makes Scotland's whisky so special: a blend of snow melt, peaty water and carefully malted barley. A Scotsman will never ask for 'Scotch' – unless, perhaps, he is abroad and in danger of being served with a foreign impostor.

Drambuie is a whisky liqueur, very drinkable for those who enjoy 'stickies'.
Gingermac, or whisky-mac, is a mixture of whisky and ginger wine which slips down easily on cold days.

Scotsmen prefer to drink seriously, in bars, though wine bars and English-type pubs are mushrooming. You may hear someone ordering 'a pint of heavy and a chaser'. This will be a pint of bitter and a dram of whisky – the accepted way to spin out the precious *uisge beatha* – the 'water of life'.

Often the dram is not sipped and savoured, but tossed down in a single reviving gulp. In the old days, when the licensing laws were restrictive, there was no time for leisurely drinking. Now licensing laws in Scotland permit public houses to stay open for 12 hours a day, or longer with special extensions, but not all of them choose to do so. Generally, a bar will be open from 11am to 2.30pm, and from 5pm to about 11pm, with reduced hours on Sunday. Most city centre bars will stay open till at least midnight, and residents in licensed hotels can buy drinks at any time. People under 18 may not be served drink in a public house or restaurant, nor may they be sold alcohol in a shop. Some establishments provide special family rooms where children can join their parents, but they must not drink alcohol here. Landlords risk losing their licences if they break the law in this respect.

Slàinte (pronounced slahn-tchuh) is Gaelic for 'health', and is often heard as a toast. For restaurant price categories, *see* p.40.

Travel

Getting There

By Air

Scotland has a reasonable choice of direct air links with cities in the UK, Canada (Toronto), America (New York and Chicago) and Europe. Tourists from other countries must fly via one of the international airports in England (*see www.visitbritain.com*).

Several charter flights serve Scotland during the summer from various countries. Consult your travel agent or *www.visitscotland.com*.

From the UK

British Airways fly from Heathrow, Gatwick and London City to Edinburgh, Glasgow and Inverness. **Scot Airways** fly from London City to Edinburgh and Dundee. **easyJet** fly from Gatwick, Luton and Stansted to Edinburgh, Glasgow, Aberdeen and Inverness. **BMI** fly from Heathrow to Edinburgh, Glasgow, Aberdeen and Inverness. **Ryanair** fly from Stansted to Glasgow Prestwick. **Flybe** fly from London City to Edinburgh. **Flyglobespan** fly from Stansted to Edinburgh and Glasgow.

From North America

Continental fly from New York to Glasgow and Edinburgh; **American Airlines** fly from Chicago to Glasgow; and **US Airways** fly from Philadelphia to Glasgow. **Air Canada** fly daily from Toronto to Glasgow; **Air Transat** fly from Toronto to Glasgow, Edinburgh and Aberdeen, from Calgary to Glasgow and from Vancouver to Glasgow; **Zoom Airlines** fly to Glasgow from Toronto, Calgary, Halifax, Ottawa and Vancouver.

Transport to/from the Airports

The main airports in Scotland are Aberdeen, Edinburgh, Glasgow and Inverness, with good connections from each airport to the city. Cars can be hired from the airports, either in advance through your travel agent or through the airport information desks on arrival. Aberdeen, Edinburgh and Glasgow airports have *bureau de change* facilities.

Aberdeen, t 0870 040 0006, *www.aberdeenairport.com* (7 miles): coach at peak times; taxi £10, or £5 to Dyce Station for fast and frequent trains to Aberdeen and Inverness.

Edinburgh, t 0870 040 0007, *www.edinburghairport.com* (8 miles): taxi £15, coach every 10mins at peak times.

Glasgow, t 0870 040 0008, *www.glasgowairport.com* (8 miles): taxi £12, coach every 15–30mins.

Inverness, t (01667) 464 000, *www.hial.co.uk* (8 miles): taxi £9, regular coach service except Sun.

Airline Carriers

UK

BMI, t 0870 6070 555, *www.flybmi.com*.
British Airways, t 0870 850 9850, *www.britishairways.co.uk*
easyJet, t 0871 244 2366, *www.easyjet.com*
Flybe, t 0871 700 0535, *www.flybe.com*.
Flyglobespan, t 08705 561 522, *www.flyglobespan.com*
Ryanair, t 0906 270 5656, *www.ryanair.com*
Scot Airways, t 0870 606 0707, *www.scotairways.co.uk*

USA and Canada

Air Canada, t 888 712 7786, *www.aircanada.ca*
American Airlines, t 800 433 7300, *ww.aa.com*

Air Transat, t 1 866 847 1112, *ww.airtransat.com*
Continental Airlines, t 1 800 231 0856, *www.continental.com*
US Airways, t 1 800 943 5436, *www.usairways.com*.
Zoom Airlines, t 1 866 359 9666, *www.flyzoom.com*.

Charters, Discounts and Special Deals

For information, search *www.expedia.com* and *www.priceline.com*, or in the UK:
STA Travel, 117 Euston Road, London NW1, t 08701 600 599, *www.statravel.co.uk*
Scotsell Ltd, t (0141) 558 0100, *www.scotsell.com*

Prestwick, t (01292) 479 822, *www.gpia.co.uk* (30 miles to Glasgow): taxi £50, train every 30mins, hourly coach.

By Train

For timetable information, which ticket to buy and route-planning details by national rail services – try **National rail enquiries, t** 08457 48 49 50, *www. rail.co.uk*; alternatively, *www.thetrainline.com* offers tickets for sale online, and also has a useful journey planner and timetable facility.

There are frequent high-speed trains from all parts of England to Edinburgh, Glasgow, Aberdeen and Inverness, with connections to regional stations. London to Edinburgh takes 4½ hours, to Glasgow about 5 hours. There are frequent trains with air-conditioned carriages, 1st and Standard classes, with dining facilities and a buffet service.

ScotRail's **Caledonian Sleeper** is the overnight service between London Euston and Edinburgh, Glasgow, Aberdeen, Inverness and Fort William (*every night exc Sat; single and twin berths*).

Sleeper reservations can be made at any mainline station in the UK, or through travel agents or BritRail offices. Lower fares are offered for reclining seats.

Eurostar, t 08705 186 186, *www.eurostar. com*, is the high-speed passenger rail service operating between Paris, Brussels, Lille, Calais and London Waterloo. Journey time from Paris is 3 hours; from Brussels 2 hours 40 minutes.

In London, transfer to King's Cross or Euston stations for trains to Scotland.

Eurotunnel, t 08705 353 535, *www.euro tunnel.com*, operates non-stop throughout the year, taking 35 minutes between Calais/Coquelles and Folkestone. Terminals have shops and services. Trains carry cars, motorbikes, camper vans and coaches.

By Ferry

There are frequent ferry services from the continent and Northern Ireland to the north of England, within easy reach of Scotland:

DFDS Seaways, t 0870 252 0524, *www. dfdsseaways.co.uk*, (Sweden, Denmark and Norway).

Fjordline, t (0191) 296 1313, *www.fjordline.co.uk* (Norway).

P&O Irish Sea, t 0870 242 4777, *www. poirishsea.com* (Northern Ireland).

P&O Ferries, t 0870 598 0333, *www.ponsf.com* (Belgium, Netherlands).

SeaCat, t 08705 523 523, *www.seacat.co.uk* (Belfast–Troon, Scotland).

Smyril Line, t (298) 345 900, *www.smyril-line.fo* (Faroe Islands).

Stenaline, t 08705 70 70 70, *www.stenaline. com* (Amsterdam and Northern Ireland).

By Coach

Eurolines, t 0870 514 3219, *www.eurolines. com*, is an express coach network which links more than 500 places in 25 countries. They connect with **National Express** in London, **t** 08705 80 80 80, *www.nationalexpress.co.uk*, for Scotland.

The journey from London to Edinburgh takes about 8hrs, and to Glasgow about 7½hrs, including 'comfort stops'.

By Car

An excellent network of motorways means that you can drive comfortably from London to Edinburgh in 7hrs, sticking to the 70mph speed limit. The M1, A1(M) and A68 is the quickest route to Edinburgh, and the M1, M6 and A74/M74 to Glasgow.

Getting Around

In remote areas, consult the tourist office for the best way of getting around, or visit *www.pti.org.uk*.

By Air

There is an excellent network of airways within the country with daily flights connecting the islands and most of the regional airports with Edinburgh, Glasgow, Aberdeen and Inverness. Most of the internal flights are operated by **British Regional Airways, t** 0845 773 3377, *www.britishairways. com*. Book well in advance for special offers and ask for details of discount fares and air passes. British Regional Airlines also has a **Scottish Air Pass** which includes five flights within the Highlands and Islands (including the Western Isles, Orkney and Shetland) for about £170. This must be bought at least 7 days in advance and before you arrive in Scotland.

Eastern Airways, t 0870 366 9100, fly throughout the Highlands and Islands, and **easyJet, Go** and **Ryanair** offer good 'no frills' prices. **British Airways** and **British Midland** both offer air passes. For further details, contact the **Scottish Tourist Board's Information Service, t** 0845 225 5121, *www.visitscotland.com*.

By Train

As well as the main inter-city routes, branch lines run through the very best of highland scenery. Trains run as far as Thurso and Wick in the far northeast, via Inverness and Lairg, and to Oban, Fort William, Mallaig and Kyle of Lochalsh in the west. Aberdeen–Inverness, Glasgow–Stranraer, Glasgow–Oban and Perth–Inverness are all beautiful journeys. The **Kyle Line** runs from Inverness across a lovely stretch of country to Kyle of Lochalsh. The famous **West Highland Line** from Glasgow to Fort William and on to Mallaig, on the *Jacobite*, a restored steam train, is worth doing just for the beauty of the journey, and the trains themselves. The **Royal Scotsman** is a delightfully self-indulgent luxury train

Rail Information

See generally *www.rail.co.uk* for all about services, times and operators.
First ScotRail Enquiries, t 0845 601 5929, *www.firstscotrail.com*.
 GNER, t 08457 225 225, *www.gner.co.uk*; for east coast services via Edinburgh.
National Rail Enquiries, t 0845 48 49 50,. *www. rail.co.uk*.
Royal Scotsman, t (0131) 555 1344, *www.royalscotsman.com*.
The Trainline, *www.thetrainline.com*; to book all rail tickets online.
Virgin, t 0870 789 1234, *www.virgintrains.co.uk*; for west coast services via Glasgow.

offering 2- and 4-night rail tours of Scotland from Edinburgh (*April–Oct*).

Passes and Railcards

BritRail Pass, *www.britrail.net*: unlimited access to Britain's entire rail network. You **must** buy your pass before you arrive.
Freedom of Scotland Travelpass, *www.firstscotrail.com*: unlimited travel on all scheduled train services within Scotland, all Caledonian MacBrayne scheduled ferry services, and various Scottish Citylink coach services.
Highland Rover: available for rail travel in the Highlands – includes reduced-rate ferry travel Oban–Mull, and Mallaig–Skye.

Also look into the **Young Person's Railcard**, *www.youngpersons-railcard.co.uk*, for 16–25s, and mature students in full-time education, **Senior Railcard**, *www.seniorrailcard.co.uk*, for those 60 and over, and **Family Railcard**, *www.family-railcard.co.uk*.

All of these passes offer 1/3 discount on most fares with a 60% discount for children for leisure travel in Britain.

By Ferry

Scotland has 130 inhabited islands, most of them around its west coast. Of these, 22 are served by **Caledonian MacBrayne** ferries. The summer timetable runs from Easter to mid-October, with reduced service in the winter. Reservations are advised and often obligatory. MacBrayne's, or CalMac as it is known, also offers economy **Island Hopscotch** tickets, and

Ferry Information

Caledonian MacBrayne, t 0870 565 0000,
   www.calmac.co.uk.
Corran Ferry, t (01855) 841 243 Ardgour–
   Nether–Lochaber (no reserv necessary).
Glenelg-Kylerhea Ferry, t (01599) 511 302,
   www.skyeferry.co.uk.
NorthLink Orkney and Shetland Ferries Ltd,
   www.northlinkferries.co.uk. Aberdeen and
   Scrabster to Orkney, Aberdeen to Shetland.
John O'Groats Ferries, t (01955) 611 353,
   www.jogferry.co.uk; to Orkney.
Orkney Ferries, t (01856) 872 044, *www.orkney
   ferries.co.uk;* inter-island ferries.
Serco Denim, t (01496) 840 681; Islay–Jura.
Western Ferries, t (01369) 704 452,
   www.western-ferries.co.uk; Firth of Clyde.

Island Rover tickets for unlimited travel over a set period for considerable savings.

For sailors there is probably nowhere in the world more beautiful (or challenging) than around Scotland's islands, and there are many sheltered anchorages from which to explore.

Cruises

The **Hebridean Princess, t** (01756) 704 704, *www.hebridean.co.uk,* offers 6- or 7-day cruises around the Highlands and Islands off the west coast. This floating luxury hotel has a crew of 30 serving 40 passengers.

Caledonian MacBrayne runs afternoon and evening cruises around the west coast.

By Bus

There is a good network of coach services in Scotland. **Scottish Citylink, t** 08705 50 50 50, *www.citylink.co.uk,* is the main operator, travelling to 190 destinations. The **Citylink Smart Card** and **Citylink Explorer Pass** give good discounts. **Stagecoach, t** (01463) 239 292 (Inverness) and **t** (01862) 892 683 (Tain), also have special offers and good bargains. There are many local bus companies throughout the Highlands and Islands and a number of saver tickets. Ask at the TIC. In the more remote areas, the **Postbus** carries fare-paying passengers, **t** (0131) 228 7407.

Special summer bus services also operate in 'scenic' areas with names like: The Trundler, The Heather Hopper and The Speyside

Rambler – TICs will have details. There are numerous coach touring companies offering scheduled itineraries, ranging from luxury with first-class accommodation, to budget tours with basic accommodation. Check on *www.visitscotland.com.*

The following minibus companies run tours from Edinburgh for 'independent travellers': **The Haggis Backpackers, t** (0131) 557 9393, *www.haggis-backpackers.com;*
Rabbie's Trail Burner Tours, t (0131) 554 2612;
Go Blue Banana, t (0131) 220 6868.

By Car

Good main roads will take you north from Edinburgh and Glasgow: the M90/A9 from Edinburgh to Inverness (and on to John O'Groats), and the A82 Glasgow to Inverness via Loch Ness. There are two toll bridges in Scotland: Forth and Tay; others are now free. The 12 National Tourist Routes signs have white lettering, with a brown background and a blue thistle.

Overseas driving licences are valid for a year in Britain. Green card insurance and car registration documents are necessary if you bring your own car.

Car hire firms operate from the airports and stations, and it is worth considering local firms: usually, the more rural, the better the bargain. A car is essential for anyone wishing to explore the Highlands and larger islands. You drive on the left in Scotland, as in the rest of the British Isles, and by law drivers and all passengers must wear seat belts. Road signs are similar to those in Europe. There is a speed limit of 70mph on all motorways and dual carriageways and 60mph on other roads outside built-up areas. A single yellow line by the kerb means you can't park by day; a double yellow line (and zigzag lines by pedestrian crossings) means no parking at any time. The police are hot on drink-driving and speeding.

Main roads are generally good, although many are not dual carriageways. In rural areas there are many single-track roads with bays ('passing places'). These should not be used for parking, but are for cars to pull into, to allow others to pass. In the far north, remember there are not many petrol stations and that some remain closed on Sundays.

Specialist Tour Operators

There are literally hundreds of special-interest tour operators in the UK and USA. The Scottish Tourist Board publishes an excellent free brochure, *Adventure and Special-interest Holidays in Scotland*, or you could try the Scottish Tourist Guide Association, t (01786) 447 784, *www.stga.co.uk*, for experienced guides and advice. Or visit *www.visitscotland.com* for a fuller list.

In the UK

Amethyst Travel, Comrie, t (01764) 670 509, *www.amethyst-travel.com*. Golf, sightseeing, heritage and themed holidays.

Bobsport (Scotland) Ltd, Edinburgh, t (0131) 332 6607, *www.bobsport.co.uk*. Salmon fishing, skiing, golf and shooting holidays.

Celtic Trails, Edinburgh, t (0131) 448 2869, *www.celtictrails.co.uk*. Short residential courses and day tours – themes include Druids, Celtic saints, Merlin and the Earth energy system.

David Urquhart Travel, t 08457 000 400, *www.davidurquharttravel.co.uk*. Short-break coach holidays of up to five days, including hotel accommodation.

Ghillie Personal Travel, Edinburgh, t (0131) 336 3120. Individually tailored holidays, sometimes in private castles, with themed activities.

Golf Vacations UK, 39 Carlisle Street, Carlisle, t (01228) 527 136, *www.golfvacationsuk.com*. Organizes tailor-made golfing trips to the major championship courses in Scotland.

Lomond Walking Holidays, Stirling, t (01786) 870 456, *www.biggar-net.co.uk/lomond*. Guided walking holidays with budget accommodation.

Rob Roy Tours, Edinburgh, t (01620) 890 908, *www.robroytours.com*. Walking, cultural and wildlife tours, mainland and islands.

Scotsell Ltd, Glasgow, t (0141) 558 0100, *www.scotsell.com*. Scottish island holidays, with ferries included. Western and Northern Isles, self-drive touring, hotels/self-catering.

In the USA

Abercrombie and Kent, Oak Brook, Il, t (800) 323 7308, *www.abercrombiekent.com*. Up-market holidays.

Atlantic Golf, Stamford, CT, t (203) 363 1003, *www.atlanticgolf.com*. Specializes in golfing holidays.

Backroads, Berkeley, CA, t (510) 527 1444, *www.backroads.com*. Cycling holidays.

Caravan Tours, t (800) 621 8338. All-inclusive holidays from New York.

Celebrity Tours Inc, Mount Kisco, NY, t (914) 751 2198, *www.celebritytours.net*. Golfing vacations.

Continental Airlines Vacations, Ft Lauderdale, FL, t (800) 301 3800, *www.coolvacations.com*. City breaks.

Extraordinary Places, Bellevue, WA, t (425) 641 9284, *www.eplaces.com*. Bespoke tours and holidays with a focus on culture.

Scots-American Travel Advisors, Vero Beach, FL, t (772) 563 2856, *www.scotsamerican.com*. A range of tours.

Hitchhiking

It is neither more nor less chancy to thumb a lift in Scotland than anywhere else. In populated areas, be extremely wary. On the Islands, however, locals will invariably stop and offer a lift without being thumbed; it is part of their instinctive hospitality.

Practical A–Z

06

Climate

Unpredictability is the main drawback in Scotland, with wide contrasts in one place in a day. When the weather is good, no other country compares. When the weather is bad, Siberia would be preferable.

Places in the north of the country have an average of 18–20 hours of daylight in summer, and in the far north, in mid-summer, it is never completely dark. Resorts on the east coast are noted for their hours of sunshine, yet in spite of the Gulf Stream, the sea is *gelid*.

The west is wettish and mild, while the east is drier with a more bracing climate and colder winds. An unfortunate side-product of the moist, mild weather in the west is the 'midge', a virulent breed of gnat that has been known to reduce grown men to gibbering wrecks under its vicious attacks. Midges are at their worst in warm, humid conditions; they hide when it is windy, and sometimes, in very bright sunshine. Anyone contemplating camping or picnicking during midge season should have the strongest possible repellent. The surest means of escape is to take to the sea – they won't follow a boat offshore.

Eating Out

You can choose between *haute cuisine*, good plain cooking at a reasonable price, bar meals, and fast food. In the cities, meals are served at fairly flexible hours, but in smaller places lunch is 12.30–2pm, and dinner is 7–9pm. If you know you will be late, it is wise to make arrangements in advance. Some of the country's best restaurants are found tucked away in out-of-the-way places. It is usual to leave a tip of 10–15%.

See also **Food and Drink**, pp.29–32.

> **Restaurant Price Categories**
> *expensive* over £30
> *moderate* £15–30
> *inexpensive* under £15

Historic Scotland

Historic Scotland (HS) is a division of the Scottish Education Department, **t** (0131) 668 8800, *www.historic-scotland.gov.uk*. It is responsible for the care and upkeep of many of the country's historic ruins, buildings and sites. Wherever possible, this book gives an idea of opening dates and times, but these change from year to year and should be checked in advance. There is an 'Explorer' ticket for reduced entrance to places of historic interest. Many castles, historic houses and smaller museums close for the winter, however. 'Doors Open Day' is Scotland's contribution to 'Heritage Open Days', two weekends every September when many buildings are open free to the public; get details from local tourist information centres.

Maps

There are plenty of road atlases, available from filling stations and bookshops. For more detail, get the Ordnance Survey Landranger maps (scale 1:50,000); for walking, the Explorer maps (1:25,000) are ideal.

National Trust for Scotland

Many of Scotland's historic buildings and much of its conserved land are under the care of the National Trust for Scotland (NTS), a charity formed in 1931 to promote the preservation of the country's heritage. Over a hundred properties, including castles, small houses, islands, mountains, coastline and gardens, come under the protection of the NTS. Most are open from April to October, and admission varies. Annual membership admits you free to all NTS properties, and to all National Trust properties in England, Wales and Northern Ireland. Prices range from £35 adult, £12 for 25 years and under, £57 family, and £26 over 60 years. There are also one- and two-week touring passes offering savings. Contact the National Trust for Scotland Head Office, 28 Charlotte Square, Edinburgh, EH2 4ET, **t** (0131) 243 9300, *www.nts.org.uk*.

Public Holidays

New Year's Day is the only statutory public holiday in Scotland. Bank Holidays are mainly for banks only and include: 2 January, the

Friday before Easter, the first Monday in May, the first Monday in August, and 25 and 26 December. Most towns and districts have local public trades' and other holidays which vary from place to place and from year to year.

Smoking

Smoking is now banned in enclosed public spaces, including pubs, restaurants and clubs.

Sports and Activities

The **Scottish Sports Council**, Caledonia House, South Gyle, Edinburgh, **t** (0131) 317 7200, *www.sportscotland.org.uk*, can provide information on sports and activities throughout Scotland. The website *www.activity-scotland.co.uk* is also a useful resource, and Visit Scotland lists extreme sports on *www.wannabethere.com*.

For full details of water sports on offer, get the *Scotland Holiday Afloat* booklet from the Scottish Tourist Board.

Canoeing

This is possible all round the coast and on many of the rivers, where the fast flow is often ideal for 'white-water' canoeing. The Scottish Sports Council (*see* above) runs outdoor courses which include canoeing.

Climbing and Walking

From the gentlest stroll to the toughest climb, Scotland's scenery is unbeatable, and the choice is endless. Unfortunately, some people still set out ill equipped and with insufficient skills and knowledge of the terrain, and often get into difficulties. Frequently it falls to the brave men and women of the mountain rescue services to extricate these foolhardy people.

Here are a few simple **rules** that could save lives, money and tempers:

1. Get a weather forecast for the area.
2. Plan your route carefully.
3. Tell someone where you are going, when you will return, and how many are with you.
4. Take appropriate clothing and equipment.
5. Always carry a map.

It would be impossible to list the literally thousands of walks and climbs in the Highlands and Islands. There are 279 peaks

over 3,000ft (914m) – seven of them over 4,000ft (1,230m) – in Scotland. These are called **Munros**, after the mountaineer Sir Hugh Munro who first listed them. 'Munro bagging', as it is called, is a popular pastime and most of them are reasonably accessible, often within easy reach of public roads.

There are coastal footpaths, nature and woodland trails, and long-distance footpaths, including the **West Highland Way**, which runs for 95 miles from Milngavie on the outskirts of Glasgow to Fort William at the southern end of the Great Glen. The nanny state has published a leaflet trying to spoil the fun of this walk: no dogs on a few stretches (even on a lead), how to pee without upsetting the environment, etc., so be prepared! There are places to stay along the way. The **Speyside Way** also runs for 30 miles, from Spey Bay to Ballindalloch, then a further 15 miles to Tomintoul.

Ski lifts for walkers are available at Cairngorm, Glencoe and Glenshee. They are open for hill walkers out of season only and give easy access to the higher terrain.

The Scottish Tourist Board issues a booklet, *Walking*, with details of walks, places to visit, etc. The **Mountaineering Council of Scotland**, The Old Granary, West Mill Street, Oerth PH1 5SE, **t** (01738) 638 227, *www.mountaineering-scotland.org.uk*, is a useful organization, as are the **Scottish Rights of Way Society** (Scotways), 24 Annandale Street, Edinburgh EH7 4AN, **t** (0131) 558 1222, *www.scotways.com*, and the **Ramblers Association Scotland**, Kingfisher House, Auld Mart Business Park, Milnathort, Kinross KY13 9DA, **t** (01577) 861 222, *www.ramblers.org.uk/scotland*.

Curling

Scotland's traditional winter game has been played for over 450 years and is described as 'a sort of bowls on ice'. These days it's usually played on indoor rinks. For information on where to go to watch or participate, contact the Scottish Sports Council, *see* above.

Diving

The wonderful clarity of the sea around the coast, full of colourful sea animals and plants, makes Scottish waters among the best in the world for diving. The places listed here are outstanding. **Scapa**, in Orkney, has four ships of the sunken German fleet, scuttled at the end of the First World War, which offer marvellous scope for wreck diving. The waters around **Oban** are also excellent. The **Sound of Mull** is littered with wrecks, and there is sub-aqua cliff scenery. **Ailsa Craig**, the **Firth of Clyde** and the **Summer Isles** are also ideal for diving. For more information contact the **Scottish Sub-aqua Club**, 40 Bogmoor Place, Glasgow, G51 4TQ, **t** (0141) 425 1021, *www.scotsac.com*.

Fishing

The salmon fishing season varies from river to river, starting in January in some places and as late as March in others. Trout fishing is from mid-March to early October. Sea fishing is extensive, with such a length of coastline. Porbeagle shark, halibut, cod, bass, hake, ling, skate and turbot are but a few of the many species of fish you can expect to find. There is never a shortage of charter boats or, in most places, of experienced locals to take you out. There is no closed season: weather and availability are the only limitations. Ask at your hotel, or in the tourist information centre.

Also try: **Central Scotland Anglers Association**, 53 Fernieside Crescent, Edinburgh EH17 7HS, **t** (0131) 664 4685; **Scottish Anglers National Association**, National Game Angling Academy, The Pier, Loch Leven, Kinross KY13 8UF, **t** (01577) 861 116, *www.sana.org.uk*; and the **Scottish Sports Council** (*see* p.41).

Also, *see* Topics, 'Fishing', pp.18–20.

Gliding

Gliding is possible in some areas and most clubs offer temporary membership and instruction. *See* Scottish Sports Council, p.41.

Golf

The monarch is **Gleneagles**, in the lee of the Ochils, though **Nairn** has a highly regarded links course, host to more than one of the Scottish Championships. **Boat of Garten**, in the Spey Valley is a relatively short course and is a joy to play. North of Inverness, **Fortrose** and **Muir of Ord**, Rosemarkie, and **Strathpeffer Spa** all offer a pleasant 18 holes, but **Tain** is the choice if time is short. **Royal Dornoch** held the first Amateur Championships in 1985.

On the islands, Arran has seven courses – **Blackwaterfoot, Lamlash and Brodick** are the pick of these. Then there is **Machrihanish** on the Mull of Kintyre and the **Machrie** on Islay.

Pony Trekking

There are many pony-trekking centres – local tourist information centres will give addresses, and tourist maps mark them with a horseshoe. The Scottish Tourist Board publishes *Pony Trekking and Riding Centres in Scotland*.

Sailing

Sailing off the west coast of Scotland and among the western and northern islands can be tricky, and proper maritime charts are essential, but it is well worth it. There are innumerable sheltered anchorages far from any human habitation, with only sea birds and sheep for company, or perhaps the eerie sound of seals calling to each other.

On the water in Scotland is a directory of water-sports facilities in Scotland, which lists firms that hire boats of all categories, together with information about slipways, chandlers, moorings, canals, and so on. It is available from the Scottish Tourist Board. You can also try the **Royal Yachting Association (Scotland)**, Caledonia House, South Gyle, Edinburgh, EH12 9DQ, **t** (0131) 317 7388, *www.ryascotland.org*.

uk, or **North of Scotland Yachting Association**, Mayfield, Victoria Road, Forres, IV36 3BN, **t** (01309) 676 931 or **t** (01343) 850 334, *www.nsya.org.uk*.

Shinty or Shinny

Scotland's version of Irish hurling is said to derive from cries used in the game: *shin ye*, *shin t'ye*. It's vaguely like hockey, with a leather ball and curved sticks.

Shooting and Stalking

No game shooting is allowed on Sundays and a certificate is required by anyone owning or using either a rifle or a shotgun.

Before you shoot game you must get a game licence, which is available in post offices throughout the country.

Some hotels will arrange shooting and stalking, and local tourist boards will advise on contacting estates and on shooting seasons.

Skiing

On the many good days, skiing in Scotland is good fun, amongst some of the most beautiful scenery in the world, though the snow is increasingly unreliable; *see* the relevant sections of the guide for particular ski areas. **Ski Hotline Scotland**, **t** 09001 654 654, *http://ski.visitscotland.com*, gives information on road and snow conditions and weather forecasts for the five ski centres.

Surfing

The north of Scotland can lay claim to some of the best surfing waves in Europe – the northernmost section from Bettyhill almost to John O'Groats has a reputation for the most consistent swells and variety of breaks. There are very few local surfers, but they are very friendly.

Tourist Offices

Scotland is divided into regions covered by Area Tourist Boards; each with its own Tourist Information Centre that publishes a free brochure with local information and a fully comprehensive accommodation guide. Readers should use these to supplement this book's recommendations. Information centres also advise on routes, sporting permits and local events, and will book accommodation. For visitor information and bookings by telephone, **Visit Scotland** (the national tourism agency) provide an **information hotline** for the whole of Scotland: **t** 0845 22 55 121. Often, calls to local tourist information centres are simply forwarded to this number. The administrative head office of Visit Scotland is at Ocean Point One, 94 Ocean Drive, Leith, Edinburgh EH6 6JH, **t** (0131) 472 2222.

The Visit Scotland Centre, 19 Cockspur Street, London, SW1 5BL, **t** (020) 7930 8661 (*open Mon–Sat throughout the year*), provides information and route planning. It also has a travel agency for accommodation and transport.

For drivers using the M6 route north, **Southwaite Tourist Information Centre**, in the Southwaite Service Station, a few minutes south of the border near Carlisle, offers full information on all areas in Scotland, as well as an accommodation service.

The main **Tourist Information Centre** for the whole of Scotland is Edinburgh Marketing, Princes Mall, 3 Princes Street (*personal callers only*). Run with American Express and Europcar, it offers advice, accommodation and travel booking, route planning, a Scottish bookshop, currency exchange and car hire.

These are the area tourist boards:

Argyll, the Isles, Loch Lomond, Stirling and Trossachs Tourist Board, 41 Dumbarton Road, Stirling FK8 2QQ, **t** 08707 200 620, *www.visitscottishheartlands.com*

The Highlands of Scotland Tourist Board, Peffery House, Strathpeffer, IV14 9HA, **t** (01997) 421 160, *www.visithighlands.com*.

Orkney Tourist Board, 6 Broad St, Kirkwall, Orkney, KW15 1NX, **t** (01856) 872 856, *www.visitorkney.com*.

Perthshire Tourist Board, Lower City Mills, West Mill St, Perth, PH1 5QP, **t** (01738) 450 600, *www.perthshire.co.uk*.

Shetland Islands Tourism, Market Cross, Lerwick, Shetland, ZE1 0LU, **t** (01595) 693 434, *www.shetland.com*.

Western Isles Tourist Board, 26 Cromwell St, Stornoway, Isle of Lewis, HS1 2DD, **t** (01851) 703 088, *www.visithebrides.com*.

Tracing Your Ancestors

A large number of exiled Scots, and descendants of exiled Scots, return hoping to trace their family history. Write to the **Keeper of the Records of Scotland**, National Archives of Scotland, Her Majesty's General Register House, Princes Street, Edinburgh, EH1 3YY, **t** (0131) 535 1314, *www.nas.gov.uk*, with all the information you have on your ancestors. Many clans have their own historian/library and will give advice. The **Scottish Genealogy Society Library and Family History Centre**, 15 Victoria Terrace, Edinburgh, EH1 2JL, **t** (0131) 220 3677, *www.scotsgenealogy.com*, or the **Scottish Roots Ancestral Research Service**, 22 Forth Street, Edinburgh EH1 3LH, **t** (0131) 477 8214, *www.scottish-roots.co.uk*, are worth a try.

For one of the best genealogists for the Western Isles, contact Bill Lawson, Taobh Tuath, Isle of Harris, **t** (01859) 520 488, *www.hebrides.com/org/genealogy*.

For an American genealogist, try Mark Kennedy Windover, Williamstown MA, t 800 634 5399, *www.windover.com*.

The **Highland Folk Museum** in Kingussie is running a root-finding project. Call Paul Basu, t (01540) 662 435, for details.

Where to Stay

The choice of accommodation in Scotland ranges from a few superb, luxury hotels to simple bed and breakfasts, or self-catering, and the price is not always a reliable guide. The **Scottish Tourist Board** (STB) accommodation guides give full details of price and facilities. This guide gives only a very small selection.

As little as £18 a night can buy bed and breakfast in a clean house, with a warm welcome and a good breakfast, while £120 can buy a night in a four-poster bed. Over £200 can buy a suite with a Jacuzzi.

You can rent a whole house or cottage from £100 a week to well over £1,000. Prices vary seasonally: single rooms are usually more expensive, per head, than double. A static caravan costs from £50 a week, and camp sites charge from about £5 a night for visiting caravans.

Camp-site facilities vary enormously, though often the scenery makes up for primitive plumbing. Many bed and breakfast places serve an evening meal, and all hotels provide full service.

Don't be put off by the lack of en-suite bathrooms in the smaller hotels and B&Bs – this is invariably made up for in the friendly hospitality. Often, 'public bathroom' means sole use of a bathroom across the passage.

STB Accommodation Gradings

An impartial team of inspectors visits hotels, guest houses, bed and breakfast and self-catering establishments, to assess their quality. They award classifications ranging from one to five stars, depending on the standard and facilities. Full details can be obtained from the Scottish Tourist Board (*www.visitscotland.com*). Visitors should be aware that these awards are based on a set range of standards and facilities – they do not necessarily apply to character and soul. It is therefore possible to opt for a five-star hotel

Hotel Price Ranges

Prices change frequently. In this guide accommodation is loosely graded into three categories, based on the price of bed and breakfast for one person in a single room.
expensive £80 at the bottom end of this range, and at the other end, the sky's the limit.
moderate about £30 to £80 should buy you a comfortable night.
budget as little as £15 a night, if you are lucky, otherwise up to about £30.

only to find yourself in a double-glazed bedroom crammed with gadgets, totally lacking in atmosphere. Equally, a slightly shabby ex-shooting lodge, with blazing log fires instead of central heating, pure cotton sheets, early-morning tea brought to you, and delicious home cooking, may be excluded.

Wolsey Lodges

Wolsey Lodges are private homes where guests are made welcome as friends, entertained as family and often dine with their hosts and other guests. The atmosphere is generally like an informal country house party. The standard of cooking is high, usually done by the hostess or host, using as many local ingredients as possible. There is often a trust bar. Some houses are licensed, but if not, guests may bring their own drink.

Prices vary but are always reasonable for what is offered.

Youth Hostels

Scottish Youth Hostel Association hostels are marked on most maps by a triangle. Anyone over the age of five may use a youth hostel. For full details, write to the **Scottish Youth Hostel Association**, 7 Glebe Crescent, Stirling, FK8 2JA, t (01786) 891 400. To find out about the availability of rooms at a variety of hostels at the same time, you can phone central reservations on t 08701 553 255. Or you can book online at *www.syha.org.uk*. There are also a large number of independent hostels/bunkhouses/bothys, and it is well worth getting brochures from Scottish Tourist Board Information Centres.

Perthshire:
Gateway to the Highlands

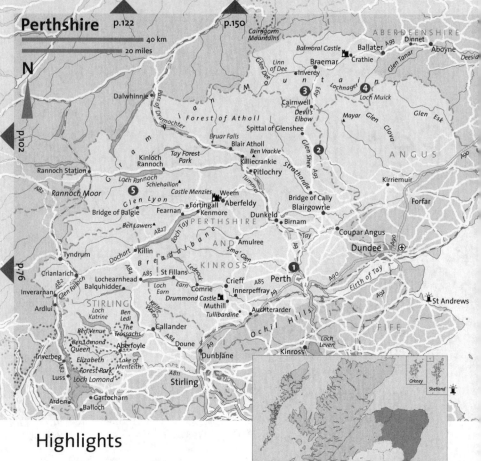

Perthshire

p.122
p.150
p.102
p.76

40 km
20 miles

N

ABERDEENSHIRE

Cairngorm Mountains

Balmoral Castle · Ballater · Dinnet · Aboyne
Braemar · Crathie · Glen Tanar · Deeside
Linn of Dee · Inverey
Dalwhinnie · Lochnagar · Loch Muick
Cairnwell · Mayar · Glen Clova · Glen Esk
Devil's Elbow
Forest of Atholl · Spittal of Glenshee
Bruar Falls · ANGUS
Blair Atholl · Ben Vrackie
Kinloch Rannoch · Tay Forest Park · Killiecrankie · Kirriemuir
Rannoch Station · Schiehallion · Pitlochry
Loch Rannoch · Castle Menzies · Weem
Rannoch Moor · Glen Lyon · Aberfeldy · Bridge of Cally · Forfar
Bridge of Balgie · Fearnan · Fortingall · Kenmore · Dunkeld · Blairgowrie
Ben Lawers · Birnam
PERTHSHIRE · Coupar Angus
AND · Dundee
Tyndrum · Dochart · Killin · Amulree · Sma'Glen
Breadalbane · KINROSS
Crianlarich · St Fillans · Crieff · Perth
Inverarnan · Glen Falloch · Lochearnhead · Balquhidder · Loch Earn · Comrie · Innerpeffray · Firth of Tay
Ardlui · STIRLING · Drummond Castle · Auchterarder · St Andrews
Loch Katrine · Ben Ledi · Muthill · Tullibardine
The Trossachs · Callander · Ochil Hills · FIFE
Ben Venue · Ben Lomond · Aberfoyle · Doune · Loch Leven
Inverbeg · Queen Elizabeth Forest Park · Lake of Menteith · Dunblane · Kinross
Luss · Loch Lomond · Stirling
Arden · Gartocharn
Balloch

SCOTLAND
Orkney
Shetland
NORTHERN IRELAND
ENGLAND

Highlights

1 Scone Palace, near Perth
2 Skiing in Glen Shee
3 Britain's highest main road – the A93 to Braemar – a spectacular route
4 Lochnagar's inspiring White Mount
5 Breathtaking scenery around Lochs Tummel and Rannoch

Perthshire and its borders represent the overture to the Highlands. Some of the scenery is grand enough, but the traveller is beckoned onwards, aware that this is a mere foretaste of what lies beyond. The city of Perth is the rather stern dowager who, late in a long life, is making a valiant effort to adjust to the 20th century – some time after the 21st century began. With Royal Deeside to the northeast, the area attracts well-born settlers and its estates offer a variety of expensive sport. To the southwest, the Trossachs lure and cater for too many people – best avoided by seekers of peace and solitude who should head north and northwest. Here, with the massive Grampians, torrential rivers, dark mysterious lochs and the moonscape to the west of Rannoch, you can get away from it all and begin to discover the Highlands proper.

Perth

We very soon came upon Perth, the situation of which is quite lovely;
it is on the Tay, with wooded hills skirting it entirely on one side,
and hills are seen again in the distance, the river winding beautifully.
Albert was charmed, and said it put him in mind of the situation of Basle.

Queen Victoria, on first seeing Perth, September 1842

Perth is the self-styled gateway to the Highlands. Reached in a flash from Edinburgh and Glasgow, it is an ideal centre from which to explore the more popular areas of the Southern Highlands. Parts of this area are not, strictly speaking, truly Highland, but they masquerade it well enough to serve as a fitting prelude to the northern hills.

Coming down into Perth from the M90 you get a fine view of the town – it is in fact the same as that extolled not only by Queen Victoria (quoted above), but also by Sir Walter Scott in the first few pages of his introduction to *The Fair Maid of Perth*. Two wide green parks, North and South Inch, unfold on either side, with a collage of

Tourist Information

Perth: Lower City Mills, West Mill Street, PH1 5QP, **t** (01738) 450 600, *www.perthshire.co.uk*. For good city maps and planned walks.

Sports and Activities

Bells Cherrybank Centre, **t** (01738) 472 818. Visitor centre for Bells Whisky – houses the National Heather Collection.

Noah's Ark, Old Gallows Road, Perth, **t** (01738) 445 568. Excellent indoor adventure play area. Each session is 1½ hours (adults free), and there is a restaurant.

Noah's Ark Indoor Karting is next door – also has a fast-food café. *Open daily 10–6.30.*

Perthshire Activity Days, **t** (01577) 861 186. Can arrange a large number of outdoor activities. All ages catered for.

Perth Leisure Pool, Glover Street, **t** (01738) 635 454, and a **Health Oasis**, **t** 635 454, for every sort of self-indulgence. *Open daily; adm.*

Perth Mart Visitor Centre, off the A85 to Crieff, East Huntingtower, **t** (01738) 474 170. Celebrates Scotland's farming heritage. *Open daily Mon–Sat 9–5 Sun 10–5; adm.* The **Perth Bull Sales**, in February and October, attract farmers from all over Britain, and they pay astronomical prices for the best bulls in the land. The sales are great fun and in the summer they stage the Highland Farm Life Show, which children enjoy.

Perth Repertory Theatre, **t** (01738) 472 700. Varied, with high standard of performance – with bar, coffee house and restaurant.

The Perth Sculpture Trail runs for about a mile along the river. Details at the tourist office.

Perth Playhouse Cinema, **t** (01738) 623 126. Has been refurbished and is now a 7-screen multiplex cinema.

Splash, Stanley, 5 miles north, **t** (01887) 829 706. Excellent for white-water rafting – over a fairly easy 5-mile stretch of the river Tay.

Where to Stay and Eat

Isle of Skye Toby Hotel, 18 Dundee Road, **t** (01738) 624 471, *www.isleofskye perth.co.uk* (*moderate*). Large and impersonal, yet comfortable and closely situated to town. Some rooms have views of the Tay.

Lovat Hotel, Glasgow Road, **t** (01738) 636 555, *www.scotlandshotels.co.uk* (*moderate*). Comfortable rooms and good food in both restaurant and bistro.

Queen's Hotel, Leonard Street, **t** (01738) 442 222, *www.scotlandshotels.co.uk*

spires reaching for the sky. 'Inch' derives from the Gaelic for island: in times of flood the Inches were cut off from the town.

Perth was the first place where the river could be bridged easily. It was a thriving port in the old days and is now an important livestock market at the centre of a productive agricultural area. First linen and then cotton were once the chief manufacturing industries. Perth used to be renowned for fulling and dyeing the cloths: Pullars of Perth is still here, though much less important now than it used to be. Bells Whisky has its administrative headquarters in the town. Its fine setting earned Perth the title 'the Fair City' (although it's also known as St John's Toun – the football team is St Johnstone) and recent refurbishment has done much to restore it to that status. When a new Marks and Spencer store was being built in the High Street some time ago, the remains of a medieval market were unearthed, resulting in a valuable stay of execution for several fine buildings. Now, with a bypass easing traffic congestion in the town centre, traffic-free shopping streets, and floral displays, Perth is once again an attractive place, particularly when the sun is shining. If you poke around, you can still find traces of the past: there are some splendid late-Georgian terraces, especially around the Inches, with charming vistas of the river.

(*moderate*). Extensive leisure facilities, with good food, near the bus and train stations.

Ramada Jarvis Hotel, West Mill Street, **t** (01738) 628 281, *www.ramadajarvis.co.uk* (*moderate*). A converted *c*. 15th-century water mill in a quiet yet central area, with comfortable rooms and two restaurants.

The Royal George Hotel, Tay Street, **t** (01738) 624 455, *www.theroyalgeorgehotel.co.uk* (*moderate*). On the river bank; Queen Victoria stayed here.

Salutation Hotel, 34 South Street, **t** (01738) 630 066, *www.strathmorehotels.com* (*moderate*). One of several hotels claiming to be the oldest in Scotland – has strong Jacobite connections (it was briefly Prince Charles' headquarters).

Sunbank House Hotel, 50 Dundee Road, **t** (01738) 624 882, *www.sunbankhouse.com* (*moderate*). An early Victorian house with views of the Tay – a short walk from the town centre. Good food.

The nicest accommodation is in fact on the city's perimeter:

Ballathie House Hotel, Kinclaven, Stanley, north of Perth, **t** (01250) 883 268, *www.ballathiehousehotel.com* (*expensive*). Overgrown Victorian shooting lodge over-looking the Tay. Won a Macallan 'Taste of Scotland' award for its cuisine; offers activities such as salmon fishing.

Campsie Hill, near Guildtown, near Perth, **t** (01821) 640 325, *campsie@globalnet.co.uk* (*moderate*). Wolsey Lodge that is still very much a family home with the emphasis on hospitality and relaxation.

Murrayshall House Hotel, Scone, **t** (01738) 551 171 (*moderate*). Has two 18-hole golf courses within its 300-acre grounds. Comfortable, with wholesome food.

Overkinfauns, off the A90 to Dundee, **t** (01738) 860 538, *www.overkinfauns.co.uk* (*budget*). Friendly guesthouse in a farmhouse overlooking the Tay. Delicious dinners by arrangement.

Eating Out

Let's Eat, 77 Kinnoull Street, **t** (01738) 643 377 (*moderate*). Has won many awards – very good food in a bistro-type atmosphere.

Let's Eat Again, George Street, **t** (01738) 633 771 (*moderate*). Reasonably priced, especially for bar meals, and seafood. Near Tay Street.

Betty's, 67 George Street. Tearoom serving memorable home-made cakes and snacks.

Greyfriars, South Street. Intimate and convivial – one of the best pubs in Perth.

Mucky Mulligan's, 97 Canal Street, **t** (01738) 636 705. Lively Irish pub serving food: an excellent choice.

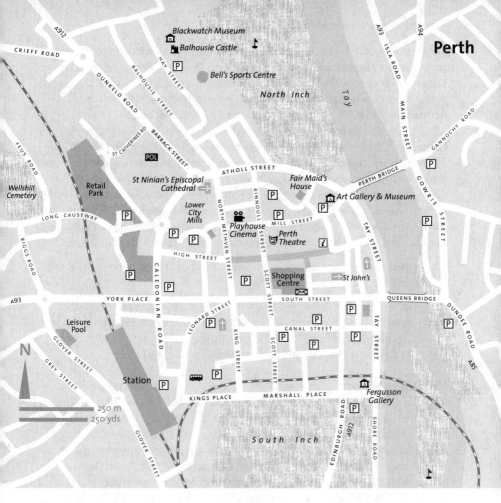

History

Traces of an old city wall in Albert Close, off George Street, indicate there was a Roman camp here, although Perth doesn't appear in the records until the 12th century. The name derives from *Aber-tha* – the mouth of the Tay, which became 'Bertha' in Roman times, and then Perth.

A devastating flood destroyed Old Perth in 1210, remembered in the song:

Says the Shochie to the Ordie,
'Where shall we meet?
'At the cross o' Perth,
When a' men are fast asleep.'

William the Lion granted a Royal Charter to the town that was built in its place the same year. It was the capital of Scotland and a town of ecclesiastical importance until the middle of the 15th century: Greyfriars, Blackfriars, Whitefriars and Carthusians all had establishments within the walled city. James I, unpopular for his draconian attempts to subdue his fractious subjects, was assassinated at Blackfriars in 1437. (A 16th-century legend tells the story of Catherine Douglas, Catherine 'Bar-Lass', who supposedly tried to bar the door to the murderers by using her arm as a bolt in the hasps.) John Knox initiated the Reformation in Perth in 1559, which saw the destruction of many sacred treasures, including the Abbey of Scone.

The mysterious drama of the Gowrie Conspiracy took place in 1600 in Gowrie House, now demolished. James VI was lured to an upstairs room by the Earl of Gowrie and his brother Alexander Ruthven (rhymes with 'driven'), and his life was in some way threatened. From an upstairs window he shouted for his lords, who rescued him, killing Gowrie and Ruthven in the scrimmage. The affair provoked much speculation, with hints of homosexual motivation mingling with suggestions that the king staged the event to rid himself of the brothers, whose ruthless political ambition was notorious. Andrew Lang, the Victorian journalist, reported an old Scottish lady as declaring:

It is a great comfort to think that at the Day of Judgement we shall know the whole truth about the Gowrie Conspiracy at last.

Legend has it, albeit hotly refuted by music historians, that Gaetano Donizetti (1797–1848), the prolific composer of bel canto, was descended from a Perthshire adventurer named Izatt, or Izett, who served with the Spanish army in Italy and was known as Don Izetti. There are still Izatts or Izetts around in Perth today.

Visiting the Town

St John's Kirk (*open Mon–Fri 10–12 and 2–4*) was founded in 1126 by David I. The present building dates from the 15th century. The War Memorial Chapel was designed by Robert Lorimer when the church was restored in 1923. Edward III is said to have killed his brother, the Earl of Cornwall, here in 1335. It was in this now plain church that John Knox preached his iconoclastic sermon in 1559, urging his followers to purge the churches of idolatry; this sermon led to the destruction of many of the churches and monasteries in the area and helped fuel the Reformation. St John's had at least 40 richly decorated altars dedicated to saints and it is heartbreaking to think of the treasures that were lost. The church is also used for festival concerts and theatre – check either in the Tourist Information Centre or in the church.

The **Fair Maid's House** (*closed at present*), standing on the site of a 13th-century monastery, can be seen from outside. It is behind Charlotte Street in North Port and was the home of virtuous Catharine Glover, the Fair Maid herself. **Balhousie Castle**, a heavily restored 15th-century Scottish Baronial castle beyond Rose Terrace, on the west side of North Inch, was the home of the Earls of Kinnoull. Now the regimental headquarters of the Black Watch, it houses its **Regimental Museum** (*open May–Sept Mon–Fri 10–4.30; Oct–April Mon–Fri 10–3.30*). The Black Watch – so called because of their dark tartan – was raised in 1739 to help the government pacify the restless Highlanders who were gathering momentum for their final bid for independence in 1745. The museum has a comprehensive display of the history of this famous regiment, with uniforms, weapons and photographs recording its honours and triumphs.

Brave Bargain at the Battle of the Clans

One of the more colourful events in the city's history was the Battle of the Clans in 1396, woven by Scott into the convoluted story of *The Fair Maid*. This was a contest between the Clan Ha, or Kay, ancestors of Clan Chattan, and Clan Quhele (pronounced 'wheel'; probably ancestors of Clan Macmillan), to establish who should take precedence in battle – a hotly disputed honour in those swashbuckling days. Thirty men from each side were to fight in a tournament on the North Inch, watched by King Robert III, his wife and the court. At the last moment, one of the Clan Ha lost his nerve and fled. The rule was that the two sides must be matched man-for-man, so a small bandy-legged blacksmith, Hal o' the Wynd, offered to stand in, for the fee of half a French crown. All but one of the Quhele Clan were slaughtered. Among the survivors of the Clan Ha was the blacksmith who, for such a meagre price, had done more than anyone else to secure the victory.

Perth Art Gallery and Museum, in George Street (*open all year Mon–Sat 10–5*), one of the oldest museums in Britain, often has some very fine paintings of local interest, as well as good examples of Perth silverware and furniture. It also has exhibits on the natural and social history of the town and its surroundings. **Fergusson Gallery** in the Round House in Marshall Place (*open all year Mon–Sat 10–5*) is devoted to the work of the Scottish painter and leader of the Scottish 'Colourist' movement, J. D. Fergusson (1874–1961) and his contemporaries. A Perthshire man, who worked mostly in France, Fergusson's statuesque round-bosomed women are not to everyone's taste, but his landscapes are lovely and some of his sculpture very fine.

The **Round House** used to be the city waterworks and from a distance resembles a mosque with its minaret. It still has a spherical water monument in front inscribed *Haurio et haereo* – 'I draw water and hold it'. **Lower City Mills**, West Mill Street (*open April–Nov Mon–Sat 10–5; adm; mill shop open all year*), is a splendidly restored Georgian oatmeal mill which once produced the porridge for prisons all over Britain. It is still working, with its massive waterwheel driven by the Town's Lade (millstream).

Branklyn Garden, off Dundee Road (*www.branklyngarden.org.uk; open Mar–Oct daily 9.30–sunset; adm*) was designed in 1910 by John Renton, a local estate agent, and his wife. Skilful planning and unexpected vistas make the 2-acre gardens seem much larger. At **Bridgend**, at the east end of Perth Bridge, take note of an old toll house which still has the notice of charges for sheep, horses, etc., which put inflated modern prices to shame.

Scone Palace, pronounced 'Scoon', (*www.scone-palace.co.uk; open April–Oct daily 9.30–5.30; adm*) 2 miles north of Perth on the A93, is a 19th-century restoration of 16th-century and earlier buildings. A popular tourist attraction, this neogothic pile is of historical rather than aesthetic interest, though it has some fine porcelain, ivories and memorabilia (including Marie Antoinette's writing desk). Prince Albert is said to have used the ancient bog-oak floor of the long gallery as a curling rink. Probably once a Pictish capital, Scone became an important centre of the Celtic church. Kenneth Macalpine brought the Stone of Destiny here from Dunstaffnage in 850 (*see* 'The Stone of Destiny', pp.8–9). Edward I stole what he thought to be the stone, now called the Stone of Scone, installing it in Westminster Abbey, but coronations continued here until that of Charles II in 1651. Alexander I established a priory of Augustinian canons here in 1120, which became an abbey in 1160. This and its adjacent palace were destroyed by John Knox's followers after his sermon in St John's in 1559.

The **Perth Hunt Racecourse**, the most northerly in Britain, is in the palace grounds. Steeplechase only, the Perth Races (*April/May and Aug/Sept*) attract many runners, drawn by the quality of its old-established turf. Also within Perth's environs is the **Caithness Glass Factory** (*www.caithnessglass.co.uk; open Mon–Sat 9–5, till 6 mid-June–Sept; Sun 10–5 (12–5 Dec–Feb); glassmaking Mon–Fri 9–4.30 all year and at weekends July and Aug*), off the bypass at the turn-off to Inverness, where you can watch glassware being made, buy it from the shop, or try it in the restaurant.

Climb **Kinnoull Hill** for an excellent bird's-eye view of Perth and the countryside around it. From here, you can define the geological 'Highland Line' that divides the Highlands from the Lowlands. The two follies, very visible from the A90, were built by the Earl of Kinnoull and by Lord Gray, owner of Kinfauns Castle, to make work for the local poor and in memory of a visit to the Rhine.

Huntingtower Castle (*open April–Sept daily 9.30–6.30; Oct–Mar Mon–Wed, Sat and Sun 9.30–4.30; adm*) is 3 miles northwest of Perth on the Crieff Road. Built by the Ruthven family in the 15th century and formerly called House of Ruthven or Ruthven Castle, this was the scene of the Ruthven Raid in 1582 when the Earl of Gowrie and several Protestant nobles captured and held 15-year-old James VI for 10 months as a hostage against a demand that some of the royal favourites be dismissed (*see* the Gowrie Conspiracy, p.50). In 1670 it passed to the Earl of Atholl, whose grandson, Lord George Murray, Prince Charles' commander, was born here in 1694. The castle fell into ruin but was rescued by the state in 1900 and still has very fine painted walls and ceilings. Nearby, the **Perth Mart and Agricultural Centre** (*open all year*) has a visitor centre, restaurant and shops. Find out when the famous Bull Sales are on – an experience not to be missed (*see* 'Sports and Activities', p.47).

Elcho Castle (*open April–Sept daily 9.30–6.30; adm*), a ruin 4 miles southeast of Perth on the south bank of the Tay, incorporates a defensive structure and palace-like comforts. The square tower with a crow-stepped gable dates from when James III granted the lands of Elcho to John de Wemyss in 1468. The huge kitchen has a fireplace as big as a small room, and the bedrooms had *en-suite* garderobes.

Around Perthshire

Perth to Balmoral

Blairgowrie to Braemar

Blairgowrie is a popular tourist centre (especially with golfers) about 16 miles north of Perth on the A93, beside the fast-flowing Ericht Water. Old mills stand along the river, some derelict, some converted into dwellings (*at least one is open to the public*). The Highlands beckon, and there is skiing to the north, at Glenshee. This is also the centre of the Scottish soft fruit industry thanks to the fertile soil. With rivers cascading through steep mountain glens and sudden glimpses of snow-capped peaks massing on the horizon, it's magical walking country.

While you are in the area, you should climb one of the many surrounding hills: make a detour east from Blairgowrie on the A962 to Kirriemuir and take the B955 north up Glen Clova. Go right to the end of the road where there is a car park near the youth hostel and have a go at Driesh and Mayar, part of the great rolling tableland of the White Mounth, south of Deeside. A track called Jock's Road goes on past Acharn through Glen Doll. Ignore all side tracks, including the fork where Jock's Road branches right to Deeside. Cross the White Water and walk along Fee Burn up towards Corrie Fee. The rest is obvious and you can choose where you go towards the top. Allow about 6 hours if you want to enjoy the summits.

From spring to autumn, the A93 to Braemar – Britain's highest main road – is a spectacular route. It once included the Devil's Elbow, a hair-raising zigzag that trapped large vehicles and was often cut off by snow. This has now been ironed out, but you can still see bits of it as you flash past on the new road. As you look across to

Tourist Information

Blairgowrie: 26 Wellmeadow, **t** (01250) 872 960,*www.perthshire.co.uk. Open all year.*

Braemar: The Mews, Mar Road, **t** (013397) 41600. *Open all year.*

Crathie: Balmoral Castle Car Park, **t** (013397) 42414. *Open end Mar–mid Nov.*

Where to Stay and Eat

Ballathie House, Kinclaven, near Blairgowrie, **t** (01250) 883 268,*www.ballathie-house-hotel.co.uk (expensive)*. Excellent food, lovely atmosphere and fishing available.

Kinloch House Hotel, by Blairgowrie, **t** (01250) 884 237, *www.kinlochhouse. com (expensive)*. Well-appointed, early-Victorian country house. The focus is fishing and the cuisine is high class.

Angus Hotel, Blairgowrie, **t** (01250) 872 455, *www.theangushotel.com (moderate)*. Rambling, convenient and very comfortable, with pool, sauna, solarium and spa bath, as well as golf and fishing.

Ashintully Castle, Kirkmichael, north of Blairgowrie, **t** (01250) 881 237, *www.ashintully.com (moderate)*. Dating from 1583, this secluded Wolsey Lodge in 3,000 acres is now run as a sheep farm and sporting estate. Cordon bleu food; outdoor activities.

Bamff House, Alyth, Blairgowrie, **t** (01828) 632 992, *www.bamff.co.uk (moderate)*. Splendid hotchpotch of additions to this *c.* 16th-century town house. Comfy and hospitable, with dinner by arrangement.

Craighall Castle and Craighall Rattray Estate, Blairgowrie, **t** (01250) 874 749, *www.craighall.co.uk (moderate)*. Spectacularly positioned B&B in 300 acres overlooking a gorge.

Dalmunzie House Hotel, Spittal o'Glenshee, **t** (01250) 885 224, *www.dalmunzie.com (moderate)*. Sprawling country house with a 9-hole golf course and relaxed atmosphere, only five miles from the slopes.

Moorfield House Hotel, Myreriggs Road, Coupar Angus, near Blairgowrie, **t** (01828) 627 303 *(moderate)*. Family run, friendly and comfortable.

Rosemount Golf Hotel, Golf Course Road, Rosemount, Blairgowrie, **t** (01250) 872 604, *www.rosemountgolf.co.uk (moderate)*. Quiet hotel specializing in golf holidays – nice gardens and warm welcome.

the remains of the old road, spare a thought for Queen Victoria, who used to travel up here with her entourage in their carriages, before they braved the new railway. They changed horses at Blairgowrie, stopped for lunch at the inn at Spittal of Glenshee, and trundled on north through the magnificent scenery. Escorted by locals on foot in case they got into difficulties, they negotiated the Devil's Elbow to reach Cairn Wall (Cairnwell), which marked the watershed. From here it was easier going for the horses, as they carried the royal party on to Braemar and Balmoral.

Glenshee is one of Scotland's main ski resorts. Its challenging pistes are often icy and demanding – especially the Tiger run, which is best left to experienced skiers – but in the right conditions there is scope for every ability. There are three valleys and four mountains with the largest network of lifts in Scotland – 26 in all. Weather conditions can be extreme, roads sometimes becoming impassable in snow. For skiing information, ring the Blairgowrie Tourist Information Office or visit *http://ski.visitscotland.com*. **Strathardle** forks off northwest of Glenshee from **Bridge of Cally**, on the A924, where the River Ardle and Black Water converge: another good launching pad for climbs and walks in lovely surroundings.

Braemar, some 17 miles north of Glenshee on the A93, has the record for Britain's lowest recorded temperature at −27°C. Royal Deeside is certainly scenic, although it is both too popular and too smart for some tastes, falling into the category of 'Designer Highlands'. **Braemar Castle** (*open April–Oct Sat–Thurs 10–6; July–Aug daily 10–6; last entry 5.30pm; adm*) is a massive, turreted fortress built by the Earl of Mar in 1628. It was burnt by the Farquharsons in 1689 and garrisoned by the English after the Jacobite risings in 1715 and 1745 to protect the military road from Perth. The castle has barrel-vaulted ceilings, a sinister pit prison, spiral stairways and gun loops. Look for the carved graffiti on the internal woodwork, left by off-duty soldiers in the 18th century. Keen Jacobites should visit the **Invercauld Arms**, on the spot where the Earl of Mar raised the Jacobite standard in 1715: a plaque commemorates the occasion.

Braemar Royal Highland Gathering is held every year on the first Saturday in September, drawing upwards of 20,000 people. It includes all the traditional events, both athletic and musical, together with plenty of stalls and sideshows. The Royal Family attend the games, which might be why it is one of the biggest events of its kind in Scotland, though perhaps one of the least reminiscent of those original games in the 11th century, when Malcolm Canmore held contests to find the best soldiers for his struggles against the Normans. For less showy, more authentic Highland Games, you must head north and west, away from the more popular areas.

Lochnagar is a good hill to climb if you have a spare day – it takes about 8 hours, and you need a good map. The north peak of the White Mounth has a fascination for artists and poets as well as climbers. It even inspired today's Prince of Wales to write a children's story. Start at Invercauld Bridge where the A93 crosses the Dee, 3 miles east of Braemar. Take one of the two forest roads by the bridge into Ballochbuie Forest, bought by Queen Victoria to keep it from being felled. Take the right fork after about half a mile, and cross over the next intersection. Keep left at the hairpin bend, passing the Falls of Garbh Allt, and rejoin the forestry road. The view at the top is lovely.

A circular tour of about 12 miles west from Braemar, through the wooded Dee Valley, includes the **Linn of Dee**. A 'linn' is a waterfall, a gorge, or a pool below a waterfall – this is all three, and consequently very popular. The narrow, rocky gorge is about 150 yards long. The river boils through this bottleneck in a tumultuous frenzy, filling the air with noise and a haze of spray. You won't find solitude here, though, unless it's early or late in the day. Follow the track west along the Dee to White Bridge, where it crosses the river and turns away to the south. You can walk for miles along here, with tracks leading off up into the hills to the east.

Another good walk from the Linn of Dee is the track south from Inverey, up Ey Water to the Colonel's Bed (less than 2 miles). The Colonel was John Farquharson of Inverey, known as the Black Colonel, who rode his horse up sheer rock slopes and used to summon his servants by firing at a wall-mounted shield which rang like a bell when hit by the bullet. The Colonel's Bed is a ledge of rock in a gorge through which the Ey runs. He hid here after his castle had been burnt down by government troops following the Battle of Killiecrankie in 1689.

Balmoral

*www.balmoralcastle.com; grounds and paintings in ballroom
and coach house open April–July daily 10–5; adm.*

Balmoral Castle, about 9 miles northeast of Braemar, is so familiar from photographs and chocolate boxes that its reality is almost an anticlimax. The parts of the castle open to the public include paintings, works of art and a tartan collection in the ballroom; an exhibition of royal heraldry, commemorative china, photographs and wildlife in the carriage hall, and carriages in the stables. In the grounds are the gardens, walks, gift shops, a café, pony trekking and pony-cart rides (if ponies are free).

Queen Victoria lost her heart to Balmoral in 1848 when it was 'a pretty little castle in the old Scottish style', leased by Victoria and Albert on the advice of their doctor as the perfect place for those with rheumatism. In the early days of their marriage, the family holiday at Balmoral was the highlight of the year, but as the royal children multiplied, it became clear that the castle was inadequate. In 1852 they bought the Balmoral estate of some 17,400 acres for 30,000 guineas, demolished the old castle and built the present one. The result, vast and imposing in pale grey ashlar, capable of housing well over 100 people, is not beautiful but has a certain endearing solidity. Albert oversaw the landscaping of the grounds, working from a model made from sand, and they are now well endowed with every sort of statue and memorial to various members of the royal household, including dogs. There were to be only seven autumn holidays in the new castle before Albert died of typhoid in 1861, and during these Victoria collected enough happy memories to last her through her long, lonely widowhood. Her visits to Balmoral became an almost sacred memorial to her beloved Albert, and, imposing as it now seems, one should picture how it must have been before it was more accessible to the public and seething with security precautions. In those halcyon days, the Queen was able to roam freely and she drew strength from 'this dear paradise'. You can walk up the hill behind the house to one of her favourite haunts – the monument to Albert. Balmoral is still the Royal Family's holiday home.

Crathie Church, just north of the castle, was built in 1895 to replace a series of previous churches whose origins date from the 9th century. The Royal Family attend the Church of Scotland Sunday service here, ensuring a good turnout of fellow worshippers during their annual holiday. This is where the royals made their first appearance following the death of Diana, Princess of Wales. Princess Anne, the Princess Royal, married her present husband Commander Tim Laurence here. In the graveyard beside the Dee, by the ruins of an older kirk, is buried John Brown, Queen Victoria's devoted servant and companion after Albert's death. Theirs was a unique relationship (beautifully portrayed in the film *Mrs Brown*) – despite his abrasive tongue and his weakness for a dram, Brown was the Queen's most loyal subject, helping to soften the grief of her widowhood.

Perth to Pitlochry

Perth to Dunkeld

The A9 is the main road north from Perth with good stretches of dual carriageway interspersed with frustrating single-lane sections. Like many Scottish roads, however, it is well landscaped.

Birnam

Be lion-mettled, proud, and take no care,
Who chafes, who frets, or where conspirers are:
Macbeth shall never vanquish'd be until
Great Birnam wood to high Dunsinane Hill
Shall come against him.

William Shakespeare, *Macbeth*, Act IV, Scene 1 – witches' prophecy

Birnam, about 14 miles north of Perth, bypassed by the main road, is familiar to all lovers of Shakespeare. From Birnam Hill, Dunsinnan, or Dunsinane Hill – opinions vary on the spelling – is about 12 miles to the southeast. Macbeth, in his castle on Dunsinane Hill, confidently believed the witches' prophecy that he was immortal until 'Birnam Forest come to Dunsinane'. Meanwhile, Malcolm had his soldiers camouflage themselves with branches from the trees in Birnam Wood and march on Dunsinane. A messenger brought the news to Macbeth: 'As I did stand my watch upon the hill, I look'd toward Birnam, and anon methought the wood began to move.' There are remains of a fort on Dunsinane Hill which was probably Macbeth's, and some of Birnam Wood is thought to date from the original forest. Queen Victoria, whose yardstick for approval was Prince Albert's, recorded of Birnam: 'Albert said, as we came along between the mountains, that to the right, where they were wooded, it was very like Thüringen, and on the left more like Switzerland.'

The **Beatrix Potter Exhibition** (*www.birnaminstitute.com; open daily 10–5; adm*) is in Birnam. The writer and her family spent long summer holidays in the area and here she developed her passion for wildlife. It was also from here that she wrote a picture letter to a friend and called it *The Tale of Peter Rabbit*. A delightful place for her fans.

Dunkeld

A mile or so on from Birnam, Dunkeld (the fort of the Celts) is an old cathedral town with an ecclesiastical history that goes back to the Celtic Church, possibly as far back as the time of St Columba. Sheltered by wooded hills and straddling the River Tay, the town is a popular centre for fishermen.

When Norsemen drove the monks from Iona in 792, they fled here and founded an abbey in which they enshrined holy relics of their founder, St Columba. Columba himself may have come to Dunkeld, possibly a few years before his death when he met up with St Mungo to discuss parish boundaries, and it is believed that the two men may have founded some sort of religious establishment then. There is a St Colm's Well nearby, though Scotland has many St Colm's Wells not necessarily related to a visit from the saint himself. Dunkeld suffered badly during the Covenanting Wars. It was here that the Cameronians, extreme Covenanters, held the town against a troop of Highlanders in 1689. Triumphant after Killiecrankie, the Highlanders stormed the town, whereupon the Cameronians set fire to most of its buildings, driving the Highlanders out and eventually securing supremacy for William and Mary.

Dunkeld Cathedral (*open daily*), dating from the early 12th century, is a substantial ruin on shady lawns beside the river. It took about 200 years to build and was

Tourist Information

Dunkeld: The Cross, **t** (01350) 727 688.
Pitlochry: 22 Atholl Road, **t** (01796) 472 215/ 472 751.

Where to Stay and Eat

Hilton Dunkeld House, Dunkeld, **t** (01350) 728 333, *reservations.dunkeld@hilton.com* (*expensive*). Former home of the Duke of Atholl, on the banks of the Tay in 280 acres with every sort of comfort and leisure facility – fishing available.

Kinnaird, Dunkeld, **t** (01350) 482 440, *www.kinnairdestate.com* (*expensive*). Ex-shooting lodge run as a private country house with all the trimmings.

Pitlochry Hydro Hotel, Knockard Road, Pitlochry, **t** (01796) 472 666, *www.shearings holidays.co.uk* (*expensive*). Imposing, but very comfortable building above the town. Owned by Shearings.

Pine Trees Hotel and Garden Restaurant, Strathview Terrace, Pitlochry, **t** (01796) 472 121, *www.pinetrees-hotel.co.uk* (*expensive–moderate*). Victorian country house in 19 acres – has garnered awards for its cooking and warm welcome. No smoking throughout.

Atholl Palace Hotel, Atholl Road, Pitlochry, **t** (01796) 472 400, *www.athollpalace.com* (*moderate*). Large pile in 48 acres surrounded by a wooded park. Not very cosy, but plenty of indoor and outdoor activities.

Knockendarroch House Hotel, Higher Oakfield, Pitlochry, **t** (01796) 473 473, *www.knockendarroch.co.uk* (*moderate*). Country house in mature gardens with good views. Only three minutes walk to town. Relaxed and comfortable; no smoking.

Auchnahyle, near Pitlochry, **t** (01796) 472 318, *www.auchnahyle.co.uk* (*moderate–budget*). Hospitable Wolsey Lodge in an 18th-century farmhouse surrounded by fields and lovely views – delicious food.

reduced to a ruin during the Reformation. The choir has been restored and is now the parish church. The nave and great northwest tower date from the 15th century. The recumbent effigy in the choir is thought to be that of Alexander Stewart, the notorious 14th-century 'Wolf of Badenoch'. Ironically, Stewart earned his sobriquet for being a keen destroyer of towns and churches, including Elgin Cathedral, in retaliation for being excommunicated for abandoning his wife.

The **Little Houses** lining Cathedral Street were built after the destruction of the town in 1689 and were saved from demolition by the National Trust for Scotland in 1950. Well restored and privately occupied, these harled cottages with outside stairs form a delightful approach to the cathedral and give this area an old-world charm.

Niel Gow, the well-known 18th-century fiddler immortalized in portrait by Raeburn, was born at Inver, south of the Tay below Dunkeld. A ferry crossed the river here until Thomas Telford built the bridge downstream in 1809. If you are addicted to sentimental restoration, the **Hermitage**, also called Ossian's Hall, is off the A9 just after Dunkeld. This folly built by the Duke of Atholl in 1758 lies along a well-trodden trail, less than a mile from where you leave your car. It was probably once very charming in a whimsical way, when it used to have mirrors reflecting the water. It is worth the stroll for the dramatic view of the Falls of Braan, from the folly.

A couple of miles northeast of Dunkeld, the **Loch of the Lowes**, formed by receding glaciers, is a nature reserve where ospreys can be watched from a hide. These large brown and white sea eagles, cousins to the falcon, are common in America where they nest on every available navigation mark in the estuaries and wreak havoc on the fish. Here they are a rare, protected species, though their numbers are increasing now that their nesting sites are fiercely protected by law. Eventually they will probably become as much of a threat to fishing as cormorants and herons. The **Wildlife Centre** (*www.swt.org.uk; open April–Sept daily; adm*) has an observation deck and shop.

Pitlochry

Thirteen miles north of Dunkeld on the A9, Pitlochry lies in the heart of Scotland, cradled by hills, with Ben Vrackie (2,759ft/849m), looming to the north. With above-average sunshine and below-average rainfall, this has been a popular holiday town since Queen Victoria, staying at Blair Atholl nearby, declared it to be one of the finest resorts in Europe. The royal stamp of approval resulted in many fine houses and mansions being built in the area, with spas that are now hotels. Today it is hard to believe it was once a remote hamlet; there were no roads north of Dunkeld until General Wade built his network of military roads after the Jacobite uprisings. Despite its popularity, it retains a leisurely, strolling atmosphere and is a good base from which to explore the Highlands. The rivers Tummel and Garry converge from their valleys into Loch Faskally to the north, hurrying through the town to join the Tay at Ballinluig to the south. The main street is cheerful with its bright façades, hotels, shops and distilleries.

Not far off the road, the **Hydroelectric Dam and Fish Ladder** (*open daily 10–5.30*) has an observation chamber to see the ingenious method of ensuring the salmon cycle is not broken. A visitor centre and exhibition (*open Easter–Oct daily*) describes activities throughout Scotland, particularly around the Loch Tummel area.

There are distilleries in the area, open to visitors with conducted tours and usually with the offer of a free dram. The **Edradour Distillery** (*www.edradour.co.uk; open Mar–Oct Mon–Sat 9.30–6, Sun 11.30–5; Nov–mid-Dec Mon–Sat 9.30–4; tours in winter depend on weather*) is the smallest in Scotland, hidden in the hills less than 3 miles east of Pitlochry. A small complex of white-washed buildings under neat grey slate roofs, tucked into a hollow beside the Edradour Burn, it was founded in 1825 by local farmers. After a conducted tour of the distillery, virtually unchanged since Victorian times, you get your free dram in front of a peat and log fire in a cosy barn. Close by, there is also the **Blair Atholl Distillery** (*t (01796) 482 003; open Easter–Sept Mon–Sat 9–5, Sun 12–5, Oct–Nov and Mar Mon–Fri 9–5, Dec and Feb restricted hours – ring first*).

Walking in this area is endlessly rewarding; every path you choose reveals fresh beauty and unexpected views. There are waterfalls and gorges, festooned with lush ferns, woods and hills and rivers running fast and shallow over rocky beds.

Perth to Crieff

Crieff

Crieff (from *Crubha Cnoc* – Hill of Trees) is about 16 miles west of Perth on the A85 and used to hold the biggest cattle tryst in Scotland in the days when sturdy black cattle were the principal currency of the Highland economy. In the summer, drovers from all over the Highlands and Islands would drive their herds over inhospitable, almost impassable tracks to the market to sell to men from the south. The fair earned such a reputation for violent behaviour that it was moved to Falkirk in the 1770s. The town was sacked and destroyed by Highlanders during the Jacobite rebellion and little remains from before the 19th century. Later, a bleaching and tanning industry brought prosperity to its people and it became a popular spa town in the 19th century, attracting a number of good schools into the area, including Morrison's Academy. Echoes of its Victorian heyday linger on in the **Crieff Hydro Hotel** (*see* p.60), perched above the town and embellished with glass domes and pavilions, which opened in 1868 as the Strathearn Hydropathic, 12 years after the arrival of the railway.

Crieff today is an attractive, lively town on the south-facing foothills of the Grampians, looking down over the valley of the River Earn. The Knock of Crieff (911ft/280m), a wooded hill with footpaths and good views from the top, dominates the north. The **Crieff Visitor Centre** (*t (01764) 654 014, open April–Oct daily 9–5, Nov–Mar 10–4*) in Muthill Road is a popular attraction. It incorporates Perthshire Paperweights, Scotland's oldest working pottery, a showroom, an audiovisual presentation and a garden centre, as well as a factory shop and a licensed restaurant. Further along Muthill Road is the **Stuart Crystal Factory Shop** and a **Falconry Centre** (*open June–Sept daily 10–6, Oct–May Mon–Sat 10–5, Sun 11–5*). The **Strathearn Gallery and Pottery**, 32 West High Street (*open Mon–Sat 10–5, Sun 1–5*), is a gallery of contemporary art and a working pottery. The **Glenturret Distillery** (*open Mon–Sat*

Tourist Information

Crieff: Town Hall, High St, **t** (01764) 652 578.
Dunblane: Stirling Rd, **t** (01786) 824 428. *Open May–Sept.*
Auchterarder: 90 High St, **t** (01764) 663 450.

Where to Stay and Eat

The Gleneagles Hotel, near Crieff, **t** (01764) 662 231, **freephone** (UK) 0800 328 4010, *www.gleneagles.com* (*expensive*). With world-renowned golf courses, a reputation as one of Scotland's best hotels and everything a hedonist could desire.

Crieff Hydro Hotel, Crieff, **t** (01764) 655 555, *www.crieffhydro.com* (*moderate*). Set in 800 acres high above the town, with its own golf course, riding school and sports hall. The brasserie has an AA rosette. Well geared towards families.

The Four Seasons Hotel, St Fillans, on Loch Earn, **t** (01764) 685 333, *www.thefourseasonshotel.co.uk* (*moderate*). Highly acclaimed restaurant and a member of the Scotch Beef Club – private chalets too.

Kippenross, Dunblane, **t** (01786) 824 048 (*moderate*). A small family estate, not in the Highlands but near enough to make it worth the detour as a place to stay. No smoking.

Murraypark Hotel, Connaught Terrace, Crieff, **t** (01764) 653 731, *www.murraypark.com* (*moderate*). Pink-stoned Victorian house in attractive grounds. Very friendly and does good food.

Leven House Hotel, Comrie Road, Crieff, **t** (01764) 652 529 (*budget*). Pleasant, old-fashioned little house with a garden.

Meadow Inn Hotel, Burrell St, Crieff, **t** (01764) 653 261, *meadowinn@barbox.net* (*budget*). Lively town-centre hotel on a corner site. Convivial and very convenient.

Merlindale (formerly Lediffton House), Perth Road, Crieff, **t** (01764) 655 205, *www.merlindale.co.uk* (*budget*). Georgian house close to the town centre, proud of its cordon bleu cooking.

Royal Hotel, Comrie, **t** (01764) 679 200, *www.royalhotel.co.uk* (*moderate*). Good place to go for stylish good food with a splendid pub-bar.

10–6, last tour 4.30; adm) is also worth a visit – it's the oldest distillery in Scotland, established in 1775; it's home of the Famous Grouse Experience.

Around Crieff

Innerpeffray Library (*open Feb–Nov Fri–Wed 10–12.45 and 2–4.45, Sun 2–4; adm*), 4 miles southeast of Crieff off the B8062, is the oldest lending library in Scotland, with the ruins of Innerpeffray Castle a few hundred yards away (*not open to the public*). It is hard to believe that in Roman times this was on the main route from England to the north. The first Lord Madderty (or Madertie) built the castle in 1610 as his family home. About 50 years later his grandson, the 3rd Lord Madderty, established a library in St Mary's chapel in the burial ground nearby, along with a school. In his will in 1691 he bequeathed 5,000 Scots *merks* (about £277) in trust to the library and school. His nephew and heir, William Drummond, 2nd Viscount Strathallan, honoured his uncle's wishes in spite of legal difficulties, and added to the endowment to preserve the library and maintain the school. The last books were borrowed in 1968, and now the library is only available for reference and as a museum for bibliophiles. Some 3,000 of the 4,400 books are pre-1800 and include many rare and priceless works. Some belonged to Montrose, including the Bible he carried throughout his campaigns, which bears his signature. There are 'Treacle Bibles' – those printed in early times before treacle was translated as balm. There are the collected works of King James VI (James I of England), and there is a borrower's record book in which, among others, were numerous loans, mostly historical and religious, to James Michell, student, who went on to be tutor to Sir Walter Scott. **St Mary's Chapel**, rebuilt in 1508 on an earlier site, is charmingly unspoilt and bare, with a medieval altar and traces of painted frescoes.

Drummond Castle Gardens (*open May–Oct 2–6; adm*) is about 3 miles south of Crieff on the A822. The castle (*not open to the public*) dates from about 1490. James IV came here often, courting Margaret Drummond. Some say they were secretly married; she almost certainly had his child. She and her two sisters were poisoned in the castle, probably by those who saw her as a threat to the king's marriage to Margaret Tudor. All three are buried in Dunblane Cathedral, commemorated by brass plaques. The castle is set in a designed landscape and is renowned for its terraced gardens created by John Drummond, 2nd Earl of Perth in 1630, influenced by French and Italian designs and recreated in 1832. The gardens, with topiary yews and hollies, many statues, sculpture and architectural features, is best appreciated from above – it was also used as the setting at the end of the film *Rob Roy*.

There is a pretty excursion from Crieff along the A822 up the **Sma' Glen** towards Amulree. The River Almond thunders down from the hills on its way to meet the Tay above Perth, with rapids and waterfalls and a good salmon leap at Buchanty Spout in Glenalmond, on the B8063.

On the right of the A822, about a mile south of Newton Bridge, you can see **Ossian's Stone**, by the river. It doesn't look much but is said to have once marked the grave of Ossian, the legendary Gaelic hero and bard who spent many years in fairyland until he was baptized by St Patrick. It was moved here by General Wade's road-builders when it blocked the path of one of their constructions. Traces of a prehistoric burial, found when they lifted the stone, were given a reburial in a secret place by local Highlanders who were convinced they were indeed the remains of the poet. Wordsworth thought so too:

In this still place, remote from men
Sleeps Ossian, in the narrow Glen.

Three miles south of Crieff is a conservation village with late 18th–19th-century houses. Pronounced Mew-Hill, from Moot Hill – Hill of Meeting – **Muthill** has a small museum (*t (01764) 652 578*), and the ruins of a pre-Reformation church with a *c.* 12th-century Norman tower. **Tullibardine Chapel**, a couple of miles east, is a complete 15th–16th-century cruciform church, founded as a collegiate church in 1445. It has been a burial vault for the Drummond Earls of Perth since the Reformation.

Comrie, 6 miles west of Crieff along the River Earn, is an attractive conservation village. At Hogmanay, villagers parade around by torchlight with much revelry. This has its roots in the ancient pagan fire festivals, held to drive off evil spirits. As it lies on the Highland Line, more seismological tremors have been recorded here than anywhere else in Britain, though in recent years tremors have done little more than rattle the village teacups. **Earthquake House**, built in 1874, houses one of the world's earliest seismometers, though the exhibits are only on view from outside.

Drummond Trout Farm and Fishery, a mile west of Comrie off the A85 (*open summer daily 10–10; winter daily 10–5*) is a good day out. There are ponds, rod hire, a salmon ladder with an underwater camera, and a farm shop (*open daily*) with fish, game and venison. The 100-acre **Auchingarrich Wildlife Centre**, in Comrie (*t (01764) 679 469; open mid-Mar–mid-Nov; adm*), contains an amazing collection of animals, including arctic foxes, wallabies and llamas. From Easter to October you can watch eggs hatch.

Just north of Comrie up Glen Lednock is the **Devil's Cauldron**, an impressive waterfall that carries the River Lednock down towards the River Earn. This road takes you on up the glen to the pretty Loch Lednock, which is a reservoir. **St Fillans**, about 5 miles west of Comrie, is a cluster of houses and hotels around the eastern end of Loch Earn, very popular for water sports in summer and best avoided if you prefer solitude. The A85 takes you along the north of the loch to **Lochearnhead**. There are quite a few places to stay around here, as well as people keen to hire boats and sell craft of all sorts. Halfway along the southern shore road is the start of a good climb up Ben Vorlich, a popular Munro in the area. From Lochearnhead you can take the A85 westwards to Crianlarich, or the A84 14 miles south to Callander.

West of Pitlochry

Pitlochry to Rannoch

If you take the B8019 west from Pitlochry, you should hum Harry Lauder's famous song 'The Road to the Isles': 'by Tummel and Loch Rannoch and Lochaber I will go...'. The drive out to Rannoch Station, on the northern side of lochs Tummel and Rannoch, to where the road ends and back along the south side, is a 65-mile round trip.

The scenery is beautiful, so you won't be alone during the tourist season. The great cone of **Schiehallion** dominates the landscape to the south, there is a kaleidoscope of vistas through the trees and the moonscape wasteland of Rannoch Moor stretches away to the west. Loch Tummel is less dramatic than Loch Rannoch, its gentler scenery reshaped by hydroelectric development. **Queen's View**, 2 miles up from the dam, was so called before Queen Victoria visited it in 1866: perhaps Mary, Queen of Scots also stood on the promontory and looked down on the water glinting in the sunlight far below during one of her royal tours.

Where to Stay and Eat

The Dunalastair Hotel, Kinloch Rannoch, t (01882) 632 218, *www.dunalastair.co.uk* (*moderate*). Large and comfortable, with fishing available.

Loch Rannoch Hotel, Kinloch Rannoch, t (01882) 632 201, *www.lochrannoch-hotel.com* (*moderate*). Victorian shooting lodge, now a convivial hotel with good food.

Bunrannoch House, Kinloch Rannoch, t (01882) 632 407, *www.bunrannoch.co.uk* (*budget*). The place to stay if you can get in. A tall, thin, Victorian ex-shooting lodge – offers hospitality at its best, with excellent cooking. Good value.

The Rannoch Smokery, Kinloch Rannoch, sells all sorts of delicious smoked game and meat, and excellent pâté.

The **Tay Forest Centre** (*open April–Oct daily; donation box*) is at the southeast corner of the loch. Here you can learn about the geography and ecology of the area. Harry Lauder's Road to the Isles was the old, much-used route to the west across the moors; the modern road ends at Rannoch Station. One hopes he had stout, waterproof boots and a good map: it is about 13 or 14 miles across to the A82, east of Glencoe, and if you don't stick to the path you'll finish up in a bog.

If you want exercise, Schiehallion is fun, easy and takes less than 5 hours. The best way goes from Schiehallion Road, the minor road that crosses its northern slope to link with the B846 to Kinloch Rannoch. Start from the Braes of Foss car park, just east of the farm of that name, and follow the path. There's a path or marker cairns all the way. It is interesting to note that while the Astronomer Royal was doing a few experiments on the estimation of the mass of the Earth in 1774, one of his helpers, Charles Hutton, looked at Schiehallion with its regular cone shape and, with a flash of inspiration, invented contour lines for maps.

Pitlochry to Killin

Pitlochry to Aberfeldy

Five miles south of Pitlochry, the A827 takes you 10 miles west to Aberfeldy and then out through Strath Tay to Loch Tay and a choice of two roads to Killin, one north and one south of the loch. Both are attractive drives, especially in late summer, but for a more dramatic route, take the B846 from Aberfeldy north of the Tay and branch off at Keltneyburn to Fortingall, where you follow the sign to Glen Lyon. At Bridge of Balgie you can easily reach the base of Ben Lawers and carry on down to Loch Tay at Milton Morenish (*see p.66*). Much of this area is part of **Breadalbane**, a large, beautiful tract of land once dominated by the Campbells of Glenorchy, later the Earls of Breadalbane, whose lands extended from the east coast to the west coast.

Let Fortune's gifts at random flee,
They ne'er shall draw a wish frae me,
Supremely blest wi' love and thee
In the birks of Aberfeldie.
Robert Burns, 'The Birks of Aberfeldie'

Aberfeldy is a pleasant little town on the Urlar Burn at its confluence with the River Tay. Burns' poem might refer to the silver birches beside the burn above the town, which is claimed as the local beauty spot, but some say Burns may have been writing about the *birks* (beeches) of Abergeldie. Dorothy Wordsworth averred that while there were lots of beeches on the Dee at that time, there were none at all on the Tay. General Wade's bridge over the Tay, designed for him by William Adam, is said to be Wade's finest bridge. The **Black Watch Monument**, on the south bank, was erected in 1887 to commemorate the regiment's founding in 1739. There is the ubiquitous restored water mill in Mill Street, working until recently and now housing a bookshop and gallery (open daily). The **Glengoulandie Deer Park**, Aberfeldy, on the

Tourist Information

Aberfeldy: The Square, t (01887) 820 276.
Killin: Breadalbane Folklore Centre,
t (01567) 820 254. *Open Mar–Nov daily; Feb
Sat and Sun.*

Sports and Activities

Croft-na-Caber, on the south side of Loch
Tay, t (01887) 830 588. Very good watersports
centre, with white-water rafting, water-skiing,
windsurfing and lots more. They also provide
chalet accommodation and a restaurant.

Where to Stay and Eat

Farleyer House, nr Aberfeldy, t (01887) 820 332,
www.farleyer.com (expensive). Gracious 15th-
century country house in 30 acres of garden
– good salmon fishing.
Ailean Chraggan Hotel, Weem, by Aberfeldy,
t (01887) 820 346 *(moderate)*. Small and
friendly, with south-facing rooms. Excellent
food, especially if they've been to the west
coast for fresh fish. Can arrange fishing.
Ardeonaig, on the south of Loch Tay, t (01567)
820 400, *www.ardeonaighotel.co.uk*
(moderate). Great hospitality, good food and
beautiful scenery.
Fortingall Hotel, t (01887) 830 367, *www.
fortingall.com (moderate)*. Splendidly
informal, cosy, unspoilt and not too grand.

Invervar Lodge, Glenlyon, Aberfeldy,
t (01887) 877 206 *(moderate)*. Splendid B&B
with dinner if ordered (bring your own
booze). Self-catering also available.
Kenmore Hotel, t (01887) 830 205,
www.kenmorehotel.com (moderate). Said by
some to be Scotland's oldest inn, with an
original poem by Robert Burns.
Morenish Lodge Highland House Hotel,
looks south over Loch Tay, near Killin,
t (01567) 820 258, *www.morenishlodge
hotel.co.uk (moderate)*. Built in 1750 as a
shooting lodge. A comfortable, attractive
haven with very good food.
Quinach House, Aberfeldy, t (01887) 820
251/237 *(moderate)*. Very friendly family-run
country house hotel in 3-acre garden.
Comfortable, and good food.
Dall Lodge Country House Hotel, Killin,
t (01567) 820 217, *www.dalllodgehotel.co.uk*
(moderate–budget). Country mansion with
great views.
Killin Hotel, Killin, t (01567) 820 296,
*www.killinhotel.com (moderate–
budget)*. Homely and good value, with a
bistro overlooking the riverbank.
Falls of Dochart Hotel, Killin, t (01567) 820 270
(budget). Overlooking the Falls of Dochart –
an 18th-century coach house with good
food and friendly owners.
Morenish House, Killin, on the north side of
Loch Tay, t (01567) 820 220 *(budget)*. An old,
beautifully converted and well-equipped
farmhouse – nicest self-catering in the area.

B846 (*t (01887) 830 495; open 9am to one hour before sunset; adm*), is a good trip for
children and adults. As well as deer there are Highland Cattle and rare breeds of
domestic animals.

Castle Menzies, pronounced 'Ming-ies' (*open April–mid-Oct Mon–Sat 10.30–5, Sun
2–5; adm*), is a mile west of the town on the north side of the Tay past Weem. Weem,
which gets its name from a cave, now blocked up, is said to have an underground
passage through to Loch Glassie. Castle Menzies is a 16th-century, Z-plan fortified
tower house with carved gables over its dormers. The central block has flanking
towers at diagonally opposite corners, and the west wing was added in 1840 together
with the present entrance porch, designed by William Burn. The Menzies family lived
here for 400 years but it became almost derelict until it was rescued in 1972. The
arduous task of restoration has had praiseworthy results, and has not been
over-restored or filled with the irrelevant and bogus clutter so prevalent in some clan
centres. There is Prince Charlie's Room, complete with four-poster bed, where the

prince stayed for two nights on his way to Culloden in Febuary 1746. The chief, Sir Robert Menzies, took no part in the Jacobite cause but was sympathetic to it and entertained his guest with a day's hunting. Among the memorabilia in the castle are a claymore believed to have been used by a Menzies at Bannockburn, a cast of Mary, Queen of Scots' hand, and two ancient shoes found in the walls during restoration. One of the turret rooms has an en-suite garderobe with no less than three holes.

Continue west a few miles along the Tay and turn left before Keltneyburn; after 3 miles you reach **Kenmore** at the head of Loch Tay, built for estate workers of Taymouth Castle in 1760 by the fourth Earl of Breadalbane, now a conservation village.

Taymouth Castle

Taymouth Castle, one of the most magnificent of Scotland's neo-Gothic palaces, has had a long and complex architectural history. The 20th century saw it used as a Polish hospital during the war and a civil defence school, then it sat largely disused for decades, its deteriorating condition causing considerable angst to conservationists. Thieves robbed it of some of its fittings. Eventually it was sold and the new owners have spent much money on repairing it. Although it is not open to the public, you can see the castle from the outside by driving through the gate to the golf course which surrounds it and along the drive.

Head of the Campbells of Glenorchy, the first Earl of Breadalbane was described as: 'grave as a Spaniard, cunning as a fox, wise as a serpent and slippery as an eel'. In 1733 he employed William Adam to smarten up what was then Balloch Castle, a 16th-century keep. Adam added two classical wings to the medieval tower. In 1799 the 3rd Earl demolished most of the old castle, leaving only Adam's two wings. From then on a succession of architects altered and added to the castle. James Gillespie Graham, with help from Augustus Pugin, remodelled the interior with an extensive and richly carved library and a great Gothic chapel with splendid woodwork screens. Much of the plasterwork executed by Bernasconi in 1809 still remains. Queen Victoria came here on her first Highland tour in September 1842. She was delighted by the castle and its lovely surroundings and by the hospitality of Lord Breadalbane who laid on a fantastic welcome with kilted Highlanders, pipers and guns, bonfires and fireworks. A whole new wing had been built in her honour with painted and gilded ceilings, and she was the first to dine in the new dining room and sleep in the new apartments. The grounds were embellished with pavilions and parterres by Adam, and some of the follies still survive, including a quartz-covered rustic dairy, now a private house, which delighted Victoria – 'a kind of Swiss cottage... very clean and nice'.

Before leaving Kenmore, turn left out of the gate to the castle and follow the loch round on the minor road a few hundred yards to the Crannog (*t (01887) 830 583, www.crannog.co.uk; open mid-March–Oct daily 10–5.30, Nov Sat–Sun 10–5.30 (last entry), winter by appointment; adm*). It would be easy to miss; it looks like a makeshift boat house or shelter, but is in fact a brilliant reconstruction of a crannog based on careful underwater research. The stone lumps we see in lochs today and call crannogs are now thought to be built-up detritus from after the huts were erected. Excavations have proved this theory correct. The dwellings' role seems to have been defensive –

one narrow causeway surrounded by water affording more protection than a land-based building.

West from Fortingall

Fortingall is little more than a hamlet, but it contains Glen Lyon House, seat of the perpetrator of the massacre of Glencoe, unusual English Arts and Crafts-style thatched cottages, and the much publicized 'oldest living thing in Europe'. The latter is a pathetic vestige of a 3,000-year-old yew tree (some say 9,000) in the churchyard, enclosed by railings and propped on stones. It isn't much to look at, but it is awe-inspiring to think that it was here in the time of King Solomon and that its circumference once measured over 60ft. The inner core is gone, burnt out long ago by Beltane fires apparently, and all that is left is a fragmented shell, reminiscent of 'coppicing'. Of much greater interest, though seldom mentioned, is the rough stone font outside the church porch on the right, attributed to Adamnan, St Columba's biographer and champion, who did as much for the Celtic Church in the 7th century as his better-known predecessor. Traditionally, Pontius Pilate was born in Fortingall, son of a Roman officer who had been sent on a peace mission to the Picts in Dun Geal, a fort on the rocky hill behind the village, and who married a local lass.

If the spirit of Adamnan (the little Adam) intrigues you, continue west on the twisty road from Fortingall, about 10 miles along beautiful Glen Lyon to 19th-century **Glen Lyon Church** at Innerwick. They say Adamnan ended his days here. He came to these parts from Iona some time before 704 and established a church at Milton Eonan just west of here; its bell now hangs behind a grid in the porch of the church. If you want to bag a Munro, leave your car opposite the church and walk along the marked track north into the hills, 8 miles due north to Loch Rannoch, through the steep-sided Lairig Chalbhath. Someone will need to pick you up at Carie, the other end.

From Innerwick, drive on west for a mile and turn left – due south – at **Bridge of Balgie**. The lush prettiness of Glen Lyon is rapidly replaced by a desolate moonscape with more Munros to conquer. **Ben Lawers** towers to the east (3,984ft/1,226m); at its foot is the National Trust for Scotland's Visitor Centre, from which the climb takes about 3 hours. On a clear day you can see from the Atlantic to the North Sea. There are masses of mountain flowers and birds, including kestrel, buzzard, red grouse, golden plover and curlew. Don't be intimidated by the somewhat dog-in-the-manger attitude you may detect in the visitor centre. Conservationists are not over-anxious for you to explore the area for fear of the damage you might do. Pictures illustrate how to walk on paths, not verges; notices command you to keep dogs on leads; advice is given on what to wear and take if you climb the hill. This mountain detour takes you down to **Loch Tay**, a long, dark snake of water with water sports, as well as excellent fishing. Go west on the A827, through Morenish, about 5 miles to Killin.

Killin is attractively grouped around an old bridge astride the Falls of Dochart, which carry the River Dochart in a tumble of falls and rapids, swirling down through the village into Loch Tay. This is not in Perthshire, but is only a whisker into Breadalbane. White-harled cottages with pretty gardens, jolly hotels and tartan-hung tourist traps complete the picture-postcard scene. On a fine day when there is snow on the hills around, there is an almost alpine feel, no doubt remarked upon by Prince Albert when he and Queen Victoria first visited in 1842. On **Inchbuie**, or *Innes Bhuidhe* (the Yellow Island), the lower of the two islets below the old bridge, is the burial ground of the MacNabs, an aggressive clan who lived at nearby Kinnell until they emigrated to Canada in the 19th century, oppressed by the more powerful Breadalbane Campbells of Glenorchy. These Campbells lived at 16th-century **Finlarig Castle**, hidden among trees on a primrose-carpeted mound, half a mile north of Killin past the cemetery, and now a rather sinister ruin. All that remains is a stark keep, a building with a coat of arms on it (possibly a chapel), as well as a gruesome 'beheading pit' near the tower. It was the privilege of the gentry to be beheaded, while the common people were hanged from a tree. St Fillan, who died around 777, is thought to have lived nearby – eight 'healing stones' in the Breadalbane Folklore Centre bear his name.

The **Breadalbane Folklore Centre** (*open Mar–May and Oct daily 10–5, June and Sept daily 10–6, July–Aug daily 9.30–6.30; adm*) gives a good insight into the life and legends of Breadalbane, and gives details of local nature and wildlife. You can get the key to the MacNab burial ground on Inchbuie here. **Moirlanich Longhouse**, on the Glen Lochay road, off the A827 northwest of Killin (*open Easter Sun and May–Sept Wed and Sun 2–5; adm*) dates from the mid-19th century and is a good example of the old buildings in which the family and their livestock lived, together under one roof.

From Killin you can continue on west to Crianlarich and the coast, south to Callander and the Lowlands, or back eastwards to Pitlochry along the south side of Loch Tay.

Pitlochry to Blair Atholl

Pass of Killiecrankie

Six thousand Veterans practised in War's game,
Tried Men, at Killicranky were arrayed,
Against an equal Host that wore the Plaid,
Shepherds and Herdsmen – Like a whirlwind came
The Highlanders, the slaughter spread like flame.
                    from a sonnet by William Wordsworth

Continuing north from Pitlochry, the A9 climbs along the upper slope of the Pass of Killiecrankie, a section of road that cost a great deal of money and took considerable engineering skill to construct. It clings precariously to the densely wooded gorge where, far below, the River Garry cuts its way through to join up with the Tummel. At the far end of the pass, about 3 miles from Pitlochry, a **National Trust for Scotland Visitor Centre** (*www.nts.org.uk; site open all year, centre open daily April–Oct 10–5.30*) has a pictorial description of the history of the Battle of Killiecrankie. John 'Bonnie Dundee' Graham of Claverhouse and his brave Jacobite Highlanders charged the British Army under General Mackay in 1689, in an attempt to depose William of Orange and restore James VII/II to the throne. Outnumbered more than two to one, Claverhouse's strategic cunning won the day. Waiting until the setting sun was in the eyes of their enemies, the Highlanders charged them with shot and broadsword until the dead and dying choked the pass. The British were almost annihilated by the Highlanders, but casualties were great on both sides and Claverhouse was mortally wounded. His death left his army leaderless and ensured the victory three weeks later at Dunkeld of the government troops, who had fled to Aberdeen and recruited a new army.

Bonnie Dundee had his darker side – descended from Robert III and a staunch Royalist, he commanded a Troop of Horse raised to suppress the Covenanters' conventicles during the notorious Killing Times. He was also known as 'the Bluidy Clavers' for the atrocities he committed, although it is said that he urged moderation in order not to alienate the people of Scotland. His wife came from a Covenanting family but the final four months of his life, spent rallying the Jacobite cause, established him as a brave, charismatic Highlander. Walk down to the river from the visitor centre, past the terrifying **Soldier's Leap**, an 18-foot jump across the gorge, said to have been made by one of Mackay's soldiers, escaping from the Highlanders.

Blair Castle

t (01796) 481 207, www.blair-castle.co.uk;
open mid-March–Oct daily 10–5.30, last entry 4.30pm; adm.

Three miles north of Killiecrankie, the new road bypasses the village of Blair Atholl giving a good view of Blair Castle from across the river. This white, turreted baronial castle, home of the Dukes of Atholl, dates from the 13th century, though it has been much Victorianized. In 1267 John Comyn of Badenoch built a tower on Atholl land while the then Earl of Atholl was away on duty. The earl was justifiably annoyed and complained bitterly to King Alexander III, but the tower remained, now incorporated as Cumming's Tower into the present castle which grew round it. It underwent a series of alterations, including the decapitation of its top storeys in the mid-18th century. Queen Victoria described it as 'a large plain white building' and David Bryce, one of Scotland's leading Victorian architects, was commissioned to baronialize it. This he did, with the help of his brother John, adding the imposing entrance, the castellations and other embellishments so admired by his contemporaries. The effect, though hardly beautiful, is certainly splendid.

The castle has seen many royal visitors: Edward III; Mary, Queen of Scots, who was entertained by a deer and wolf hunt in which 360 deer and five wolves were killed; Claverhouse before the Battle of Killiecrankie (his body lay here before burial in the churchyard of old St Bride's Church in Blair Atholl); Prince Charlie, on his march south in 1745; and Cumberland, who garrisoned his troops here the following year, during which time the Duke of Atholl's brother, Lord George Murray, inflicted severe damage on the castle in his attempts to win it back for the Jacobite cause. When Queen Victoria visited the castle in 1844, she and Prince Albert explored the area enthusiastically, escorted by Lord Glenlyon, heir to the Duke of Atholl. Later, she presented his bodyguard of Highlanders with a pair of colours, bestowing on him the privilege of being the only British subject allowed to retain a private army, the Atholl Highlanders. This honour was revived in 1966 by the late Duke of Atholl, and the army numbers some 50 men who appear on parades and have their own pipe band. Membership is highly-prized and consists of former servicemen, local lairds and kinsmen of the late Duke.

The castle is one of Scotland's top historic attractions. Look for the Tapestry Room, hung with tapestries and furnished with a sumptuous four-poster bed topped by two vases of ostrich feathers. The Old Scots Room is reconstructed in the style of a simple cottage living room, complete with box bed, cradle and spinning wheel. The castle is stuffed with the usual historic memorabilia, as well as portraits by Lely, Ramsay and Raeburn. There is even a natural history museum – one of the highlights is a rather moth-eaten and tired-looking, though quite endearing, 18th-century stuffed polar bear at the bottom of a stairwell. The self-service restaurant is licensed and there is a separate dining room for private parties of up to 50 people. You can even use the ballroom for up to 200 people; a noble setting for a knees-up, its panelled walls bristling with a forest of antlers and acres of ancestral portraits under a timber-ribbed roof.

If this feast of history gives you dyspepsia, take a stroll to the **Bruar Falls** about 3 miles to the west, where the River Bruar cascades down through rocky chasms and over gleaming slabs of granite. Robert Burns came up here when he was a guest of the Duke of Atholl. He was so disgusted by the bare moorland that then surrounded the falls that he dashed off a poem, 'The Humble Petition of Bruar Water', and dispatched it to the Duke:

> *Would then my noble master please,*
> *To grant my highest wishes,*
> *He'll shade the bank wi' towering trees,*
> *And bonnie spreading bushes.*

This plea found its mark and inspired the fourth Duke to plant the trees now growing there. Walk on beyond the falls up the path for another mile or so, through birches and rhododendrons. A bridge takes you over the stream and down the other side, making a round trip of just over 2 miles.

You can't miss the **House of Bruar** (*www.houseofbruar.com*), which stands prominently beside the A9 at Blair Atholl. People drive miles to visit this serious shopper's paradise, dubbed 'the Harrods of the North'. In a spectacular building, there are dozens of different shops: country clothes, cashmere, tweed, woollens, china and glass, gifts, a gourmet food hall, a restaurant, a wild-flower nursery and a library.

Beyond Blair Atholl

The drive from here to Newtonmore takes you through a diversity of true Highland scenery. The road is so good and fast now that one is through in a flash without realizing what lonely grandeur and solitude lie beyond. (General Wade was responsible for this route.) After the Drumochter Pass, you come to **Dalwhinnie Moor**, a place of the utmost desolation, especially in the old days when the previous road wound tortuously across it. The intrepid German writer, Theodor Fontane, described crossing Dalwhinnie in a coach in 1858, packed so tightly on to the roof that those on the outside had only one cheek on the seat. He called it 'the Grampian waste' and said it was the most lonely country he had ever seen. Beware the A889 from Dalwhinnie to Laggan: a European road assessment programme has dubbed it 'the most dangerous road in Europe, with almost double the accident rate of the next most dangerous'.

The Trossachs and Breadalbane

Callander

Callander, 34 miles from Crieff and some 40 miles from Perth, is a popular tourist centre for the Trossachs. It is a sturdy town, overshadowed by Ben Ledi to the northwest. Television addicts might recognize the *Tannochbrae* of *Dr Finlay's Casebook*, and scenes from *The Country Diary of an Edwardian Lady*. There are lots of good walks around here. For a quick stroll, go up to the Bracklinn Falls about a mile to the northeast, on Keltie Water. They say Sir Walter Scott once rode his horse across here for a bet. (To give someone *keltie* is to force a large alcoholic drink on a teetotaller or to give a double dose of punishment.) The Falls of Leny, a couple of miles on up the A84, are rather overrun, but you can climb Ben Ledi (2,875ft/884m) from here, on a reasonable path. During the tourist season, Callander offers ceilidhs, open-air pipe band concerts and Highland dancing, as well as wildlife slide shows. The Callander International Highland Games are in August.

The Trossachs: A Literary Introduction

It has to be said that if it hadn't been for Sir Walter Scott, and to a lesser extent Wordsworth and his sister Dorothy, the Trossachs would never have appeared so indelibly on the tourist map, although travellers had become obsessed by the idea of the Highlands since the publication of James Macpherson's 'translation' of Ossian's epic in 1762. When *The Lady of the Lake* was first read by an avid public, the Trossachs became the 'in' place and its unsurpassed beauty became legend. They flocked here from the south and eulogized the places where fair Ellen Douglas was courted by James V, disguised as James Fitzjames. The 'beauty spot' image stuck, heartily

Tourist Information

Callander: Rob Roy and Trossachs Visitor Centre, Ancaster Square, **t** 0870 720 0628, *www.visitscottishheartlands.com*. Includes a Rob Roy exhibition (*open Mar–May and Oct–Dec 10–5, June 9.30–6, July–Aug 9–7, Sept 10–6, Jan–Feb 11–4.30; adm*).

Tyndrum: Main Street, **t** 8070 720 0626, *www.visitscottishheartlands.com*. Open April–Oct.

Where to Stay

Ben Doran Hotel, Tyndrum, **t** (01838) 400 373 (*expensive*). Comfortable and good.

Monachyle Mhor, Balquhidder, **t** (01877) 384 622,*www.monachylemhor.com* (*expensive*). Pink-harled farmhouse with views and great food. The bar is the locals' choice.

Royal Hotel, Tyndrum, **t** (01838) 400 272 (*expensive*).

Roman Camp, Main Street, Callander, **t** (01877) 330 003, *www.roman-camp-hotel.co.uk* (*expensive–moderate*). Mixture of 17th century, Victorian and modern. Not noisy, and with nice, relaxed atmosphere, enhanced by cosy log fires. Excellent food.

Arden House, Bracklinn Road, Callander, **t** (01877) 330 235, *www.ardenhouse.org.uk* (*moderate*). Small hospitable guesthouse in a good position above the town.

Bridgend House Hotel, Callander, **t** (01877) 330 130, *www.bridgendhotel.co.uk* (*moderate*). A mock Tudor face hides an 18th-century heart. On the road but friendly and comfortable.

Creagan House, Strathyre, near Balquhidder, **t** (01877) 384 638, *www.creaganhouse.co.uk* (*moderate*). Delightful overgrown cottage; peaceful and welcoming with excellent food.

Invertrossachs Country House, near Callander on Loch Venachar, **t** (01877) 331 447 *www.invertrossachs.co.uk* (*moderate*). Large characterful Edwardian house set in 33 acres of woods and gardens. With self-catering apartments.

Lake Hotel, Port of Menteith, **t** (01877) 385 258, *www.lake-of-menteith-hotel.com* (*moderate*). With a splendid conservatory restaurant overlooking the water.

Leny House, Callander, **t** (01877) 331 078 (*moderate*). Very comfortable country mansion in parkland with good views and B&B.

The Lodge House, Crianlarich, **t** (01838) 300 276, *www.lodgehouse.co.uk* (*moderate*). Very friendly guesthouse – good base for walkers.

Lubnaig Hotel, Callander, **t** (01877) 330 376, *www.lubnaighotel.co.uk* (*moderate*). Small, private hotel in a nice garden – excellent.

Stronvar House, Balquhidder, **t** (01877) 384 688, *www.stronvar.co.uk* (*moderate*). A once-delightful hotel with early 17th-century origins, converted to self-catering.

Invervey Hotel, Tyndrum, **t** (01838) 400 219 (*budget*). A convivial and lively opton in the heart of Tyndrum.

Leny Estate, contact Mrs F. Roebuck, Leny Estate Lodges, Leny House, Callander, **t** (01877) 331 078, *www.lenyestate.com*. First-class self-catering establishments, from houses to log cabins.

Eating Out

Myrtle Inn, south of Callander on A84, **t** (01877) 330 919. (*moderate*) Probably the best place to eat in this area.

Ben Ledi Café, on the main street near the square, Callander. Good plain food.

The Café, Brig O'Turk, **t** (01877) 376 267. Very popular: book in advance.

The Green Welly Stop, Tyndrum **t** (01838) 400385. Good café for snacks, soups and outdoor gear.

endorsed by innkeepers and hoteliers, assisted by the fact that the area was conveniently situated for the densely populated towns to the south.

Although the tourist brochures tend to refer to the whole area between Callander and Loch Lomond as the Trossachs, in fact the Trossachs proper is only the gorge that runs from Loch Achray to Loch Katrine, a rugged pass barely a mile long. Locals give two meanings for this name: 'bristly country' or 'the crossing place'. It is narrow, rocky, rather bosky and unremarkable, but now and then you get a hint of the magic that so enchanted Scott. The road twists and climbs through gorse, bracken and emerald green moor, past rhododendrons, with a number of inviting footpaths leading off.

Loch Katrine

Nine miles west of Callander, this loch was the main setting for *The Lady of the Lake*, with Ellen's Isle named after its heroine. From April to September, the Victorian steamer *Sir Walter Scott* runs two to three 45-minute trips per day along the length of the loch from Trossachs Pier to Stronachlachar (*t (01877) 376 316*). As you pass Ellen's Isle, remember how, when James Fitzjames blew his horn to summon help:

> *From underneath an aged oak,*
> *That slanted from the islet rock*
> *A Damsel guider of its way,*
> *A little skiff shot to the bay*
> *That round the promontory steep*
> *Led its deep line in graceful sweep...*

A prosaic guide will tell you that this loch is also Glasgow's water supply. Because of this, there is a large notice at the pier forbidding you to swim, paddle, picnic, fish, camp, light fires or throw coins into the loch. To get the best view of the loch, forget the boat trip and put on your boots. There is a splendid, very easy climb up **Ben Venue** (2,393ft/736m). It's just over 5 miles and takes under 5 hours. Take the track from behind the Loch Achray Hotel (about 8 miles west of Callander on the A827) and head west through the Pass of Achray. It can become quite boggy in places, but the views from the two peaks are well worth the climb.

Aberfoyle

Aberfoyle, 5 miles south of the Trossachs, is another bustling tourist centre for the area. Walter Scott made his first notes for *Rob Roy* in the village manse. A **Scottish Wool Centre** (*open daily; adm*) tells you all about the role of sheep over the past 2,000 years, with a children's farm, shop and restaurant. **Queen Elizabeth Forest Park Visitor Centre**, just before Aberfoyle (*drive and visitor centre open daily 10–6*) is a modern stone building with an ornamental lake, walks and all the usual displays illustrating flora and fauna. The park lies to the west, all 75,000 acres of it. Although very much Designer Highlands, it still has bits off the beaten trail and some good hills to climb with staggering views: Ben Lomond (3,192ft/974m) and Ben Vrackie (1,922ft/591m) are two of the best. **Ben Lomond** is the most southerly Munro, ascended by two well-trodden paths, one from Rowardennan Hotel at the northern end of the road on the eastern side of Loch Lomond – the B837 – and the other from the south end of Loch Dhu, off the B829, west of Aberfoyle. Ben Lomond is so popular that it is in danger of becoming too much of a 'theme park', causing conservationists to wring their hands as erosion worsens. However, it will remain a splendid summit from which to view

Balquhidder: Rob Roy's Grave

A famous man is Robin Hood,
The English ballad-singer's joy!
And Scotland has a thief as good,
An outlaw of as daring mood;
She has her brave Rob Roy.
      'Rob Roy's Grave' by William Wordsworth

Balquhidder, about 10 miles north of Callander on Loch Voil, is the burial place of Walter Scott's Rob Roy MacGregor. Born in 1671 and so called for his red hair (from the Gaelic *ruadh* (roy – red), he fought under 'Bonnie Dundee' at Killiecrankie in 1689 when he was 18 and was known for his exceptionally long, almost simian, arms and skill with a broadsword. The Protestant MacGregors were notorious, extorting 'blackmail' in their territory in return for protection. In 1694, when their name was proscribed (not for the first time), Rob Roy took the name Campbell, having married a Mary Campbell the year before. For a while he lived honestly enough as a prosperous cattle dealer, but he was accused of embezzlement in 1711, when a sum of £1,000 which he had borrowed was stolen by his chief drover, a Macdonald. He was outlawed and so began his legendary exploits, depicted by Scott. He rallied Clan Gregor to the Jacobite cause in 1715, eventually submitted to General Wade in 1725, converted to Catholicism and finally died in his bed in 1734. Legend has him visited on his deathbed by an enemy, for whom he insisted on being dressed in full armour, saying: 'It shall never be said that a foe saw Robert Roy MacGregor defenceless and unarmed.' After the man had left, Rob instructed a piper to play *Ha til me tulidh* – 'We Return No More' – and died before the tune was finished. You can't miss his grave in Balquhidder churchyard: Clan Gregor have been unable to resist the temptation to do it up. The 'MacGregor Despite Them' refers to the proscription of the clan.

the Arrochar Alps, the Southern Highlands, and their famous loch. Even Gerard Manley Hopkins noted the threat in 1880:

What would the world be, once bereft
Of wet and wilderness?
Let them be left, wildness and wet;
Long live the weeds and the wilderness yet.
      'Inversnaid' by Gerard Manley Hopkins

Inchmahome Priory

t (01877) 385 294; open daily April–Sept 9.30–6.30; weather dictates the running of the ferry, for which you pay; entrance to the priory is free.

Take the A81 southwest from Callander for 6 miles to Lake of Menteith to reach the romantic ruin of the priory, founded for Augustinian monks in 1238, though there may have been a Celtic monastery here before. Look out for the whimsical, weathered remains of the two figures of the 13th-century Earl and Countess of Menteith in the chapter house. In the choir is the grave of Robert Cunninghame Graham, the 'rebel laird' of the estate who travelled extensively, married a Chilean poetess, was imprisoned for 'illegal assembly' in 1887, was elected first president of the Scottish Labour party in 1888, and wrote many travel books, essays and short stories. He was a close friend of both Joseph Conrad and W.H. Hudson and his *Mogreb-el-Acksa*, which tells of his attempt to reach the fobidden city of Tarouddant in Morocco, was claimed by Bernard Shaw as his inspiration for *Captain Brassbound's Conversion*. Inchmahome was also the refuge for Mary, Queen of Scots, before she was sent to France to grow up out of range of Henry VIII's 'Rough Wooing'.

Crianlarich and Around

The A84 north from Callander to Lochearnhead and then the A85 north and west take you to Crianlarich. This is all excellent walking and climbing country with good paths. The village of Crianlarich is tucked into moorland about 12 miles southwest of Killin, isolated but by no means desolate, as this is where the rail lines from Oban and Fort William join up on their progress south. The station, unmanned and ramshackle, has in its midst, like an oasis in the desert, a cosy café for waiting travellers. The 95-mile West Highland Way passes by on its way from Milngavie (pronounced Mull-guy) to Fort William, and this is a favourite staging post. If you like a purpose to your walk, go a couple of miles on up the A82 and take the track just north of the school house at Castlebridge, across the River Fillan. The ruin here is that of St Fillan's Priory, associated with St Adamnan. Or you can take a track east to Loch Dochart to see the ruin on an island of a early 17th-century castle built by 'Black Duncan' Campbell of Glenorchy, which was destroyed almost at once by his rivals, the Macnabs. For James Hogg fans, Glen Dochart was the setting for *Spectre of the Glen*. Three road-routes meet here: south to Loch Lomond, northwest to Oban and Fort William, northeast to Pitlochry.

Five miles north of Crianlarich on the A82, **Tyndrum** nestles in a glacial valley where the cattle drovers used to meet on their way to Falkirk and Crieff markets, a bleak-enough tryst. Tyndrum means 'the House on the Ridge'. Lately, there has been a shift to tourism, with accompanying outsized hotels. It is now a place to stop en route to the western Highlands, and there are well over a dozen Munros within conquering distance. Take a good map and stick to the accepted codes of practice to spend happy weeks in these hills.

Southwestern Highlands

08

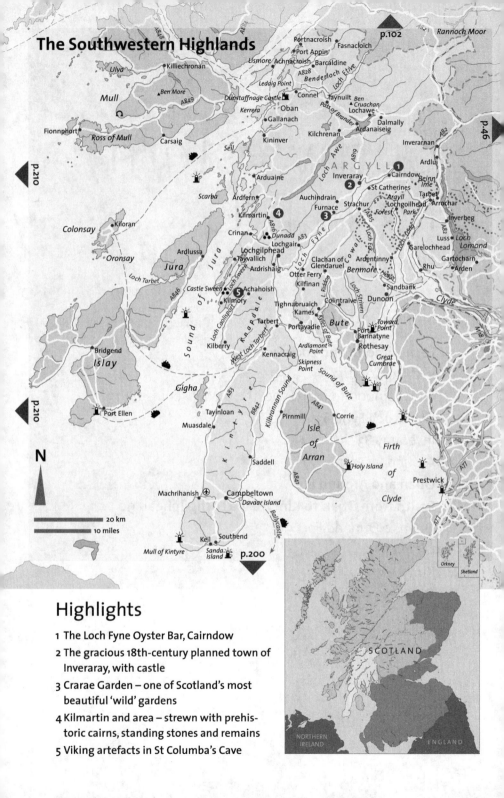

The Southwestern Highlands

p.102
p.46
p.210
p.210
p.200

Rannoch Moor
Portnacroish
Port Appin Fasnacloich
Lismore Achnacroish Barcaldine
Killiechronan Benderloch Loch Etive
Ulva
Ben More Leddig Point Connel
Mull Dunstaffnage Castle Taynuilt Ben Cruachan
Kerrera Oban Lochawe
Fionnphort Gallanach Pass of Brander Dalmally
Ross of Mull Kilchrenan Ardanaiseig
Carsaig Kininver Kilchrenan
Inverarnan
Seil Loch Awe Ardlui
ARGYLL Cairndow
Arduaine Inveraray Beinn
Scarba St Catherines Ime
Ardfern Auchindrain Argyll Tarbet
Kilmartin Furnace Strachur Forest Arrochar
Colonsay Kiloran Crinan Lochgoilhead Inverbeg
Oronsay Dunadd Loch Fyne Luss Loch
Ardlussa Lochgair Lomond
Jura Lochgilphead Clachan of Cowal Garelochhead
Loch Tarbet Tayvallich Glendaruel Ardentinny Gartocharn
Ardrishaig Benmore Rhu Arden
Otter Ferry
Kilfinan
Castle Sween Achahoish Sandbank
Kilmory Tighnabruaich Colintraive Dunoon Clyde
Loch Caolisport Kames Toward
Bridgend Tarbert Portavadie Bute Point
Islay Kilberry Ardlamont Port Rothesay
Kennacraig Point Bannatyne
Gigha Skipness Great
Point Sound of Bute Cumbrae
Tayinloan Pirnmill Corrie Firth
Muasdale Kilbrannan Sound Isle
Port Ellen Saddell of of
Arran Clyde
Holy Island Prestwick
Machrihanish Campbeltown
Davaar Island
Keil Southend
Mull of Kintyre Sanda
Island

N

20 km
10 miles

Highlights

1 The Loch Fyne Oyster Bar, Cairndow
2 The gracious 18th-century planned town of Inveraray, with castle
3 Crarae Garden – one of Scotland's most beautiful 'wild' gardens
4 Kilmartin and area – strewn with prehistoric cairns, standing stones and remains
5 Viking artefacts in St Columba's Cave

Orkney Shetland

SCOTLAND

NORTHERN IRELAND ENGLAND

The further west you go in the Highlands, the more beautiful the scenery becomes. The southwestern Highlands, for the purposes of this book, cover the area from Crianlarich and Tyndrum west to and around Oban, south round the Kintyre Peninsula, back to Crianlarich encompassing the Cowal Peninsula and Loch Lomond.

Argyllshire, until recently embraced by Strathclyde, was where the ancient Dalriada Scots from Ireland settled and formed their powerful kingdom. Here, Columba landed to spread the Christianity St Ninian had introduced at Whithorn more than one and a half centuries earlier. As well as dozens of prehistoric burial mounds, stones and cairns, the coast is punctuated with the remains of fortresses and watchtowers, built to defend the land from invasion by sea.

The climate becomes milder the further west you go and supports gardens where exotic foreign plants thrive; many of these are open to the public. Some of the coastal scenery is as magnificent as you could hope for, and the further north you go the better it gets, partly because it becomes less populated. Inland around Loch Lomond, the cities are too close to allow much solitude – the hills and glens well-trodden but undeniably beautiful. Large areas are remote and wild still – serpentine sea lochs eat into the land to form long peninsulas and narrow isthmuses. Moor, hill and forest are fringed by miles of beaches, with many islands lying off the coast like stray pieces of a jigsaw. Fishing, farming and tourism are the main industries.

Loch Lomond and Loch Fyne

Loch Lomond

The A82 south from Crianlarich, through Glen Falloch and down the west side of Loch Lomond, takes you through some impressive mountainous scenery, but by the time you get to Balloch you are definitely in the urban hinterland of Glasgow.

Loch Lomond

Oh, I'll tak the high road,
An' you'll tak the low road,
An' I'll be in Scotland afore ye
But me and my true Love will never meet again
On the bonnie, bonnie banks o' Loch Lomond.

The song 'Loch Lomond' was composed in Carlisle jail during the aftermath of Culloden by the Jacobite Donald MacDonell of Keppoch, awaiting a trial that ended in his brutal execution. The English were capricious in their distribution of justice: some prisoners were arbitrarily sent to the gallows, others set free and told to walk home. MacDonell, fairly sure of his fate, wrote that his spirit would return to Scotland on the 'high road', swinging on the gallows, faster than his living companions on the low road. (Some sing the first two lines differently: 'You'll tak the high road' – the normal route – 'And I'll tak the low road' – of death – the first version is the original.)

Tourist Information

Balloch: Balloch Road, **t** 0870 720 0607, *www.visitscottishheartlands.com*.

Sports and Activities

Sweeney's Cruises, **t** (01389) 752 376.

The Maid of the Loch, on the pier at Balloch, is a paddle steamer/visitor centre. *Open Easter–Oct 11–4; free.*

Loch Lomond Shores, Balloch, **t** (01389) 721 500, *www.lochlomondshores.com*. New visitor centre with films, special events, restaurants, cafés and shops.

Loch Lomond Water Ski Club at Balloch, **t** (01389) 753 000, runs courses April–Sept.

Where to Stay and Eat

Ardlui Hotel, Ardlui, **t** (01301) 704 243/269, *www.ardluihotel.com* (*moderate*). Cosy country house hotel on the banks of Loch Lomond – two restaurants, boat moorings.

Rowardennan Hotel, Rowardennan, east side of Loch Lomond, **t** (01360) 870 273, *www.rowardennan.co.uk* (*moderate*). Dates from 1869 – friendly and comfortable.

The Cottage, Auchendennan, Arden, **t** (01389) 850 287 (*moderate–budget*). With just two bedrooms and a garden, located near Duck Bay.

Drovers Inn, Inverarnan, on the west side before the river widens into the loch, **t** (01301) 704 234, *www.thedroversinn.co.uk* (*moderate–budget*). Atmospheric inn dating from 1705. Inside are low-lit, highly characterful rooms with bare floorboards, pungent with the smell of wood smoke. Dusty curiosities throughout.

Inverbeg Inn, near Luss on Loch Lomond, **t** (01436) 860 678, *www.inverbeginn.co.uk* (*moderate–budget*). Stands on Loch Lomond and has a great atmosphere.

The Old School House, Gartocharn, **t** (01389) 830 373, *bertiearmstrong@compuserve.com* (*moderate–budget*). Hospitable Wolsey Lodge in rural setting, with good cook/hostess.

Loch Lomond Youth Hostel, Arden, **t** (01389) 850 226, *www.syha.org.uk* (*budget*). Scotland's grandest youth hostel – a haunted 19th-century Baronial mansion with palatial porch.

Rowardennan Youth hostel, Rowardennan, **t** (01360) 870 259 (*budget*). Not very grand, but well-organized and fairly secluded.

The Gardeners Cottages, Arden house estate, **t** (01389) 850 601, *www.gardenerscottages.com*. Two to three well-equipped self-catering cottages in a wooded estate (sleeps 2–6).

The Stagger Inn, opposite the Drovers Inn, Inverarnan, **t** (01301) 704 274 (*moderate–inexpensive*). Good plain food, and a shop.

Loch Lomond is the largest freshwater lake in Britain – 24 miles from north to south – but only the third longest, after Lochs Awe and Ness, and the third deepest, after Lochs Morar and Ness. Its northern end is a long, thin neck, little more than an estuary for the River Falloch, widening to as much as 5 miles in the south. At first the road is twisty and narrow – a nightmare in summer – but the newish stretch further south is better and gives excellent views of the loch with the hills on the far side dominated by Ben Lomond. There are tourist traps galore on this road, especially in the over-prettified estate-village of **Luss**, which even has a kilt shop and bagpipe works. A number of marinas offer all kinds of water activity and launching slips for your own boat.

A grand entrance on the main road heralds **Rossdhu House**, a classical mansion on the shores of the loch in a landscaped park. It was built in 1773 for the Colquhoun family who have owned most of the land around here for 900 odd years. It is now an exclusive golf club attached to a 600-acre course, attracting rich celebrities such as Sean Connery, Clint Eastwood and Gerald Ford. The smartened-up ruins of the

15th-century castle decorate the 18th green, and the clan chapel, complete with chieftains' bones, presides over the game from some yew trees.

On the eastern shore of Loch Lomond, you can drive from Aberfeldy to the Inversnaid Hotel, or up as far as the Rowardennan Hotel from the south. This is fine walking country and includes one of the most popular routes up Ben Lomond. The best time to see the loch is in the early morning, when the mist clings to the glassy water as the sun rises over Ben Lomond. In the spring, bluebells carpet the ground under oak woods. Because of its accessibility from Glasgow, the loch is crowded with boats of all sorts in the summer; some say too many and that the washes from the speed boats will cause erosion. Even Queen Victoria noted the tourist traffic – large coaches with outside seats, full of tourists. She was reminded of Switzerland when she went cruising down the loch in 1869 and thought it magnificent – remarkably like Lake Lucerne, with truly alpine scenery. Dr Johnson, on the other hand, visiting the loch 'in the rainy season', found nothing more than uncultivated ruggedness, but thought it would have been splendid in 'a happier climate' to own one of its islands.

The loch has more varieties of fish than any other in Scotland, including trout, salmon, sea trout, gigantic pike and freshwater herring, descended from sea herring trapped here after the last Ice Age. A number of cruise boats operate, weaving between the 30 or so small islands scattered over the southern end. **Inch Cailleach** (Island of the Old Women) was the burial place of the fierce MacGregor clan. It belongs to Scottish Natural Heritage and has trails and woodland paths. Ruined **Lennox Castle**, on Inch Murrin (Isle of Spears), the largest island, was where the Duchess of Albany retired after James I had slaughtered her family in 1425.

Loch Lomond to Loch Fyne: the Cowal Peninsula

Cowal derives from Comhal, who was an ancient Dalriadic Scot. To get the best from Cowal you must walk or go by boat, but you can get an overview of what is on offer from your car. The A83, between the heads of Loch Long and Loch Fyne, cuts across the north of it, encompassing gloriously high, wild places which earn it a place here, in spite of the more pacific areas to the south and southwest. It attracts many climbers, sailors and holiday-makers but, apart from some coastal resorts, is not too crowded.

North Cowal

A third of the way south down Loch Lomond, you can turn right on to the A83 and drive westwards around the head of Loch Long, through Glen Croe and Glen Kinglas to the head of Loch Fyne. **Tarbet**, meaning isthmus, is where King Haakon IV's Vikings pulled 50 galleys from Loch Long into Loch Lomond in 1263. They then navigated the River Leven into the Firth of Clyde, and sailed down to Largs where, thanks to a bad equinoctial gale, many of the ships were wrecked and Haakon got his comeuppance from Alexander III. That was more or less the end of the Viking threat to Scotland.

Arrochar, on Loch Long where the Vikings began their 1½ mile haul, used to be a centre for cattle rustling. Robert Burns was unimpressed, writing that it was 'a land of

Tourist Information

The Cowal Peninsula and Dunoon: *www.cowal-dunoon.com*.
Dunoon: 7 Alexandra Parade, **t** (01369) 703 785, *www.scottishheartlands.com*.

Sports and Activities

Cowal Highland Gathering, t (01369) 703 206, *www.cowalgathering.com*. This 100-year-old annual event is the largest in the world, held on the last Friday and Saturday in August, at the same time as The World Highland Dancing Championships.

Castle Toward Outdoor Centre, by Dunoon, **t** (01369) 702 267. Offers multiactivity breaks, learning holidays and expeditions.

Where to Stay

Creggans Inn, on the shores of Loch Fyne, Strachur, **t** (01369) 860 279, *www.creggans-inn.co.uk* (*expensive*). Once owned by the late Sir Fitzroy Maclean.

Ardfillayne Country House, West Bay, Dunoon, **t** (01369) 702 267 (*moderate*). Comfortable Victorian country house in 16 acres of woodland with sea views.

Drimsynie House Hotel and Leisure Complex, Lochgoilhead, **t** (01301) 703 247 (*moderate*). A Victorian mansion overlooking Loch Goil, with golf course, leisure facilities and good food.

Enmore Hotel, Kirn, Dunoon, **t** (01369) 702 230, *www.enmorehotel.co.uk* (*moderate*). Small luxury hotel with lovely sea views, squash courts and good food.

Kilfinan Hotel, Kilfinan, **t** (01700) 821 201, *www.kilfinan.com* (*moderate*). Very comfortable old coaching inn – exceptionally good food.

The Royal Hotel, Tighnabruaich, **t** (01700) 811 239, *www.royalhotel.org.uk* (*moderate*). On the shore of the Kyles of Bute – very hospitable, fish and game a speciality.

Cobbler Hotel, Arrochar, on the banks of Loch Long, **t** (01301) 702 238 (*budget*). Friendly hotel in 4 acres of landscaped gardens, with dinner dances and bingo.

Colintraive Hotel, Colintraive, **t** (01700) 841 217, *www.colintraivehotel.com* (*budget*). Cosy, hotel with large bedrooms and lovely views.

Kames Hotel, by Tighnabruaich, **t** (01700) 811 489, *www.kames-hotel.com* (*budget*). A family hotel. Lovely views over the Kyles of Bute. Real ales and malts, good seafood.

Eating Out

Chatters, 58 John Street, Dunoon, **t** (01369) 706 402 (*moderate*). Excellent food. *Open Wed–Sat*.

The Oystercatcher, Otter Ferry, **t** (01700) 821 229 (*moderate*). Delightful pub – French-born chef is renowned for his seafood dishes. Free moorings for those arriving by boat. Best to book.

savage hills, swept by savage rains, peopled by savage sheep, tended by savage people'. Now it is a picturesque holiday village with flower baskets and trim B&Bs.

About a mile beyond Arrochar and into the **Arrochar Alps**, there is an excellent path up **Ben Arthur** (2,950ft/900m), known as the Cobbler because of its resemblance to a cobbler bent over his last. It is not too rough underfoot and fairly easy to find your way. The summit is not for vertigo sufferers. Ben Ime, Beinn Narnain, Ben Vane and Ben Vorlich march away to the northeast – all Munros, over 3,000ft (923m).

Doubling and doubling with laborious walk,
Who that has gained at length the wished-for height
This brief, this simple wayside call can slight
And rest not thankful?

William Wordsworth, 1803

The pass between Loch Long and Loch Fyne rises to 860ft (262m) and is called the **Rest and be Thankful**, after the inscription on a stone seat at the top. This was the military road built by William Caulfield over the pass between 1746 and 1748. According to Dr Johnson, who came this way in 1773, the milestones for the new road were removed by locals who said they would 'have no new miles'. In 1875 Queen Victoria, delighted as ever by the resemblance to Switzerland, descended from her coach and walked down the zigzag pass into Glen Croe. The A814 from Arrochar skirts the eastern side of Loch Long.

The B828 south from the Rest and be Thankful takes you through dramatic Glen Mhoir along the River Goil, with the road dropping from 1,000ft (308m) to sea level in 3 miles, joining with the B839 down to Lochgoilhead. Unfortunately, the village is now dominated by the Drimsynie Leisure Centre, just to the west. Five miles down the west side of the fjord-like loch is **Carrick Castle**, a 14th-century ruin on a promontory. This was where the Campbells of Argyll kept their documents and their prisoners. A remote enough place in those days, the shell of the keep is still aloof and impressive, even with the rash of water-sport enthusiasts nearby. James IV used it as a resting place when hunting wild boar in the area (Cowal is the last recorded place in Britain to have had indigenous wild boar). The 8th Earl of Argyll fortified the castle in 1681, preparing for an attack by Cromwell which never came. The road ends here and you can see where the loch joins up with Loch Long to the southeast.

The area within the triangle formed by the Rest and be Thankful, Loch Long and Loch Goil is known by the unlikely name of **Argyll's Bowling Green**. It measures 8 miles by 4, includes 10 major summits and is only accessible on foot (the name actually comes from *baile na greine* – sunny settlement). You must retrace your route to 3 miles north of Lochgoilhead, where you can take the left fork and continue on the B839 west through Hell's Glen, a steep hanging valley running out to Loch Fyne.

Loch Fyne washes around the western curve of the Cowal Peninsula and is renowned for sea fishing, oysters and good sailing. The B839 joins the A815 south and you can drive down the eastern shore through a string of villages, with the Argyll Forest Park stretching away to the hinterland. Alternatively, keep on the A815 at Strachur and drive southeast down narrow Loch Eck, hedged in by steep, wooded slopes. Branch left at the Whistlefield Hotel and take the long way round, through Glen Finart to **Ardentinny**, a picturesque village with good beaches on Loch Long.

The road hugs the shore to Strone Point and back northwest along Holy Loch. Don't anticipate a spiritual experience here; until 1992 **Holy Loch** was the deep-water anchorage for the American submarine base, gone now. It is 'Holy' because of an incident in the 12th century when a ship, carrying earth from the Holy Land intended as sacred foundations for Glasgow Cathedral, foundered in a storm as it tried to round the headland into the sheltered Clyde. The name might also come from the 15th-century church at Kilmun, on the north shore, dedicated to St Mundus, a 7th-century disciple of St Columba. Only the original tower survives.

Benmore Botanic Garden, Benmore (*open Mar–Oct daily 10–6; adm*) is barely 2 miles north of the head of Holy Loch on the A815. Planted in the last four decades of the 19th century and made over to the nation in 1928, it is now an offshoot of the

Royal Botanic Garden in Edinburgh. It is more of a park than a garden, with a splendid grass avenue of sequoias (giant Californian Wellingtonias) leading to grounds ablaze with azaleas in May and June. Its 250 species of rhododendron flower from March to September and are thought by many to be one of the best collections in the world. This interesting and spectacular garden also has some of the largest trees in Britain.

Dunoon

Dunoon, just a village until the early 19th century, is now a holiday base for the gregarious who intend to explore Cowal, and has long been the destination for generations of Glaswegians taking their summer break '*doon the watter*'. The long, low sprawl of the town, washed by the Firth of Clyde, is backed by a crescent of blue-green tree-covered hills. It has a lively holiday resort atmosphere in summer, with its busy esplanade and rows of seaside boarding houses and hotels. In winter it goes into hibernation. Two ferry companies operate the 20-minute crossing of the Clyde to Gourock. Dunoon stands on the threshold of fine walking and climbing country and also makes a good base for some idyllic sailing routes. For those who prefer to let someone else take the helm, there are cruises on the Firth of Clyde in the summer.

Only a trace remains of **Dunoon Castle**, on Castle Hill, dating from the 14th century. It was built on the site of an earlier fort, with a colourful history that kept it bouncing back and forth between English and Scottish hands. Edward I took it – Robert the Bruce snatched it back; Edward Balliol had a turn – to be ousted by Robert II. In 1471 the Earls of Argyll were made Honorary Keepers by James III, on condition they paid the Crown the fee of a red rose whenever demanded. When Queen Elizabeth II visited Dunoon in 1958, she was presented with a red rose without having to demand it.

Castle House Museum (*www.castlehousemuseum.org.uk; open Easter–Oct Mon–Sat 10.30–4.30, Sun 2–4.30; adm*) in Castle Gardens opposite the Pier, was built in 1822 in the Gothic style with grandiose crenellations. There are exhibits of local history, with delightful furnished Victorian rooms and a lot else. The 2-mile **Ardnadam Heritage Trail** starts at Sandbank, 2 miles northeast of the town – it is dotted with information boards on the local flora and fauna and pointing out the site of an Iron Age roundhouse. Less than 4 miles north of Dunoon, beyond Hunter's Quay, **Lazaretto Point** was the quarantine station for servicemen fighting in the Napoleonic Wars.

South Cowal

Toward Castle (with the stress on the first syllable, 'tow', to rhyme with 'now'), 8 miles south of Dunoon and just west of Toward Point, was the stronghold of the Lamont clan. In 1646 the bloodthirsty Campbells of Argyll surrounded the castle, captured a large number of the clan and dragged them off to Dunoon where they were hanged. In the words of a contemporary observer: the Campbells 'most barbarously, cruelly and inhumanly murdered several, young and old, yea, sucking children, some of them not one month old'. (The tree that served as the gallows was later felled and was said to gush blood from its roots.) Following this massacre, the castle was deserted and fell into the ruins that remain today. In 1906, the victims' descendants erected a Celtic cross in Tom-a-Mhoid Road near Castle Hill.

To explore the rest of the peninsula by car, take the B836 west from the head of Holy Loch to the head of Loch Striven and on to the A886. Here, turn left and take the new road down the east side of Loch Riddon to **Colintraive** – meaning 'Strait of Swimming', from the time when the drovers used to swim their cattle across here. (In the recent past, people have tried to retrace the old drovers' routes with modern cattle. One difficulty was to actually persuade the beasts to brave these deep passages of water.) A car ferry runs from Colintraive to Bute and there are splendid views across the Kyles of Bute to Tighnabruaich. You can get down to Strone Point, but there is no road right up the western shore of Loch Striven.

Return to the head of Loch Riddon on the A886 and take the A8003 down its west side, with good views high above the Kyles of Bute. **Tighnabruaich** – 'house on the hill' – and **Kames** are two popular resorts looking across the Kyles to the Isle of Bute. A minor road runs on down to Ardlamont Point, the most southerly tip of the peninsula, rising to 205ft (63m). The waters of Loch Fyne, Kyles of Bute, Sound of Bute and Kilbrannan Sound meet in a flurry beyond the headland.

From Ardlamont, go north 4 miles to Millhouse and then west 2 miles to **Portavadie**, from where a ferry runs across to Tarbert on the Kintyre Peninsula. With deep water offshore, it was chosen as an oil-platform construction site and £14 million was spent building an enormous dry dock that no one then seemed to want – eventually the sea wall was breached, and the £14 million investment washed away.

From Millhouse take the B8000 north through Kilfinan, a hamlet whose hotel has 16th-century vaults and whose church stands on a Celtic site. **Otter Ferry**, 3 miles to the north, takes its name from the Gaelic *oitir* – a sandbank (yachtsmen beware!). The Norsemen who fought in the Battle of Glendaruel in 1100 beached their longships side by side on the sand bar, clambered ashore and marched over the pass into Glendaruel, 5 miles to the east. There they were slaughtered by the Scots who threw their bodies into the river – 'ruel' is a corruption of the Gaelic for 'blood flowed'.

West Loch Fyne

The A83 west from Arrochar on Loch Long, and the A819 south from Dalmally take you to Inveraray on the northwest shore of Loch Fyne. **Ardkinglas Woodland Garden** (*open daily dawn–dusk; adm*) is on a hillside just beyond Cairndow at the head of the loch with views over the loch. It has one of the finest collections of conifers in the British Isles, including five 'champion trees', one of which, known as the 'mightiest conifer in Europe', dates back to 1790. The **Tree Shop** sells specimen trees, indigenous Highland trees and shrubs, as well as woodwork, basketwork and unusual gifts.

Inveraray

Inveraray is one of the few planned Highland towns – it's certainly the most gracious. The 18th-century town's tall, elegant, white terraced houses were designed by John Adam and Robert Mylne, and are now embellished with an overwhelming

Tourist Information

Inveraray: Front Street, **t** 0870 720 0616, *www.visitscottishheartlands.org*.

Cairndow: Here We Are, beyond Cairndow, next to the Loch Fyne Oyster Bar (*see below*), *www.hereweare-uk.com*. In a new building of local oak – a visitor centre/community resource centre, with local exhibits.

Where to Stay

Ardanaiseig Hotel, Kilchrenan, **t** (01866) 833 333, *www.ardanaiseig.com* (*expensive*). Scots Baronial mansion set in wooded grounds overlooking Loch Awe. Log fires, fresh flowers, every sort of comfort, as well as excellent food. Very memorable.

Taychreggan, Kilchrenan, on the shores of Loch Awe, **t** (01866) 833 211, *www.taychreggan hotel.co.uk* (*expensive*). Old inn, with comfortable rooms and excellent food.

Argyll Hotel, Front Street, Inveraray, **t** (01499) 302 466, *www.the-argyll-hotel.co.uk* (*moderate*). The Argyll Arms overlooking Loch Fyne where Johnson and Boswell stayed. Well modernized and comfortable.

Cairndow Stagecoach Inn, Cairndow, **t** (01499) 600 286 (*moderate*). Historic coaching inn on Loch Fyne, with a modern sauna, solarium and gym.

Bridge of Awe Lodge, Taynuilt, **t** (01866) 822 642 (*moderate–budget*). Wolsey Lodge catering for fishermen. Comfortable and welcoming, with good food.

Fernpoint Hotel, Inveraray, by the pier, **t** (01499) 302 170 (*moderate–budget*). Georgian house with executive suites. Unremarkable public rooms, but varied, good food.

Loch Fyne Hotel, Inveraray, **t** (01499) 302 148 (*moderate–budget*). Relaxed and comfortable, with very much a Highland atmosphere.

Killean Farmhouse, Inveraray, **t** (01499) 302 474 (*budget*). This is a large, attractive farmhouse with good B&B. They also do self-catering.

Braleckan House, Inveraray, **t** (01499) 500 662, *pcrawford@quista.net* (*moderate–budget*). Restored 19th-century building on a family farm, with two peaceful and well-equipped self-catering houses.

Eating Out

The Loch Fyne Oyster Bar beyond Cairndow, **t** (01499) 600 264 (*moderate–expensive*). A superb restaurant in an old farm building. Its founder is a passionate food and wine buff. An attached shop sells fresh and smoked sea food including oysters from the local beds, mussels and salmon. It's very popular so book ahead. *Open daily from 9am (kipper breakfasts), last orders from mid-Mar–Oct 9pm, Nov–mid-Mar 8pm*.

display of tartan and Highland-related souvenir tourist-traps. In South Main Street the architecture becomes distinctly more austere, with massive, three-storey tenements for the 'poorer labouring class' lining the road. Old Inveraray was clustered round the former castle, close to where the present one stands today, half a mile to the north, and was little more than a village. It was burnt down in 1644 by Montrose, and in 1741 the 3rd Duke of Argyll began work on both the new town and the castle. The duke decided his new castle deserved more privacy, and planted the new town in its present, more attractive position. John Adam is thought to have been responsible for building the Great Inn (now the Argyll Hotel), where Johnson and Boswell are reputed to have stayed during their tour in 1773. Johnson pronounced it 'not only commodious, but magnificent'. Boswell is more expansive: 'Dr Johnson owned tonight that he got as good a room and bed as at an English inn.' They 'supped well', and Johnson, whom Boswell had not seen drink any fermented liquor during their travels together, called for a gill of whisky, saying 'Come, let me know what it is that makes a Scotchman happy!'

The Town

The church on the island in the middle of the main street was built in 1798 with one side for Gaelic services and the other for English, in use until the 1950s; the Gaelic part is now the church hall. The **Bell Tower All Saints Episcopal Church** (*open May–Sept 10–1 and 2–5; adm*), built in 1866, has a detached 126ft (39m) tower built in 1913, which offers good views across town and has a peal of 10 bells. The bells are the second heaviest in the world and are rung in memory of the Campbells who died in the First World War; a complete peal takes 4 hours to ring.

Inveraray Jail (*open daily April–Oct 9.30–6, Nov–Mar 10–5; adm*), in Church Square, is one of the best examples of reconstructed history in Scotland. Guides dress as warders and prisoners, and realistic waxwork models talk in this 19th-century courthouse and gaol. There are also replica cells, an exhibition of tortures, and a court room where you can sit in and listen to the trial of a farmer accused of fraud – a good springboard for the imagination. The **Maritime Museum** (*open daily April–Sept 10–6, Oct–Mar 10–5; adm*) includes a three-masted schooner, the *Arctic Penguin*, with maritime displays and memorabilia.

Inveraray Castle

Open April–Oct Mon–Thurs and Sat 10–1 and 2–5.45, Sun 1–5.45; adm.

Inveraray Castle was built between 1741 and 1785 to replace a great tower house nearby, now demolished, that was home to the Earls and Dukes of Argyll since the 15th century. The Campbell clan who lived here dominated the history of Scotland for centuries and became synonymous to some, notably the clan Donald, with the word 'enemy'. They transferred their allegiance from Balliol to Bruce at an opportune moment, and from then on became the lawkeepers and policemen for the government, involving amongst other things a relentless struggle to tame the lawless Lords of the Isles. They were amply rewarded for their loyalty to the crown, often with lands forfeited by the proud Macdonalds, who refused to be tamed. They were ruthless in their duties, but there is no doubt that they helped control the chaotic anarchy of *Gaidhealtachd* – Gaeldom. That it was a Campbell – Robert, of Glenlyon, a drunken bankrupt – who was chosen to implement the outrageous massacre of the Glencoe Macdonalds in 1692 (*see* pp.109–10), sealed the loathing that Clan Donald felt for Clan Campbell.

The present castle stands four-square, greenish and imposing, in a dry moat surrounded by formal gardens, with some of the finest internal neoclassical decoration in Britain. Perhaps overawed by the prospect of his son's marriage to Queen Victoria's daughter in 1871, and a visit from the queen herself in 1875, the 8th Duke lost his head and commissioned the aggrandizement of his castle, resulting in four witches' hats, perched on the four corner towers, and an additional floor with gabled dormers. The central hall soars to 90ft and contains a magnificent collection of arms and armour. The castle also houses splendid Beauvais tapestries and fine paintings by Gainsborough, Batoni and Opie.

Dr Johnson was much struck by its grandeur and elegance on a visit, commenting: 'What I admire here, is the total defiance of expence [sic]).' When Queen Victoria first visited in 1847, the Marquess of Lorne, afterwards 9th Duke of Argyll, stood outside to greet her, aged two, 'a dear, white, fat, fair little fellow with reddish hair, but very delicate features'. When she returned, in 1875, Lorne was her son-in-law.

Around Inveraray

Auchindrain (*open April–Sept daily 10–5; adm*) is 5½ miles southwest of Inveraray on the A83. When the Duke of Argyll brought Queen Victoria here in 1875, he gave her a brief homily on the old system of 'village communities', on which the crofting townships were based. The people lived in a close-knit group and the farm was divided into pasture and arable. The pasture was held in common by all the families and the arable was divided by lot every year so each family had a turn at each plot of soil. When this practice was revised and families persuaded to divide the arable and hold it in perpetuity, Auchindrain remained the only communal tenancy township in Scotland to survive on its ancient site in the original form. Restoration began in 1963 and the whole village has been preserved, furnished and equipped in the style of the periods through which it existed. What you see here is much as it would have been when Queen Victoria saw it. It's been sanitized, of course, but each cottage, barn and farm building has been imaginatively restored. You should allow at least an hour to stroll around and inspect it all.

Furnace, a couple of miles further on, is an unhappy reminder of the troubled times that the 18th century brought. It is so called from the charcoal-burning smelting furnace founded by the Duke of Argyll to help the local economy. It was established here to make use of the trees felled by order of the Hanoverian government to deprive rebel Highlanders of somewhere to hide as they clung to the Jacobite cause.

Crarae Garden (*open daily Easter–Sept 10–5, winter daylight hours only; adm*), 10 miles south of Inveraray, just past Furnace, is one of Scotland's most beautiful 'wild' gardens. Cumlodden estate was handed over to Captain (later Sir) George Campbell in 1926. His mother had already started planting exotic species in this wooded glen, and soon Crarae became George Campbell's lifelong interest. From 1926 he began to plant the banks of the Crarae Burn, cutting back the natural oak, birch, rowan, alder and hazel and replacing them with exotics, protected from the prevailing southwesterly winds by periphery conifers. Gradually Sir George increased his plantings by taking in land on either side of the glen until, today, the garden covers some 40 acres. He preferred to plant groups of one species together, resulting in the spectacular drifts of colour both in spring, with the azaleas, and in autumn, when the decorative hardwoods turn. The gardens lead you up the Crarae Burn, crossing and recrossing its tumbling water, through the banks, dramatic with slabs of colour and texture. A Neolithic chambered cairn, dating back some 4,500 years and once of considerable size, was excavated in the 1950s and is now a feature of the gardens.

The A83 takes you on down Loch Fyne to Lochgilphead. The A819 from Inveraray takes you north through Glen Aray to Dalmally and Loch Awe. **Loch Awe** is well named, narrow and darkly brooding, dominated to the north by Ben Cruachan

(3,689ft/1,126m) and dotted with ancient remains. Legend claims there was a 'well of youth' in a corrie high on Ben Cruachan, guarded by the goddess Bheithir. Every day she bathed in the magic waters and one evening she forgot to replace the capstone to the well. All night the crystal water flowed down the hillside, flooding the valley, and in the morning – there was Loch Awe. Bheithir was banished and cursed with immortality by the irate gods; she is now Cailleach Bheithir, the winter hag of death and darkness and you hear her icy voice echoing round the chasms of Ben Cruachan on winter nights. Loch Awe is fed by the rivers Orchy and Strae to the north. Its outlet, the River Awe, runs through the Pass of Brander to Loch Etive and the sea. Loch Awe is one of the largest freshwater lochs in Scotland, renowned for its huge brown trout. Not so long ago, before there were sensible roads, Loch Awe was a major waterway for the area with regular steamer services and ferries.

Kilchurn Castle, best seen from a distance – sticking out into the north end of the loch on a peninsula – is a recently stabilized ruin dating back to 1440 when it was a five-storey tower house built to guard Glen Orchy and Glen Strae. During the Jacobite Rising it was garrisoned by Hanoverian troops with the consent of the anti-Jacobite Campbells who owned it. It was unroofed in 1775 and is now a picturesque shell, reflected in the waters of the loch with Ben Cruachan beyond, a scene painted by Turner and many others.

There are boat trips on the loch from the pier beside the Loch Awe Hotel, on the northwest tip of the loch. When the level of the loch is low, traces of several crannogs – man-made islands – can be seen, where early settlers built dwellings for protection against attack. Some of the islands were used as clan burial grounds, especially Inchail, where there is a 13th-century ruined chapel and several graves of the Macarthur clan. **St Conan's Church**, in Lochawe village west of Kilchurn, is a synthesis of architectural styles from ancient Roman to Norman, designed at the turn of the 20th century by an eccentric Campbell. At the mouth of the River Awe, on the A85, inside the hollow mountain of Ben Cruachan, a glistening subterranean empire, the **Cruachan Power Station** (*open daily Easter–Nov 9.30–5, July–Aug 9.30–6; adm*) gives a guided tour. You can see how the generating station works, using water from the Cruachan Reservoir to power turbines, which then supply electricity.

The **Pass of Brander** is a geological fault some four to six million years old, carved out by the receding Ice Age to form a gorge through which the River Awe squeezes itself into Loch Etive. In 1309 the Black Douglas, fighting for Robert the Bruce, vanquished John MacDougall of Lorne who, fighting for Edward II, had set up an ambush for Bruce's army in the Pass. As Bruce approached almost certain disaster, the Black Douglas led his men down from the summit of Ben Cruachan in a ferocious stampede, to slaughter the MacDougalls. The Pass was too narrow for more than one horseman at a time, and the surviving MacDougalls fled in panic, impeding and killing each other in their frenzy to get over the bridge; many were drowned. John MacDougall escaped down the loch in his galley. You can drive all the way round the loch, and continue south to Lochgilphead or north to Taynuilt (*Tigh an Uilt* – House by the Burn) and on to Oban.

Oban and Around

Oban – the Little Bay – is the gateway to the isles. It is unashamedly a holiday resort in summer, when its streets seethe with visitors and traffic, but quiet and provincial

Tourist Information

Oban: Argyll Square, **t** 0870 720 0630, *www.visitscottishheartlands.com*.

Sports and Activities

The Corryvreckan, **t** (01631) 770 246, *www.corryvreckan.co.uk*. A 64-foot sailing boat with experienced crew and good food.

The Hebridean Princess, **t** (01756) 704 704, *www.hebridean.co.uk*. A luxurious (and expensive) ways to see the Western Isles.

Where to Stay

Isle of Eriska Hotel, Ledaig, 20 minutes' drive north of Oban, **t** (01631) 720 371, *www.eriska-hotel.co.uk* (*expensive*). This Scottish Baronial pile, situated on a 300-acre island, is connected to the mainland by a bridge. It is an amazingly luxurious hotel – with leisure facilities and wonderful wildlife.

The Falls of Lora Hotel, Connel Ferry, **t** (01631) 710 483, *www.fallsoflora.com* (*expensive–budget*). Solid old building overlooking Loch Etive – log fire in the bar, and a wide selection of malts.

Ards House, Connel, **t** (01631) 710 255, *www.ardshouse.com* (*moderate*). Small, very cosy hotel – glorious sea views.

Caledonian Hotel, Station Square, Oban, **t** (01631) 563 133, *www.obancaledonian.com* (*moderate*). One of the splendid old hotels – large and dependable.

Dungallan House Hotel, Gallanach Road, Oban, **t** (01631) 563 799, *www.dungallanhotel-oban.co.uk* (*moderate*). Victorian villa with glorious views over Oban to the Isles. Friendly, with good food.

Foxholes Country Hotel, Lerags, south of Oban, **t** (01631) 564 982, *www.hoteloban.com* (*moderate*). In a quiet glen with good views – comfortable.

Kimberley Hotel, 13 Dalriach Road, Oban, **t** (01631) 571 115, *www.kimberley-hotel.com*

(*moderate*). 19th-century house with spectacular views and great hospitality.

Manor House, Gallanack Road, Oban, **t** (01631) 562 087, *www.manorhouseoban.com* (*moderate*). Built in 1780 – attractively furnished, with good food (*see* 'Eating Out').

The Barriemore Hotel, Corran Esplanade, Oban, **t** (01631) 566 356, *www.barriemore-hotel.co.uk* (*budget*). Friendly, restored Victorian B&B overlooking the bay.

Glenbervie Guest House, Dalriach Road, Oban, **t** (01631) 564 770 (*budget*). Comfortable Victorian villa close to town and overlooking the bay; good food.

Lerags House, near Oban, **t** (01631) 563 381, *www.leragshouse.com* (*budget*). Lovely Georgian country house on Loch Ferchan.

The Old Manse Guest House, Dalriach Road, Oban, **t** (01631) 564 886, *www.obanguesthouse.co.uk* (*budget*). Detached Victorian villa with sea views in a quiet area close to the town centre. *Closed Dec and Jan*.

Eating Out

The Barn, Lerags, **t** (01631) 564 618 (*moderate*). Nice atmosphere.

The Boxtree, 108 George Street, Oban, **t** (01631) 563 542 (*moderate*). Cheerful, good value bistro.

Hawthorne Cottage, Benderloch, **t** (01631) 720 452 (*moderate*). Old croft house in a cosy setting.

Manor House, Oban, **t** (01631) 562 087 (*moderate*). The best place to eat in Oban.

Waterfront Restaurant, Railway Pier, Oban, **t** (01631) 563 110 (*moderate*). First-class seafood and local beef and venison – splendid atmosphere overlooking harbour.

The Studio, Craigard Road, Oban, **t** (01631) 562 030 (*moderate*). Reasonably priced and candlelit. *Open April–Oct 5–10pm*.

Onorio's, George Street, Oban. Famous for its fish and chips.

A shed on the pier, Oban. Sells delicious fresh takeaway seafood snacks.

in winter. Before the Victorians developed Oban into an important port and the principal town in Argyll, it was a mere hamlet with one inn. Now it is crammed with shops, hospitals and schools serving a wide area. Hotels, guesthouses and neat villas offering bed and breakfast are numerous; cafés and restaurants are busy and there is a fairly lively nightlife offering discos, public ceilidhs and other amusements. In spite of this, Oban remains truly West Highland and unspoilt.

The Town

The town rises steeply from a crescent-shaped bay, its main street fronting the harbour whence ferries, fishing boats and pleasure craft come and go between the islands. The quays are thronged with people, cars and freight, loading and unloading from the ferries. High above the bustle stands **McCaig's Tower**, a large replica of the Colosseum built in 1897 at a cost of £5,000. A banker, McCaig erected it to give work to the many unemployed in the area and to create a museum and observation tower as a memorial to his family. Never finished, it remains a prominent landmark. Walk up here at sunset for views of the Morvern Hills across the island-studded sea. The Catholic See of Argyll and the Western Isles has its well-attended cathedral, **St Columba's**, in town. Although this area is predominantly Protestant, there are still communities left untouched by the Reformation.

The first National Mod was held here in 1892, and has returned since. Because Oban is the main port for many of the islands, you will often hear Gaelic spoken on the pier or in the streets and shops. The **Argyllshire Gathering** in August is one of the major Highland Games and much less 'smart' than those around Royal Deeside.

Oban is a popular base for **scuba divers**, with air supplies in the town and good diving locations in the surrounding waters. The Sound of Mull is littered with wrecks, and the waters support a wealth of marine life beneath dramatic cliff scenery. The area is also ideal for sailing, offering some fairly challenging, but breathtakingly beautiful, stretches, especially south through the Firth of Lorne to the Sound of Jura, past the infamous Corryvreckan whirlpool (*see* p.217). There is plenty of wet-weather entertainment in the area: a **Seal and Marine Centre** (*open daily from 10am*); **Rare Breeds Farm** (*open April–Oct 10–4; adm*); and **Oban Distillery** (*t (01631) 572 004; open Mon–Sat 9.30–5, later in summer*).

Kerrera Island

From a point a couple of miles south of Oban on the Gallanach road, a foot ferry (*t (01631) 563 665; run on demand, takes 3 minutes*) runs across to Kerrera, the 4-mile-long island sheltering Oban from the worst of the southwesterly gales that rip up the Firth of Lorne. Alexander II came here in 1249 with a fleet to try to evict the Norsemen who held the island. He was taken ill and died in Horseshoe Bay. Kerrera was a droving station between Mull and the mainland; cattle had to swim across from its northern tip to the mainland. **Gylen Castle** is a ruin on the cliffs overlooking Port a' Chastell on the south coast. Built in 1582, this was the second stronghold of the MacDougalls after Dunollie (*see* p.90), and was besieged and burnt by General Leslie and his Covenanters in 1647. It is currently being consolidated for its MacDougall owner. There is a monument to David Hutcheson on the northern hammerhead; he masterminded the ferry services between Oban and the Hebrides before Caledonian MacBrayne got the monopoly. **Dunollie Castle**, the ruin on a promontory guarding the north entrance to Oban harbour, was the ancient stronghold of the MacDougall Lords of Lorne, one of the oldest clans in Scotland. **Ganavan Sands** is a good place to stretch your legs while waiting for the ferry to the Outer Isles after a long journey, but is not the place for a quiet day on the beach.

South from Oban to Kintyre via Lochgilphead

The A816 swoops south from Oban, flirting here and there with the sea, dipping and rising for 37 miles, with magnificent views as it kisses the coast. There are numerous side roads, tracks and footpaths, almost all of which are worth exploring. Walk up any of the glens to the east of the road and discover remote lochans hidden in the hills and wild moorland. Wherever you go to the west, you will get to the sea and miles of empty beaches with sand, rocks and cliffs, and enchanting views of the islands.

Oban to Dunadd Fort

About 6 miles south of Oban, at Kilninver, you can go west out to **Seil Island**, with its famous humpbacked 'bridge over the Atlantic' designed by Telford in 1792. Just over the bridge is *Tigh na Truish* – the House of the Trousers – where Highlanders who had been off the island in the days of proscription would change back into the forbidden tartan kilts. It is now an informal inn (*see* 'Where to Stay and Eat', below). Seil and its surrounding islands are known as the Slate Islands; slate was extracted as long ago as

Where to Stay and Eat

Ardifuir, Duntrune Castle, near Kilmartin, t (01546) 510 271 (*moderate*). A comfortable 19th-century farmstead, with good food.
Barcaldine Castle, nr Oban, t (01631) 720 598, *www.barcaldinecastle.co.uk* (*moderate*). Spacious, comfortable accommodation in a fairy-tale castle; *see* also p.100.
Galley of Lorne, Ardfern, t (01852) 500 284, *www.galleyoflorne.co.uk* (*moderate*). Traditional Highland inn on Loch Craignish: comfortable and good value, with log fires, reasonably priced food and a good range of malts. Dogs welcome.
Loch Melfort Hotel, Arduaine, t (01852) 200 233, *www.lochmelfort.co.uk* (*moderate*). Wonderfully placed by the water's edge. Has 23 comfortable bedrooms and a reputation for excellent local shellfish and game.

Tigh-na-Truish, Isle of Seil, t (01852) 300 242 (*moderate*). A delightful inn that offers B&B rooms and one self-catering cottage (sleeps 2).
Corranmor House, Ardfern, t (01852) 500 609, (*budget*). B&B rooms in a glorious position on the waterfront. Located on a working farm with charming hosts – dinner by arrangement.
Culfail Hotel, 15 miles south of Oban on the A816, t (01852) 200 274 (*budget*). The food is very popular with locals.
Duachy Farm, Kilninver, t (01852) 316 244, *gillian.cadzow@tesco.net* (*budget*). A cosy and friendly B&B, on a trout loch, with boat.
Poltalloch Estate, in the castle grounds, t (01546) 510 283. 6 charming and well-equipped self-catering cottages (sleeps 2–5).
The Cairn, Kilmartin, t (01546) 510 254 (*moderate*). Excellent bistro/restaurant.

the 16th century and was an important industry, supporting the local population while creating some rather ugly blemishes. Easdale, just off the west coast, was particularly badly scarred, until a violent storm in 1881 flooded the quarries and hastened the decline and demise of the prosperous works.

An Cala Garden, on Seil Island (*open daily April–Oct 10–6; adm*), is a coastal garden designed in the 1930s to be looked at as the foreground to a wonderful vista of sea and islands. It is an unexpected gem nestling amid the slate.

The National Trust for Scotland's **Arduaine Gardens** (*open all year 9.30–sunset; adm*) is about 20 miles south of Oban on the southwest side of Loch Melfort. It is most colourful in late spring and early summer with a blaze of rhododendrons and azaleas, but it is an all-season garden, with informal lawns and shrubberies and a wild woodland area. In the lower garden there are streams and ponds and lovely mixtures of texture and colour. Sheltered as they are from the strong winds that prevail around here, some of the ornamental trees and shrubs grow to a gigantic size.

About 30 miles south of Oban, around the little village of **Kilmartin**, history has left a remarkable detritus of cairns, standing stones and prehistoric remains. Throughout an area stretching 4 miles south to Dunadd, Stone and Bronze Age remains abound, many with information boards. Some of the cists have been reconstructed, with carvings on the walls, but they are far easier to understand and appreciate after a visit to the award-winning Museum of Ancient Culture at **Kilmartin House** (*www.kilmartin.org; open daily 11–4; adm*), next to the church. The ticket lasts all day, so an overview obtained here can be followed up by a visit to the sites and then a return to the museum to study particular attractions in depth. As an excellent intro-duction to exploring some of the 150-plus prehistoric sites close by, this is a place worth making a detour to visit, even if you're not passionate about archaeology. Start with the 12-projector audiovisual presentation on the Kilmartin Valley; much of the music for this is recorded on replica prehistoric instruments, such as the Bronze Age horn (over 2,500 years old) and the Pictish triple pipes, modelled on carvings in early Christian stones like the one from Ardchattan Priory. There's a large three-dimensional map of the various ancient sites (which light up at the touch of a button) with a time chart showing the world perspective and environmental changes over the past 13,000 years. Then come displays of artefacts and models from the first settlers (about 9,000 years ago) to the early historic period. Some of the genuine artefacts are replicated, enabling you to see them as new. The hands-on exhibits include a quern stone to grind corn, a flint axe and animal furs. Music from listening posts brings it all to life: ringing rocks, pottery drums, cow horns, an Iron Age trumpet and monastic chanting.

At **Ardfern** there is a large **marina**, signed from the main road.

Dunadd Fort

Dunadd Fort to the west of the A816, 4 miles south of Kilmartin, is only special if you are fascinated by Scotland's ancient history, and the myths and uncertainties that surround it. Dunadd was the capital of the kingdom of Dalriada from the 6th to the 9th centuries, a powerful political centre and the headquarters of early missionaries, including St Columba, until Kenneth Macalpine moved the capital to Pictland. A rocky hillock above a meandering river is all that is immediately obvious, but careful search will reveal a rock with carvings of a boar, some Ogham (ancient Irish) inscriptions (now protected by fibreglass) and... a footprint. Historians believe this to be the place where kings were crowned, and that St Columba crowned Aidan here in 574, using the Stone of Destiny as the throne. The footprint is indisputable and only the most prosaic could resist the urge to stand in it and imagine those ancient ceremonies on this lofty site. In fact, crowning didn't come in until much later, but the ceremony of enthronement was elaborate. In those days, *mormaers* owned their kingdoms and the High King was their overlord – King of Scots but not of Scotland. At the enthronement, each *mormaer* filled a shoe with earth from his kingdom and poured a little into this footprint, carved here on this rock at Dunadd. The King sat on the Stone of Destiny and put his foot over this cocktail of Scottish soil, thus establishing his overlordship. Archaeological findings include many brooches and intricate metal work, backing up the tradition that this was a royal residence.

It's about 5 miles south to Lochgilphead, but fun to branch off on the way, west to Crinan, along the B841 that follows the canal.

Knapdale

Kintyre and Knapdale run south from Lochgilphead like a giant lobster claw, with Knapdale just managing to cling onto the long pincer of Kintyre. This part of the west coast, on the Gulf Stream, is unbelievably lush in the summer. Autumn is glorious, with a wonderful range of colours painting the densely wooded hills. So too is spring, when the rhododendrons and azaleas are in bloom against the soft new green and the sparkle of water. Perhaps the best time of all, though, is November, when a light dusting of snow covers the last autumn leaves and the water shows steel-grey against hills etched in white. It is possible to drive most of the way round the coast of Knapdale from Lochgilphead and across its middle from Inverneil to Achahoish. Along the coast, each mile opens up a fresh view to the islands of Jura and Islay in the west, or down through layers of hills to distant lochs and the sea.

The Crinan Canal

The Crinan Canal slices through the top of Knapdale from Ardrishaig on Loch Gilp to Crinan on the west coast, cutting out the often treacherous passage round the Mull of Kintyre, once a severe hazard for fishing fleets, commercial puffers and passenger craft. The 9-mile stretch of canal – opened in 1801 with 15 locks, rising to 64ft (19.5m) – was designed by Sir John Rennie, though Thomas Telford was called in to iron out a few teething troubles and got much of the credit. With the decline of the herring industry and the introduction of good road networks, it lost most of its commercial traffic and is now mainly used by pleasure boats, saving the sailor 130 miles. Gliding down the canal is a peaceful way to pass a fine day, though you have to work the lock gates yourself. In 1847 Queen Victoria sailed down the canal in a decorated horse-

Tourist Information

Lochgilphead: Lochnell Street, **t** (01546) 602 344, *www.visitscottishheartlands.com*. Open April–Oct.

Where to Stay

Crinan Hotel, Crinan, **t** (01546) 830 261, *www.crinanhotel.com* (*expensive*). Renowned for its lovely position overlooking the sea towards the Sound of Jura – sunset over the islands is memorable – and for its comfort and excellent food, supplied daily by fishing boats unloading a short distance from the kitchen.

Cairnbaan Hotel, by Lochgilphead, **t** (01546) 603 668 (*moderate*). Delightful small hotel right on the Crinan Canal. Excellent food and comfort.

Knock Cottage, at Lochgair, a little way up the west side of Loch Fyne, **t** (01546) 886 331 (*moderate*). Wolsey Lodge in 10 acres of secluded wild gardens, loch and field with lovely views over the sheltered anchorage of Lochgair to Loch Fyne and the Cowal Hills. An old croft house with attractive modern additions, very cosy and friendly and the food is delicious.

Lochgair Hotel, Lochgair, by Lochgilphead, **t** (01546) 886 333, *www.lochgair.com* (*moderate*). Family-run, with boats for fishing. Warm welcome.

Ormsary Estate Lodges, Ormsary, near Loch Caolisport, **t** (01880) 770 222 (*budget*). Fifteen comfortably furnished and well-equipped self-catering lodges, with lovely views to the west in one of the most beautiful locations to be found in Kintyre (sleeps 2–6).

Castle Sween (Holidays) Ltd, Ellary, Lochgilphead, **t** (01880) 770 232, *www.ellary.com*. Has cottages, chalets and caravans, mostly in lovely positions (sleeps up to 8).

Where to Eat

North Beachmore Farm Restaurant, near Muasdale, signed off the A83 (*moderate*). Overlooking the Sound of Gigha – serves very good food.

The Smiddy, Smithy Lane, Lochgilphead, **t** (01546) 603 606 (*moderate*). A vegetarian bistro-style establishment, with excellent home cooking.

Tayvallich Inn, Tayvallich, **t** (01546) 870 282 (*moderate*). Overlooking Loch Sween and specializing in delicious fresh sea-to-plate-fresh seafood. Memorable for its seafood platter, mussels, scallops and warm welcome. There's a tiny bar, and tables in a bay window or outside, weather permitting. Worth a detour.

The Westward (*moderate*) at the Crinan Hotel, *see above*. People travel from far and wide to eat at this seafood restaurant. The bar food is equally good – same chef – but cheaper and in a more relaxed atmosphere.

Kilberry Inn, Kilberry, **t** (01880) 770 223 (*budget*). Roadside inn serving delicious food and with 2 inexpensive rooms.

drawn barge, ridden by postilions dressed in scarlet, on her way to the Western Isles: 'We glided along very smoothly and the views of the hills were very fine indeed; but the eleven locks we had to go through (a very curious process, first passing several by rising, and then others by going down) were tedious...'.

It is fun to walk along the canal when there is traffic on the water, and watch the boats passing through the locks, not much more than 5 miles from the A816. **Crinan** itself is a pretty hamlet on a rocky peninsula with a sheltered harbour and the final, tidal gate between the canal and the open sea.

The left turn in Bellanoch, just before Crinan, and then right on to the B8025, takes you down the west side of Loch Sween and from anywhere along here your feet will take you to stretches of remote coast, with rocks, sand and cliffs, liberally dotted with prehistoric remains. The eastern road along Loch Sween goes past Castle Sween to

Kilmory. **Castle Sween** is sadly best avoided if you are looking for ruins in fine scenery: it is surrounded by a huge caravan park. The castle was built to guard the entrance to Loch Sween from the eastern shore and some say it is the oldest stone castle on the Scottish mainland. Dating from the 11th century, it is a great sprawl of a ruin, Norman in style, with buttresses. Still visible are the old ovens, the well and the original drain and rubbish chute in the wall of the round tower, down which everything, including sewage, was indiscriminately cast. The castle was a stronghold of the MacSweens who held the coast as far as Skipness. Robert the Bruce captured it in 1315 when the MacSweens sided with the English, and installed the McNeills of Argyll to maintain it, one of whom married a MacMillan. Thus Knapdale became MacMillan territory. The castle was destroyed in 1647 by Royalists, fighting for Charles I.

Two and a half miles on from Castle Sween, 13th-century **Kilmory Knap Chapel** is at the southern end of the peninsula. A glass roof protects the sculpted stones inside and the tall, very fine 15th-century **MacMillan's Cross**, elaborately carved with a crucified Christ on one side and a hunting scene on the other. It was probably made by monks from the monastery at Kilberry before the Reformation, after which masons were allowed to depict only 'Emblems of Mortality' – skulls, hourglasses, angels – with the result that many of the more elaborate embellishments died out. Unfortunately the track across to Loch Caolisport is private and has a locked gate, so you must go all the way back to the canal and down to Lochgilphead, to explore further south.

Lochgilphead to Kilberry

A couple of miles down the A816 from the Crinan turn-off, Lochgilphead, at the head of Loch Gilp, is a holiday resort as well as the shopping centre for the area, with plenty of shops down the wide main street that was once the market place. This was a fishing village until the Crinan Canal opened in 1801 and it became a popular stopping-off place for boats. Loch Gilp is an expanse of mud flats at low tide. The population expanded to supply services for people passing through the canal: a lunatic asylum and a poorhouse were built. Now it is a busy town and the regional headquarters. The Mid Argyll Show takes place here in August.

Ardrishaig, a couple of miles south of Lochgilphead, stands at the southern end of the Crinan Canal. Passengers on the ferry from Glasgow used to transfer to a canal boat here for the journey up the canal to Crinan, where other ferries took them to Oban, Fort William and, after the Caledonian Canal opened in 1822, to Inverness. This was a thriving fishing village during the herring boom in the 19th century, providing work for people supplying the fishermen, and also for women gutting the fish.

Today Ardrishaig has a somewhat different character, its centre having been completely rebuilt in the 1970s. However, it has a pretty lighthouse and some old villas above. It is a good base for cycling and walking – the canal banks making a popular route for both purposes. The late John Smith, who led the Labour Party for a short time before his tragically early death in 1994, was brought up here. **Loch Fyne Miniature Railway Society** runs a train along the green (*weekends from 11–6; adm*).

To avoid the main road if you are going on down into Kintyre, take the B8024 a couple of miles south of Ardrishaig, which follows the more scenic west-coast route.

At Achahoish, less than 5 miles from the turning, fork right, round the head of Loch Caolisport, pronounced – and sometimes spelt – Killisport.

Here is enchantment. Just over 3 miles along the road, overlooking a tiny bay, is **St Columba's Cave** behind the ruins of a 13th-century church and the tumbled stones of previous dwellings. There are in fact two caves in a cliff. The smaller is thought to have been a hermit's cell and the larger has an altar on a rock with crosses carved above. Strong local tradition holds that St Columba landed here on his way to Iona. A number of other places on the coast lay similar claims and, given the frailty of his craft and the notorious weather conditions in these parts, he may have made several landfalls before he finally decided on Iona. There is an almost tangible spirituality about this place, in spite of archaeological vandalism (a 19th-century laird cleaned out the cave and deposited a tip of debris from it outside). In 1959, when some of this tip was being restored to the cave, a sewing needle made from horn was discovered and the archaeologists moved in. A wealth of artefacts, including Viking weighing scales, was found, some of which dated back to 8000 BC.

Kilberry (about 12 miles from the cave, although you have to return to where you turned off and rejoin the B8024) has a splendid collection of 9th- and 10th-century stones gathered up from the surrounding area and housed under cover in a steading just north of the hamlet, signposted Kilberry Stones from the road. Marion Campbell, the archaeologist who collected the stones, used to live in Kilberry Castle, a brooding pile (medieval in origin, remodelled in the 19th century by David Bryce), which has belonged to the Campbells of Kilberry for centuries. The road takes you on southwards round Knapdale and up the west side of West Loch Tarbert.

Kintyre

Tarbert

An isthmus between East and West Loch Tarbert, straddled by the village of Tarbert, joins Kintyre to Knapdale. Here, in 1098, Malcolm Canmore struck a bargain with the Norwegian King, Magnus Barelegs, who was harassing him. He told Magnus he could claim any western island he could get to by boat with his rudder down. Magnus had his Viking henchmen tow him the mile across the isthmus in a boat – and claimed Kintyre as his. History doesn't relate the damage done to his rudder.

Tarbert comes from *an tairbeart* – isthmus; there are several in Scotland. This one has an attractive bay with a backdrop of hills, popular with sailors, especially when regattas are held on Loch Fyne. It used to be a thriving ring-net herring-fishing port and still has a small fishing fleet, but tourism is the main source of income now, together with a bit of yacht- and boat-servicing. Take the signed footpath to **Tarbert Castle**, renovated by Robert the Bruce in 1325, but keep in mind that it is now no more than a pile of stones with a good view.

The A83 zips down the west coast of Kintyre through villages and hamlets, most of which cater for summer visitors. The landscapes and seascapes are similar to those of Knapdale, cut by wooded glens rising to hilly moorland.

Tourist Information

Campbeltown: Mackinnon House, The Pier, **t** 0870 200 609, *www.visitscottish heartlands.com.*

Where to Stay and Eat

Stonefield Castle Hotel, Tarbert, **t** (01880) 820 836 (*expensive*). Comfortable hotel in wooded grounds with stunning views. The AA and RAC gave Stonefield's restaurant three stars – Egon Ronay agrees with them.

Columba Hotel, Tarbert, on the waterfront, **t** (01880) 820 808, *www.columbahotel.com* (*moderate*). Comfy, with a gym and a sauna.

Skipness Castle, by Tarbert, **t** (01880) 760 207, *sophie@skipness.freeserve.co.uk* (*moderate*). Nicely furnished, with spectacular views and good food, from the estate (a working farm) and fresh from the sea.

Ardshiel Hotel, Kilkerran Road, Campbeltown, **t** (01586) 552 133 (*budget*). Family-run hotel, with traditional home cooking served in a garden restaurant – 175 malts to sample in front of a cosy open fire.

Tarbert Hotel, Tarbert harbour, **t** (01880) 820 264 (*budget*). Popular for après-sailing gatherings and yarn-swapping.

West Loch Hotel, beyond Tarbert on the A83, **t** (01880) 820 283, *www.westlochhotel.co.uk* (*budget*). Friendly 18th-century former coaching inn. Glorious views and good food.

The Anchorage, Tarbert, **t** (01880) 820 881 (*moderate*). Excellent restaurant on the quay, some say the best in the land, especially for seafood.

Net Store, Tarbert. Very popular bar with visiting yachtsmen, as well as locals.

The Whitehouse Old School Tearoom, Kennacraig, near the ferry to Islay. Good home-made baking and snacks. *Closed Tues.*

Campbeltown

Campbeltown is 38 miles south of Tarbert at the head of Campbeltown Loch on the east coast, a haven for boats in a westerly gale and subject of that hopeful song: 'O Campbeltown Loch, I wish you were whisky...' This is a holiday town and boating centre and, like most coastal settlements in these parts, was once an important herring port. Of its 34 distilleries, only two remain in business. Although less than 40 miles from Glasgow as the crow flies, Campbeltown is about 135 miles by road. Despite its Victorian appearance, it was founded in 1607. The 7th Earl of Argyll brought in Protestants from the Lowlands – mainly Ayrshire and Renfrewshire – in an attempt (known as the 'Plantation Policy') to pacify what was then a rather troublesome area. James IV had trouble here too and built Kilkerran Castle, now in ruins, in 1498 when he was desperately trying to bring the Lords of the Isles to heel. Rather sad is the **Campeltown Cross**, a truly splendid, intricately carved stone cross dating from 1380 and brought from Kilkivan near Machrihanish to be the market cross. It now stands on a roundabout. There is the usual **Heritage Centre** (*t (01586) 551 400; open April–Oct Mon–Sat 11–5, Sun 2–5; adm*) showing the cultural and economic development of Kintyre. There is also the **Campbeltown Museum** (*open Tues and Thurs 10–1, 2–5 and 5.30–7.30; Wed, Fri and Sat 10–1 and 2–5*), which is free and shows geological and archaeological specimens from Kintyre.

It would be a pity to visit Campbeltown and not venture out to the caves on **Davaar Island**, off the southeastern point of the loch. You walk the mile across a shingle spit – the Dhorlin – at low tide. It is marked by buoys and you must get the tides right (any local will tell you), or you will be cut off until the next low tide – you have about 6 hours, which is more than enough. The cave of most interest is on the eastern side of the island, the seventh cave along to your right. In 1887 Archibald Mackinnon had a dream which inspired him to paint an El Greco-like Crucifixion here, secretly, on the rock, lit by a shaft of light that streams into the cave through an aperture. In 1934, when he was 80, he returned to the cave and restored the painting.

Machrihanish to Keil

Machrihanish, 6 miles west of Campbeltown and fully exposed to the fury of Atlantic gales, is a holiday village with a hotel, golf course, camp site, sandy beaches, and a token airport. There are good walks across the moorland to the south and lovely coastal stretches, but beach-lounging can be breezy. **Southend**, 10 miles south of Campbeltown on the south coast, is another holiday village and nothing special: a golf-course and sandy beaches with dunes covered in marram grass, useful for shelter from the wind. Nothing remains today of Dunaverty Castle, which once stood on the vicious rocks here. Three hundred of Montrose's men, fighting the cause of Charles I, were besieged in the castle by the merciless Covenanter General, David Leslie. The Royalists, mostly Irish mercenaries, were forced by thirst to surrender and were then shamefully massacred. **Sanda Island**, a couple of miles off the south coast from Southend, is where Robert the Bruce is said to have hidden in 1306 on his way back from Rathlin Island, spurred on towards Bannockburn by the spider. There is the ruin of a chapel dedicated to St Ninian, some crosses and a holy well, suggesting that he or his missionaries got to this area ahead of Columba.

Keil, a couple of miles west of Southend, has the ruin of a 13th-century chapel below the cliffs just before the point, built to honour St Columba, for this is yet another of the places where he is said to have first landed on his way to Iona. His 'footsteps' are 'burnt' into the rocky hump just past the ruins.

The Mull of Kintyre

The Mull of Kintyre, the southern tip of the peninsula, is a rocky extremity with a lighthouse and sheer cliffs, dramatic in westerly gales. You must walk the final 1½ miles or so and it is particularly stirring on a fine, blustery day. Ireland is only about 13 miles away, and when visibility is good you feel you could almost swim across. The Mull of Kintyre was put on the map by Paul McCartney, who owns a house here and wrote the popular song about the area.

The B842 from Campbeltown takes you back along the east coast, a lovely drive up Kilbrannan Sound, with good walks in the hinterland. **Saddell Abbey and Castle**, about 13 miles north of Campbeltown, was a Cistercian abbey founded in 1160 by Somerled, King of Man and the Isles, with monks from Mellifont in Ireland. Somerled is thought to be buried here, and there is a grave slab bearing his effigy. Stones from the monastic buildings were used to build the castle in 1508, a typical tower house by the bay, burned by the English and subsequently rebuilt and extended. It is now owned by the Landmark Trust and available for holiday lets rather than open to the public on a daily basis. It has a pit prison, entered by a trapdoor in the entrance passage – not a cosy resting place for miscreants. Visitors can look from the outside and are asked to leave their cars at the top of the drive.

About 19 miles on, take the B8001, right, about 3 miles out to **Skipness Point**, where the ruins of a large 13th-century castle and chapel command the bay, built by the MacSweens to guard the Kilbrannan Sound. In 1537 the then chatelaine, Janet Douglas Lyon, Lady Glamis, was burnt for witchcraft, accused of poisoning her husband and plotting to kill King James V. He was in the process of ridding his kingdom of the Douglases, a threat to his supremacy, and poor Janet was born a Douglas.

Oban to Appin

It is a 7-mile ferry crossing from Oban to Achnacroish on **Lismore Island** (*4 times daily Mon–Sat, 50 minutes*), but the most popular route is from Port Appin, about 18 miles north off the A828. This crossing is about a mile. Lying at the entrance to Loch Linnhe, between Morvern and the hammerhead of the Benderloch Peninsula, Lismore is 10 miles long and 1½ miles wide, a limestone sliver overlaid with heather.

Lismore

Because of its strategic position and its fertile soil, Lismore has always been an important place. Its Christian tradition goes back to St Moluag who, in the 6th century, is said to have cut off his finger and thrown it ashore in order to beat St Columba to claim the land. (They were rivals, one being a Pict and the other a Celt. This self-mutilating feat of foolhardy ambition is also claimed by the Irving clan, one of whose ancestors is said to have done the same with his hand – hence the red hand device on their crest – in order to be first ashore at what is now Irvine, in Ayrshire.) St Moluag's pastoral staff is preserved in Bachuil House towards the north of the island. *Lios mor* means 'great garden' or 'enclosure'. When the Roman Church succeeded the Celtic church in 1200, Lismore became the centre of a bishopric, until 1507 when Luther stirred up the Reformation. The parish church incorporates the remains of the

Where to Stay and Eat

Airds Hotel, Port Appin, t (01631) 730 236, *www.airds-hotel.com* (*expensive*). Country house with sea views – family-home atmosphere, with excellent food.

Invercreran Country House Hotel, Glen Creran near Appin, t (01631) 730 414, *www. invercreran.com* (*expensive*). A well-run, comfortable country house with good food.

The Frog at Dunstaffnage Bay, Dunstaffnage, t (01631) 567 005, *www.widemouthedfrog. com* (*moderate*). Restaurant with rooms overlooking the marina. Good atmosphere.

Pierhouse, Port Appin, t (01631) 730 302, *www.pierhousehotel.co.uk* (*moderate*). The old ferry inn, with delicious seafood.

Fasgadh Guest House, Port Appin, t (01631) 730 374 (*budget*). Modern bungalow on a croft in the village, with beautiful views.

Lochside Cottage, Fasnacloich, Appin, t (01631) 730 216, *www.broadbent.fsnet.co.uk* (*budget*). Wolsey Lodge on the shore of Loch Baile Mhic Chailen – peaceful, and friendly with good food. No smoking.

Appin House, near Appin, t (01631) 730 207, *www.appinhouse.co.uk*. Self-catering (sleeps 2–6; £200–800 pw).

Kinlochlaich House, Kinlochlaich, t (01631) 730 342, *www.kinlochlaich-house.co.uk*. In the grounds of a huge garden centre. A country house with self-catering units (sleeps 2–5; £163–459 pw).

miniature cathedral and there is a ruined castle residence where the bishops lived at Achadun on the southwest end of the island. *The Book of the Dean of Lismore*, a 16th-century collection of Gaelic poetry, is in the National Library of Scotland, in Edinburgh.

Lady's Rock, off the island's southwest tip, is where in 1527 a MacLean of Duart marooned his discarded wife, a daughter of the Earl of Argyll. Gallant men from Lismore rescued her and returned her to her father, who took dire revenge on the MacLeans.

Lismore suffered badly during the Highland Clearances and the population dwindled from about 1,500 in 1775 to 600 by 1885. Today only about 140 people live here and you can still see the ruins of all the old croft houses, whose occupants subsisted on what they could get from the land, from the limeworks and from fishing.

Dunstaffnage Castle and Around

Dunstaffnage Castle (*open April–Sept daily 9.30–6.30; Oct–Mar Mon–Sat 9.30–4.30, Sun 2–4.30; adm*) is 4 miles north of Oban just off the A85, on a massive crag guarding the entrance to Loch Etive. A splendid ruin, it seems to grow out of the rock with parts of it over 60ft (18.5m) high and the walls more than 10ft (3m) thick, but its ancient glory is somewhat marred by a marine laboratory and housing developments. Its position, guarding both sea access to Loch Etive and Lorne, and the main route from the Lowlands to the Hebrides, made Dunstaffnage of vital strategic importance. The first fort was founded around the 1st century BC, and is said to have been a recruiting centre for soldiers to fight the Romans.

The present ruin dates from the 13th century and was built by the MacDougalls. Robert the Bruce captured it in 1309 and from then on it was usually in the hands of the Campbells of Argyll, who waged bitter battles against Macdonalds, MacLeans and Camerons from here. Flora Macdonald was held prisoner here for a few days after helping Prince Charles in 1746. Tradition holds that the Stone of Destiny came here from Dunadd, staying until Kenneth Macalpine moved it to Scone in an attempt to draw together his kingdom of Picts and Scots. The Early Gothic chapel in the woods is said to be of great architectural interest, with dog-toothed carving on its windows.

The Connel Bridge crosses the crooked finger of Loch Etive at the Falls of Lora, where sea and loch are in constant turmoil, trying to pour in and out through a bottleneck over slabs of rock. Connel comes from *conghail* – tumultuous flood.

If you keep to the A85, along the south side of Loch Etive, you come to Taynuilt, after about 5 miles. **Bonawe Iron Furnace** (*open April–Sept daily 9.30–6.30; adm*) is signed from the village and is well worth the detour. The old iron-ore smelter, of great importance during the Napoleonic Wars, has been excellently preserved by Historic Scotland. It may not sound it, but it is fascinating for anyone interested in the industrial and related social history of the country. The Lorne Furnace Company was founded in 1753, using the plentiful and cheap supply of charcoal from surrounding oak and birch woods. Iron ore came in by boat and was processed into pig iron, with the River Awe providing power to drive the furnaces. This was an industrial community with cottages, a school, a laundry and everything needed to serve the workforce. Some buildings as well as the furnace can be seen.

Benderloch and Appin

Turn right just over the Connel bridge and head along the northern shore of Loch Etive for about 5 miles to **Ardchattan Priory Gardens** (*open April–Oct daily 9–6; adm*). The priory, founded by Duncan MacDougall, Lord of Lorne (who built the present Dunstaffnage), was for Valliscaulian monks. In 1309 Robert the Bruce summoned local chiefs here for a conference after he had captured Dunstaffnage, and it was one of the last parliaments to be held in Gaelic. After the Reformation, the Campbells of Cawdor acquired the property and it remained with their descendants. The gardens are at their best between July and September, with shrub roses, herbaceous borders and potentillas. From Ardchattan, continue to Inveresragan and then north on the B845 to the A828.

Barcaldine Castle (now a bed and breakfast; *see p.90*), an L-shaped fortalice overlooking Loch Creran, was built in 1609 by Duncan Campbell of Glenorchy and known as 'the black castle' because of its dark stones. It played a tragic part in the events that led up to the Massacre of Glencoe (*see pp.109–10*). There are secret passages and a ghost. Barcaldine also has a **Scottish Sealife and Marine Sanctuary** (*t (01631) 720 386; open all year 9–6 in summer, 10–3 in winter; adm*), with talks, feeding times, a marine hospital, shop and restaurant.

Heading north again, you reach **Appin**, with its particularly satisfying combination of rugged hills and spectacular coast line. (*See* Ballachulish for the Appin Murder, p.107). **Port Appin**, on the flat, marshy peninsula off the southwest tip of Appin, is an attractive little place with a pier and lovely views across the islands of Loch Linnhe. The passenger ferry to Lismore runs from here. Linnhe Marine Water Sports Centre, at Lettershuna just to the east, is a family-run place with a variety of boats and courses.

Castle Stalker – *Caisteal Stalcair*, Castle of the Hunter – off Portnacroish, a few miles north (*t (01631) 730 234; open by appt; adm includes boat*), is a popular postcard/calendar picture on its small island at the mouth of Loch Laich. Former seat of the Stewarts of Appin, it dates back to about 1540 when it was built by Duncan Stewart of Appin for his kinsman, James IV, to protect the Stewart lands and to serve as a hunting lodge. It passed temporarily out of Stewart hands in the 17th century when its owner gave it to a neighbouring Campbell as payment for an eight-oared galley. It was forfeited after the Battle of Killiecrankie and garrisoned by Hanoverian troops during the '45 Jacobite rising. A small, grey tower house built over a pit prison, it has been well restored and you get a good view of it from the road.

Keep an eye out for the seals basking on the rocks around here: they flop down into the water if disturbed, and then pop up and stare balefully at intruders with their great velvety eyes.

Central West Highlands

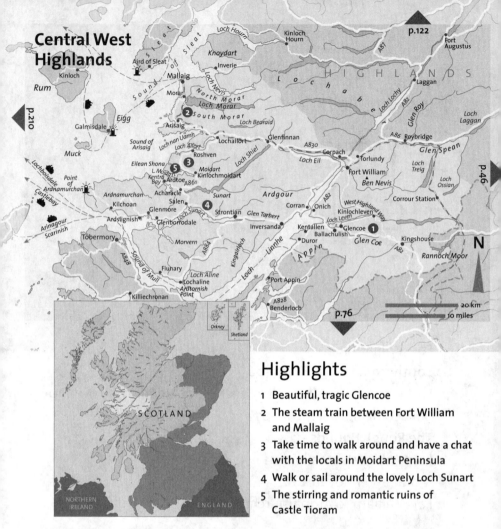

Central West
Highlights

p.122

HIGHLANDS

Kinloch Hourn
Fort Augustus
Loch Hourn
Knoydart
Inverie
Aird of Sleat
Kinloch
Mallaig
Morar
North Morar
Loch Nevis
Laggan
Glen Roy
Loch Lochy
p.210
Loch Morar
South Morar
Loch Beoraid
Loch Laggan
Eigg
Arisaig
Glenfinnan
A830
Roybridge
A86
Galmisdale
Sound of Arisaig
Lochailort
Loch nan Uamh
Loch Ailort
Corpach
Glen Spean
Muck
Roshven
Loch Shiel
Loch Eil
Torlundy
Loch Treig
Eilean Shona
Moidart
Kinlochmoidart
Fort William
Loch Ossian
Point of Ardnamurchan
L. Moidart
Kentra Bay
Ardtoe
A861
Ben Nevis
p.46
Ardnamurchan
Acharacle
Sunart
Ardgour
Corrour Station
Castlebay
Kilchoan
Salen
Strontian
Glen Tarbert
Corran
Onich
West Highland Way
Arinagour Scarinish
Ardslignish
Glenmore
Inversanda
Kentallen
Kinlochleven
Corrour Station
Tobermory
Glenborrodale
Ballachulish
Glencoe
Kingshouse
Morvern
Duror
Glen Coe
A82
Rannoch Moor
Sound of Mull
Kingairloch
N
Fiunary
Loch Aline
Lochaline
Ardtornish Point
Port Appin
A828
Killiechronan
Benderloch
p.76
20 km
10 miles

SCOTLAND

NORTHERN IRELAND

ENGLAND

Orkney
Shetland

Highlights

1. Beautiful, tragic Glencoe
2. The steam train between Fort William and Mallaig
3. Take time to walk around and have a chat with the locals in Moidart Peninsula
4. Walk or sail around the lovely Loch Sunart
5. The stirring and romantic ruins of Castle Tioram

Here is a Highland cornucopia: the highest hill with its skiing resort; the saddest glen still mourning its infamous massacre; the aptly named Rough Bounds; the many waymarkers on the Jacobite trail; glorious land- and seascapes; an enigmatic murder; poets and bards; saints and villains. The climate tends to be damp, but when the sun shines, all else is forgotten. Away from the more popular areas around Fort William are some truly remote corners – you might easily spend days without seeing a soul.

Fort William

North from Oban, Crianlarich or Callander, Fort William is a good centre from which to explore the central west Highlands. It is the southern entrance to the Caledonian Canal, tourist resort, shopping centre for the whole of the area and hub of several routes; it is also the northern end of the West Highland Way, the 95-mile hike from

Milngavie in Glasgow. Not surprisingly, the town seethes with summer holiday-makers and provides all the facilities needed for climbing, hiking and boating. It lies in the lee of Ben Nevis, Britain's highest mountain (*see* p.105), a forbidding but seductive lump with several routes to the top of varying degrees of difficulty.

History

The first fort was built by General Monk in 1655, an earth construction that proved to be of insufficient strength when put to the test by rebellious Highlanders later in the century. Rebuilt after 35 years, in stone, it was called after the new king, William of Orange, and withstood Jacobite attacks in 1715 and 1746. The scruffy settlement which grew up beside it was variously named: Maryburgh, after the wife of King William; Gordonsburgh, after its Gordon lairds in the 18th century; and Duncansburgh, after Sir Duncan Cameron of Fassifern, who owned it in the 19th century. Finally it reverted to the original name of the fort. (For Gaelic speakers it is still *An Gearasdan* – the Garrison.) The fort was demolished in the 19th century and a patch of grass edged with sections of stone rampart is all that remains today. It made way for the railway which used to run along the lochside to terminate in the centre of the town. (Later,

Tourist Information

Cameron Square, t 0845 225 5121, *www.visithighlands.com*.

Where to Stay

Inverlochy Castle, Torlundy, 3 miles north of Fort William, t (01397) 702 177, *www.inverlochy.co.uk* (*expensive*). Victorian pile – one of Scotland's top hotels (for old Inverlochy Castle history, *see* p.105).

Ashburn House, Achintore Road, Fort William, t (01397) 706 000, *www.highland5star.co.uk* (*moderate*). Modernized, comfortable Victorian house on Loch Linnhe, near town centre. Good food.

The Grange, Grange Road, Fort William, t (01397) 705 516, *www.thegrange-scotland.co.uk* (*moderate*). Comfortable Victorian guesthouse on Loch Linnhe.

Moorings Hotel, Banavie, Fort William, t (01397) 772 797, *www.moorings-fortwilliam.co.uk* (*moderate*). Four-star hotel at the western end of the Caledonian Canal, with mountain views and good food.

Distillery House, Nevisbridge, North Road, Fort William, t (01397) 700 103, *www.stayin-fortwilliam.co.uk* (*budget*). Welcoming 4-star guesthouse, offering complimentary shortbread and whisky to guests.

Tangasdale, Corpach, t (01397) 772 591 (*budget*). Gaelic-speaking bungalow owners, with warm hospitality.

Snowgoose Mountain Centre at Corpach, t (01397) 772 467, *www.highland-mountain-guides.co.uk*. Well-equipped, inexpensive self-catering apartments in an old smithy and forge overlooking Loch Linnhe (sleeps 2–12). The train to Mallaig passes close by.

Eating Out

Inverlochy Castle, Fort William, t (01397) 702 177 (*expensive*). Exceptionally good food (*see* above).

The Crannog Seafood Restaurant, The Underwater Centre, Fort William, t (01397) 703 919 (*moderate*). Memorable, reasonably priced meals. Seafood virtually from sea to plate.

No. 4, Cameron Square, Fort William, t (01397) 772 797 (*moderate*). Excellent reputation.

Lochaber Siding, Fort William Station, t (01397) 701 843 (*inexpensive*). A splendid coffee shop/travel centre with excellent home baking, proper tea (not in tea bags) and quality local crafts.

this part of the line was replaced by the present dual carriageway. The new station was built near the site of the fort. The small Victorian town that mushroomed around the railway is sturdy and busy rather than architecturally gracious. Its limits have spread beyond the streets of genteel gabled villas to suburbs of modern houses built to serve the various industries that have been developed on Fort William's doorstep.

The Town

The **West Highland Museum** in Cameron Square (*www.westhighlandmuseum. org.uk; open all year Mon–Sat 10–4/5; July–Aug Sun 2–5 also; adm*) is one of the most rewarding ways of spending a few hours in the town, not just on a wet day. This is a traditional museum and carefully preserves traditional features such as its new display cases modelled on those of the 1890s, but with modern lighting. It is almost a 'museum of a museum', enhanced by modern technology with an amazingly wide range of exhibits in a series of well-laid-out rooms. The first thing to look for is the Ballachulish Goddess dating from 600 BC: a tall, graceful statue with quartz eyes, carved from black alder and found under 4ft of peat by Loch Leven. The best known exhibit is the 'anamorphic' portrait of Prince Charles, used in the days when loyal Jacobites toasted 'the king across the water' – a smear of paint on a tray, meaningless until you view its reflection on the side of a metal cylinder (or on the curved side of a wine glass if you were making a secret toast), when it is transformed into a recognizable portrait. (There are two more of these anamorphic paintings in the museum, both 'naughty pictures'.) Another highlight is the 'Black Gun of Misfortune', one of the four guns alleged to be *the* gun used in the Appin Murder (*see p.107*). This one, a long Spanish weapon, was found in a hollow tree near Lettermore shortly after the murder and is most likely to be the true claimant to the dubious honour. There are also Jacobite relics, Montrose's helmet, and the re-erected interior of the governor of the fort's house.

You can also pass a contented hour or so leaning over the rails beside the long ladder of locks that bring the **Caledonian Canal** down to the level of the sea and into Loch Linnhe at Corpach. The canal was opened in 1882 to allow vessels to avoid the Pentland Firth and marauding French privateers in the Napoleonic Wars. It is used now by fishing boats and pleasure craft and the gates are hydraulically operated. The eight locks at Banavie, **Neptune's Staircase**, rise 72ft in 500 yards, which presented Thomas Telford with an enormous problem when he built the canal. You can still see the original lock-keepers' houses, with bow windows that enabled the keepers to see the canal in both directions from inside. **Loch Linnhe** is always busy with pleasure boats in the summer and is fringed with moorings as well as a great many hotels and guesthouses running some way out of the town.

The northern suburbs are not attractive, rather dominated by a huge paper factory and lots of warehouses. **Ben Nevis Woollen Mill**, on Belford Road, 10 minutes' walk from the town centre, is a good stopping-off place for woollens, tartans, gifts, snacks and clan/tartan research. You can also collect your official certificate for completing the 95-mile West Highland Way here. **Treasures of the Earth** (*open daily 10–5; adm*), on the A830 Corpach Road out of Fort William, is a rather sparkly crystal and gemstone exhibition in an 'ultraviolet' setting. *See p.111 for the* **Jacobite Steam Railway**.

Inverlochy Castle, now a crumbling ruin at the mouth of the Loch, has been stabilized by Historic Scotland. Its moat was filled by the river on which it stands, and its rectangle of curtain walls with four corner towers is thought to date from the 13th century, probably built by John Comyn of Badenoch. Later it passed to the Bruces and then to the Gordons of Huntly. It is likely that there was an earlier structure on this strategic site, sometimes connected with Banquo, Thane of Lochaber, thanks to Hector Boece. The historian Boece wrote a *History of Scotland* in 1527, inventing colourful stories to embroider an already colourful story. Holinshed used Boece as a primary source, and Shakespeare used Holinshed – hence the many legends that now flesh out the bare bones of fact. Also according to Boece, Inverlochy was once a prosperous, cosmopolitan city where King Achaius signed a treaty with Charlemagne in 790. Boece blames the Vikings for the lack of any surviving tangible evidence. (*Inverlochy Castle is not to be confused with the Victorian pile mentioned on p.103.*)

The **Battle of Inverlochy** in 1645 was the third of Montrose's great victories, before his defeat and execution. He had made a Christmas raid on his enemies, the Covenanting Campbells, at Inveraray and was marching his men back up the coast to the Great Glen. When they got to Fort Augustus (Kilchumein, in those days), he heard that the Earl of Argyll was behind him, garrisoned at Inverlochy with 3,000 men. He led his men back through the hills and descended on the Covenanters at dawn from above Inverlochy Castle. Argyll, with a dislocated shoulder, watched from a galley while the castle surrendered and 1,300 of his men were massacred as they fled. Montrose wrote to Charles I: 'I am in the fairest hopes of rendering this kingdom to your Majesty's obedience, and shall be able to come to your Majesty's assistance with a brave army.' History was to prove him wrong and within five years both Charles I and Montrose were dead, the latter having been executed for fighting for the cause of Charles II, who turned his back on his loyal subject in his hour of need.

Around Fort William

Aonach Mor ski area (*www.skiclub.co.uk*), developed in 1989, is accessible off the A82, 7 miles northeast of the town. It has the only cable car in Scotland – the Nevis Range gondola – and is a popular and fast-expanding ski resort. Although the weather is unpredictable, there are some excellent runs for all standards and the Corrie Dubh holds snow late in the season. The gondola runs daily throughout the year and gives access to a restaurant, bar and shops at 4,006ft, as well as lofty walks in the summer. There is also some of the most challenging rock climbing in Scotland shere.

From the summit of **Ben Nevis** (4,406ft/1,344m) on a clear day you can see Ben Lomond near Glasgow, the Cairngorms, the Cuillins in Skye and the Outer Hebrides. The tourist route to the top starts at Achintee Farm about a mile southeast of the town on the way into Glen Nevis. It is well signposted and well trodden. This was a pony trail in the 19th century, leading to the weather observatory at the top. In 1911 an Edinburgh motor dealer drove a 20-horsepower Model T Ford up here, taking five days. You are advised to allow about 7 hours to get there and back. 'Running the Ben', usually on the first Saturday in September, started in 1895, and about 500 runners compete. The record is 1 hour, 25 minutes, 34 seconds. A local octogenarian did it in 3 hours. For the less energetic, **Glen Nevis**, through which the Water of Nevis runs, circles the southwestern base of the Nevis range. The Glen gets better the further in you go. It narrows dramatically and becomes less frequented; the scenery is almost primeval, with waterfalls, narrow gorges and tracks up into the hills at several points.

South from Fort William

Fort William to Ballachulish: Loch Linnhe and Loch Leven

After the strip of lochside hotels southwest of Fort William, the A82 zips down Loch Linnhe about 7 miles to the Corran Narrows, where the slim head of the loch narrows to a mere channel before opening into the sea. A ferry crosses to Ardgour, cutting out a huge loop for those heading west. Whenever you can, abandon your car, consult your map, and take off into the hills on any of the tracks marked. A network of tracks lead north from Loch Leven and Kinlochleven at the head of the loch.

Kinlochleven sits somewhat incongruously at the head of Loch Leven below a backdrop of mountains. A settlement of three houses was transformed into a thriving town in 1904 by the founding of an aluminium works here – an interesting display at the **Visitor Centre** (*open all year*) tells **'The Aluminium Story'**. (A suggestion that the town be renamed Aluminiumville was not adopted.) Nearby there is a waterfall rated as one of the best in Scotland, descending past Mamore Lodge from the top of a cliff to drop 210ft (60m) into a hidden gorge. At **North Ballachulish** (pronounced Balla-hoolish), 13 miles south of Fort William, a bridge spans the narrows between Lochs Linnhe and Leven where, not so long ago, a small car ferry used to slither and slide on the fast current. Many tales are told of this intrepid vessel's exploits, like the time it ran aground one Hogmanay because the skipper had swallowed some holly. Today you are over the bridge and away before you know it.

The village of **Ballachulish**, 2 miles to the east, grew up around Scotland's biggest slate quarry, still full of slate but no longer in use, because imported slate is much cheaper. The slate works have been landscaped and there is now a large hotel by the loch, The Isles of Glencoe Hotel (*see* 'Where to Stay and Eat', p.108). Ironically, not one slate on its vast slate roof comes from Ballachulish! Go on into Glencoe village and take the A82 into the famous glen.

Ballachulish to Glencoe

Although it is always awe-inspiring, Glencoe can show a benign face when the sun shines. You will find creaming burns and falls, glistening rocks, hidden lochans and glens with surprise pockets of wild flowers and dramatic views. But when the weather closes in and cloud swirls down off the raw, steep-sided peaks slashed by white scars of cascading water, and the wind moans in the corries, an aura of doom and melancholy pervades the place. This is Glencoe – the Glen of Weeping.

The Appin Murder

Doubling back west towards Oban through South Ballachulish on the A828, you can contemplate one of Scotland's unsolved mysteries. In South Ballachulish, a monument on a hillock just above the bridge is inscribed: 'Erected in 1911 to the memory of James Stewart of Acharn, or James of the Glens, executed on this spot Nov. 8, 1752, for a crime of which he was not guilty.' The story behind it inspired Robert Louis Stevenson to embellish the truth in his novel *Kidnapped* and its sequel *Catriona*.

Colin Campbell of Glenure, known as the Red Fox, was factor and rent collector to several Jacobite estates which had been forfeited after Culloden. The Campbell clan had fought on the English side and were loathed as traitors by loyal Jacobites. On 14 May 1752, only six years after Culloden, when feelings were still raw and tempers high, Campbell crossed the ferry with three companions with the order to evict some Stewart tenants in Appin, in favour of some Campbells. This eviction order had been disputed by the staunchly Jacobite James Stewart. As well as three children of his own, he had staying with him his protégé Allan Breck – Allan the Pockmarked – who had fought for the English at Prestonpans, changed sides and fought with the Jacobites at Culloden, for which he was now outlawed. Campbell and his companions rode from the ferry along the old road that cut across the hill to Kentallen. At about 5pm a shot rang out and put paid to Colin Campbell of Glenure. His companions set off for help, where they saw James Stewart busy on his land. On hearing the news, Stewart is alleged to have remarked: 'Whoever is the culprit, I shall be the victim.' He was prophetic. The prime suspect, Allan Breck the outlaw, had vanished.

The day after the murder, James Stewart was arrested as an accessory and taken to Inveraray. He was tried by a 15-person jury that included eleven Campbells, presided over by their chief, the Duke of Argyll. James Stewart was taken to a hillock above the Ballachulish ferry on a wild November day and hanged, after a long and impassioned valedictory to his gathered clan, begging them not to seek vengeance. It was forbidden to cut down his body which hung in chains from the gallows for three years, guarded by soldiers to prevent the Stewarts taking it away for burial. At one point it fell from the chains but still the bitter sentence prevailed and the bones were wired together and rehung. When it fell again, in 1755, the bones were rescued and are thought to be buried lovingly among the Stewarts of Ardsheal in the graveyard at Keil. Some say that the murderer's name is passed down from father to son by the Stewarts of Appin; if so, then at least one person today must know the truth. Four existing guns have been claimed to be the murder weapon: the most likely is the one in the museum at Fort William (*see* p.104). The rough stone on Stewart's memorial came from his farm at Acharn. Another memorial cairn, in the woods above the road about a mile west of Ballachulish, marks the site of Campbell's murder. At Duror, a Lochaber bank barn stands close to the ruin of James Stewart's house.

Tourist Information

Ballachulish: t (01855) 811 296. *Open April–Oct.*

Where to Stay and Eat

The Lodge on the Loch, Onich, t (01855) 821 237, *www.lodgeontheloch.com* (*expensive*). Has a lovely position on the loch; the restaurant has two AA rosettes.

Kingshouse Hotel, Glencoe, t (01855) 851 259, *www.kingy.com* (*expensive–budget*). Provides excellent facilities for hikers, climbers and skiers – some leave their backpacks to be transported to their next staging post. Its 'outward-bound' atmosphere could put off those seeking solitude.

Ardsheal House, Kentallen of Appin, t (01631) 740 227, *www.ardsheal.co.uk* (*moderate*). 16th-century house on a hill looking across Loch Linnhe, with strong Jacobite connections, rebuilt *c.* 1760. Very welcoming atmosphere – a conservatory dining room overlooks the garden, and there is a billiard room. Excellent food, with local ingredients, a good selection of wines and malt whiskies.

Ballachulish Hotel, Balluchulish, t 0871 222 3415, *www.freedomglen.co.uk* (*moderate*). Right on the loch and very good value.

Ballachulish House, Ballachulish, t (01855) 811 266 (*moderate*). Antique furniture and family photograph albums give a lived-in feeling; all the bedrooms (with en-suite bathrooms) are like the best spare rooms in a private house. The food is excellently prepared, with fresh local ingredients, and a good wine list.

Cuilcheanna House, Onich, off the A82, t (01855) 821 226, (*moderate*). A small hotel – lovely views, welcoming hosts.

The Isles of Glencoe, on Loch Leven near Glencoe, same numbers as the Ballachulish Hotel (*moderate*). Heated pool, sauna, steam room and solarium.

Moor of Rannoch Hotel, near Kinloch Rannoch, t (01882) 633 238, *www.moorofrannoch.co.uk* (*moderate*). One of the best places in the area: fantastic food, eaten by a roaring fire in a panelled dining room; very friendy hosts.

Onich Hotel, Onich, t (01855) 821 214, *www.onich-fortwilliam.co.uk* (*moderate*). Overlooks Loch Linnhe – one of the best hotels on the A82.

Calasona, Onich, t (01855) 821 291 (*budget*). Comfortable, modern B&B run by a friendly young local couple. Stunning scenery.

Clachaig Inn, 2 miles east of Glencoe village, t (01855) 811 252, *www.clachaig.com* (*budget*). Hotel/hostel with all the facilities you want when hobbling in, soaking wet and freezing cold, after a day in the hills, though don't stay here for peace and solitude.

Druimgrianach, Duror, t (01631) 740 286 (*budget*). A family-run B&B, on Loch Linnhe, with lovely views and friendly people.

Glencoe Youth Hostel, Glencoe, t 0870 004 1122, *www.shya.org.uk* (*budget*). Marvellous base for walkers and climbers.

Ardgour House, by Fort William, t (01413) 376 669, *ardgour.house@unforgettable.com* (*£2825–£4195/mth*). Self-catering mansion in 6 acres with fishing, heated pool, sauna and billiards (sleeps 22).

Carefree Holidays Glencoe, Clachaig, Glencoe, t (01855) 811 679. Well-appointed self-catering chalets in lovely scenery, with the inn close by for snacks (sleeps 4–6).

Invercoe Highland Holidays, Invercoe, Glencoe, t (01855) 811 210, *www.invercoe.co.uk*. Self-catering stone cottages, mobile homes or lodges (sleeps 2–6).

The **Glencoe Folk Museum** (*open May–Sept daily 10–5.30*) in the village is an absorbing local collection. The Massacre Memorial is a tall, slender Celtic cross where a small group of people meet on 13 February each year to honour the clan. The **National Trust for Scotland Visitor Centre** (*open Mar–Oct; site always open*), in the glen, set back to the left of the road as you drive east, tells the story of the Massacre. It also has a shop, and gives advice on walking or climbing, with rangers available. **White Corries Ski Centre** (*http://ski.visitscotland for snow reports*), a little further on, has the longest vertical descent in Scotland – 2,600ft (793m) – and plenty of challenging skiing on Meall a' Bhuiridh, for those who aren't put off by capricious weather. Snow tends to linger long in Glencoe and the skiing season sometimes continues well into spring.

The **Devil's Staircase** is a zigzag track, part of the West Highland Way and former military route constructed by Caulfeild in the 1740s, climbing from Altnafeadh, across a ridge and down to Kinlochleven. It is a steepish walk with views to Buachaille Etive Mor. The 17th-century **Kingshouse Inn**, on the left beyond the Pass, is said to be one of Scotland's oldest licensed inns. It was used as a barracks for the troops of George III after Culloden, hence its name, and has a colourful history. Dorothy Wordsworth wrote in her journal in 1803: 'Never did I see such a miserable, such a wretched place – long rooms with ranges of beds, no other furniture except benches, or perhaps one or two crazy chairs, the floors far dirtier than an ordinary house could be if it were never washed.' The supper, when it came, was 'a shoulder of mutton so hard that it was

The Massacre of Glencoe

Everyone knows a version of the stirring story of the Massacre of Glencoe, unquestionably a hideous blemish on the honour of some members of the government of the day. When William and Mary succeeded James VII/II in 1689, the Jacobites posed a powerful threat to their stability. In an attempt to bring the rebellious clans in line, it was decided that the chiefs must sign an oath of loyalty to the crown by 1 January 1692. The order was issued on pain of death and, after much hesitation, most of the chiefs obeyed, having received agreement from the exiled King James VII. Maclain of Glencoe was the chief of a small branch of Clan Donald and an obstinate old diehard. By the time he reluctantly conceded, it was too late. Starting off, he went the wrong way, to Fort William, where he learnt that the governor of the garrison was not empowered to take his oath. In filthy weather he then set off for Inveraray, but was delayed on the way by a blizzard and was stormbound at Barcaldine Castle (*see* p.100). He arrived after the deadline and the Sheriff, Campbell of Ardkinglas, was off duty nursing his New Year hangover. The oath was eventually sworn and accepted, but the delay was seized upon by the government as a pretext for dealing a short, sharp shock to Highland chiefs who might have had their fingers crossed while swearing their oaths. The Macdonalds of Glencoe were perfect scapegoats: their loyalty to the Jacobite cause was known to be extreme, their numbers were small, their glen so enclosed that escape would be difficult, and they had a reputation among their neighbours as scoundrels. It was believed that their extermination, while being a lesson to some, would also be a relief to many.

The Secretary of State for Scotland, John Dalrymple, Master of Stair, masterminded the plan and it was endorsed by King William (who was not told, when the order was presented for his signature, that Maclain had eventually signed the oath, albeit late). Two companies of the Earl of Argyll's Regiment, recruited from the Campbell Clan, were ordered to Glencoe under the command of Robert Campbell of Glenlyon, an elderly alcoholic who had been forced into the army by bankruptcy caused partly by impossible to chew the little flesh that might have been scraped off the bones'. In spite of its isolation, Kingshouse received many visitors, and its taproom was notorious. At the turn of the 20th century, labourers working on the Black Water Reservoir used to drop in on their way to and from work; many who had imbibed too freely were lost and perished in the hills.

Rannoch Moor stretches away into the distance to the east beyond the Pass: a vast, swampy moonscape, unpopulated except by birds. It is bleak, even in summer. In the late 19th century an expedition to survey this most desolate of terrain prior to the construction of the West Highland Railway ended in disaster; a group of top railway executives set out over the moor in their best suits, got lost and separated from each other, and had to spend the night out in the bog. Some nearly died of exposure. The route chosen for the West Highland Line across Rannoch Moor takes it from Rannoch

the depredations of the Glencoe Macdonalds. The Campbells moved into the glen on 1 February 1692; the Macdonalds, who had been evading their taxes, were obliged to accommodate them. The unwritten laws of hospitality by which all Highlanders were bound, ensured that the Campbells were safe among their enemies and well tended. In the harsh climate of mid-winter, the Campbells and Macdonalds cohabited in uneasy peace. Campbell of Glenlyon received his final order:

> *You are hereby ordered to fall upon the rebels the Macdonalds of Glencoe and put all to the sword under 70. See that this be put into execution without fear or favour, or you may expect to be dealt with as not one true to King or Government, nor a man fit to carry a commission in the King's service. Expecting you will not fail in the fulfilling hereof as you love yourself.*

At dawn on 13 February about 40 of the clan were slaughtered, including Maclain, his wife and two of his sons. Some believe that the Campbells were not as ruthless as portrayed; their military strategy did not go according to plan and quite a few Macdonalds managed to escape. Tradition has it that Glenlyon's piper played *People of This Glen* as a warning to the Macdonalds and that some of the Campbells passed oblique cautionary signals to their hosts concerning the danger of sleeping in the glen that night. The lasting disgrace of this massacre is the unforgivable betrayal of trust, that of guest versus host. In the recriminations that followed, the massacre came to be represented as a Battle of the Clans – Campbells against Macdonalds, rivals since the beginning of time. In fact it was a cynical act of genocide in an attempt to enforce obedience to the law on a proud, independent, if roguish people. It failed and brought lasting dishonour and contempt upon its perpetrators. It is interesting that when Queen Victoria visited Glencoe in 1873, she wrote in her journal: 'The place itself is one which adds to the horror of the thought that such a thing could have been conceived and committed on innocent sleeping people. How and whither could they fly? Let me hope that William III knew nothing of it.'

Station to Tulloch via Lochs Ossian and Treig, far from human habitation and any road. Because of the boggy terrain the track was floated on a platform of timber piles and brushwood. You need a good map if you plan to walk through to the Grampians.

Loch Ossian is about 17 miles northeast of Glencoe, tucked into a valley surrounded by hills and inaccessible by public road. There is a **youth hostel** and the train stops at Corrour Station, but the energetic should attack it on foot. It is an easy 10-mile tramp from Black Corries Lodge, over the shoulder of Stob na Cruaiche, around the eastern end of the Blackwater Reservoir and along the railway. There is a café at the station.

The Rough Bounds

The Rough Bounds – *Garbh-chriochan* – is the name given from time immemorial to that southwestern corner of the Highlands, west of Fort William, between Loch Sunart in the south and Loch Hourn in the north. This was the heartland of the Lords of the Isles, accessed by sea and guarded at every headland by a fortress. Much of the interior is still reached only by the old hill tracks on which intruders were ambushed. It is said that when one of the Glengarry chiefs travelled into the Rough Bounds with his family, he packed his younger children into creels tied on to sturdy ponies; if one child weighed more than another, stones were used to even the balance.

At one time the whole of the *Garbh-chriochan* belonged to various branches of the Macdonald clan. Because of its inaccessibility, the people remained largely Jacobite: Moidart and Morar are mostly Catholic today, despite great persecution in the 18th century. When a hardy old warrior who had been 'out' in the '45 met George III, he assured the king he regretted nothing, although added: 'What I did for the Prince, I would have done as heartily for your Majesty, if you had been in the Prince's place.'

Fort William to Mallaig

The **Jacobite Steam Railway** (*t (01463) 239 026, t (01524) 737751 (bookings), www.steamtrain.info; runs June–mid-Oct Mon–Fri, plus Sun in Aug; trains depart at 10.20am and return at 4pm; adm*) offers day trips from Fort William to Mallaig west along Loch Eil, skirting Loch Nan Uamh where Prince Charles landed, and northwards along the gleaming Sands of Morar, stopping at Glenfinnan. To explore and walk, however, take your car for what is one of the most beautiful routes in Scotland.

Glenfinnan

About 4 miles west of Loch Eil you come into Glenfinnan where three glens meet at the head of Loch Shiel against a layered backdrop of grape-blue hills. Here, on bleak, swampy wasteland, stands **The Prince's Monument**, a gaunt column topped by a statue of the Prince, erected by Macdonald of Glenaladale in 1815. It commemorates the raising of Prince Charles' standard on 19 August 1745 – the beginning of Bliadhna Tearlach – Charlie's Year. The **National Trust Visitor Centre** (*open daily April–Oct 10–5, mid-May–Aug 9.30–6; adm*) has excellent maps showing the progress of the Prince's

Where to Stay and Eat

Camusdarach, between Arisaig and Morar, t (01687) 450 221 (*expensive*). A delightful, spacious B&B with its own beach (where some of *Local Hero* was filmed). Hospitable, very good value – camp site on the property.

Arisaig Hotel, Arisaig, t (01687) 450 210, *www.arisaighotel.co.uk* (*moderate*). Early 18th-century house near the jetty, with good bar meals and a nice craft-and-book shop.

Glenfinnan House Hotel, Glenfinnan, t (01397) 722 235, *www.glenfinnanhouse.com* (*moderate*). Victorian mansion overlooking Loch Shiel. Highland hospitality, with spontaneous ceilidhs.

Old Library Lodge and Restaurant, Arisaig, t (01687) 450 651, *www.oldlibrary.co.uk* (*moderate*). 200-year-old stable with cosy rooms and bistro meals.

The Prince's House, Glenfinnan, t (01397) 722 246, *www.glenfinnan.co.uk* (*moderate*). Small, comfortable and family-run inn, dating from 1658. Local ingredients are used for the meals; especially good seafood.

Garramore Hotel, South Morar, t (01687) 450 268 (*budget*). This family-run Victorian sporting lodge overlooks a lush woodland garden and a family of peacocks. An excellent bed and breakfast; book ahead.

Glenfinnan Dining Car/Glenfinnan Sleeping Car, by Glenfinnan Station, t (01397) 722 295, *glenstat@hege-hernes.demon.co.uk* (*inexpensive*). An imaginative restoration of a 1950s railway carriage, and a delightful place for a meal or cream tea. Bring your own alcohol. Basic sleeping for up to 10 people in four compartments of the dining car. *Dining car open June–Sept; sleeping car open all year.*

army throughout the Rising. The Glenfinnan Games are held every August on the nearest Saturday to the 19th, and are splendidly Highland.

Trains still stop at **Glenfinnan Station**. The building has been converted into a **Museum** (*open June–Sept 9.30–4.30*) with a 'diner' carriage (*see* 'Where to Stay and Eat', above). The **Glenfinnan Viaduct** is an impressive landmark and a considerable engineering feat. When built (1897–1900) it was the longest, and first mass-concrete, viaduct in Britain. Nearby, the Gothic-style **Catholic church** overlooking Loch Shiel, must be the most beautifully sited Catholic church in Scotland.

Glenfinnan gets its name from St Finnan who came from Ireland to spread Christianity. Climbing Ben Resipol from Loch Sunart, he looked down upon Loch Shiel and saw a green island in the narrows where the loch turns west. Here he built a cell. The ruins of old foundations can still be seen on St Finnan's Isle, which became an important burial ground for the chiefs and clansmen of this region. It is still in use as a burial place and one of the most sacred places in the West Highlands. Islands were used for burials partly to protect the dead from predators such as wolves.

West of Glenfinnan

Halfway up the northern shore of Loch Shiel, inaccessible **Glenaladale** runs down from the hills. Now, only the ruins of the Macdonalds of Glenaladale, a loyal Jacobite clan, populate this remote glen. In 1772, Captain John Macdonald of Glenaladale took 300 of his clansmen to Prince Edward Island (now Canadian), where he had acquired some land. This expedient evacuation was due to disillusionment with prospects in the West Highlands, and to the fact that Catholics in Scotland were being forced into Protestant education. Resettlement meant freedom and possible prosperity.

The road westwards twists through a bleak, unpeopled landscape, with superb views to the Small Isles. Between Borrodale and Arisaig it plunges into woodland, where banks of rhododendrons make it riotously colourful in early summer. **Loch nan Uamh** – pronounced 'naan ooa' – Loch of the Caves, to the west of the road beyond the head of Loch Ailort, is where Prince Charles arrived from Eriskay on 25 July 1745, at the start of his campaign to restore the Stuart throne, accompanied by only seven companions. These **Seven Men of Moidart** who had sailed from France with the Prince were: William Lord Tullibardine, the titular Duke of Atholl who had lost his title after the 1715 Rising; Sir Thomas Sheridan, Prince Charles's 70-year-old tutor; Aeneas Macdonald, a friend; John William O'Sullivan, a soldier of fortune who was later blamed bitterly by Lord George Murray for his part in the tragedy of Culloden; Sir John Macdonald, a lieutenant colonel in the Irish Brigade of the French army; Colonel Francis Strickland, whose father had gone to France with James VII in 1688; and the Reverend George Kelly, a clergyman who had refused to take the oath of allegiance to King William while James VII lived, and was thus banned from the church – a 'non-juror'. A cairn on a crag beside the road commemorates the occasion, although nobody knows exactly where they landed. A year later, broken and defeated, the Prince embarked for France from this same place, leaving behind him many corpses, shattered hopes, vicious reprisals for generations to come, and the destruction of *Gaidhealtachd* (Gaeldom). You can still see the cave he is reputed to have hidden in.

The Jacobite Rising of '45

It is perhaps easier to recall the past if you turn your back on this 19th-century folly and look down the loch and up into the hills. When the Prince arrived here in the middle of the morning there was no one to greet him but two shepherds. Somewhat disconsolate, he took shelter in a nearby hut. After a while he was joined by about 150 Macdonalds and by James Mor MacGregor, son of Rob Roy. (MacGregor was a double agent, acting as a spy for the Lord Advocate in Edinburgh, and at the same time pledging the allegiance of his clan to the Prince and bringing him the welcome news that the Camerons were already on their way.) It was crucial to the cause that Cameron of Locheil joined them, for he was a man whose great influence would sway the decisions of other clans. Though unenthusiastic about the uprising, this powerful chief was brave and loyal, declaring: 'I'll share the fate of my Prince.' Now, in the still afternoon, the waiting clans already committed to the young Prince heard the skirl of pipes. They turned to watch as Locheil marched down from the hills, leading 700 of his clansmen to join the Prince. (The well-known 'March of the Cameron Men' was composed by Mary Maxwell Campbell in 1829, to commemorate this event.) Locheil's action encouraged other clans and in the late afternoon a great red and white silken banner was unfurled. The Prince's father, the son and only male heir to James VII, was proclaimed King James of Britain, with Prince Charles Edward Stuart as his Regent.

Whatever misguided dream may have influenced this final Jacobite rising, it is tempting, when standing in this romantic setting, to forget its aftermath and feel staunchly Jacobite. When Queen Victoria came here in 1873, she revealed her strong sympathies for the Jacobite cause and noted: 'And here was I, the descendant of the Stewarts and of the very king whom Prince Charles sought to overthrow, sitting and walking about quite privately and peaceably.'

The knobbly, mottled sepia-grey hills of South Morar, though rather gloomy, offer unrivalled views across to Eigg and Rum. **Arisaig**, at the head of Loch nan Ceall, has a very sheltered anchorage and is a peaceful holiday village popular with 'white settlers' (the Scots' term for incomers – usually English). Yachts lie at anchor around the bay and a privately operated passenger ferry, **Murdo Grant** (*t (01687) 450 224, www.arisaig.co.uk; sailings April–Sept and charter*) runs from Arisaig to the islands. In this largely Catholic area, the stark tower of the church of St Mary is a prominent landmark. Beside it is the medieval ruin of Kilmory church, and in its graveyard lies Alasdair MacMhaigsthir, born about 1698, one of the greatest of the Gaelic poets, who took the Jacobite side in 1745 and was tutor/bard to the Prince. **Borrodale House**, once a hotel, is a large, restored farmhouse whose core dates from about 1745 when it was possibly the home of the Macdonald of Borrodale who entertained Prince Charles.

Morar and Knoydart

Morar is the peninsula between the Sound of Arisaig to the south and Loch Nevis to the north. Loch Morar, cutting right across its heart, is the deepest freshwater loch in Europe – over 1,000ft (308m) – separated from the sea by only a few hundred yards over which the road and railway jostle for space. Its monster, Morag, rivals the Loch

Tourist Information

Mallaig: t (01687) 462 170. *Open all year; reduced hours in winter.*

Where to Stay and Eat

Doune Stone Lodge, on the western tip of Knoydart, t (01687) 462 667, *www.doune-knoydart.co.uk* (*moderate*). Only accessible by sea – they collect you by boat from Mallaig. It's a custom-built lodge without too many frills.

Morar Hotel, Mallaig, t (01687) 462 346, *www.morarhotel.co.uk* (*moderate*). Log fires, excellent views and good home cooking. Local fishing can be arranged.

Pier House, Inverie, Knoydart, t (01687) 462 347 (*moderate*). Guesthouse with a tearoom and restaurant serving delicious lobster and other seafood.

West Highland Hotel, Mallaig, t (01687) 462 210, *www.westhighlandhotel.co.uk* (*moderate*). A friendly, sprawling, traditional Highland hotel with panoramic views – where freshly caught seafood is served daily.

Achnaluin, Mallaig, t (01687) 462 131 (*budget*). Special, very reasonable B&B in an old croft house. Traditional Highland atmosphere.

Loch Morar House, Beoraid, t (01687) 462 823, *macmairi2@aol.com* (*budget*) A spacious, spotless new house plainly decorated in pine, no artificial bedding, linen napkins and memorable breakfasts.

Sheena's Backpackers' Lodge, overlooks the harbour, Mallaig, t (01687) 462 764 (*budget*). Comfy place with dormitory bedrooms and a covered timber veranda – offers fresh seafood and home baking.

Western Isles Guest House, East Bay, Mallaig, t (01687) 462 320, *westernisles@aol.com* (*budget*). Small and quiet, near the harbour.

Creageiridh, in Knoydart near Inverie, t (01747) 852 289, *www.creageiridh.co.uk* (*budget*). A splendid self-catering house (sleeps 10). They meet you off the boat and transport you, and will rent you a Land Rover.

Glashoille Holidays, Mallaig, t (01333) 360 251. Self-catering 6-bedroom house in a glorious setting on the water (sleeps 11).

Old Forge, Inverie, t (01687) 462 267. Britain's remotest pub; adjacent restaurant.

Ness Monster. Less famous but more sinister; Morag's appearance is said to herald the death of a Clanranald Macdonald. It was beside this loch that Simon Fraser, 11th Lord Lovat, known as the Old Fox of the '45 (*see* Beauly, pp.167–9), was finally captured as he lay, so it is said, on two feather beds by the water's edge.

Mallaig

About 10 miles north of Arisaig, Mallaig is the terminus for the railway and the road, and a busy fishing and ferry port. Unpretentious, it makes few concessions to the many tourists waiting here for boats, trains and buses. The **Heritage Centre** (*open summer Mon–Sat 11–4, winter Tues–Sat 12–5; adm*) on the site of the old Railwaymen's Hostel, has exhibits about the people and history of the Rough Bounds, with videos and fascinating old photographs. The **Marine World**, near the harbour (*open Mon–Sat 9–6, Sun 11–6; adm*) has tanks of sea creatures, with informative exhibits.

Fishing boats pack into the harbour, bombarded by gulls and surrounded by all the clutter of their trade – Mallaig deals mainly in prawns these days. One or two of the old fish-curing sheds survive, along with a quantity of modern replacements. Buying fresh fish is not as easy as it should be. Your best bet is to chat up one of the boats. Mallaig was Gavin Maxwell's mainland base in *Harpoon at a Venture*, where he struggled against the odds to establish a shark-fishing industry on the island of Soay just after the Second World War. He landed his first 'kill' in this harbour, in front of a large crowd of tourists – a 25ft female basking shark, 18ft in circumference.

Caledonian MacBrayne's ferry ticket office is on the quay. Ferries depart from Mallaig to Ardvasar in Skye, the Small Isles, and Castlebay and Lochboisdale in the Outer Isles. Ask around for a lift across Loch Nevis to Knoydart, or ring Bruce Watt (*t (01687) 462 320*), who does the trip to Inverie three times a week.

Knoydart

One of Scotland's most isolated inhabited peninsulas, inaccessible by road, Knoydart is the northern extent of the Rough Bounds. This remote mountainous lump, washed by Loch Nevis (Heaven) to its south and Loch Hourn (Hell) to its north, thrusts westwards into the Sound of Sleat with a track across from its only village, Inverie, to Barrisdale on Loch Hourn, about 8 miles north. From here it is another 6 miles round the loch to the nearest road at Kinloch Hourn. The track from Inverie takes you through Glen Dulochan, between two Munros. It's a good tramp on a fine day, but for shopping, one must go to Mallaig, travelling by boat.

Knoydart's history is rather gloomy. It belonged to the Macdonells of Glengarry, large numbers of whom lived in the area until it was 'cleared' by Josephine Macdonell in 1853 and they were shipped to Nova Scotia in the wake of the potato famine. During the 20th century the land was sold repeatedly, none of its new owners staying for long. In 1948 squatters calling themselves the Seven Men of Knoydart tried to appropriate the land but were dispossessed by the then owner. Successive buyers came, exploited, and departed. Inspired by events in Assynt and the Isle of Eigg, the residents (none of whom are descendants of Knoydart people) made a successful buyout bid, and have already sold off the laird's house in Inverie.

Fort William to Ardnamurchan

Loch Ailort to Loch Sunart

Travelling west from Fort William on the A830 to the head of Loch Ailort, take the A861 southwest through Moidart – from *midard*, heights of the sea spray. The road is satisfactory for getting you from A to B and for a superficial overview, but to discover the true essence of the place, you must walk, climb and scramble; and you must take time to stop and talk to the slow, courteous, highly intelligent local people. Even today, the inhabitants of Moidart are mainly Catholic, living in peaceful harmony with their Protestant neighbours west of the River Sheil in Ardnamurchan.

Loch Ailort snakes its way out from Inverailort to the Sound of Arisaig. Approaching by boat can be a tricky business, with fluky winds bouncing off the hills in all directions. **Inverailort Castle**, at the head of the loch, has as its core an elegant Georgian house, much impaired by subsequent Victorian additions and now in need of restoration. Like many other large houses in the area, it played an important role in the activities of the Special Forces, later the Commandos, in the war. Its late owner, Mrs Francis Cameron-Head, was a devout Catholic, one of the last of an old school of

Tourist Information

Kilchoan: t (01972) 510 222. *Open Easter–Oct.*
Strontian: t (01967) 402 131. *Open April–Oct.*

Where to Stay and Eat

For self-catering, *see Kinlochmoidart*, p.117.

Kilcamb Lodge, Strontian, t (01967) 402 257, *www.kilcamblodge.co.uk* (*expensive*). In an idyllic setting overlooking Loch Sunart. A friendly, lovely place to stay, with convivial company as well as excellent food.
Meall Mo Chridhe Country House, Kilchoan, t (01972) 510 238, *www.westcoastscotland.co.uk* (*expensive*). Imposing 18th-century manse, now an up-market guesthouse. Excellent food, with seafood and game.
Cuildarroch, near Lochailort on the Road to the Isles, t (01687) 470 232 (*moderate*). Wolsey Lodge with a family-home atmosphere and excellent food.
Dalilea House, near Acharacle, t (01967) 431 253, *www.westcoastscotland.co.uk* (*moderate*). Hospitable old laird's house in nice setting, with excellent food.
Feorag House, Glenborrodale, t (01972) 500 248, *www.feorag.co.uk* (*moderate*). A 5-star guesthouse on the shores of Loch Sunart and offering a soothing haven of tranquility and comfort.
Belmont, Acharacle, t (01967) 431 266 (*budget*). Very comfortable B&B in a former manse.
Clanranald Hotel, Acharacle, t (01967) 431 202, *www.clanranaldhotel.co.uk* (*budget*). The place to go for local atmosphere. A homely hotel and bar with plenty of character and not many frills.
Fasgadh, at Drimnin, opposite Tobermory, t (01967) 421 347, *www.west-scotland-tourism.com/fasgadh-holidays* (*budget*). A B&B with wonderful views and outstanding hospitality. A foot ferry runs every Friday to Tobermory. Self-catering caravan. Dinner by arrangement.
Otterburn, Strontian, t (01967) 402 138, *otter-burnbb@aol.com* (*budget*). Highly recommended. A hospitable, comfortable B&B with lovely loch views.
Glenmore Holidays, near Acharacle, t (01972) 500 263/254, *www.michael-macgregor.co.uk* (£275–£775pw). Two self-catering houses and a cottage – fine sea views (sleeps 2–8).
Ariundle Centre, t (01967) 402 279, near Ariundle (*moderate–inexpensive*). Excellent food. *Evening meals in summer (bring your own bottle).*

eccentric Highland gentry (though actually of Irish birth). She kept open house here until she died and her table always had extra places set for unexpected visitors, including parties of orphans and deprived children. Her husband, who died many years before her, was a well-known Gaelic scholar.

Roshven House overlooks the southern entrance to Loch Ailort. In 1855 Professor Hugh Blackburn and his wife Jemima, an illustrator whom Ruskin pronounced the best artist he knew, set about restoring and rebuilding the plain Georgian house that survives at its core. The book *Jemima* by Rob Fairley gives an intriguing account of Jemima Blackburn's life, reproducing many of her beautiful watercolours of the West Highlands and the birds and flowers found around Roshven.

This part of Moidart was accessible only by boat from Inverailort, or on foot, until 1966 when the road (A861) was built. The road turns south now and takes you down to Loch Moidart and eastwards along the loch to **Kinlochmoidart**. The house, recently restored to the highest standards, is available for comfortable holiday lets (*t (0131) 468 8535*). The baronial mansion was built between 1882 and 1884 by fashionable Glasgow architect, William Leiper. Its predecessor, the home of the Macdonalds of Kinlochmoidart, stood nearby until the 1980s. On this site, in an even earlier house (burnt down in 1746), Prince Charles stayed for a week in August 1745 before going on to raise his standard in Glenfinnan. Here he waited while the clans were rallied to his cause, and worked his charms on the chiefs reluctant to take part in the Rising. Traditionally, he sailed in through the north channel of Loch Moidart and landed on the flat stretch of its northern shore. The **Seven Men of Moidart** mark this spot – five large beech trees plus two saplings to replace those blown down in gales.

The road then takes you inland about 6 miles to **Acharacle** (the 'ch' is guttural) where Loch Shiel narrows into its river and flows out under Shiel Bridge to the sea, or you can walk round the southern shore of Loch Moidart. St Adamnan mentions the River Shiel in his biography of Columba, and describes how some of Columba's companions caught five salmon. Predicting a larger catch, he urged them to try again; they obeyed and caught a fish '*mirae magnitudinis*', of extraordinary size. Adamnan calls the Shiel '*fluvius piscosus*', a river abounding in fish. Acharacle is a scattered village typical of many contemporary crofting settlements with a good mix of former thatched houses (many now relegated to barns), later gabled dwellings and modern bungalows. There is nothing twee about the genuine Highland vernacular style.

At Shiel Bridge a narrow road twists and turns out to the South Channel of Loch Moidart, to one of the most stirring, romantic ruins in Scotland. **Castle Tioram** – pronounced 'Chiram', meaning 'dry land' – stands high on a rocky islet overlooking Eilean Shona, reached on foot by causeway at low tide. This stronghold of the 13th and 14th centuries was the seat of the Macdonalds of Clanranald. John of Islay, descended from Somerled, married his cousin Amie, who inherited Moidart, Arisaig and Knoydart from her father, one of Robert the Bruce's most faithful followers. Amie was divorced by John and retired to Moidart, where she extended Castle Tioram to its present form in about 1353. Her son became the first Captain of Clanranald and the castle has always been associated with that clan. It was captured once by the cunning Campbells but swiftly retaken by the Clanranalds. In later sieges considerable damage was done and several cannonballs were found lodged in the walls in the 19th century. The castle was burnt in 1715 by its staunchly Jacobite chief, Allan Mor of Clanranald, to save it from falling into English hands. He stood on the wooded hill on the mainland opposite and watched Tioram burn before going off to fight at Sheriffmuir. (His other castle, Ormacleit in South Uist, also went up in flames on the night of Sheriffmuir, due to overenthusiastic stoking of fires in the kitchen.) Workmen clearing debris from the Tioram fire found a lump of metal with faint fragments of canvas or leather sticking to it, containing a number of solid silver Spanish dollars dating from the 17th century. The Moidart people have a tradition that a murder of unusual atrocity was once committed in the dungeon and that the blood of the victim can never be wiped from the soil. To this day there's a constant oozing from the ground near the door, which turns a dark rusty colour on contact with the air and looks suspiciously like blood. Chemical analysis has proved that it isn't.

In 1984 these ancient walls became the setting for a gathering of Clanranald Macdonalds from all over the world. They were entertained by the present chief in the roofless banqueting hall, roasting whole lambs in the old hearth, and for a few hours the castle lived again, vibrant with pipe music, songs and laughter. The next day an open-air Mass was celebrated in the courtyard to rededicate the Clanranald banner, said to have survived Culloden. The ruin came on the market in the late 1990s. The Captain of Clanranald sent out the 'Fiery Cross' (two crossed sticks, charred at two ends and originally dipped in goat's blood – a traditional call to arms in the Highlands), in an attempt to persuade Macdonalds of Clanranald all over the world to buy it for the clan. He was outbid. The new owner, Lex Brown, planned a sympathetic restoration, with a dwelling for himself and a centre for Clanranald Macdonalds. He spent vast sums in research for his project and had almost total support from local people. However, the government turned down his application despite the fact that it would have generated employment in an area where jobs are scarce.

Another road west from Acharacle goes out to Kentra Bay and Ardtoe, a sheltered, sandy haven that has been turned into a vast sea-water reserve for white-fish farming. South again across the eastern neck of Ardnamurchan, the road comes down to Salen on the north shore of Loch Sunart.

Loch Sunart

Loch Sunart is a perfect, safe anchorage for boats. There can be few more satisfying experiences than sailing out of this lovely loch early on a fine morning, the wind on your quarter, the sun on your back, watching the whole island-studded Minch open up ahead. **Strontian** – *sron-an-t Sidhean*, Point of the Fairies – at the head of the loch, caters well for visiting yachts with a well-stocked boat chandler. The rare mineral strontium, was discovered here in 1787. (Sir Humphry Davy, the inventor of the miners' safety lamp, realized its potential in the early 19th century; it gives fireworks their dazzle, and produces the isotope Strontium 90.) The Strontian Lead Mines, opened in 1722 and manned by French prisoners of war, provided bullets for the Napoleonic Wars.

It was just off Strontian, in Loch Sunart, that the Floating Church anchored in 1843 during the 'Disruption', when the Free Church broke from the Church of Scotland. The local laird refused to let members of the breakaway church build a new kirk on his land, so they bought an old ship on the Clyde, fitted it up and towed it to Loch Sunart. For 30-odd years the congregation rowed out to their services.

Although some earlier buildings survive, the heart of Strontian is characterized by a 1960s development of houses, pleasantly sited round a central green. **Ariundle Centre**, near the village centre, is a restaurant (*see* 'Where to Stay and Eat', p.116), with weekend craft courses and a craft/bookshop selling knitwear and tweeds.

Heading westwards from Salen, the B8007 hugs the northern shore of Loch Sunart and finishes up at Ardnamurchan Point – Point of the Great Ocean. On the way is the **Natural History Centre**, at Glenmore (*t* *(01463) 791 575; open April–Oct Mon–Sat 11.30–5.30, Sun 12–5.30*). There are good wildlife exhibitions here as well as home baking, books and gifts.

Ardnamurchan

The rugged, wind-lashed peninsula of **Ardnamurchan**, familiar to west-coast yachtsmen as the most westerly point on the mainland of the British Isles, has a diverse landscape. The soil is poor, eroded by retreating ice in the last Ice Age, but manages to support trees to the east, giving way to heathery moorland presided over by the volcanic plug of Ben Hiant. Once well-populated, this area lost most of its inhabitants during the Highland Clearances (*see* **Topics**, p.21). The ruins of many old crofting townships can still be seen, while a good number of surviving cottages have been gentrified or turned into holiday homes.

Northwest Ardnamurchan provides exceptional views and there are good sandy beaches. At Ardslignish, about 8 miles from Salen, there is a tall pillar of red granite carved with a cross, thought to have been erected by St Columba in honour of the Irish saint, Ciaran, who died in 548. The 13th-century ruin of **Mingary Castle**, another 8 miles on, was once the stronghold of the Maclans of Ardnamurchan, kinsmen of the Lords of the Isles. It stands on a rocky cliff from which its walls rise sheer on the seaward side, guarding the entrance to Loch Sunart and to the Sound of Mull. James IV came to Mingary to receive the homage of the Lords of the Isles in 1495, and was peeved by their lack of enthusiasm. The Campbells got their hands on the castle in the 1600s, but Alasdair Macdonald managed to capture it for Montrose in 1644. General Leslie took it back and it reverted to the Campbells; in 1745 it was garrisoned by government soldiers who built a barracks within the walls. From **Kilchoan**, the largest settlement on the peninsula, a ferry runs to Tobermory on Mull once a day.

Ardnamurchan Point, about 22 miles from Salen, is wild, heatherclad bedrock with a lighthouse at its tip (*www.ardnamurchan.u-net.com; open daily April–Oct 10–5.30*). This listed building was designed in 1848 by Alan Stevenson, one of the famous Stevenson family who were the architects/engineers of most of the western seaboard's lighthouses. Ardnamurchan Lighthouse Trust has a display in the principal keeper's house showing the keeper's living quarters in the 1940s. The assistant keepers' cottages are now holiday lets with a café and gift shop in stables nearby.

This dramatic headland takes the full force of westerly gales and can present quite a challenge to small boats. Johnson and Boswell, having waited for a fair wind to take them from Skye to Coll, finally embarked on a kelp boat. Dr Johnson did not have a happy voyage: 'We were doomed to experience, like others, the danger of trusting to the wind, which blew against us, in a short time, with such violence, that we, being no seasoned sailors, were willing to call it a tempest. I was sea-sick and lay down.' Boswell, having stayed on deck and flattered himself that he was a good sailor, became worried as the tempest increased and, as they rounded Ardnamurchan Point, changed direction and forced them to tack. It was on this trip that Boswell, anxious to help in the boat, was handed a rope and told to hang on to it until further notice. He did so, reflecting later that as the rope was fixed to the top of one of the masts, pulling it would have achieved nothing, the object having been to keep him out of the way and divert his fear by making him feel busy: 'Thus did I stand firm to my post, while the wind and rain beat upon me, always expecting a call to pull my rope.'

Morvern is the heel of this southwest corner, washed by Loch Sunart to the north, the Sound of Mull to the west and Loch Linnhe to the east. Sparsely populated, it clings to the mainland at Glen Tarbert, the 5-mile isthmus between Strontian and Inversanda. The largest granite quarry in Scotland is at Glensanda. **Lochaline**, on the southern shore, means 'the beautiful loch' and so it is. It faces across the Sound of Mull to Fishnish Point, linked by a fairly frequent car ferry taking 15 minutes. Silica sand has been mined here since 1939 and is used for making optical glass.

Ardtornish House (*garden open Wed–Mon 9–5; adm*) is a striking landmark at the head of Loch Aline, a Victorian mansion designed by Alexander Ross in the late 19th century and described as 'a suburban villa afflicted with elephantiasis'. Set in a designed landscape, the garden is full of unusual and exotic plants, shrubs and trees, with some of Scotland's earliest concrete estate buildings.

You must walk to **Ardtornish Castle**, on a point a couple of miles east of Loch Aline. Built in 1340 and restored in 1910, it was for many years a stronghold of the Lords of the Isles. Its walls, which gave massive shelter and protection in the days when enemies stormed in from the sea, are nearly 10ft thick. John, 1st Lord Macdonald of the Isles, died here in 1387 and it was his great-grandson the 4th Lord, also John, who received ambassadors from Edward IV of England here in 1462, and signed the Treaty of Ardtornish, a somewhat futile agreement that was hardly of much value. When the English failed in their conquest, James IV was quick to start dismantling the Lordship.

Fiunary, 5 miles west of Lochaline, was the home of George Macleod, the left-wing Presbyterian who re-established a community on Iona in 1938. He was a controversial man, full of good intentions but not always tactful – he tried to introduce bishops into the kirk in the interests of church unity. He refused to use his title when he succeeded to a baronetcy in 1924, but chose the title Baron Macleod of Fiunary when created a life peer in 1967. The house – an old manse – is now falling into dereliction. It was the home of the original Rev Norman Macleod in 1775, from whom descended no fewer than six moderators of the Church of Scotland. There are good views across the Sound of Mull from this road, which peters out a few miles to the north at Drimnin.

Central Highlands

10

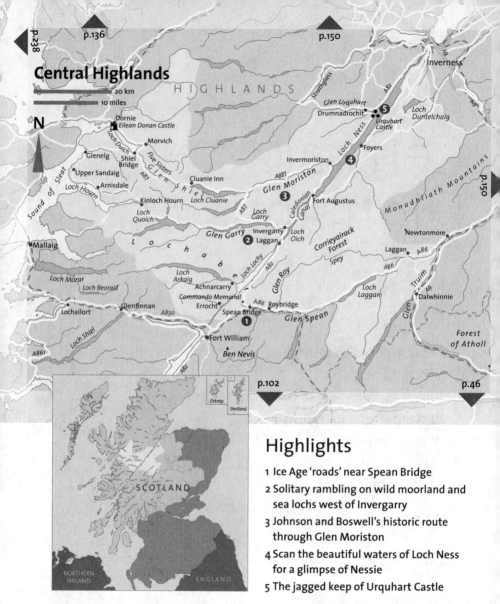

p.238

p.136

p.150

Central Highlands

20 km
10 miles

N

p.102

p.46

Highlights

1 Ice Age 'roads' near Spean Bridge
2 Solitary rambling on wild moorland and sea lochs west of Invergarry
3 Johnson and Boswell's historic route through Glen Moriston
4 Scan the beautiful waters of Loch Ness for a glimpse of Nessie
5 The jagged keep of Urquhart Castle

The Great Glen – Glenmore Albin – *Gleann mor na-h Albin* – is that diagonal slash across the Highlands from Loch Linnhe in the southwest to Inverness and the Moray Firth in the northeast. It was carved out by receding ice in the last Ice Age, leaving a chain of lochs and rivers, now linked by the Caledonian Canal. Even before the canal, the Great Glen provided a route north as early as the time of St Columba. Although the route to Inverness is a well-worn trail, it offers many detours into less frequented glens and hills. As you go northeast the climate changes from the benign pearly dampness of the west to a more bracing easterly bite which can be diamond-hard and bright in winter.

Fort William to Invergarry

Lochaber

Lochaber, the region from Loch Leven to Glen Garry and out west to Moidart, has always been synonymous with the names Macdonald and Cameron. This territory, including the Nevis range and part of the Rough Bounds, was a seething turmoil of Jacobite unrest and has witnessed many a ferocious battle.

The A82 from Fort William follows one of General Wade's roads to **Spean Bridge**. To the west of the road you pass some rather unexpected ranch-style buildings, weathered, with 'Great Glen Cattle Ranch' emblazoned on their walls. During the post-war years of hardship and shortage around 1946, Mr Joseph William Hobbs, an Englishman who had spent many years on ranches in Canada, bought 10,000 acres here, revitalized what had been poor land and turned it into a highly successful Canadian-style ranch, producing 'beef in quantity'. It was a great success and he was given the Freedom of Fort William for his efforts. He lived at **Inverlochy Castle**, a baronial mansion built in 1863, which is now the Inverlochy Castle Hotel (*see* below).

Tourist Information

Spean Bridge: t (01397) 712 576. *Open Easter–Oct.*

Sports and Activities

Fishing Scotland, Roybridge, **t** (01397) 712 812, *www.fishing-scotland.co.uk*. Fly-fishing tuition in lovely scenery.

Where to Stay and Eat

Glengarry Castle Hotel, near Invergarry, **t** (01809) 501 254, *www.glengarry.net* (*expensive*). Built as a baronial mansion (1866–9) in a lovely setting overlooking Loch Oich. Sumptuous furnishings. Good food, with pretty gardens and a resident ghost. Tennis and rowing. *Open Easter–early Nov.*

Inverlochy Castle Hotel, near Fort William, **t** (01397) 702 177, *www.inverlochy. co.uk* (*expensive*). *See* p.103. Not to be confused with ruined Inverlochy (*see* p.105).

Corriegour Lodge Hotel, Loch Lochy, **t** (01397) 712 685, *www.corriegour-lodge-hotel.com* (*moderate*). Friendly, comfortable Victorian hunting lodge with loch views.

Glenspean Lodge Hotel, Roybridge, **t** (01397) 712 223, *www.glenspeanlodge.com* (*moderate*). Turreted Highland lodge in 5 acres. Panoramic views and good food.

Invergarry Hotel, Invergarry, **t** (01809) 501 206 (*moderate*). Built in 1885 – very picturesque with a friendly atmosphere. Locals frequent the bar.

Old Pines Restaurant with Rooms, Spean Bridge, **t** (01397) 712 324, *www.oldpines.co.uk* (*moderate*). Delightful, informal family home – excellent food.

Tomdoun Hotel, near Invergarry, **t** (01809) 511 218, *www.tomdoun.com* (*moderate/budget*). 19th-century coaching inn, unpretentious and very Highland.

Drumlaggan, Balgowan, just beyond Laggan, **t** (01528) 544 242 (*budget*). Idyllic 'retreat with a difference', between the ski slopes of Aviemore and Fort William. Charming hosts with much knowledge of the surroundings.

Invergloy House, Spean Bridge, **t** (01347) 712 681, *www.invergloy-house.co.uk* (*budget*). Peaceful B&B in a converted coach house and stables.

The Old Station Restaurant, Spean Bridge, **t** (01397) 712 535 (*inexpensive*). Good seafood and snacks, home baking and meals. The train still stops here. *Open Tues–Sun 11–5.30, and dinner Fri and Sat till 9pm.*

It is not generally known that John Buchan's famous novel *John Macnab* is based on a true story connected with this place. An officer in the Cameron Highlanders, Captain James Brander-Dunbar of Pitgaveny near Elgin, together with some fellow officers, bet Lord Abinger that they could 'poach a stag, a salmon and a grouse' from his estate, undetected, and lay them at the door of Inverlochy Castle. By various means they carried out their objective and the *gralloch* – viscera – of the stag was delivered at breakfast the next day, on a silver dish from which the cover was removed by the butler. Proof of this story remains at Pitgaveny: the stag's head, labelled 'Poached in Inverlochy 1887'; a framed cheque made out to J. B. Dunbar, poacher; and a copy of Buchan's book signed 'To John Macnab from John Buchan'.

Spean Bridge Mill (*t (01397) 712 260; open daily*) has weaving demonstrations, a Clan Tartan Centre, a gift shop and a restaurant. Just northwest of Spean Bridge is the impressive bronze **Commando Memorial** by Scott Sutherland, erected in 1952. To the northwest lies Achnacarry, home of the Camerons of Lochiel, which served as their headquarters during the Second World War. At **Highbridge**, a couple of miles west of Spean Bridge, one of General Wade's most remarkable bridges was built across the 100ft gorge of the River Spean. Most of the bridge's original structure is in ruins and a later metal bridge no longer spans the gap, but the site is spectacular; in summer the river seems little more than a stream, but when it is swollen with snow melt and rain, it is an awesome torrent. It was here that the first 'engagement' of the '45 Rising occurred – it is said that the outcome decided those of the chiefs who had not yet committed themselves.

And wild and high the 'Camerons' Gathering' rose,
The war-note of Lochiel, which Albynn's hills
Have heard, and heard, too, have her Saxon foes:
Now in the noon of night that pibroch thrills,
Savage and shrill! But with the breath that thrills
Their mountain pipe, so fill the mountaineers
With the fierce daring which instills
The stirring memory of a thousand years,
And Evans', Donald's fame rings in each clansman's ears.
From 'Childe Harold's Pilgrimage' by Lord Byron

At Achnacarry, off the B8005 at the southwest end of Loch Lochy, the **Clan Cameron Museum** (*www.clan-cameron.org; open Easter–mid-Oct daily, pm only*) covers the history of this proud clan, described by General Wolfe as the 'bravest clan among them' in his description of Culloden. Though not one of the largest clans, the Camerons made up for their small numbers by acts of chivalry and honour. They were always loyal to the Stewart cause. Archibald, brother of Donald, the 19th chief, known as 'the Gentle Lochiel', was captured and executed in 1753, the last man to die for the Jacobite cause.

Achnacarry Castle has been the home of the Camerons of Lochiel since the 1660s and the present house, designed by James Gillespie Graham, dates from 1802. The previous house was burnt down in reprisal for Gentle Lochiel's sympathies at

Lowlanders Defeated at Highbridge

Two companies of the Royal Scots were on their way to Fort William as reinforcements at a time when it was known that local people were hatching mischief. The soldiers were mostly new recruits and as they approached the high bridge they heard bagpipes and discovered that 'a party of Highlanders' was in possession of the bridge. Macdonald of Keppoch, having heard of the march, had dispatched Macdonell of Tirandrish to set up an ambush here. The Highlanders numbered only about ten, but were sited cunningly to give the illusion of a larger force. The sound of the pipes skirled out from the high ground across the river, and Captain Scott, in command of the Royal Scots, sent his batman and a sergeant across the bridge to scout. The Highlanders disposed of the unfortunate pair and then leapt about brandishing their weapons and holding out their plaids between them, terrifying the raw recruits. Captain Scott, deeming it expedient to retire, turned his troops about and marched back the way they had come. As they hurried up Loch Lochy between the hills and the water, their retreat was harried by the Highlanders, who fired on them from above with five old hunting guns between them. Keppoch summoned more men to head them off and they were trapped at Laggan just south of Invergarry. With some soldiers dead and several wounded, Keppoch persuaded Captain Scott, also wounded, to surrender before there was a blood bath. His white gelding was dispatched to Prince Charles in Moidart, and Scott was imprisoned at Achnacarry. Here, Lochiel 'treated him more as a brother than an enemy and a prisoner', while Lady Lochiel dressed his wounds herself. The wavering chiefs decided in favour of the prince. The affair is remembered in the pibroch 'The Rout of the Lowland Captain'.

Culloden; only an ivy-covered stump of it survives, near the stables. A row of magnificent beech trees follows the line of the river at Achnacarry. It is said that Lochiel was planting a formal beech avenue here when news of Prince Charles' landing at Loch nan Uamh came to him. In a frantic rush to join the Prince, he heeled the young seedlings into a temporary trench intending to deal with them on his return. He never came back.

Five miles to the southwest off the B8004, lies **Erracht**, the home of Alan Cameron, who, in 1793, raised the 79th Highlanders – the Cameron Highlanders, subsequently amalgamated and re-amalgamated to become what is now the Highlanders.

Glen Roy leads off the A86 about 3 miles east of Spean Bridge at Roybridge. The River Roy tumbles through wooded gorges to meander across the valley floor, bare hills rising on either side. Stop at the large observation car park some way along and look up the valley. Horizontal lines run across the upper hillside, each line exactly matched by one on the opposite side of the valley. These **Parallel Roads** mark the receding shoreline of an ice-lake in the late Ice Age, and are geologically famous for their clarity. Among the scientists who puzzled over these scars was Charles Darwin. Several secret glens lie up beyond the track and there are marvellous walks here.

The **Corrieyairick Pass** was an important military route and it was once possible to take a carriage through to Fort Augustus on Wade's road, today a track. Built to facilitate troop movements between the Highland forts, this route was used by Prince Charles in August 1745. General Cope was preparing to march his men through the pass on their way to Fort Augustus when he heard that the Prince, who now commanded a force of about 3,000 men, planned to ambush him there. Fully aware that it would be suicidal to attempt to force his way over this high, wild spot against men who knew every inch of it, Cope abandoned the plan. The Prince was thoroughly put out when Cope failed to materialize. All he got for his efforts was the capture of a few deserters from Cope's army, who told him of their general's change of plan.

From Roybridge the A86 is a lovely drive, winding through Glen Spean to Loch Laggan and into the Spey Valley. About three-quarters of the way along Loch Laggan on its opposite shore, stands **Ardverikie House**, an astonishing pile which replaced an attractive shooting lodge where Queen Victoria had stayed with Prince Albert for about a month in 1847. They were looking for a Highland retreat and were much taken with the place, complete with murals by Landseer. The royal party stretched the capacity of the house so much that the host's four eldest children were moved out of their cosy nursery into rather cramped quarters in the home farm. Four-year-old Claud was so outraged by this that when he was presented to the Queen in his party kilt, he refused to bow and instead stood on his head, revealing the secret all Sassenachs long to know. He was suitably chastized and promised to apologize. But the Queen had not been amused and her expression so unnerved him that he stood on his head again and was banished for the duration. (In later life he became an MP and Lord of the Treasury, and in 1887 ADC to the Queen for 10 years.) It rained continuously during the royal visit and they decided not to buy the house, which unfortunately burnt down in 1873. *Monarch of the Glen* was filmed here recently.

From Kinlochlaggan you reach **Laggan**, a scattered settlement with two prominent churches, one a ruin. It is a good base from which to explore the Monadhliath Mountains and for excellent walks to the west (over the Corrieyairick Pass) and to Glen Roy. The route runs through Strath Mashie into the Spey valley where the river, having gathered volume in its tumble from the hills, meanders over Strath Spey past Newtonmore (*see* p.167) and down to the sea. Just outside Laggan on the Dalwhinnie Road, look for the pottery/gift shop/tearoom – lots of good stuff here.

On the A82 further up the west side of Loch Oich, **Tobar nan Ceann** is the 'well of the heads' marked by a monument beside the road. An obelisk supports the bronze heads of seven men, held together by a dirk through their hair. Beyond, steps lead through a damp tunnel to a sinister well. Alasdair Macdonell, 12th chief of Keppoch, and his brother Ranald were murdered by their ambitious uncle Alastair Buidhe in 1663. For a while, none of their kinsmen dared to avenge the murder, but the Keppoch Bard, Ian Lom Macdonell, poured forth such a torrent of invective against the murderers that Sir James Macdonald of Sleat felt obliged to do something. He dispatched Ian Lom up the valley of the Spean to Inverlair, west of Loch Laggan, where the murderer and his six sons were hiding. Justice was done. The seven men were beheaded and their heads were carried in a sack to Invergarry. Before presenting them to Macdonell of Glengarry (as a reproach for not having done the deed himself), Ian Lom washed them in the well on Loch Oich. The monument was erected by the 15th and last chief

Macdonell of Glengarry in 1812. Inscribed in English, Gaelic, French and Latin are the words: 'this ample and summary vengeance'. The heads were buried in a little glade in Invergarry, the bodies at Inverlair. Some years ago the bodies were exhumed to prove the truth of the gory tale: seven headless skeletons were discovered, without coffins.

The ruin of old **Invergarry Castle** stands perched on a rock rising sheer from the waters of Loch Oich in what was a position of great strength. The rock is known as *Creag an Fhithich* – the Raven's Rock – which used to be the war cry of the Macdonells of Glengarry whose stronghold this was. Tradition holds that the castle was created with stones passed from hand to hand by a chain of clansmen from Ben Tigh, some 7 miles away. Built in the early 17th century for the Macdonells of Glengarry, it was razed in 1654 by General Monk, who reported that he had 'burned Glengaries new House' and that 'the remaining structure I order'd to be defaced by the pyoneers.' However, it was repaired by 1691 and described as 'ane extraordinary strong house. It is fortified and cannot be taken without great cannon.' At around this time, a detachment of redcoats were sent from Inverness to take the recently rebuilt castle. Glengarry himself was at home, looking out from a castle window with his armourer. He waited until the column of invaders was nicely lined up, then told his armourer to fire through the window. He picked off enough of the enemy to send them scurrying back to Inverness. In 1727 it was occupied briefly by an Englishman, Rawlinson, who was manager of the local iron smelter. The story of how he 'invented the kilt' is hotly denied by Scots purists. Rawlinson noticed the discomfort of his men working in the heat dressed in their *breacan feile* – belted plaids – and suggested they cut the cloth so that the upper portion could be removed leaving only the *feile beag*, 'philibeg' or 'little kilt' we know today. Many refute this 'ridiculous' theory, arguing the *feile beag* was worn before Rawlinson was a gleam in his father's eye. Prince Charles stayed at the castle during his escape from Culloden in 1746 – it was blown up by Cumberland's forces in retaliation. Never rebuilt, it is now in danger of crumbling away.

Invergarry was built as an estate village in the 1860s by its new owner, Edward Ellice, who already owned Glen Quoich. Ellice, by the standard of many Victorian estate owners, was a good landlord, providing solid cottages, a school, hotel, hospital and church. The picturesque buildings survive today, most with the Ellice monogram incorporated into their fabric. The **Glengarry Visitor Centre** (*t (01809) 501 424*), on the site of the old inn by the Invergarry Hotel, has exhibitions of local and natural history, and up-to-date information on tourist attractions and facilities in the area.

Invergarry to Kyle of Lochalsh – a Detour

At Invergarry the A87 takes you west to Kyle of Lochalsh (*see* p.137), the stepping stone to Skye. This is an excellent road along the north side of Loch Garry, over high moorland with sweeping views. It cuts through a wild, mountainous area which can only be explored on foot with a proper map – in these more remote areas you can walk all day and not see a living soul, surrounded by Munros galore, glens and waterfalls, secret lochans, and a number of good tracks.

Where to Stay and Eat

Conchra House Hotel, Ardelve, **t** (01599) 555 233, *www.conchrahouse.co.uk* (*moderate*). Modernized 'country house' hotel overlooking Loch Duich and Eilean Donan. Built in the 1760s, with Jacobite connections. Adjacent self-catering cottages are very comfortable (**t** (01599) 555 752), *www.conchra.co.uk*.

Glenelg Inn, Glenelg, **t** (01599) 522 273 (*moderate*). A conversion of former stables. Excellent, and very convivial.

Loch Duich Hotel, Dornie, near Kyle of Lochalsh, **t** (01599) 555 213, *www.lochduich.f9.co.uk* (*moderate*). Well-known landmark in a superb position overlooking Eilean Donan Castle and Skye. Quality accommodation, with good food.

Mrs Margaret Cameron, Marabhaig, Glenelg, **t** (01599) 522 327 (*moderate*). Clean, comfortable B&B with lovely views.

Skiary, Loch Hourn, **t** (01809) 511 214 (*moderate*). A guesthouse in the wilds, only accessible by boat (run by your host) or on foot. No electricity, but very cosy.

Ratagan Youth Hostel, Glen Shiel, **t** 0870 004 1147, *www.syha.org.uk* (*budget*). In a stunning position surrounded by Munros. Perfect for climbers.

Five miles west of Invergarry, a single-track road leads to **Loch Hourn**, Loch of Hell. Despite its name, this is a glorious sea loch snaking out towards Skye, steep-sided and treacherous for sailors in certain winds. The road, which runs for miles through a landscape that was once an inspiration to the artist Landseer, is much bleaker since the damming of Loch Quoich by the Hydroelectric Board. It stops at Kinloch Hourn but there are a number of good walks including a track north through the hills to Glen Shiel. Another goes west, partly inland and partly following the north shore of Loch Hourn. In summer, the old farm steadings at Kinloch Hourn offer scones and tea. The A87 runs north of Loch Cluanie into Glen Shiel, dominated by the Five Sisters of Kintail that rear vertically on each side.

At **Shiel Bridge**, on Loch Duich, 10 miles west of Cluanie, a narrow, twisting road branches off left and climbs over the **Mam Ratagan** – *mam* being Gaelic for Pass – the only way to Glenelg by land. This was the route taken by the drovers bringing cattle from Skye down to trysts at Falkirk and Crieff. The beasts swam or were towed across the swirling channel from Kylerhea on precarious floats. This was also an important military route and when Johnson and Boswell travelled this way in 1773, soldiers were still working on it. The gaunt ruin of **Bernera Barracks**, built in 1722 and used until after 1790, lies north of Glenelg village. Boswell eyed Bernera as he shepherded Dr Johnson towards what proved to be very poor lodgings: 'I looked at them wishfully, as soldiers have always everything in the best order.' Poor Boswell: the inn (now gone) was not a success. 'The room was damp and dirty, with bare walls, and a variety of bad smells.' Their discomfort was eased somewhat by a local laird who, knowing the inn, sent them rum and sugar to help them through the ordeal.

Glenelg Candles is a modern, all-timber Scandanavian-style structure in the garden of Balcraggie House, almost worth a visit for the building alone, though there is a good gift shop and café here, with excellent home baking. **Glen Beag** runs east off a narrow road 2 miles south of Glenelg. Here you can see two of the most splendid examples of Iron Age brochs: **Dun Telve** and **Dun Troddan**, built to provide shelter and refuge for the chiefs, their people and their livestock. Their double walls are pierced by a single small entrance, easily defended, and honeycombed with galleries, in which the people lived, leaving the central enclosure for the animals. Dun Telve is the best preserved, over 10m in height, the bell-shaped outline very clear. At the end of the road a track leads to Dun Grugaig, an earlier fort, perched on the brink of a steep gorge.

Not far south of Glen Beag is **Sandaig**, with its islands; the house where Gavin Maxwell lived with his otters was on the beach below Upper Sandaig – it was burnt to the ground and its site is marked by an inscription set into a rock. In his well-known books, such as *Ring of Bright Water* and *The Rocks Remain*, Maxwell called the place *Camusfeàrna* (bay of the alders) in order to protect his privacy. His ashes were buried here and one hopes that his restless spirit has found peace at last in one of the most beautiful corners of the west coast. There are many genuine *Camusfeàrnas* in

The Battle of the Shirts

On up the A82 from Spean Bridge, the road hugs Loch Lochy until the Caledonian Canal links it with Loch Oich at Laggan. This isthmus was the site of a famous battle – *Blar na Leine* – the Battle of the Shirts, fought between the Macdonalds and the Frasers in 1544. The Clanranald Macdonalds had rejected their legitimate chief Ranald in favour of a renowned leader, John of Moidart, and Ranald had been sent to his mother's kinsmen, the Frasers, to be brought up. When John was taken hostage by James V, Ranald reappeared to claim his heritage. He insulted his clan at Castle Tioram by rejecting the feast they had planned in his honour and announcing that 'a few hens would be amply sufficient to celebrate the event', thus earning for himself the name 'hen chief' and banishment by his people. This was too much for his protector, Lord Lovat, who with the help of Huntly descended on Loch Lochy, intent on taking revenge. John of Moidart, recently escaped from captivity, enlisted the help of the Camerons and the Glengarry Macdonalds and prepared for battle. They assembled on the shore of a lochan beneath Ben Tigh and fed on oatmeal (a small quantity of which each man carried tied up in his plaid) mixed with water from the loch. Each man then drove a stick into the peat moss, a common practice before battle, how many had been slain being indicated by the number of sticks not retrieved afterwards. The battleground is now partly under water since Loch Lochy was raised several feet during the making of the canal. Here, 300 Frasers took on and were considerably outnumbered by John of Moidart and his men. Because it was an intensely hot July day, the men threw off their plaids, jackets and vests, and fought in their shirts which were knee-length 'tunics'. Lovat's son, the Master of Lovat, who had been left safely at home by his father, appeared on the scene and was killed almost immediately, fuelling the fury of the Frasers. Fighting chest-to-chest, the combatants were 'felled on each side like trees in a wood'. Ranald, the 'hen chief', fought like a hero but was killed by a dishonourable trick – his assailant crying out to him to beware of a man behind, and then killing him from behind when he spun round. Of the 1,000 men engaged, only 12 survived – all Macdonalds. The Frasers perished to a man, leaving the clan leaderless – fortunately 80 of the gentlemen's wives were pregnant at the time and each one, it is said, produced a male heir.

Scotland, causing some confusion. The rough road goes on down to Arnisdale and Glen Corran on Loch Hourn, 10 miles or so to the south.

Back on the A87, stop at Morvich, at the head of Loch Duich. From here you can walk about 7 miles to the truly spectacular **Falls of Glomach**, past a couple of smaller waterfalls by way of introduction. The 370ft (114m) torrent thunders down in two cascades over a projecting rock into a stomach-churningly deep chasm. The sides of the gorge are hung with lush green ferns and foliage and the air sparkles with moisture. Don't expect to be on your own here. There is a National Trust for Scotland Visitor Centre at Morvich with audiovisual exhibitions and information.

Eilean Donan Castle (*www.eileandonancastle.com; open Easter–Sept daily 10–5.30; adm*) is one of the most photographed castles in Scotland and familiar to anyone who has seen the film *Highlander*. Standing on a rocky island reached by a causeway in Loch Duich, it was built on the site of an ancient fort in 1230 by Alexander II who hoped to re-establish Scottish rule after the defeat of the Vikings at Largs. The castle became the seat of the MacKenzies, Earls of Seaforth, but what you see today is modern – a loose 20th-century interpretation of a medieval castle, not entirely accurate but nonetheless attractive.

The old castle was garrisoned by Spanish troops and used as an administrative base in 1719, supporting one of the Jacobite attempts to regain the throne for the Stuarts; in reprisal it was bombarded by English warships whose efforts reduced it to a complete ruin. Thus it stood for 200 years, until its complete 'reproduction' was commissioned in the 1930s. It is dedicated as a war memorial to the Clan Macrae, who held the castle as constables to the Earl of Seaforth – the 'MacKenzie coat of mail'. Among other things housed in the castle, there are interesting Jacobite relics.

Invergarry to Inverness

Continuing on from Invergarry, up the A82 to Aberchalder, the canal connects Loch Oich with Loch Ness, 5 miles to the northeast at Fort Augustus.

Fort Augustus

Fort Augustus, at the southern end of Loch Ness, is the halfway halt in the Great Glen, a popular tourist centre with an ancient history. This was a base for St Columba and the early missionaries when travelling from Iona to convert the east coast. Their names survive in the place names of churches, wells, hills, cemeteries and dwellings throughout the district. The Gaelic name *Cille-Chumein*, which the village of Fort Augustus bore for 1,300 years, and by which it is still known to Gaelic speakers, derives from St Cummein, a successor of Columba. He built a church here, among other things, whose ancient Celtic bell survived until 1559. The Dowager Lady Lovat, whose son and husband were killed in the Battle of the Shirts in 1554, came on a pilgrimage to the battlefield. On their return they took the bell for their own church. A sudden storm got up in Loch Ness and the oarsmen threw the bell into the loch as a peace

Tourist Information

Fort Augustus: the Car Park, **t** (01320) 366 367, *www.visithighlands.com*. Open April–Oct.

Where to Stay and Eat

Cluanie Inn, Kintail, Glen Moriston, **t** (01320) 340 238, *www.cluanieinn.com* (*moderate*). Cosy rooms and reasonable food – ideal base for a walking/climbing holiday.

Foyers Hotel, Foyers, **t** (01456) 486 216, *www.foyershotel.co.uk* (*moderate*). Larger than Foyers Bay House, below.

Glenmoriston Arms Hotel, Invermoriston, **t** (01320) 351 206, *www.glenmoristonarms. co.uk* (*moderate*). Has a jolly Highland atmosphere and offers good value.

Inchnacardoch Lodge Hotel, overlooking Loch Ness near Fort Augustus, **t** (01320) 366 258, *www.inchnacardoch.com* (*moderate*). Comfortable, with good views.

The Lovat Arms, Fort Augustus, **t** 0845 450 1100, *www.lovatarms-hotel.com* (*moderate*). Delightful and old-fashioned, friendly and comfortable, with good food.

Old Pier House, Fort Augustus, **t** (01320) 366 418 (*moderate*). One of the nicest places to stay in the area: 100-year-old Highland farmhouse on the shore of Loch Ness. The Gaelic-speaking musical family also run it as a riding centre. Boats and mountain bikes for hire, fishing. *Open April–Halloween*.

Polmaily House, Drumnadrochit, **t** (01456) 450 343, *www.polmaily.co.uk* (*moderate*). Splendid, comfortable country house hotel, with good food, tennis, pool and riding.

Drumnadrochit Hotel, Drumnadrochit, **t** (01456) 450 218, *www.loch-ness-scotland.com* (*budget*). Hideous modern glass house, but handy for monster-spotting.

Farr Mains, by Inverness, **t** (01808) 251 205, *c&jmurray@farrmains.freeserve.co.uk* (*budget*). Comfortable family home with Highland hospitality, dinner if wanted – you may get to feed the llamas.

Foyers Bay House, Lower Foyers, **t** (01456) 486 624, *www.foyersbay.co.uk* (*budget*). Small, quiet and friendly, with a garden and reasonable food.

Glenurquhart House Hotel, near Drumnadrochit, **t** (01456) 476 234 (*budget*). In the lovely glen and offering true Highland hospitality.

The Old Parsonage, Croachy, to the east of Loch Ness, **t** (01808) 521 441, *oldparsonage@btinternet.com* (*budget*). Nice, family run B&B.

Mrs Mackintosh, Achmony, Drumnadrochit, **t** (01456) 450 357, *www.achmonyholidays. co.uk* (£350–550 pw). Detached, well-equipped, self-catering timber chalets, around a 30-acre birch wood (sleeps 2–6).

The Gondolier, Fort Augustus, **t** (01320) 366 262 (*expensive–moderate*). Up-market Highland food.

The Bothy Bite, Fort Augustus, by the side of the locks, **t** (01320) 366 710 (*moderate–inexpensive; accommodation budget*). A pleasant eatery within an old smithy, with backpackers' accommodation as well.

The Lock Inn, Fort Augustus, **t** (01320) 366 302 (*moderate–inexpensive*). Beside the canal and popular with locals.

offering to the spirit of the lake. The boat was saved and from then on people would take water from where the bell was thrown and use it for medicinal purposes.

There is a pre-Christian crannog, **Cherry Island** – *Eilean Mhuirich* (Maurice's Islet) – a mile up Loch Ness from the town. When the canal was made, however, Loch Ness was raised by some 9ft, submerging much of the remains. A chief of Glengarry came courting a Fraser here, it is said, during a deadly feud between the Macdonalds and the Frasers. Stories vary, but he and his seven-strong bodyguard, or 'tail', came to an untimely end – his body was flung into the water, his 'tail' buried close by.

Fort Augustus marked the extremity of Fraser lands and was the setting for many territorial battles against the men of Lochaber. During the 18th century it was the hub of General Wade's road network, a fort having been built just behind what is now the Lovat Arms Hotel to protect the entrance to Loch Ness (part of the wall can still be seen). After 1715 the English garrisoned the fort in the hope of controlling the turbulent Highlanders, and when General Wade started work, a much more substantial fort was built on the same design as those at Ruthven, Bernera and Inversnaid. Traces of this can now be seen incorporated in the present abbey buildings – little remains but the dungeons and ancient bastions.

Wade named his new fort after William Augustus, Duke of Cumberland, a fat schoolboy of eight, son of George II, who was to go down in history as Butcher Cumberland. Jacobites gained control of the fort in 1745 until after Culloden, when the 'Butcher' took up residence and used it as a headquarters from which to wreak his atrocious revenge on the Highlands. From here he issued commands that were to tyrannize and destroy any fight that was left in a defeated people, including many who were innocent. Johnson and Boswell stayed with the Governor of the Fort during their tour in 1773, and it was still garrisoned when the Caledonian Canal was opened in 1822, with the ladder of locks now a focal point in the middle of the town. The fort was sold in 1867 to Lord Lovat, descendant of the 'Old Fox of the '45' who was imprisoned in the dungeons here before his execution in London. Lovat gave the fort to the Benedictines, who established a monastery, opened a boys' public school in 1878 and an abbey in 1882. The school closed in 1993, and at the end of the 20th century, with the monks gone, the abbey was sold to a private owner, a heartbreaking loss for the Catholic community.

The **Clansman Centre** (*t (01320) 366 444, www.scottish-swords.com; open April–Oct daily; adm*), beside the bridge over the canal, shows how the clans lived in the Highlands, and includes clothing and weapon demonstrations and a talk in a Highland turf house. You can even be photographed in authentic Highland costume.

Loch Ness

Loch Ness is world famous, thanks to Nessie, but it is also extremely beautiful. It is so long and narrow – it is about 23 miles long, an average of a mile wide and reaches depths of 900ft (278m) – that its steep wooded banks form a wind-funnel, causing surprisingly rough waters at times. Before General Wade got to work building roads in the region, Loch Ness was the main artery of communication between the east and west, and even after the roads, Butcher Cumberland kept galleys to patrol the water.

The A82 is the busy main road along the west side of Loch Ness, giving plenty of opportunity to view the loch, but not many stopping places. On the east side, the B862/852, part of it the original Wade road, is much less busy, very attractive, but with fewer views of the loch, some sections being inland. About 10 miles north of Fort Augustus, this road forks: the left branch goes to **Foyers**, where there is a splendid waterfall (except in drought) and attractive woodland walks. The origin of the hotel or 'Kingshouse' here is that of the 'General's Hut' mentioned by Dr Johnson in his journal. Such houses were established at intervals along the roads as they were being built, to house the officers in charge of the labouring troops. In 1773 this one was 'now a house of entertainment for passengers, and we found it not ill stocked with provisions.' From **Inverfarigaig**, about 3 miles northeast of Foyers, there are a number of excavated remains of burial chambers, forts and cairns, some in good condition, including a vitrified Iron Age fort at Ashie Moor, west of Loch Duntelchaig.

Glen Moriston

The A887 runs west through Glen Moriston, from Invermoriston, about 7 miles north of Fort Augustus and this was the route Johnson and Boswell took on their way to Skye. They stayed in the glen; Johnson distributed largesse to a party of soldiers who were mending the road, as a result of which they turned up at the inn, got drunk and 'left blood upon the spot and cursed whisky next morning'.

A cairn stands beside the road near Achlain in memory of a brave, loyal Jacobite, Roderick Mackenzie, a travelling merchant who had the dubious honour of being a Prince Charlie look-alike. He was shot by government troops who mistook him for the Prince, and had the presence of mind to cry out, as he died, 'Villains, you have

The Loch Ness Monster

Feelings run high over Nessie – the Loch Ness Monster – known to the cognoscenti as Nessiteras Rhombopteryx. Sceptics may scoff, but St Adamnan records a sighting of her in his biography of St Columba, when they were sailing up the loch to convert Inverness. Columba, it seems, had a calming effect on her when she threatened one of his monks who was swimming across the mouth of the Ness to fetch Columba a boat. The monster appeared with 'one hideous roar' and made for the swimmer. Columba raised his hand, invoked the name of God and made the sign of the cross, saying: 'Thou shall go no further nor touch the man; go back with all speed.' The monster was terrified, according to Adamnan, and fled 'more quickly than if it had been pulled back with a rope...' and she has never been troublesome again. It must be remembered, however, that Adamnan was writing some hundred years after the event, and viewed St Columba through very rosy spectacles. Setting aside whisky-induced hallucinations, and wishful-thinking sightings, many eye-witness accounts of Nessie come from people whose honesty and integrity are beyond doubt. A 16th-century chronicle describes 'a terrible beast issuing out of the water early one morning about midsummer, knocking down trees and killing three men with its tail.' Curiously, considering how much traffic there used to be on the loch in the old days, almost all sightings have been recent. A monk who was organist at Westminster Cathedral saw her in 1973, and several monks at Fort Augustus Abbey have seen her. In 1961 thirty hotel guests saw two humps appear in an explosion of surf and cruise half a mile before sinking. Bertram Mills was sufficiently convinced to offer £20,000 to have Nessie delivered alive to his circus. However logical and phlegmatic one is, it is impossible to drive down Loch Ness without scanning its dark waters hopefully. Anyone who spends a night at anchor in a boat on the fringes of the loch will find themselves starting up in the darkness every time a ripple slaps the hull.

murdered your Prince!' With great rejoicing the soldiers cut off his head, perhaps in expectation of the £30,000 reward offered for it, and took it to Fort Augustus. A Jacobite prisoner who was asked to identify the head carried the deception further by swearing that it was indeed the Prince, and Butcher Cumberland took it off to London in high glee, giving the Prince enough respite to enable him to reach safety.

The Seven Men of Glen Moriston – three Chisholms, two Macdonalds, a MacGregor and a Grant – swore an oath never to surrender to the English after Culloden. They made their home in a cave in the glen and waged continuous war on Hanoverians and against Highlanders who acted as guides and informers to the army. They evaded capture and did much damage to their enemies. On 29 July 1746 Prince Charles was brought to them in Glen Moriston and they hid and entertained him for three weeks. When he said goodbye, he gave each man three guineas and shook his hand. Afterwards, Hugh Chisholm refrained from giving his right hand to any other person. The A887 joins up with the A87 which runs between Invergarry and Kyle of Lochalsh.

About 7 miles up Loch Ness from Invermoriston on the A82, a simple modern cairn beside the road is a memorial to John Cobb, who was killed on the loch in 1952 trying to beat the world water-speed record in his jet-propelled boat *Crusader*. Travelling at 206mph, it is believed his boat hit floating debris. It disintegrated in a great burst of spray. The memorial is inscribed in Gaelic: 'Honour to the brave and to the humble.'

Urquhart Castle (*www.historic-scotland.gov.uk; open daily April–Sept 9.30–6.30, Oct–Mar 9.30–4.30; adm*) stands on the southern tip of Urquhart Bay, just south of Drumnadrochit. There is free parking off the road from which you get an excellent overview if you can't face the crowds. The castle is impressive – a jagged keep surrounded by crumbling walls which rise sheer from the water, against a backdrop of loch and hills. Built in the 12th century on the site of a vitrified Iron Age fort and frequently fought over, this was once one of the largest castles in Scotland, a motte-and-double-bailey construction guarding the Great Glen. Edward I occupied it in 1296 and 1308; Robert I captured it in 1308 and it became a royal castle. But in 1509, when the Lords of the Isles were forever challenging the authority of the Crown, it was given to John Grant of Freuchie by James IV in the hope that it would help him to maintain peace. Covenanters and Jacobites tried to hold it in their turn and it was finally blown up in 1692 by government troops to save it from Jacobite hands. Romantics believe that Nessie lives in a subterranean cavern beneath the castle. The introductory film in the Visitor Centre is a must, if only for its climactic ending.

There is a choice of Loch Ness Monster exhibitions at **Drumnadrochit**, just north of Castle Urquhart. You won't learn anything from them except that, despite all our modern technology, microchips, satellites, and robots taking holiday snapshots on Mars, Nessie remains an enigma.

From Drumnadrochit the A82 hugs the loch to Loch Dochfour where the River Ness runs in tandem with the canal to Inverness and the sea. The A831 runs westwards along Glen Urquhart to Strathglass. A mile or so along this road you can take an alternative, more attractive route northwards to Inverness on the A833, over wild moor and woodland. The A831 reaches Cannich before turning north and continuing through some lovely glens, best explored separately from Beauly.

Wester Ross and the Northwestern Highlands

11

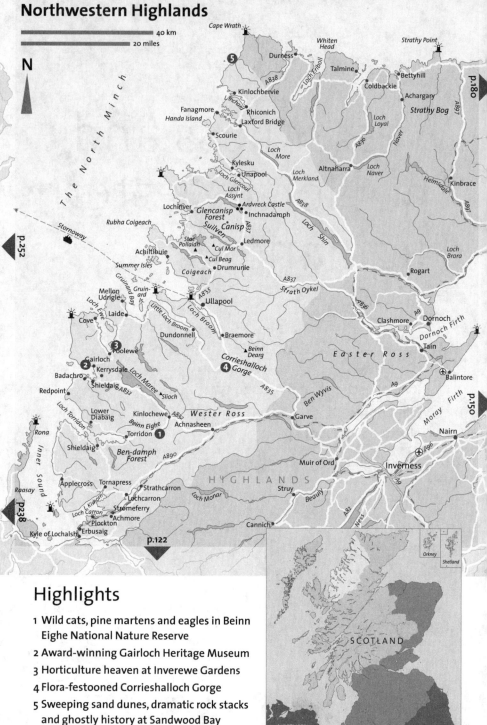

Northwestern Highlands

40 km
20 miles

N

The North Minch

Cape Wrath
Durness
Whiten Head
Strathy Point
Loch Eriboll
Talmine
Bettyhill
Coldbackie
Kinlochbervie
Achargary
Linchad
Rhiconich
Laxford Bridge
Strathy Bog
Fanagmore
Handa Island
Loch Loyal
Scourie
Loch More
Altnaharra
Kylesku
Unapool
Loch Merkland
Loch Naver
Loch Shin
Kinbrace
Helmsdale
Lochinver
Glencanisp Forest
Ardvreck Castle
Inchnadamph
Suilven
Canisp
Ledmore
Loch Brora
Rubha Coigeach
Stac Pollaidh
Cul Mor
Cul Beag
Coigeach
Drumrunie
Rogart
Achiltibuie
Summer Isles
Strath Oykel
Clashmore
Dornoch
Mellon Udrigle
Gruinard Bay
Gruinard Is.
Ullapool
Dornoch Firth
Tain
Loch Ewe
Cove
Laide
Little Loch Broom
Loch Broom
Braemore
Beinn Dearg
Balintore
Poolewe
Dundonnell
Corrieshalloch Gorge
Easter Ross
Gairloch
Kerrysdale
Badachro
Shieldaig
Loch Maree
Slioch
Ben Wyvis
Moray Firth
Redpoint
Lower Diabaig
Kinlochewe
Wester Ross
Garve
Nairn
Loch Torridon
Beinn Eighe
Torridon
Achnasheen
Rona
Shieldaig
Ben-damph Forest
Muir of Ord
Inverness
Inner Sound
Applecross
Tornapress
Strathcarron
HIGHLANDS
Raasay
Lochcarron
Struy
Beauly
Stromeferry
Loch Monar
Achmore
Plockton
Kyle of Lochalsh
Erbusaig
Cannich
Loch Carron

p.180
p.252
p.150
p.238
p.122

ORKNEY
Shetland

SCOTLAND

NORTHERN IRELAND

ENGLAND

Highlights

1 Wild cats, pine martens and eagles in Beinn Eighe National Nature Reserve
2 Award-winning Gairloch Heritage Museum
3 Horticulture heaven at Inverewe Gardens
4 Flora-festooned Corrieshalloch Gorge
5 Sweeping sand dunes, dramatic rock stacks and ghostly history at Sandwood Bay

This northwestern corner of Scotland, known as the Western Routes, offers the traveller a seaboard of unmatchable beauty, one of the few 'last wild places', once you abandon your car. There were virtually no roads in this area until General Wade's military roads were constructed in the first half of the 18th century. When the Highlands were devastated by the potato famine in the middle of the 19th century, Destitution Committees were set up to send supplies of meal and provisions to the starving Highlanders. Some of the 'Destitution Funds' collected were used to build access roads to remote communities, which also provided work for the people.

As in so much of the Highland hinterland, vast areas are totally inaccessible except on foot, but here, there are far fewer of the well-tramped byways festooned with cautionary notices. Your survival off road is up to your own common sense, equipment and experience. The climate is wild rather than harsh – mellow in the summer, gale-torn and often dramatic in the autumn and winter. The people are mainly crofters and fishermen, rapidly adding tourism to their economy.

Kyle of Lochalsh and Around

Kyle of Lochalsh: Skye's Stepping Stone

Until 1995 **Kyle of Lochalsh** was a bustling place, its car park crammed with vehicles waiting for the ferry across the Kyle, cheerful holiday-makers hanging about, stocking up in the shops. Now, with the new bridge marching across the narrow channel, few linger here.

The bridge has a foot planted firmly on Eilean Ban, a tiny island in the Kyle where the writer Gavin Maxwell lived for the last 18 months of his life. One of the rooms in his cottage has been preserved as a memorial, with some of his possessions displayed. However, suggestions for an interpretative centre based on his life and works, with the island conserved as a wildlife haven complete with closed-circuit television to spy on otters, must have that eccentric recluse turning in his grave. One wonders if there is much in the way of wildlife left now that the bridge has brought traffic roaring overhead. The **Bright Water Visitor Centre**, on the Pier at Kyleakin, on Skye (*t (01599) 530 040; open May–Nov; times vary*), runs boat trips to the island.

North of Kyle of Lochalsh

Keep to the left out of Kyle of Lochalsh and follow the road and railway to Plockton. There are lovely views west to Raasay and Skye and north to Applecross.

Plockton, southwest of Loch Carron, was laid out as a planned Highland village in 1794. Once a working fishing village, its smart stone cottages now gleam with fresh paint, and its gardens are adorned with velvet lawns, lush shrubs, birches and pines, even palm trees. Everything is neat and tidy in this 'holiday village'; the upturned fishing boats on shore and the boats on moorings seem carefully arranged for the artists who flock to capture it on canvas. There are craft shops, restaurants and lots of places to stay. From here the road follows the southern shore of Loch Carron to Stromeferry (no ferry now) and up to Strathcarron at the head of the loch. Look in at

Tourist Information

Kyle of Lochalsh: t (01599) 534 276. *Open April–Oct.*

Gairloch: Auchtercairn, t (01445) 712 130.

Sports and Activities

Mountain and Sea Guides, Applecross, t (01520) 744 394, *www.applecross.uk.com.* Hill walking, mountaineering and sea kayaking trips, from half-day trips to week-long expeditions.

Where to Stay

Loch Torridon Hotel, Loch Torridon, t (01445) 791 242, *www.lochtorridonhotel.com* (*expensive*). Baronial mansion overlooking the loch, with shooting lodge ambience.

Little Lodge, North Erradale, near Gairloch, t (01445) 771 237 (*moderate*). Small croft – nicely furnished, glorious views, good food.

Lochalsh Hotel, Kyle of Lochalsh, t (01599) 534 202, *www.lochalshhotel.com* (*moderate*). More peaceful than it used to be, with sea views – near the village centre.

Loch Maree Hotel, Loch Torridon, t (01445) 760 288, *www.lochmareehotel.co.uk* (*moderate*). A splendidly unspoilt hotel serving fine

Scottish cuisine. Also offers wildlife tours of the loch. *See also* p.140.

Shieldaig Lodge, Badachro, t (01445) 741 250, *www.shieldaiglodge.com* (*moderate*). Renowned for its excellent food and cellar. Comfy rooms, splendid situation.

Tigh An Eilean Hotel (*House of the Island*), Shieldaig t (01520) 755 251, (*moderate*). Small hotel with some sea-view rooms. Good food, great hospitality.

Craig Highland Farm, Plockton, t (01599) 544 205, *craighighlandfm@yahoo.co.uk* (*moderate–budget*). B&B or self-catering in stone cottages in glorious settings (sleeps 2–6). Seals, otters and a heronry nearby.

Kyle Hotel, Main Street, Kyle of Lochalsh, t (01599) 534 204, *www.kylehotel.co.uk* (*moderate–budget*). Friendly; on the road.

Lochcarron Hotel, Lochcarron, t (01520) 722 226, *www.lochcarronhotel.co.uk* (*moderate–budget*). Right on the water, with two 'lochside suites'. Lots of local seafood.

The Old Smiddy, Laide, t (01445) 731 425, *www.oldsmiddyguesthouse.co.uk* (*moderate–budget*). B&B, with dinner if required, in a delightful old croft house.

Plockton Hotel, Plockton, t (01599) 544 274, *www.plocktonhotel.co.uk* (*moderate–budget*). Overlooking the water, in converted terraced houses; cosy and good value.

the **West Highland Dairy** at Dailfearn Achmore, near Stromeferry, where they make speciality cheese and dairy products from cow's, goat's and sheep's milk.

Applecross, a mountainous lump to the west of Shieldaig, has no orchards. The name comes from *Aber-Crossan* – the estuary of the Crossan, now the River Applecross. St Maelrubha founded a Celtic Christian community here in 673 which lasted for 200 years until the Vikings destroyed it. Legend has him buried here as well as in a number of other nearby places. There are the remains of a 15th-century chapel which was part of the monastery, and part of a cross slab in the graveyard. Fragments of elaborate stonework survive inside the present church.

A road runs up its eastern side from Loch Kishorn to Loch Shieldaig, and then hugs the coast round to Applecross village and on down to Toscaig in the south west. From the village a road runs back to Tornapress at the head of Loch Kishorn called *Bealach-nam-Ba* – Pass of the Cattle – a steep, narrow road with hairpin bends that make the adrenalin flow, rising to 2,053ft (625m). The scenery is almost alpine, fringed by cliffs and rock spurs, with the distant hills of Skye in the west. Cattle were driven over this pass en route to the lucrative markets on the east coast. In the 18th century there were three blacksmiths working full time to prepare the cattle for the long trek

Seann Bhruthach, at Duirinish near Plockton, t (01599) 544 204, *www.highlandhideaway. co.uk (moderate–budget)*. B&B from a working croft with outstanding views and a warm welcome.

Applecross Flower Tunnel and Campsite, Applecross, t (01520) 744 268,*www.apple- cross-campsite.co.uk. (budget)* First-class facilities, festooned with wonderful blooms and scents – and delicious home-made food. *Open Easter–Oct.*

Applecross Inn, at the sea end of the Pass of the Cattle, Applecross, t (01520) 744 262 *(budget)*. A celestial seafood pub with perfect hospitality and cosy rooms.

Badachro Inn, Badachro, t (01445) 741 255, *www.badachroinn.com (budget)*. Friendly, whitewashed inn with garden on the bay.

Kerrysdale House, Gairloch, t (01445) 712 292, *www.kerrysdalehouse.co.uk (budget)*. Small and cosy.

Rua Reidh Lighthouse, at the end of a 10-mile single-track road from Gairloch to Rua (Rubha) Reidh, t (01445) 771 263, *www.scot- land-info.co.uk/ruareidh.htm (budget)*. An unbeatable position on the peninsula, near wonderful, virtually deserted beaches and cliffs. Rock-climbing courses and walking programmes for all levels of ability.

Sand Hotel, Laide, t 07854 146 184, *www. westhighlands.com (budget)*. Wonderful ocean views and access to hill walking, fishing and water sports. Also has a bistro.

Torridon Youth Hostel, near Redpoint, t 0870 004 1154, *www.syha.org.uk (budget)*.

Where to Eat

The Old Schoolhouse, Erbusaig, t (01599) 534 369, *www.oldschoohouse87.co.uk (moderate)*. Excellent dinners; cosy rooms *April–Oct.*

The Seafood Restaurant, in the long station building, Kyle of Lochalsh, t (01599) 534 813 *(moderate)*. Delicious fresh fish, also good meat and vegetarian dishes.

Seagreen Restaurant and Bookshop, Plockton Road, Kyle of Lochalsh, t (01599) 534 388 *(moderate)*. Relaxed atmosphere with garden, using local seafood and produce.

Kishorn Seafood Bar, Kishorn near Applecross, t (01520) 733 240 *(moderate)*. Deliciously tempting, fresh seafood – eat in or take away.

MacIver Shellfish, Kenmore, west of Shieldaig, t (01520) 755 367 *(moderate)*. Family-run business: choose your own lobster. Also teas and B&B.

Off the Rails, Plockton Station, t (01599) 544 423 *(moderate–inexpensive)*. Convenient and imaginative café/restaurant.

to market; their payment was the heads of all slaughtered cows. An excellent walk from Applecross village takes you northeast along the river valley, through Strath Maol Chaluim, then left to Kenmore (about 8 miles), or right to Inverbain (about 7 miles).

Loch Torridon washes the northern shore of Applecross, with Ben Damph forest to its east, beyond Ben Shieldaig and Loch Damh. There are several good hills to climb including Beinn Damh, Meall a Chinn Deirg (a Munro) and An Ruadh Stac. This is wild, rugged terrain, and very beautiful. The 26,000-acre Torridon Estate, acquired by the National Trust for Scotland, has a visitor centre at the head of Upper Loch Torridon. There is also a deer museum set up by a local man who certainly knows his deer and spares you no detail. Mountains of sandstone, 750 million years old, dominate the whole of this region with their distinctive peaks of quartzite. Queen Victoria was impressed: 'Glen of Torridon opened upon us, with the dark mural precipices of that most extraordinary mountain Ben Liughach, which the people pronounce Liarach...The mountains here rise so abruptly from their base that they seem much higher than our Aberdeenshire mountains, although, excepting Ben Sleach (3,216ft/980m) and a few others, the hills are not of any remarkable height and the level of the country or land itself is barely a hundred feet above the sea, whereas

Balmoral is eight hundred feet to begin with.' Liathach and Beinn Eighe are two of the most popular peaks to climb and there are organized hikes.

The **Beinn Eighe National Nature Reserve** (pronounced Ben Ay), northeast of Torridon, was the first of its kind to be established for the preservation and study of the remains of the Caledonian Forest. Wildlife here includes deer, wild mountain goat, wild cat, pine marten and eagles. The visitor centre at Aultroy Cottage northwest of Kinlochewe, offers advice, a local model and details of the work done on the reserve.

Driving west along the northern shore of Loch Torridon, you pass scattered crofting townships with sea views backed by massive hills. From Lower Diabaig a track continues further round the coast to the Torridon Youth Hostel and from here it is a glorious walk up the rocky, sandy coast to **Redpoint**. The A896 goes northeast through magnificent Glen Torridon, joining the A832 at Kinlochewe, then runs northwest along the southern shore of 12-mile long **Loch Maree**, dominated by Slioch on its opposite side – another Munro. Loch Maree's name derives from St Maelrubha, the monk who founded the monastery at Applecross and lived for a while as a hermit on Isle Maree in the loch. Some say he was buried here; there is certainly a burial ground.

About 8 miles on is the **Loch Maree Hotel** (*see* p.138). Little seems to have changed since Queen Victoria stayed here for six days in 1877. She enjoyed it greatly ('A very nice little house, neatly furnished'), making daily excursions to paint several of her attractive watercolour sketches. The wasps were so bad that gauze netting was put over the open windows. They also had a fair amount of rain and 'the midges are dreadful, and you cannot stand for a moment without being stung' (this was mid-September). Be warned – midges are not respectful of rank. On one of their outings, to Upper Loch Torridon, where the royal party picnicked and sketched, they passed 'a row of five or six wretched hovels, before which stood barelegged and very ill-clad children, and poor women literally squatting on the ground'. On the Sunday, there being no kirk nearby, they read prayers in the hotel, watched locals pass by on foot to church, and later set out in a 'four-oared gig' to visit Eilean Maree. They landed and inspected the well whose waters were said to cure insanity, and hammered pennies into a tree, following an ancient custom; this was a 'clootie well' – a pagan institution.

The A832 leaves Loch Maree soon after the hotel and heads westwards towards Gairloch. At **Kerrysdale**, about 10 miles beyond the hotel, the River Kerry dashes towards the sea through mossy glades and silver birches, with a few gnarled oaks and feathery rowans. A profusion of wild flowers carpets the dappled turf.

Take the very minor cul-de-sac left from Kerrysdale, past the sheltered anchorage of Shieldaig (not to be confused with the other Sheildaig on the Applecross peninsula) and the bay at Badachro. This was once a large fishing station. Now the community life is centred on a tiny, friendly shop-cum-post office. The road, built with money from the Destitution Fund, goes on to Redpoint. Heather-carpeted moorland runs down to rocky cliffs with crescents of red-gold sand below, and stunning sea views. Sit for a while on the sheep-cropped turf above the cliffs. An otter swims in the sea and builds its cone of fish remains; wheatears, ringed plovers, linnets and skylarks fill the air with song; colonies of sea birds mass on the rocks. An old man with piercing blue eyes sits on a rock sucking an empty pipe: 'You could never be bored here', he says, 'if you run out of things to do, you can just watch the weather.'

Back at Kerrysdale turn left to **Gairloch**, a well-developed holiday resort with sandy beaches and several hotels. The hub of the community seems to be the Wild Cat Stores, purveyors of fresh milk, fresh baps and local chat. Opposite is the award-winning **Gairloch Heritage Museum** (*t* *(01445) 712 287, www.gairlochheritagemuseum.org.uk; open April–mid-Oct Mon–Sat 10–5; mid-Oct–end Oct Mon–Fri 10–1.30; or by appt; adm*), well worth a visit. In only a few rooms one can learn a great deal about life in the western Highlands. The exhibits range from Pictish stones and relics to Victoriana, with the highlight being the imaginative replica of the inside of a croft house. You could easily spend a couple of hours in here.

Around Loch Ewe

Poolewe, about 5 miles northeast of Gairloch, is built around a bridge where the mighty force of water from Loch Maree thrusts its way out into Loch Ewe, forming the pool that gave the place its name. Loch Ewe was an important naval base in the Second World War and there are still gun emplacements on its west side.

An attractive dead-end road along the west side of Loch Ewe goes out to **Cove** at the mouth of the loch, where there is a cave so deep and sheltered that it was once used as a place of worship by those who had broken away from the Church of Scotland and found themselves without a kirk in which to worship. Their main complaint was their objection to the Patronage Act of 1712 which gave the local laird the right to appoint ministers regardless of the wishes of the congregation.

Inverewe Gardens (*www.nts.org.uk; garden open daily all year mid-Mar–Oct 9.30–9, Nov–mid-Mar 9.30–4; visitor centre and shop open mid-Mar–Oct daily 9.30–5; restaurant mid-Mar–Oct 10–5; guided garden walks mid-April–mid-Sept Mon–Fri at 1.30; dogs aren't allowed in the garden, and there is no shade in the car park; adm*) owned by the National Trust for Scotland, and half a mile north of Inverewe, is famous to horticulturists all over the world. It was created by Osgood MacKenzie, son of the laird of Gairloch, a Victorian who spent much of his early life on the Continent. If you can find a copy of his book *A Hundred Years in the Highlands* you will never regret buying it. Not only does it give a vivid portrait of life in the Highlands in the 19th century, but it also gives an account of how he established this remarkable garden. His mother, a splendid woman, bought him the land in 1862, and her job was to build the house. The 'policies' consisted of a peninsula – *am ploc*, The High Lump: a high bluff of Torridon sandstone jutting out into the sea, consisting mostly of sheep braes and peat hags, with a narrow strip of land down by the shore. This was to be the garden, Osgood's creation. There was virtually no soil, though in a few places 'peat and rotten rock jumbled up together, which we thought grand stuff in comparison with the rest'. They had to excavate masses of rock; the 'ploc' caught the full force of the prevailing southwesterly gales and was continually soused with salt spray. Osgood, who was 'very young and perfectly ignorant of everything connected with forestry and gardening', learnt entirely by trial and error. There were few roads and soil was carried in wicker creels. 'For four or five years my poor peninsula looked miserable, and all who had prophesied evil of it, and they were many, said "I told you so"." Plants were introduced from all over the world and he was not ashamed to admit that many of these did far better than native stock. Now there are some 2,500 species in 50 acres of woodland. The garden lies only a little to the south of the latitude that runs through Cape Farewell in Greenland – it is the proximity of the Gulf Stream together with years of hard labour and acquired expertise that have led to this exotic, subtropical paradise. Osgood's daughter, Mairi T Nic Coinnich, inherited the garden in 1922; she made it over to the National Trust for Scotland in 1952.

Gruinard Bay

Gruinard, about 11 miles north of Poolewe, has sandy beaches surrounded by hills and good views out to the Summer Isles. It is a magnificent spot with a camp site right on the beach at Mellon Udrigle. Gruinard Island, in the bay, has been much publicized over the years; in 1942 the Ministry of Defence wished to experiment with *Bacillus anthracis* (anthrax) as a weapon of biological warfare. Some scientists from Porton Down in Wiltshire descended upon the island that winter and exploded six small bombs of anthrax. They then beat a hasty retreat, leaving a flock of sheep. The sheep died within days. The island was sealed off with alarming notices warning the public not to go anywhere near it: Contaminated! It is said that anthrax spores can live on for a thousand years, but in 1987 a second team of scientists arrived, 'decontaminated' the soil, and, pronouncing it safe, restored it to its original owner.

A small sign beside the road at **Sand**, to the east of **Laide** on the southwest corner of Gruinard Bay, points out a cliff path to two caves. The largest was a meeting place for hundreds of years and was used as a church by dis-established Presbyterians as late as 1843. The smaller cave was inhabited by an old woman and her girl companion in 1885. Families evicted from their crofts during the Clearances used to take shelter here. It is an idyllic place now, but must have been much less so for those huddled together inside with what they had saved of their possessions and livestock.

The A832 skirts Little Loch Broom (the Ardressie Falls about two-thirds of the way along are worth a look), and cuts across the moors. The road from Dundonnell, by Feithean, to Braemore Junction was another of the Destitution Roads built during the potato famine. Despite its gloomy origins, it's a lovely drive today. **Braemore Junction** is at the confluence of the rivers Broom, Cuileig and Droma, known locally as 'the Valley of the Broom'. Stop at the large observation car park just before the A835 and look down into the junction of the three valleys, the steep wooded banks ablaze with colour in autumn. Less than a mile further on, a sign on the left marks the Corrieshalloch Gorge and the Falls of Measach, only a short walk from the road. An alternative approach on the A835, round the corner, has another car park and signs.

Corrieshalloch Gorge (*for up-to-date access information, see www.nts.org.uk or* **t** *(01445) 781200*) is unforgettable – a mile-long box canyon, 200ft (60m) deep and between 50ft and 150ft wide (15–46m), its sheer rock walls festooned with flora of all description. There is an observation platform from which to view the Falls of Measach, a single cascade of 150ft (46m) that seems to hang in the air like smoke. For those who don't suffer from vertigo, there is a much better view from the suspension bridge that spans the gorge, erected in the 19th century by Sir John Fowler who also designed the famous Forth Railway Bridge. The deep pools below are rich in trout, and above the roar of the falls the angry 'pruk' of ravens can be heard from their nests on a ledge opposite the viewing platform. The A835 takes you back down to the A832 at Gorstan and on to Dingwall and Inverness.

Ullapool

Ullapool is about 13 miles from the Corrieshalloch Gorge, another beautiful drive down the River Broom, with Lael Forest to the east and lumpy hills to the west across the valley. (The Lael Forest Garden Trail has over 150 different labelled species of trees and shrubs.) There are good views across Loch Broom, fringed with beaches and picturesque picnic spots. Herring fishing was the main activity here, but by 1830 herring stocks were dwindling and the industry was in decline. The railway never got there and in 1900 the enterprise was considered a 'dismal failure', its carefully designed grid-plan town downgraded to a 'dreary fishing village'. Then the road improved and east-coast trawlers in the 1920s discovered Ullapool's excellent deep-water anchorage and sheltered harbour. It became a popular rendezvous for factory ships from Eastern Europe and Russia; today you see them out at anchor in the bay.

After the boats came the tourists, and Ullapool is now a thriving holiday resort and the ferry terminus for boats to Stornoway on Lewis. Freshly painted houses, many of them dating from the 18th-century birth of the town, line the sea front in an original curving terrace, some looking down on the jumble of quays and slipways cluttered

Tourist Information

Ullapool: Argyle Street, t (01854) 612 135. *Open all year.*

Sports and Activities

Local boats visit the Summer Isles in season.
Summer Queen Cruises, Ullapool, t (01854) 612 472, *www.summerqueen.co.uk.* Offer cruises on Loch Broom and to the Summer Isles, giving the opportunity of spotting seals, bird life and dolphins.

Where to Stay and Eat

Morefield Hotel, Ullapool, t (01854) 612 161/171 (*moderate*). Good for gourmets.
Tanglewood House, Ullapool, t (01854) 612 059, *www.tanglewoodhouse.co.uk* (*moderate*). A Wolsey Lodge perched up

above Loch Broom, with panoramic views. Innovative cooking. No smoking.
The Céilidh Place, Ullapool, t (01854) 612 103, *www.theceilidhplace.com* (*moderate–budget*). Highly popular Arts Centre where you can stay, eat wonderful seafood, and sometimes listen to live music. It's also a place to visit for its coffee shop and bookshop.
Ardvreck Guest House, North Road, Morefield, near Ullapool, t (01854) 612 028, *ardvreck.guesthouse@btinternet.com* (*budget*). An excellent place overlooking Loch Broom. No licensed bar.
Ardmair Point Chalets, Ullapool, t (01854) 612 054, *www.ardmair.com* (£235–575 pw). Self-catering bungalow-type chalets and houses with lovely views (sleeps 4–8).
Mrs J. Scobie, Rhidorroch, t (01854) 612 548, *www.rhidorroch.com* (£210–380pw). Country house accommodation and converted self-catering estate houses (sleeps 6).

with small boats and fishing gear. **Ullapool Museum and Visitor Centre** (*West Argyle Street; open April–Oct Mon–Sat 9.30–5.30, Nov–Feb Wed, Thurs, Sat 11–3, March Mon–Sat 10–3; adm*) in a converted grade A-listed church, charts the development of the fishing industry and tells about life in the area from the arrival of the earliest settlers, with good audiovisuals you can watch from the old kirk pews.

There is a large range of shops, restaurants, cafés, bars and accommodation. The tourist office will arrange sea fishing and boat cruises, or you can hang about on the quay and ask someone off one of the boats. Across the loch at Lagaidh, Glasgow's Hunterian Museum has excavated a 1st millennium BC vitrified fort, an early AD broch, and remains of a 12th-century motte-and-bailey castle.

North of Ullapool

North of Ullapool you can be fairly sure that any track you take to the west will have a pot of gold at the end of it. The main road (A835/837) gives you a foretaste, but push west wherever you can. About 7 miles beyond Ullapool, turn left off the A835 at Drumrunie. A narrow single track winds out through a wild landscape of hills and lochs to the Coigeach Peninsula – you must walk the last couple of miles to Rubha Coigeach for windswept, uninterrupted views across the Minch to the Outer Isles. Down the western side of the peninsula is **Achiltibuie**, remote but a favourite spot for family holidays. There is everything from walking and climbing, to fishing, boating, lovely beaches and trips to the Summer Isles. Well-known and interesting is the **Summer Isles Garden of the Future**, or **Hydroponicum**, near the hotel (*www. thehydroponicum.com; open daily Easter–end Sept 10–6; 1 hour tours every hour on the hour; Oct Mon–Fri 11.30–3.30, tours 12 and 2; adm*). When its creator, Robert Irvine, took over the Summer Isles Hotel, he wanted to provide his guests with fresh fruit and vegetables daily. Poor communications and remote markets, combined with poor soil and an unfriendly climate for agriculture, made it almost impossible. Hence the ingenious 'hi-tech soil-less growing houses' which emulate the climates of Hampshire, Bordeaux and the Canaries. Strawberries are picked fresh daily April to October, and bananas flourish. Figs, lemons, passion fruit, vines, vegetables, flowers and herbs grow luxuriantly in greenhouses. The tour is quite instructive on solar energy.

Five miles northwest is the **Achiltibuie Smokehouse** (*open May–Sept Mon–Sat; Oct–April weekdays*), where fish and meat are cured and there is a retail shop.

The sixteen or so **Summer Isles**, scattered across the mouth of Loch Broom, were put on the map by Sir Frank Fraser Darling, a self-important ecologist who farmed the largest island, Tanera Mor, for five years during the Second World War and wrote of it in *Island Farm*. He also wrote *Natural History of the Highlands and Islands*, which experts savaged as a lack of true scholarship and knowledge. Over 100 people lived on Tanera Mor in 1881; by 1931 it was uninhabited. Some cottages are now holiday lets. Groups of self-sufficiency dreamers have tried to settle permanently, but none have lasted. Priest Island and Isle Martin are RSPB bird sanctuaries.

Tourist Information

Lochinver: Main Street, t (01571) 844 330. *Open Easter–Oct.*

Where to Stay and Eat

Inver Lodge Hotel, Lochinver, t (01571) 844 496, *www.inverlodge.com (expensive)*. Modern and luxurious, in a lovely position and excellent food, but lacks traditional character.

Summer Isles Hotel, Achiltibuie, t (01854) 622 282, *www.summerisleshotel.co.uk (expensive)*. Exceptionally comfortable country-house-style rooms in a spectacular, remote setting. *Haute cuisine* meals using foods produced on their own grounds. *Open April–Oct.*

The Albannach, Lochinver, t (01571) 844 407, *www.thealbannach.co.uk (expensive–moderate)*. Friendly place with imaginative furnishings and Victoriana. Good locally produced food served in a cosy restaurant. *Open Mar–Dec.*

Kinlochbervie Hotel, Kinlochbervie, t (01971) 521 275, *www.kinlochberviehotel.com (moderate)*. Inn overlooking the harbour. Well equipped for families, friendly, with comfortable rooms and good food: a nice place for refreshments after a walk to Sandwood Bay.

Kylesku Hotel, Loch Glendhu, t (01971) 502 231, *www.kyleskuhotel.co.uk (moderate)*. Cottage-style inn with good views and cosy, pretty rooms, and freshly caught seafood.

Newton Lodge, Kylesku, t (01971) 502 070 *(moderate)*. Wonderful position, with good food and relaxed Highland hospitality.

Old School Hotel, Inshegra, Kinlochbervie, t (01971) 521 383, *www.oldschoolhotel.co.uk (moderate)*. Loch views, with school memorabilia as decoration – meals with plenty of seafood fresh from the loch. Cheerfully furnished rooms in an annexe.

Scourie Hotel, Scourie, t (01971) 502 396, *www.scourie-hotel.co.uk (moderate)*. Fishermen's trophies adorn the walls here, all of them fish caught in one of the 250 lochs the hotel has rights to. Simple décor.

Inchnadamph Lodge, Elphin, Assynt, t (01571) 822 218, *www.inch-lodge.co.uk (budget)*. Splendid backpackers' hostel in a former Highland Shooting Lodge, with dormitories and private rooms, self-catering facilities, and an on-site shop for snacks and stores.

Lochinver House Travel Lodge, Lochinver, t (01571) 844 270 *(budget)*. Unpretentious place overlooking the harbour; few frills but inviting atmosphere.

Mr and Mrs MacLeod, Dornie House, Achiltibuie, t (01854) 622 271 *(budget)*. The best B&B in the area, in a modern bungalow with stunning views and a warm welcome. Breakfast is supreme. *Open Easter–Oct.*

Riverside Bistro, Lochinver, t (01571) 844 356 *(moderate)*. Good choice of excellent food.

Tarbet Café/Bistro, Tarbet, near Scourie, t (01971) 502 251 *(inexpensive)*. Delicious, fresh seafood and very good value.

Lilypond Café, the Hydroponicum, Achiltibuie, t (01854) 622 202. Sample delicious produce here without touring the Hydroponicum.

The **Inverpolly National Nature Reserve** spreads across the northeast of the Coigeach Peninsula, distinguished by the great lumps of Cul Beag, Stac Pollaidh and Stac Mor. The silhouette of Stac Pollaidh with its dramatic jagged ridge is familiar from photographs. The red sandstone is eroding alarmingly and several of its pinnacles have been lost in recent years – you can see chips and chunks scattered down the hillside. Stac Mor is the highest of these three and the views from the summit are stunning, but Stac Pollaidh is the most satisfying climb. There are several ways up, the shortest being a steep scramble from the car park at the bridge over the burn coming down from Coire Gorm, 5 miles along the road from Drumrunie. The path up the grassy hillside to below the summit is steep and earthy. From here you can explore the fantastic pinnacles but watch out for loose scree.

Ledmore is less than 8 miles beyond Drumrunie, where the A835 joins the A837. To the southeast the road runs 30 miles back to Bonar Bridge, through Strath Oykel. Inchnadamph at the head of Loch Assynt is about 5 miles north of Ledmore, along a passageway through the hills.

Assynt

There's a tortuous but spectacular drive to Loch Assynt and the north via the very minor road up the coast, starting from the Coigeach Peninsula. Turn right at Badagyle beyond Loch Badagyle and twist your way up to Lochinver at the head of Loch Inver, with Stac Polly, Cul Mor and Suilven towering to the east and an ever-changing seascape to the west. **Lochinver** is a holiday resort, working fishing port and the only place of any size between Ullapool and Scourie. Even in this remote place there is a visitor centre – quite a good one, with information about the local wildlife. Close by are several pleasant sandy coves. Cruises run from the village in the summer with a chance to see some of the many birds and seal colonies around the coast. The **West Highland Stoneware Potteries** (*www.highlandstoneware.com,* **t** *(01571) 844 376*), in Lochinver, is a marvellous working pottery. It has a shop, and some of the seconds are true bargains (they also have a place in North Road, Ullapool). This is a popular centre for fishermen and climbers. Suilven – the Sugar Loaf (2,399ft/738m) – was called the Pillar Mountain by the Vikings and the Grey Castle by the Gaels. It is a fairly serious scramble over not too difficult ground, easy to navigate and taking about 8 hours for the round trip. Start from the parking area at the end of the road east from Lochinver, walk through the grounds of Glencanisp Lodge and go left when you reach Loch Druin Suardalain. A good stalkers' track runs east to the hill through lochans and rocks, and from there on the way is obvious. If you don't want to climb, walk out from Inverkirkaig, a couple of miles south of Lochinver, to the Falls of Kirkaig along the signed track.

Loch Assynt, dark and mysterious, holds memories of betrayal. **Ardvreck Castle**, a jagged fang of a ruin three storeys high, stands on a turf-covered rocky peninsula on the northeast shore. It dates from the 15th century and was owned by the Macleods who had held the Assynt lands since the 13th century. There are conflicting stories about what happened here in 1650. James Graham, Marquis of Montrose, fighting for the cause of Charles II, fled here after his defeat at the Battle of Carbisdale, near Bonar Bridge. Some say he threw himself on the mercy of the Macleod laird, who then sold him to the government for £20,000 and 400 bolls of meal – which turned out to be sour. Others say that Macleod found and captured him honourably.

Whatever the truth, Montrose was imprisoned in this grim fortress before being taken to Edinburgh, tied back-to-front on his horse, where he was hung and disembowelled, without trial. (Over 200 years later a tomb and monument were erected for him, at St Giles in Edinburgh.) Charles II, for whom he had given up everything, had by now settled affairs with his lords and chose not to intervene. In the words of a biographer, Montrose 'presents a standard of honesty, generosity and decent dealing which is conspicuously absent in 17th-century Scottish politics.

Companions fought and died for him and enemies marvelled at the courage with which he met his execution.'

In caves near **Inchnadamph**, 2 miles south of Ardvreck, archaeologists have found evidence of early man, including carefully buried skeletons, charred bones and stones. They also found the bones of arctic animals going back at least 10,000 years.

Take the coast road north from Lochinver (the B869) if you've time. It's about 35 miles at a snail's pace, and though slower than the route inland via the A837 and A894, it is really stunning. At **Kylesku**, by Unapool, a bridge whips you across the narrows where Lochs Glendhu and Glencoul flow into Loch Cairnbawn and out to Eddrachillis Bay and the Atlantic. A tiny ferry used to be the only way north from here, holding up traffic for hours in the holiday season and giving time to wander and wonder. The old jetty is still a hive of activity with a very nice old inn perched above it, and chalked notices saying when fresh prawns and langoustine will be for sale. It's a favourite meeting place for seals.

Boats run from **Unapool**, down Loch Glencoul to see **Eas 'Chual Aluinn**, Britain's highest waterfall at 658ft (202m), four times the height of Niagara and higher than the Falls of Glomach in Kintail. Sometimes called 'the Maiden's Tresses', its Gaelic name means 'the splendid waterfall of Glencoul'. And very splendid it is, thundering down in staggers of glistening tresses splintered by the rocks. You can walk out to it along a track that leaves the A894 three miles short of Unapool, past Loch Gainmhich under the northern flank of Glas Bheinn. However, it is quite tricky to find and the boat trip is fun, with occasional glimpses of minke whales if you are lucky.

For a highly rewarding walk, take the stalkers' track west, about 4 miles north of Inchnadamph – there is a car park on the right – and aim for Quinag. Walk across the moor to the foot of the southeast ridge of Spidean Coinich and climb the edge of the escarpment. From here you can get to the summit of Quinag and explore its Y-shaped crests, with amazing views of the west coast.

Scourie

Scourie is about 8 miles north on the A894, a sheltered village within the arms of Scourie Bay with sandy beaches and rock pools, slightly spoiled by a camping ground overlooking the bay. The mild climate supports several varieties of orchid and an Atlantic palm. It is a trout fisherman's haven but there is much else for the outward bounder to do. Boats run from **Tarbet** (north of Scourie) to **Handa Island** (*t (01971) 502 340*), north of Scourie bay, a 760-acre lump of Torridon sandstone and moorland, with 400ft guano-splashed cliffs – an ornithologists' paradise. A variety of sea birds congregate on Handa, including razorbills, guillemots, kittiwakes and skua – watch out for the skua who dive bomb intruders remorselessly. Puffins dig their burrows in the turf and can be seen strutting about guarding their offspring in summer. This is a Scottish Wildlife Trust sanctuary, uninhabited except by a warden. A self-governing community of some 12 families lived here off potatoes, fish and sea birds until the potato famine in 1847, when they were forced to emigrate to Canada. They had their own queen, the oldest widow in the community, who reigned supreme even over mainland royalty, and the men met each morning to settle the day's business. Boats run intermittently to Tarbet until 4pm and there's also a postbus from Scourie.

The road northeast from Scourie joins the A838 at **Laxford Bridge**, another centre for fishermen. Here the A838 leading southeast heads to Lairg through rocky hills that tower menacingly over the road with sharp turns and blind summits. On a sunny day the sparkling waters of Lochs More, Merkland and Shin make this a magic drive, but on a grey, sullen day of mist and rain it can be melancholy.

Rhiconich, 4 miles north of Laxford Bridge at the head of Loch Inchard, is where the fish lorries turn off to **Kinlochbervie**, now one of Scotland's main fishing ports. As long ago as 1840, the minister of Eddrachillis remarked on the excellence of the coast's harbours and pronounced: 'they are sufficient to afford safe anchorage to the whole naval and mercantile shipping of Great Britain.' Lorries arrive at this benighted spot to collect the catches of the trawlers. It is fun to watch the boats come in after weeks at sea and unload on the teeming quays, where sometimes you can buy a bag of fish from an obliging skipper. Once loaded, the lorries set off to drive to Aberdeen for the early morning market. Many of the fishermen come from the east and set off home late on Friday night, returning at the crack of dawn on Monday. Strong currents around the northern headland make swimming extremely dangerous here – beware.

Drive on past Kinlochbervie to Sheigra where a signpost marks the start of the 4½-mile walk out to **Sandwood Bay**, a 1½-mile sweep of empty sand dunes and dramatic rock stacks considered by some to be the most beautiful beach in Scotland, although it's not safe for swimming. Sandwood's ghost has been experienced too often to be a myth. He is a bearded seaman with a peaked cap and brass buttons on his coat, thought to have been the victim of one of the many shipwrecks on this treacherous coast. Leaving no footprints in the sand, he threatened two local men who were collecting driftwood, and appeared to some men from Kinlochbervie who were looking for stray sheep. He made his presence felt to campers near Sandwood cottage, now untenanted, and on one occasion a visitor to the cottage was woken in the night by 'a thick blackness' that pressed down on him. His most recent appearance was not so long ago when he passed a honeymooning couple on the path and vanished when they greeted him. They had not been told about him beforehand. There was a settlement here, evacuated after the potato famine, and it is possible that the mortal remains of the sailor lie in the old burial ground now obliterated by sand. A great many people say they get a feeling of oppressive doom here. On a sunny day it is glorious. From Rhiconich, the 15-mile drive north to Durness is through a bleak wilderness of rock-strewn glens, forbidding hills and dark, sombre lochs.

Inverness and Around

12

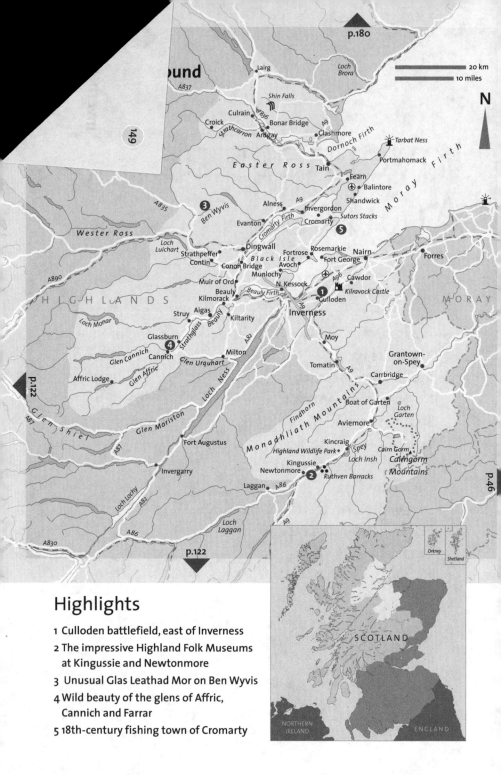

Highlights

1 Culloden battlefield, east of Inverness
2 The impressive Highland Folk Museums at Kingussie and Newtonmore
3 Unusual Glas Leathad Mor on Ben Wyvis
4 Wild beauty of the glens of Affric, Cannich and Farrar
5 18th-century fishing town of Cromarty

With the capital of the Highlands at its heart, this area is more populated and prosperous than its northern and western neighbours. Large sporting estates attract southern and foreign visitors, there is good skiing from Aviemore – and infinite scope for climbers and walkers both in the hills and in the fertile straths – and historic castles and battle sites bear witness to a violent history. Hard winters give way to often hot summers, though snow lies all year in north-facing corries. There is some good farmland here, but the economy is turning more and more to tourism.

Inverness

As the capital of the Highlands with its newly acquired 'city' status, and as the junction of many routes, Inverness – from *Inbhir* ('mouth' of) the River Ness – is a good base for exploring the north of Scotland. The river flows through the heart of the 5,000-year-old city, which was the first place where people could ford it at low tide, the sea and hills forcing travellers from all directions to pass through a bottle-neck. Being also the navigable limit of the Moray Firth, with a good sheltered harbour at the river mouth, Inverness became a focal point of trade routes. Trade brought prosperity and the threat of attack. From early times Inverness was of strategic importance – whoever controlled the ford controlled the northern Highlands.

History

Traces of ancient forts, castles and garrisons scattered in and around the town bear witness to thousands of years of struggle to gain and hold this vital area. The early population probably lived in small farming and fishing communities dotted around the coast and in the river valleys, adjacent to a hill fort where they and their livestock could seek refuge in times of danger. **Craig Phadraig**, the small hill just west of the town, has impressive remains of a 4th-century vitrified fort.

St Columba is recorded by his biographer, St Adamnan, as having visited and converted the Pictish King Brude in a castle somewhere near the River Ness in AD 565. This could have been the one on Craig Phadraig – the old Gaelic name for which was *Larach an tigh mhor*: 'site of the great house' – which was still used in Brude's time. But the fort was partially ruined by the 6th century. It is more likely that Brude's stronghold stood on Castle Hill, where the castle stands today. (According to St Adamnan, Columba's first task was to get past the king's druids, which he did by singing Psalm 46, 'God is our Refuge and our Strength', so loud that the druids gave way.)

Macbeth arrived four and a half centuries later, disposed of King Duncan and took the Crown of Scotland. His stronghold was almost certainly at the eastern end of what is still known as the Crown area of the city, and still referred to as Auldcastle. Historical fact and poetic fiction have become so inextricably interwoven around the story of Macbeth and his bloodstained journey to the throne that there are several different claims for the setting of King Duncan's murder in 1039. The most reliable sources say the deed was not done in Macbeth's castle in Inverness but in a house

Tourist Information

Castle Wynd, t (01463) 234, 353, *www.visit highlands.com*. Provides details of events in Inverness, including September's **Northern Meeting Piping Competition**.

Guide Friday, railway station, **t** (01463) 224 000. Tours on an open-top double decker bus. *May–early Oct daily*.

Ken White, t (01463) 223 168. Conducts minibus tours, including Loch Ness.

Tartan Taxis, t (01463) 233 033, *tartantaxis.org*. Tours over a wide area, including one to Skye.

Shopping

Kiltmaker Visitor Centre, 4–9 Huntly Street. Watch kilts being made by hand.

Pringle Woollen Mill, Holm Mills, Dores Road. 200-year-old weaving mill with tartan centre and restaurant. Demonstrations, displays, and excellent bargains. *Open daily*.

Sports and Activities

Cabin cruisers can be hired from the marinas and passenger cruises run in the summer.

Caley Cruisers, Canal Road, **t** (01463) 236 328, *www.caleycruisers.com*. One of the best, with a fleet of 50 cruise boats. Canal charges included (sleeps 2–8).

Loch Ness and Great Glen Cruise Co, from Top Lock, Canal Road, **t** (01463) 711 913, *www. lochnessboat.com* (*expensive*). Splendid old converted barge runs jolly 3-night cruises. *April–Oct and winter charter*.

Jacobite Cruises, t (01463) 233 999, *www.jacobite.co.uk*. Offer steamer cruises on Loch Ness.

Inverness Aquadome, Bught Park, **t** (01463) 667 500. Everything a swimmer could want, with whirlpools etc. *Open daily; adm*.

Sports Centre, Bught Park, **t** (01463) 667 505. Games, fitness classes, martial arts etc.

Inverness Cruises, Shore Street Quay, **t** (01463) 717 900. Dolphin-spotting cruises. *Mar–Oct daily*.

Edencourt Theatre, t (01463) 234 234/239 841.

Ice Rink, Bucht Park, **t** (01463) 235 711.

Warner Bros Multiplex Cinema, Eastfield Way, **t** (01463) 711 175.

Tenpin Bowling, 167 Culduthel Road, **t** (01463) 235 100.

Where to Stay

Bunchrew House Hotel, Bunchrew, 5 miles west of Inverness on the south side of the Beauly Firth, **t** (01463) 234 917, *www.bunchrew-inverness.co.uk* (*expensive*). A Victorian mansion in 15 acres – comfortable, full of atmosphere, peaceful with good food.

Culduthel Lodge, 14 Culduthel Road, **t** (01463) 240 089, *www.culduthel.com* (*expensive*). Elegant Georgian mansion on B861 overlooking the River Ness, with every possible comfort.

Dunain Park, on the road to Fort William, **t** (01463) 230 512, *www.dunainparkhotel. co.uk* (*expensive*). Quiet but convivial mansion-house hotel, with swimming pool and excellent food.

Inverness Marriott, Culcabock Road, **t** (01463) 257 106, *www.marriotthotels.co.uk*

near Elgin, though it was the one at Auldcastle that Malcolm Canmore destroyed in revenge. A new castle was built on Castle Hill in the 12th century and was much abused in subsequent years. The English occupied it in the War of Independence and Robert the Bruce destroyed it. Mary, Queen of Scots hanged its rebellious governor from the ramparts when he refused her entry in 1562. Jacobites occupied it twice and blew it up in February 1746 to keep it from government hands. Johnson and Boswell visited the site of this ruin on Castle Hill, mistaking it for Macbeth's castle, which didn't deter Boswell from having 'a romantick satisfaction in seeing Dr Johnson actually in it. It perfectly corresponds with Shakspear's description, which Sir Joshua Reynolds has so happily illustrated.'

(*expensive-moderate*). Set in an old family home, but with the full whack of facilities.

Birkwood, near Croy, t (01667) 493 376 (*moderate*). B&B in a splendid house with good views – very inviting.

Brae Ness Hotel, Ness Bank, t (01463) 712 266, *www.braenesshotel.co.uk* (*moderate*). Family-run, good-value Georgian house, with original character.

Columba Hotel, Ness Walk, t (01463) 231 391, *www.swallowhotels.com* (*moderate*). A 4-star hotel overlooking the river up to the castle. Takes bus parties and offers nightly Scottish entertainment.

Maple Court Hotel, 12 Ness Walk, t (01463) 230 330, *www.maplecourthotel.co.uk* (*moderate*). In attractive surroundings beside the river and only a few minutes from the town centre – good food.

Moyness House Hotel, 6 Bruce Gardens, t (01463) 233 836, *www.moyness.co.uk* (*moderate*). 5-star guesthouse, elegantly furnished in nice grounds, once the home of the writer Neil Gunn.

Royal Highland Hotel, Station Road, t (01463) 231 926, *www.royalhighlandhotel.co.uk* (*moderate*). Wonderfully traditional and comfortable, with an air of genteel respectability; on the expensive side though, and offers unexciting food.

The Steadings Grouse and Trout, Flichity Farr, in Strathnairn, east of Loch Ness, on the old route to Fort Augustus, t (01808) 521 314, *www.steadingshotel.co.uk* (*moderate*). In a converted farm steading – acclaimed by fishermen. Cosy comfort and warm hospitality, with excellent food.

Felstead House, Ness Bank, t (01463) 231 634, *www.jafsoft.com/felstead/felstead.html*

(*budget*). Opposite Eden Court, a family-run guesthouse – good value and friendly.

Glendruidh House, Old Edinburgh Road, t (01463) 226 499 (*budget*). Just outside the city centre, with nice views and ambience.

Taigh na Teile, 6 Island Bank Road, t (01463) 222 842 (*budget*). B&B with first-class breakfasts.

Eating Out

Dunain Park, *see* 'Where to Stay', opposite (*expensive*). Has excellent food, and the price is reasonable for what you get.

La Riviera, part of the Glenmoriston Hotel, Ness Bank, t (01463) 223 777 (*expensive–moderate*). An up-market favourite, on the river, with an Italian slant.

Café One, Castle Street, t (01463) 226 200 (*moderate*). Booking is advisable.

Hootananny, 67 Church Street, t (01463) 233651 (*moderate*). Bar/restaurant; live Scottish music.

The Mustard Seed, 16 Fraser Street, t (01463) 220 220 (*moderate*). A good reputation for food and service; overlooks the river.

River Café, 10 Bank Street, t (01463) 714 884 (*moderate*). Smallish place with an excellent fish menu; local dishes too.

Edencourt Theatre, *see* 'Sports and Activities, opposite (*moderate–inexpensive*). Good self-service food and refreshment.

The Castle Restaurant, by the main tourist information centre, t (01463) 230 925 (*inexpensive*). Excellent simple food.

Riva, Ness Walk, t (01463) 237 377. Delicious Italian food, pastries and coffee.

Chili Palmers, Queensgate. A continental-style bar with a lively atmosphere.

In the Middle Ages, Inverness developed further as a port and shipbuilding centre with important European trade links, and it became the focus for clashes between the chiefs of the Highlands and Islands and the Scottish Crown.

Mary, Queen of Scots came here in 1563, and was entranced by Highland life. She adopted Highland dress and forced some of her courtiers into plaids. General Monk, Commander in Scotland under Cromwell, built the Citadel here, a polygonal artillery fort in the harbour, using stones from the ruined abbeys nearby, and from the castle on Ormond Hill. It was obliterated after the Restoration. In Queen Victoria's time Inverness became the hub of the Highlands, with its converging routes and new railway, and grand new Highland mansions on sporting estates mushroomed.

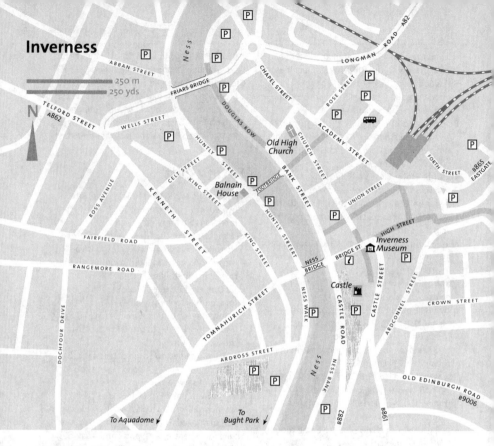

Visiting the Town

Inverness is now the communications and administrative centre for the north of Scotland. Its 19th-century castle, which houses the law courts and local government offices, looks brand new, its bare walls rising from Castle Hill like a toy fort. Although not outstandingly beautiful, Inverness has a certain sturdy charm. From the bridge below Bridge Street, you can view fishermen thigh-deep in the fast-flowing river, flanked by well-proportioned houses and churches. When the sun shines, it is a curiously Continental scene. Station Square, in the middle of the compact city centre, has a splendid war memorial statue of a Cameron Highlander, erected in 1893 to mark the centenary of the local regiment, the Camerons. Unfortunately, chain department stores mean you must often search to find traces of a more gracious past.

Inverness Museum and Gallery (*open Mon–Sat 9–5; closed local hols*) in Castle Wynd, has displays of social and natural history, Highland culture and Jacobite relics. There are exhibitions, talks and slide shows, and the Art Gallery includes views of Old Inverness. There is a shop and café. The **Castle Gallery**, in Castle Street, displays work by contemporary artists and sells a good range of up-market gifts and craft work.

St Andrew's Cathedral, south of the Ness Bridge, was the first cathedral to be built in Britain after the Reformation, in 1869. The elaborate interior includes five gold icons, presented by the Tsar of Russia. **Eden Court**, beyond the cathedral, is a glass edifice built in 1976, incorporating the 19th-century house of Bishop Eden. Inside is an 800-seat multipurpose theatre, conference centre, art gallery and an excellent restaurant. Up-river from Eden Court, **Ness Islands** form a public park spread over a series of small islands in the river, and linked by footbridges, with views towards the town.

Art.tm (*20 Bank Street, t (01463) 712 240, www.arttm.org.uk*), a very trendy art gallery, is well worth a visit, as is **Bught Floral Hall and Visitor Centre** (*Bught Lane, t (01463) 222 755; open daily; adm*), an indoor tropical garden. **Castle Garrison** (*3 Connel Court, t (01463) 243 363; open Easter–Nov Mon–Sat; adm*) relives the years of the last Jacobite rising.

Tomnahurich – Hill of the Yews, or Hill of the Fairies – is the boat-shaped hillock to the southwest. Two wandering fiddlers, Thomas and Farquhar, were lured to the place by the Fairy Queen, to play for a night's dancing. In the morning they found the town and its people strangely altered and everyone laughing at them. The 'night' had lasted a hundred years. They crept into a church for refuge – and crumbled into dust. Tomnahurich is now the city's cemetery, with many elaborate monuments clinging to the steep, wooded slopes, and a splendid viewing point. Below lie the environs of Inverness, with neat villas and gardens, and an air of solid respectability.

The northern entrance to the 19th-century **Caledonian Canal** is in the western suburbs. The canal, constructed by Thomas Telford, was a considerable feat of engineering, linking Loch Ness, Loch Oich and Loch Lochy to form a 65-mile waterway between the east and west coasts. Before its construction, large vessels circumnavigated Scotland via the Pentland Firth, a hazardous slog due to harsh conditions and marauding privateers. The canal is still used by fishing boats, but nowadays is mostly the haunt of pleasure craft, being a perfect way for sailors to explore the Great Glen.

Like a wise old sentinel on guard, 19th-century **Cameron Barracks** stands on Knockentinnel – the Rallying Hill – on the eastern edge of Inverness. From here, many a brave young Cameron Highlander walked out, newly trained, ready to give his life so that his Highland home should remain free. The Camerons joined with the Seaforth Highlanders in the early 1960s, becoming the Queen's Own Highlanders, who then joined with the Gordon Highlanders to become The Highlanders. They are now The Highlanders, 4th Battalion of the Royal Regiment of Scotland.

Around Inverness

North from Inverness

The Black Isle
Although not actually an island, being securely tied to the mainland by the 5-mile isthmus between Beauly and the River Conan, the Black Isle is sufficiently sea-girt to feel like one. Until 1982 the narrow neck of water between the Beauly and Moray

Tourist Information

North Kessock Tourist Information Centre, off the A9 just after Kessock Bridge, t (01463) 731 505.

Sports and Activities

Dolphin Ecosse, in Victoria Place, Cromarty, t (01381) 600 323. Operates dolphin-spotting cruises. You can see bottlenose dolphins in the wild at any time of year, though prior booking for cruises is recommended.

Dolphin-spotting trips, Avoch harbour, t (01381) 620 958. *Daily May–Sept/Oct.*

Majestic Cruises, North Kessock t (01463) 731 661 (or North Kessock Hotel; *see* opposite). Dolphin-spotting on the Moray Firth. *Daily in summer.*

Visitor Centre, in the tourist information centre car park, North Kessock, t (01463) 731 866. Has recordings of dolphins and seals. *Open daily April–Oct.*

Where to Stay and Eat

North Kessock Hotel, t (01463) 731 208 (*moderate*). Listed old-fashioned inn with sea views and Highland atmosphere. First-class food – imaginative and unfussy.

Royal Hotel, Marine Terrace, Cromarty, t (01381) 600 217, *www.royalcromartyhotel. co.uk* (*moderate*). Friendly, good value, on the harbour.

Braelangwell House, at Balblair, t (01381) 610 353, *www.braelangwell.co.uk* (*budget*). Comfortable Georgian house offering B&B in 50 acres, with facilities for children.

Craigiewood, North Kessock, t (01463) 731 628, *craigiewood.co.uk* (*budget*). B&B.

The Plough Inn, Rosemarkie, t (01381) 620 164 (*moderate–inexpensive*). A splendid traditional pub serving excellent meals, bar food and Black Isle beers. Great atmosphere.

The Tea Cosy, Fortrose, t (01381) 620 690. A very good café. At night it becomes **The Chanonry Restaurant** (*moderate*) serving first-class seafood.

Firths was crossed in a small car ferry which slithered over the turbulent currents between two queues of cars – a half-mile voyage often meaning as much as an hour's wait. The alternative was to drive all the way round the Beauly Firth. Now, with a link to Inverness via the Kessock Bridge, there is no ferry journey to give an impression of insularity. You are over the bridge and across the peninsula on the fast A9 without noticing, and the island feeling has gone. But things change slowly and the scattered communities retain much of their separateness. The first settlers arrived about 5,000 years ago and started leaving traces of their habitation about 1000 BC. Plenty of ancient remains – chambered cairns, duns and Pictish stones – are dotted around. No one is quite sure about the 'Black': some say it is because the climate is milder, and that frost and snow are rare, leaving the land 'black' when all around it is white. Others say the name derives from St Duthus, or Duthac (*dubh* – black) who was born in Tain around the year 1000 and did a lot of missionary work in the area.

About 45 miles of coastline strung together by attractive fishing villages encloses a district of rolling farmland interspersed with forestry and moor, with no significant heights. The Black Isle is unlike anywhere else in the Highlands and has its own, soft, singsong dialect. When the elegant, award-winning bridge was opened by the Queen Mother, opinions were divided. Locals can nip into Inverness in a matter of minutes now, but their quiet countryside has been opened up as a dormitory for the town, and offers easy pickings for itinerant vandals.

Munlochy Bay, about 3 miles up a twisting minor road from the first turning right north of the bridge, is vibrant with the cackle of geese in winter, targets for sportsmen who like to see wildfowl at the end of their guns, seeing them as a menace to the farmland on which they so voraciously graze. Ask in the village for the 'Clootie Well'. This one is not so well known as the one near Culloden, but over the years petitioners have turned the hedgerow into an extraordinary collage of filthy rags of all materials, including plastic. The origins are pagan, the superstition still strong; no one dares to remove the offerings for fear of supernatural reprisals. The **Black Isle Wildlife Park and Country Park** (*t (01463) 731 656; open Mar–Nov daily 10–6; adm*) is on your way to Munlochy, at the Croft, Drumsmittal. For those who hate to see wild animals in captivity (Highland wild cat), it's not the place, but during spring and summer you can watch chicks pecking their way out of their eggs.

Avoch (pronounced with a guttural 'ch'), 3 miles east on the A832, is a picturesque fishing village with miles of bracing walks along tidal sand flats with good views. A mile to the south on Ormond Hill, is the ruin of the castle in which Sir Andrew Murray, or de Moravia, lived. From this stronghold he raised the north against Edward I, while William Wallace was busy raising the south. He was killed as a result of wounds at the Battle of Stirling Bridge in 1297. Though he shared responsibility with Wallace for Scotland's victory over the English, his death deprived him of most of the credit. The surnames Patience and Skinner, common here, date back to when Cromwell's soldiers were in the area. The **Avoch Heritage Centre** (*open June–Sept Mon–Sat*) is also here.

Fortrose, a couple of miles on, is a pleasant, no-nonsense resort town with the strong feel of an island community. Between it and **Rosemarkie**, a mile to the north, the flat, tapering nose of Chanonry Ness, ending in Chanonry Point, protrudes into the Moray Firth, sheltering Fortrose and balancing Rosemarkie on its bridge. Rosemarkie's first church was built by St Moluag in the 6th century, together with a school, and it is said that he is buried beneath the Pictish stone in the churchyard. In the 12th century King David I authorized the building of a great cathedral, of which only the sandstone ruins remain on a well-kept green in Fortrose. Memorials here to Lord Seaforth and his family confirm the Brahan Seer's prophecy about the downfall of the House of Seaforth (*see* 'Seers, Sorcerers and Superstitions', pp.27–8). In 1880 a hoard of silver coins was dug up from the green, dating from the reign of Robert III. Cromwell recycled much of the fabric of the cathedral to build a fort in Inverness. **Chanonry Ness** has a golf course, caravan park and lighthouse; the beaches are popular in summer, with golden sands and rock pools. It also has a memorial cairn to the Brahan Seer, alleged to have been burnt here in a barrel of tar.

Groam House Museum (*t (01381) 620 961; open May–Sept Mon–Sat 10–5, Sun 2–4.30; Oct–April Sat and Sun 2–4; Easter week 2–4.30; adm*), in Rosemarkie, has local and archaeological exhibits: carved stones found in the vicinity of the church, indicating the importance of Rosemarkie in early Christian times; fragments of cross-slabs and gravestones and a particularly fine Pictish slab, all well laid out and explained. It is a good place to learn the little that is known about those elusive Picts.

Cromarty

Cromarty, on the northeastern tip of the Black Isle, about 23 miles from the Kessock Bridge, is sheltered by the great headland of the South Sutor at the mouth of the Cromarty Firth. This picturesque, 18th-century fishing town was once an important port with a magnificent natural harbour and was a Royal Burgh for several centuries. Some of its old merchants' houses are important examples of domestic architecture for the period, and rows of terraced cottages stand gable-end-on to the street, hunched against the wind, forming 'rope walks' where fisherwomen stretched out new ropes from the town's rope factory. A number of old buildings that were in danger of dereliction have been rescued and reused: the old rope works has been converted into housing; the old brewery is a small residential conference centre; fishermen's cottages and the old manse have been modernized. Escaping later development, Cromarty was designated a 'conservation area', with the result that its picture-postcard prettiness is almost too good to be true.

Sir Thomas Urquhart was one of the town's more endearing lairds, and an ardent Royalist knighted by Charles I – he fought for him at Worcester in 1641 and was imprisoned as a result. He tried to bribe his way out of prison by offering Cromwell the first complete *Universal Language* which reads as well backwards as forwards, and wrote reams of good prose and bad poetry. He was said to have died of an uncontrollable fit of laughter when he heard of the Restoration of Charles II in 1660.

Cromarty was bought in 1772 by George Ross, some of whose descendants still live here. Ross made his money as an army agent who supplied uniforms and advanced pay, always with a commission. He built the harbour, and founded several factories (cloth, rope, nails and spades), a brewery and a lace industry. He imported Highlanders to work for him and in 1783 built them a Gaelic chapel, the poignant ruins of which are on top of the hill behind the town, with an imposing monument to Hugh Miller in the graveyard – a landmark for mariners. George Ross also built Cromarty House in 1772, which stands in its own private grounds to the east, on the site of Cromarty Castle, built to watch over pilgrims coming to St Duthas. The town was on the main coastal route north from Inverness and it thrived until the decline of the fishing industry. Trade and population dwindled further with the establishment of a road and rail network bypassing this eastern outpost.

Cromarty Courthouse (*t (01381) 600 418, www.cromarty-courthouse.org.uk; open April–Oct daily 10–5; Nov, Dec and Mar daily 12–4; Jan and Feb by arrangement; adm*) is one of the town's successful restorations of an old building and it has won several well-deserved awards. It is an '18th-century experience', with a courtroom scene and animated models. From here you can hire a 'walkman tour of Cromarty' narrated by Hugh Miller himself.

Hugh Miller's Cottage (*t (01381) 600 245; open Easter–Sept daily 12–5; adm*), in Church Street, is a nostalgic journey into the past. The long, low, thatched cottage with crow-stepped gables, its tiny upper windows half-buried in the eaves, was built *c.* 1711 by the great-grandfather of Hugh Miller (1802–56). Hugh rose from simple beginnings as a stonemason and poet to become a famous palaeontologist, naturalist and journalist. He was also a radical theologian. Working at the same time as Darwin, he expounded his own God-centred theories of evolution and argued that evolution was not gradual but the result of a sudden change. As with Darwin, his work with fossils cast serious doubts on the accuracy of the Bible as history. Among much else, he wrote about the Brahan Seer in *Scenes and Legends of the North of*

Scotland. Torn apart with doubt, he shot himself on Christmas Eve 1856, having recorded 'a fearful dream'. Restored by the National Trust for Scotland, the cottage contains a museum with collections of his writings, personal belongings, geological specimens and such endearing memorabilia as the wooden chair in which his mother sat to nurse him. There is also craft work on sale in the restored cottages across the green on the seafront, including pottery, jewellery and local paintings.

The **North and South Sutors** guarding the entrance to the Cromarty Firth were once two giant cobblers ('souter' is the Scots word for shoemaker) who protected the Black Isle from pirates. Perhaps they slept whilst on duty – they were turned to stone. In the First World War the Cromarty Firth provided a sheltered harbour for half the North Sea fleet, the other half using Scapa Flow in Orkney. Charles II landed somewhere near here on his way to be crowned at Scone in 1650. The view north to the modern constructions of the oil installations at Nigg is a splendid contrast to the picturesque elegance of the old 18th-century town. A woodland walk from the village to the top of the South Sutor (where there are remains of gun emplacements from the First and Second World Wars), gives you stunning views of the Dornoch Firth, Nairn and beyond, and the Cromarty Firth. This can be surrealistic when the oil rigs are in the firth.

West from Cromarty to North Kessock

The B9163 takes you westwards along the firth and on round the perimeter of the Black Isle. To complete a circular tour, a one-track road skirts the northern shore of the Beauly Firth, 10 miles back to the Kessock Bridge. It hugs the shore for the last stretch, where tidal flats are rich in wildfowl, backed by blue-grey hills to the north with traces of snow even in late summer. The ruined castle (private, but visible from the road) behind a wall at the western end of the firth is **Redcastle**, reputed to have been one of the oldest continuously inhabited strongholds in Scotland, until it was abandoned in the 1950s. A castle called Edradour was known to have stood here for many years before William the Lion strengthened it in 1179. It passed through several hands until it was annexed by the Crown after the fall from power of the notorious Douglas family. The Mackenzies held it for 200 years from 1570. According to legend, they resorted to sorcery and human sacrifices in a vain attempt to save the land from a cattle plague, and were subsequently cursed. The present castle was built for Rory Mackenzie in 1641 and this 'new strong house of Redcastle' was besieged by Covenanting troops who 'brunt the castle to ashes, with all the good furnitur'. It was quickly repaired and the estate was sold by the Mackenzies in 1790. A gutted skeleton today, its rose-red shell rises from a wilderness behind an ivy-clad wall. Less than 50 years ago it was a splendid, lived-in castle with well-tended gardens. The present owners have resisted all attempts to save it, but are still under pressure to sell it to a buyer who would restore it.

North Kessock straggles along the shore and merges with Charlestown, its core of attractive fishermen's cottages somewhat swamped by much new development. It used to be the ferry terminal. **North Kessock Tourist Information Centre** (*see* 'Tourist Information', p.156) has a **Red Kite Viewing** television link-up so that you can watch the red kites, live, on their nests from May to August.

South of the Moray Firth: Inverness to Nairn

The south side of the Moray Firth is low-lying open farmland with views across to the Black Isle and the often snow-capped hills of Easter Ross. This is a gentle landscape compared with the ruggedness more commonly associated with the Highlands, but its soil is as stained with Highland blood as any in Scotland.

Culloden

Take the back roads, east of the A96, to Culloden, about 5 miles east of Inverness – brown tourism signs point the way. The excellent **visitor centre**, on the edge of the battlefield (*t (01463) 790 607; open daily, summer 9–5.30, winter 11–4; adm for audiovisual and cottage; site open all year*) recounts the battle which took place here on 16 April 1746, when Prince Charles Edward Stuart and his 5,000 exhausted, starving and ill-equipped Highlanders were defeated by the Duke of Cumberland, son of George II, and his 9,000 well-trained and well-equipped troops. Roughly 1,200 Highlanders fell; a large number were butchered by order of the Duke as they lay wounded; families were later rounded up, slaughtered, persecuted or exiled. Accounts of the Prince's reaction to the failure of his dreams vary: some say he tried to rally his Highlanders; some, that he had to be held back from galloping forward to a hero's

Tourist Information

Nairn: 62 King Street, **t** (01667) 452 753, *www.highlandfreedom.com. Open April–Oct.*

Where to Stay and Eat

Culloden House Hotel, 3 miles east of Inverness, **t** (01463) 790 461, *www.culloden house.co.uk* (*expensive*). Georgian mansion built around a Jacobean castle near the battlefield. Bought by an American millionaire who traces his roots back to the time of Robert the Bruce. Staying here is an extravagance – and worth every penny, including the food.

Boath House, Auldearn near Nairn, **t** (01667) 454 896, *www.boath-house.com* (*expensive–moderate*). Gracious luxury living in a lovely house amid pleasant grounds, with good food too.

Geddes House, 3 miles outside Nairn, **t** (01667) 452 241 (*expensive–moderate*). Small, comfortable mansion in a rural estate with good food.

Alton Burn Hotel, Nairn, **t** (01667) 452 051 (*expensive–moderate*). Roomy family hotel in a peaceful setting overlooking Nairn Golf Course and Moray Firth.

Claymore House Hotel, Seabank Road, Nairn, **t** (01667) 453 731, *www.claymorehousehotel. com* (*expensive–moderate*). Small and comfortable, with friendly staff.

Invernairne Hotel, Thurlow Road, Nairn, overlooking the firth, **t** (01667) 452 039, *www.invernairne.co.uk* (*expensive–moderate*). Family-run with private path to beach and good 3-night special offers.

Sunny Brae Hotel, Marine Road, Nairn, **t** (01667) 452 309, *wwwsunnybraehotel.com* (*expensive–moderate*). Cosy family hotel, overlooking the firth.

Kilravock Castle Hotel, 5 miles northeast of Culloden, **t** (01667) 493 258, *www.kilravock castle.com* (*moderate*). The emphasis is on God: grace before meals, Bible readings and comment at breakfast and dinner; no smoking or drinking – though naughty guests have smuggled in bottles and smoked up the chimney.

The Longhouse, Harbour Street, Nairn, **t** (01667) 455532 (*expensive–moderate*). Good, unpretentious restaurant. *Open Thurs–Sat and Sun lunch.*

death; other accounts are less flattering. Whatever the truth, he was led away and hidden by loyal Highlanders for five months, with a price of £30,000 on his head, until he returned to the Continent in a French frigate, to live out the rest of his life in wretched, debauched exile.

Many a Highlander who 'went out' in the Battle of Culloden with the Prince, followed his heart, not his head. It is said that there were more Scots fighting for the government at Culloden than there were fighting for the Prince. That it was an ill-advised and disastrously ill-managed battle is certain, as is the fact that it spelt the demise of a whole way of life and a social system that had endured for centuries.

On the battlefield, plaques tell which clan fought where and how the battle progressed. There are clan graves – communal burial sites with simple headstones bearing clan names, and a memorial cairn erected in 1881. On the edge of the bleak site is the Well of the Dead, where wounded Highlanders were slain as they drank water in desperation to revive themselves. A single stone bears the inscription: 'The English were buried here'. The flat stone beyond the visitor centre is called the Cumberland Stone, thought to have been the vantage point from which the Duke viewed the battle. The advance of the Redcoats was described by an eyewitness: 'It resembled a deep and sullen river, while the Prince's army might be compared to a streamlet running among stones, whose noise sufficiently showed its shallowness.' The old cottage outside the visitor centre is the only building to have survived. It has been restored as an 18th-century bothy and includes a military dressing station. It is said that 30 Highlanders were burnt alive nearby, after the battle.

Culloden House Hotel, 3 miles east of Inverness, is a Georgian mansion built around a Jacobean castle near the battlefield (*see* 'Where to Stay and Eat'). Prince Charles spent the night before the battle in a house on this site. It was the home of Duncan Forbes, the Lord President, one of Scotland's most trusted judges. His canny diplomacy dissuaded many northeastern Jacobites from taking part in the '45 Rising and, although he supported the government, he advocated leniency for the rebels after the battle. Some 30 or so Highlanders took refuge here afterwards, to be slaughtered by Cumberland's men. A mound marks the burial ground; no heather grows there now, it being a hater of chalk and calcified bones. Culloden House was destroyed by fire soon after the battle and replaced in 1772 by the present mansion.

The **Clava Cairns**, a mile east of Culloden, are a remarkable Stone Age and Bronze Age burial site, possibly dating from 2000 BC. Two of the cairns have passages leading into them; the third has curious stone strips radiating from it like the spokes of a wheel. Excavations revealed traces of cremated human bones, pottery and other remains – memorials of people who were alive nearly 4,000 years ago. A line through the two graves with passages points exactly to the spot where the sun sets at midwinter, and the geometrical accuracy with which the cairns are laid out suggests a sophisticated knowledge of mathematics and astronomy.

Kilravock Castle

Kilravock Castle – pronounced Kilrawk – (*www.kilravockcastle.com; grounds open Mon–Sat; house open end April–Sept Wed pm; adm*) is 5 miles northeast of Culloden, keeping to the back roads. In 1190 a Norman called Rose married into a local family, and settled on these lands; Kilravock has been the home of the Rose chiefs ever since. Mary, Queen of Scots was entertained in the original keep in 1562, during her Highland tour that year.

Among its relics the castle has two reminders of Culloden – a punch bowl and a pair of leather thigh boots. Rose of Kilravock entertained Prince Charles before the battle and offered him punch from this bowl. He was not a Jacobite, but the Prince had called on him and no true Highlander refuses hospitality. Shortly afterwards Cumberland appeared, flushed with the celebration of his 25th birthday and exhilarated with anticipation of the battle: 'I hear, Sir, you have been entertaining my cousin!' Rose explained, and was excused. Cumberland, for some inexplicable reason, left his boots behind. There is something wonderfully ironic about the relics left by the two men: Prince Charles, merry and charismatic, who later drowned his failure in alcohol; and Butcher Cumberland, all 18 stone of him, brash, and cruel in his jackboots.

The gardens and grounds are attractive, especially in spring. Prince Charles walked here with his host and watched young trees being planted; he remarked on the contrast between this peaceful scene and the commotion that was going on all around, as preparations were being made for the battle. Some of the beautiful old trees growing here today could be the ones he watched being planted. Kilravock is now a 'Christian guesthouse' (*see* 'Where to Stay and Eat', above).

Cawdor

Cawdor, 8 miles northeast of Culloden, is familiar to anyone who has read or seen Shakespeare's *Macbeth*, although 11th-century Macbeth was dead long before this place came into being. **Cawdor Castle** (*www.cawdorcastle.com; open May–2nd Sun in Oct daily 10–5.30; adm*), originally named Calder, home of the Thanes of Calder, dates from 1372 when William Calder built the central tower, probably replacing an older building more familiar to Macbeth. That would have been Old Calder, a Norman 'moatstead' not far north of the present castle. The Campbells of Argyll acquired the castle in 1510, one of them having abducted and married a Calder heiress. Protected by a gully on one side and a dry moat on the other, the castle is entered over a drawbridge. Domestic buildings were added in the 16th century and later remodelled; inside, it feels like a living home rather than a museum, as the Cawdors still live here.

Carbon dating has confirmed that the scrap of an ancient tree, railed off in the basement, is older than the castle, thus authenticating an old story. The original founder, Thane William, was granted a licence to build himself a fortress. He was told in a dream to load a donkey with panniers of gold and build a castle wherever it stopped. The donkey stopped for a rest in the shade of a holly tree, round which William built his castle. Don't resist buying the official guide written by a previous Lord Cawdor – irreverent descriptions of ancestors and heirlooms add humour to an otherwise fairly standard collection of memorabilia. Outside, as well as a walled garden, ablaze with colour in the summer, there is a charming, less formal 19th-century garden and a maze. There are riverside and woodland walks, a putting green and mini-golf course, picnic spots, and a restaurant and souvenir shop. You could easily spend a day here.

In a conservation area, Cawdor village, straggling round the castle grounds, is not at all typical of the rest of the Highlands – its peaceful cosiness matches that of the castle. The church is 17th-century, built in thanksgiving by the 12th Lord Cawdor after he survived a shipwreck.

Fort George

Fort George (*www.historic-scotland.net; open daily: summer 9.30–6.30, winter 9.30–4.30; adm*), about 8 miles northwest of Cawdor on the B9006, on a windswept promontory jutting out into the Moray Firth, is the most unspoilt example of an artillery fort in Europe. Built between 1748 and 1769 to replace 'Old' Fort George in Inverness which was destroyed by Prince Charles in 1746, its defences include the traditional outer works: ravelin, ditch, bastion and rampart, designed by William Skinnor who, in his day, was the leading expert on artillery fortification. Passing through the forbidding fortifications, one is brought to a delighted standstill by the mellow pink sandstone garrison buildings, their impeccable proportions mercifully unscarred by later 'improvement'.

The fort was built to house a garrison large enough to overawe Jacobite support in the Highlands, but by the time it was complete the Jacobite threat was finally dead. Instead, it became a base where a long series of regiments was mustered and equipped before embarking for overseas service. In 1881, when each British infantry regiment was allocated its own territorial recruiting area and home base, Fort George became the depot for the Seaforth Highlanders and generations of Highland soldiers trained there for service. The regiments of the garrison change every two or three years and they have the privilege of living in barracks that are the oldest in the world still occupied by a battalion of British infantry. The visitor sees splendid reconstructions of 18th-century army life, and with luck, dolphins frolicking in the Moray Firth. The **Regimental Museum of The Highlanders** (*t (01667) 462 777; open April–Sept daily; Oct–Mar Mon–Sat; donations welcome*) here includes the Queen's Own Highlanders' Collection – it contains a fascinating display of this unrivalled Highland regiment.

Nairn

Nairn, almost 9 miles east of Fort George, is a seaside holiday town, sometimes called the Brighton of the North. On the mouth of the River Nairn, it has sandy beaches along the Moray Firth, two golf courses and a reputation for a high average of annual sunshine. In Victorian times a Dr Grigor put Nairn on the map by recommending it to his patients as 'one of the healthiest spots in Britain'. Imposing houses built by retired Victorian empire-builders and trim villas with neat gardens give it an aura of old-fashioned gentility. The town lays on plenty of entertainment in the summer, and there is a Performing Arts Guild, a Repertory Theatre and a Fishertown Museum. Even so, you won't die of excitement in Nairn. **36 High Street** looks comparatively modern, but it encases a much older building which was the town house of the Roses of Kilravock. The Duke of Cumberland stayed here the night Prince Charles dined with the Roses at Kilravock (*see* pp.162).

The **Nairn Fishertown Museum** (*King Street; open May–Sept Mon–Sat 10.30–12.30*) tells the story of Nairn's fishing heritage, and **Nairn Museum** (*Viewfield Drive; open May–Sept Mon–Sat 10–4.30*) recounts local history.

Inverness South to Newtonmore

Inverness to Aviemore

The A9, part dual carriageway and part frustrating, even dangerous, single carriageway, speeds you south from Inverness. To the southwest lie the massive Monadhliath Mountains; to the southeast, Strathspey and the Grampians. **Moy**, about 12 miles south of Inverness, has long been the home of the chief of the clan Mackintosh, though Moy Hall, where Prince Charles stayed on 16 February 1746, no longer stands. Lord Loudoun, in command of the government forces in Inverness, led 1,500 men to capture the Prince. Mackintosh heard of this attack and, though no Jacobite himself, warned the Prince, who escaped wearing a Highland bonnet over his nightcap. The chief's wife, 'Colonel' Anne Mackintosh, who was an ardent Jacobite,

Tourist Information

Aviemore: Grampian Road, t (01479) 810 363, *www.visithighlands.com.*
Kingussie: King Street, t (01540) 661 297, *see website above. Open Easter–Oct.*

Sports and Activities

Strathspey Steam Railway, t (01479) 810 725, *www.strathspeyrailway.co.uk.* Runs between Aviemore and Boat of Garten. On Wednesdays in high summer you can have lunch in a restaurant car that was once in the Flying Scotsman. *Open mid-June–Sept.*
Loch Insh Watersports Centre, t (01540) 651 272, *www.lochinsh.com.* A boathouse restaurant built of telegraph poles, and pleasing log chalets. Courses in all water sports available.
Rothiemurchus Visitor Centre, near Aviemore, t (01479) 812 345, *www.rothiemurchus.net.* Vividly illustrates everyday life on a Highland estate; you can hire mountain bikes (maps, rucksacks and waterproofs etc. provided). *Open daily 9–5.30.*
Cairngorm Reindeer Centre, Glenmore, t (01479) 861 228. Guided reindeer tours. *Open daily; tours 11 and 2.30; 11 only in winter; adm.*

Loch Morlich Watersports, t (01479) 861 221, *www.lochmorlich.com.*
Kincraig Highland Wildlife Park, t (01540) 651 270 *www.highlandwildlifepark.org.* Children's paradise: wolves, lynx, otters, arctic fox, bears, etc: themed events, talks, activities, tuition and equipment hire. *Sports centre open May–Oct; park open daily; adm.*
Leault Farm, Kincraig, on the B9152, t (01540) 651 310, *www.leaultfarm.co.uk.* Demonstrations by working sheepdogs – and much else besides. *Sun–Fri, taking about 45mins; adm.*

Where to Stay and Eat

Auchendean Lodge, Dulnain Bridge, east of Carrbridge, t (01479) 851 347, *www.auchendean.com (expensive–moderate).* Seven rooms, excellent restaurant. Local chanterelles, wild venison, and their own wild strawberries; many malt whiskies.
Columba House Hotel, by the Folk Museum, Kingussie, t (01540) 661 402, *www.columba-hotel.co.uk (expensive–moderate).* 19th-century former manse with cosy atmosphere, good food and comfy rooms.

dispatched five loyal men to ambush the army. They fired their guns and made such a din shouting battle cries that Loudoun's men panicked and ran. This was 'the Rout of Moy'. The old house burnt down, replaced by a grand pile which had to be abandoned because of dry rot in the 20th century. The present Moy Hall was built in the 1950s.

For a lovely walk, turn right at Findhorn Bridge, a mile south of **Tomatin**. Drive about 5 miles up the River Findhorn and abandon your car when the road becomes a track. This will take you up the river into the very heart of the hills, remote and beautiful. You can follow any of the tributaries of the Findhorn and discover waterfalls, lochans, birds and wild flowers. At **Carrbridge**, 24 miles from Inverness and bypassed by the A9, is the **Landmark Visitor Centre** (*www.landmark-centre.co.uk; open daily April–Aug 10–6, Sept–Mar 10–5; adm*), with well-presented Highland history and a very sophisticated Adventure Park.

Aviemore, , about 7 miles south of Carrbridge, is the tourist centre and main dormitory for the Cairngorm ski resort. It used to be no more than a railway station on the main line to Inverness, without even a pub. In the 1960s however, it was chosen as the Highlands' first 'designer resort' and a series of not always beautiful structures were built.

The skiing is centred on Cairngorm (*http://ski.visitscotland.com for snow conditions*) about 9 miles to the south east, where a funicular railway runs up to the Ptarmigan

---

Dalrachney Lodge Hotel, Carrbridge, **t** (01479) 841 252, *www.dalrachney.co.uk* (*expensive–moderate*). In nice grounds, comfortable and friendly.

Duke of Gordon Hotel, Newtonmore Road, Kingussie, **t** (01540) 661 302, *www.dukeof gordonhotel.co.uk* (*expensive–moderate*). Expensively restored – you are piped into dinner. Mentioned in Queen Victoria's diary.

Eagle View Guest House, Newtonmore, **t** (01540) 673 675, *www.eagleview-guest-house.co.uk* (*expensive–moderate*). Splendid, recently redecorated place with friendly owners, comfortable rooms and good food.

Corrour House Hotel, Aviemore, **t** (01479) 810 220, *www.corrourhouse.co.uk* (*moderate*). Delightful, very friendly country house hotel, extremely good value.

Fairwinds Hotel, Carrbridge, **t** (01479) 841 240, *www.fairwindshotel.com* (*moderate*). Victorian manse in 7 acres: good value.

The Aspens, Spey Bridge, Newtonmore, **t** (01540) 673 264, *theaspens@aol.com* (*budget*). B&B.

Avondale House, Newtonmore Road, Kingussie, **t** (01540) 661 731 (*budget*). Good guesthouse.

Glengarry, East Terrace, Kingussie, **t** (01540) 661 386, *www.scot89.freeserve.co.uk* (*budget*). B&B where you will be well looked after.

Hermitage Guest House, Spey Street, Kingussie, **t** (01540) 662 137, *www.the hermitage-scotland.com* (*budget*). 4-star guesthouse in town centre.

Homewood Lodge, Newtonmore Road, Kingussie, **t** (01540) 661 507, *www. homewood-lodge-kingussie.co.uk* (*budget*). Another comfortable option.

The Oldferryman's House, Boat of Garten, **t** (01479) 831 370 (*budget*). A very cosy and relaxed B&B with dinner.

Osprey Hotel, Ruthven Road, Kingussie, **t** (01540) 661 510, *www.ospreyhotel.co.uk* (*budget*). Pleasant setting, first-class food.

Rowan House, Homewood, Newtonmore Road, Kingussie, **t** (01540) 662 153, *www.rowanhousescotland.com* (*budget*). B&B.

The Boathouse, Kincraig, near Kingussie, **t** (01540) 651 394 (*expensive–moderate*). Good place to eat. *Open April–Oct.*

The Cross, Ardbroilach Road, Kingussie, **t** (01540) 661 166, *www.thecross.co.uk* (*expensive–moderate*). Good restaurant with charming rooms. *Open Mar–Nov. Closed Tues*

Old Bridge Inn, Aviemore, **t** (01479) 811 181, *www.oldbridgeinn.co.uk* (*expensive–moderate*). Good meals.

Smiffy's, Grampian Road, Aviemore, **t** (01479) 810 190 (*inexpensive*). Great fish and chips.

Centre (**t** (01497) 861 261). There are about 30 runs spread over two valleys, with enough to challenge most people who don't mind capricious weather: it can be Arctic on the higher pistes. There are café-bars at the bottom and top, and ski hire available both at the centre and on the way there from Aviemore.

From Carrbridge, head 10 miles east to **Grantown-on-Spey**, one of Speyside's tourist centres, an attractive Georgian town at the junction of several routes. On the banks of the River Spey and surrounded by trees, the town was founded in 1776 by Sir James Grant, one of the Highland's 'improving lairds'. With the development of skiing in the hills, this area is popular all year round for holidays. The Grantown-on-Spey Highland Games are held in June.

The **Loch Garten Osprey Centre** (**t** *(01479) 831 694; open May–Aug daily 10–6; adm*), 8 miles south of Grantown-on-Spey, is known for its breeding ospreys. North Americans, accustomed to seeing these 'fish-hawks' in countless numbers nesting in their rivers and estuaries, are amused by the security surrounding Scotland's few pairs, but it must be remembered that before the mid-1950s (when one pair set up their nest in a tree at Loch Garten), they had not been seen in Britain for almost 50 years. When an over-enthusiastic egg thief robbed this precious nest in 1958, precautions had to be taken. Now, it is not so unusual to see the slow, flapping flight of one of these brown and white birds, or hear its shrill, cheeping cry. The nature reserve has a lot more than ospreys. Bird life includes blackcock, capercaillie and crossbills, and among the animals are red squirrels and deer. In winter the haunting cry of geese and the eerie honk of whooper swans float across the water.

Boat of Garten, west of the loch, is so called after the ferry that operated here until a bridge was built in 1898. It is the home of the **Strathspey Steam Railway Company**, which has its own station and some remnants of the old Highland railway (closed in 1965) and a museum of railway memorabilia. The railway reopened in 1978 and enthusiasts can travel the scenic route between Boat of Garten and Aviemore (*see* 'Sports and Activities', p.164). While you are in the area, visit the **Tomatin Distillery** (*www.tomatin.com; open Easter–Oct Mon–Fri 9–5; May–Sept, also Sat 9–1*), Scotland's largest malt whisky distillery, with guided tours and a free dram. Tomatin is derived from a Gaelic word meaning 'the hill of the juniper bushes' – curious for a whisky distillery. Also nearby, award-winning **Speyside Heather**, 6 miles from Grantown (*open all year; restriced opening Jan–Mar*), grows over 300 different heathers.

Kingussie and Newtonmore

By-passed by the A9, Kingussie (pronounced Kinyewsie) is a tourist resort 13 miles on from Aviemore, but with a different, peaceful atmosphere. Perhaps this is because it is thought to have been founded by St Columba; a church dedicated to him, of which only parts of the burial ground remain, once stood at the west of the town. The Duke of Gordon founded the present town in 1799. It was intended as a centre of woollen manufacture, but failed to prosper.

The **Highland Folk Museum** (**t** *(01540) 661 307, www.highlandfolk.com*) merits a detour. It is on two sites, Kingussie (*open April–Sept Mon–Sat 9.30–5.30; guided tours only in winter, allow 1½ hours; ring for details; adm*) and Newtonmore (*mid-April–Aug* *daily 10.30–5.30, Sept daily 11–4.30, Oct Mon–Fri 11–4.30; allow 3 hours; adm)*, 2½miles southwest, easily found by following the signs. It was founded in Iona in the 1930s and later moved here under the control of the universities of Glasgow, Edinburgh, St Andrews and Aberdeen. Beautifully arranged, the two outstanding sites include an authentic black house, built by a Lewisman as a replica of his childhood home, a clack mill (named for its 'clacking' noise) and exhibits of farming and domestic life, including a salmon smokehouse. At Newtonmore you will see a reconstructed 18th-century Highland township complete with animals.

The gaunt shell of **Ruthven Barracks** stands on a hillock east of the A9. Originally a 12th-century Norman motte on the site of a stronghold of the Wolf of Badenoch (the notorious son of Robert II), it was built after the 1715 Jacobite uprising to discourage further rebellion. Prince Charles captured it from a handful of government troops, and it was here that some 1,500 survivors from Culloden assembled to await their Prince. They waited in vain until the message came that the cause was dead and they must now fend for themselves. The following day Lord George Murray sat down in the barracks and wrote a long, bitter letter to the Prince, resentfully listing all the blunders that had contributed to their defeat. He blamed Colonel John William O'Sullivan, the plausible Irishman whom the Prince had trusted 'with the most escential things in regard to your operations', who had 'committed gross Blunders on many occasions'. It is a sad letter, written in the searing pain of defeat, lashing out with many understandable grievances and concluding with his resignation. Prince Charles never forgave him. Before disbanding to return to their homes, most of which had been razed, the loyal Highlanders blew up Ruthven to save it from the enemy. It remains, nonetheless, an important and dramatic landmark.

Newtonmore is a popular Highland holiday village which always seems to have bunting hanging along its one main street, full of hotels, guesthouses, B&Bs, craft shops and tearooms. **Waltzing Waters** at Newtonmore (*t (01540) 673 752; open daily Feb–early Dec; shows take 45 minutes starting every hour on the hour from 11–5, evening show 8.30; adm)*, is an elaborate water, light and music production which is experienced in a seated theatre. Thousands of dazzling patterns of moving water are synchronized with music – the effect is very spectacular.

West from Inverness

Beauly

Beauly, 10 miles west of Inverness, is fed by several rivers including the Glass, the Affric and the Cannich, all of which start their lives high in the hills to the southwest. The surrounding landscape is gentle, rich farmland and wooded hills.

This is Lovat country. The Lovats came to Britain with the Normans and it was their French influence that inspired the name Beauly – *Beau Lieu*. (Romantics prefer to attribute the name to Mary, Queen of Scots who, fresh from her French château, exclaimed: '*Ah, quelle beau lieu.*') The Lovats named their home Beaufort Castle, no doubt with the same French influence. The town was developed in 1840 by Thomas

Tourist Information

Strathpeffer: in the square, **t** (01997) 421 415. *Open Easter–Sept.*

Shopping

Campbells of Beauly, Beauly, **t** (01463) 782 239. Renowned tweeds, woollens, and tartans. *Open Mon–Sat 9–1 and 2–5.30, Thurs 9–1.*

Moniack Castle Winery, south of Beauly, **t** (01463) 831 080. Home-produced wines, meads and jellies. *Open Mon–Fri.*

Where to Stay and Eat

Mullardoch House Hotel, Glen Cannich, **t** (01456) 415 460, *www.mullhouse1.demon. co.uk* (*expensive*). Sporting lodge with 11 Munros on the doorstep, good food.

Achilty Hotel, Contin, **t** (01997) 421 355, *www.achiltyhotel.co.uk* (*expensive–moderate*). Comfortable with good food, log fires and lots of atmosphere.

Coul House Hotel, Contin, by Strathpeffer, **t** (01997) 421 487, *www.coulhousehotel.com* (*expensive–moderate*). Secluded and comfortable country house, with good food and candlelit dinners.

The Dower House, Highfield, a mile out of Muir of Ord, **t** (01463) 870 090, *www.thedowerhouse.co.uk* (*expensive–moderate*). Past winner of the AA's 'Best New Incomers for Scotland Award'. The food is first class – worth a detour even if you can't get a room.

Ord House Hotel, Muir of Ord, **t** (01463) 870 492, *www.ord-house.co.uk* (*expensive–moderate*). Delightful 17th-century laird's house in 50 acres.

Aigas Field Centre, Beauly, **t** (01463) 782 443, *www.aigas.co.uk* (*moderate*). Victorian mansion in magnificent surroundings, with field study programmes.

Ben Wyvis Hotel, Strathpeffer, **t** (01997) 421 323, *www.british-trust-hotels.co.uk* (*moderate*). Has the air of a spa hotel – a relaxing Victorian retreat.

Brunstane Lodge Hotel, Golf Course Road, Strathpeffer, **t** (01997) 421 261, *www.brunstanelodge.com* (*moderate*). Peaceful location, quite smart but good value.

Craigvar, The Square, Strathpeffer, **t** (01997) 421 622, *www.craigvar.com* (*moderate*). B&B with a four-poster bed.

Dunraven Lodge, Golf Course Road, Strathpeffer, **t** (01997) 421 210, *www.dunravenlodge.co.uk* (*moderate*). Cosy guesthouse.

Garden House Guest House, Strathpeffer, **t** (01997) 421 242, *www.gardenhouseguest house.co.uk* (*moderate*). Guesthouse; smoking is only allowed in the garden.

Mrs Cameron, White Lodge, Strathpeffer, **t** (01997) 421 730, *www.the-white-lodge.co.uk* (*moderate*). High-class B&B.

Priory Hotel, The Square, Beauly, **t** (01463) 782 309, *www.priory-hotel.com* (*moderate*). Attractive, well-run and comfortable hotel.

Richmond Hotel, Church Brae, Strathpeffer, **t** (01997) 421 300, *www.richmondhighland hotel.co.uk* (*moderate*). Good value.

Ardgowan Lodge Guest House, Wester Phoineas, near Beauly, **t** (01463) 741 745, *www.ardgowanlodge.co.uk* (*budget*). Part of a Victorian coach house and stables in 2 acres. Comfortable B&B, with good food.

Brockies Lodge Hotel, Kiltarlity, **t** (01463) 741 257, *www.brockieslodgehotel.co.uk* (*budget*). Good value and caters for children.

Broomhill, Kiltarlity, **t** (01463) 741 447, *www.visitscotland.com* (*budget*). A 3-star B&B.

Craigdarroch Lodge Hotel, Contin, **t** (01997) 421 265. Comfortable and friendly with separate B&B cottage, **t** (01997) 421 127.

Kerrow House, Cannich, **t** (01456) 415 243, *www.kerrow-house.co.uk* (*budget*). B&B.

Lovat Arms, Beauly, **t** (01463) 782 313, *www.lovatarms.com* (*budget*). Comfortable, informal and good value, with nice food.

The Struy Inn and **Glass Restaurant**, Strathglass (*budget; meals moderate*), **t** (01463) 761 219, *www.glassrestaurant.supanet.com*. Splendid atmosphere, good food and cosy, reasonable B&B.

Wester Moniack Farmhouse, Kirkhill, near Beauly, **t** (01463) 831 237 (*budget*). B&B.

Mains of Aigas, Strathglass, **t** (01463) 782 942, *www.aigas-holidays.co.uk* (*moderate*). Self-catering apartments in beautifully refurbished farm buildings.

Tomich Holidays, near Beauly, **t** (01456) 415 332, *www.tomich-holidays.co.uk*. Self-catering cottages and chalets (*sleeps 4–6*).

Fraser of Strichen, Lord Lovat, and a monument in the centre of the square erected in 1905 commemorates the Lovat Scouts, a special unit raised by Simon Joseph, 16th Lord Lovat in 1900 to serve in the Boer War. The Lovat Scouts became famous for their service in harsh conditions. The recruits were Highlanders, born and bred to survive and work in tough surroundings – men who had been stalkers, keepers or ghillies, in harmony with nature. In many ways they were the forerunners of today's SAS.

The charm of Beauly, once winner of the Scotland in Bloom prize for large villages, is enhanced by **Beauly Priory** (*open all year 10–5*) at the north end of the square beyond the old cross. Founded in 1230 for Valliscaulian monks from Burgundy, only the well-kept ruin of the church survives, but in the south wall there are three fine original triangular windows embellished with trefoils. The Reformation spelt its demise as a priory and in the 1650s Cromwell's soldiers removed some of the masonry to build a fort in Inverness. Among the memorials here is one to the Fraser of Lovat who was killed in the Battle of the Shirts (*see* p.129).

Perhaps the most colourful member of this family was Simon, Lord Lovat, born in about 1667. His many notorious escapades included the attempted abduction of an heiress and his subsequent marriage by force to her mother, a deed that left him convicted of high treason and outlawed. Having come into the title by devious means, he became a Jacobite agent, involved in conveying false information to the enemy. Outlawed once more, he turned government man and received a full pardon. Swearing loyalty to the Crown, however, he sent his son to fight for Prince Charles in 1745. He was beheaded, finally, in London, having conducted his own defence, and met his end with humorous dignity. 'You'll get that nasty head of yours chopped off, you ugly old Scotch dog,' taunted a Cockney woman in the crowd. 'I believe I shall, you ugly old English bitch,' he replied. Hogarth painted a portrait of him in hideous old age, just before he was helped up the steps to the scaffold. Known as 'the Old Fox of the '45', he was indisputably a rogue, traitor and hypocrite. He was also, if contemporary reports are to be believed, intelligent, witty and charming.

A small **Lovat Memorial Garden** has recently been planted, behind the bank in Beauly. The imposing Victorian Catholic church is well attended, the Catholic Lovats having attracted a large Catholic following in the area. **Beaufort Castle**, at Kiltarlity nearby, is Victorian baronial, rebuilt in 1937 and sold after the death in 1995 of '*Shimi*' – Gaelic for Simon, the previous Lord Lovat. He had made over his estates to his son, Simon Fraser, the Master of Lovat, to try to combat death duties. Unfortunately, his son could not cope with such a responsibility and a vast fortune slipped through his fingers. Both he and his brother died prematurely in 1994, within weeks of each other, their father following them to the grave a year later – a broken man.

Straths Glass, Farrar, Cannich and Affric

may want to consider this day trip

Beauly is at the junction of several routes. The A862 takes you back to Inverness along the south side of the firth with good views northwards to the Black Isle. The A833 takes you south (past Beaufort Castle) to Milton in Glen Urquhart, a pretty drive not much frequented. For a good day out, take the A831 southwest to Cannich along the River Beauly and then the Glass, where fishermen in waders stand thigh-deep in swirling waters surrounded by lichen-hung woods and gravelly islands. To the east is a ridge of high ground down to the Aird country of Lovat, while the three glens of Affric, Cannich and Farrar converge from the west. Strathglass was one of the places that suffered most in the Clearances. In the first three decades of the 19th century Elizabeth Chisholm of Strathglass, acting for her sick husband, managed to clear the land of virtually all the people whose roots had been embedded there for centuries.

At **Kilmorack**, 2 miles from Beauly, there are the remains of two Iron Age forts. Further on, at **Aigas**, there are hydroelectric dams where visitors can watch salmon being 'lifted' on their way upstream to breed. The old church here has been converted into an art gallery. At **Struy** you can go west into Strath Farrar and follow the River Farrar up to Loch Monar. From here you can walk up into the hills along any of the many tracks without disturbance.

For an interesting detour, take the left turn over the River Glass at Struy, and head back up the east side of the Beauly on the very minor Eskadale road. The peaceful little chapel of St Mary's was once the main Catholic centre for this area. In its graveyard is a memorial to an almost-forgotten episode in Scotland's history: the graves of the 'Sobieski Stuarts'. These two brothers, John Sobieski Stolberg Stuart and Charles Edward Stuart, conned Victorian society into accepting them as grandsons of Prince Charles Edward Stuart. They claimed their father, Lieutenant Thomas Allen, Royal Navy, was the legitimate son of Prince Charles by Louise of Stolberg. They called themselves Counts d'Albanie and fought for Napoleon at Waterloo. It was fashionable to support their pretensions and many did, including Lord Lovat, who established them at Eilean Aigas House, where they kept deerhounds, wrote several collections of poetry and invented tartans to impress their gullible friends. They also 'discovered' the *Vestiarium Scoticum*, an 'ancient' work on clan tartans with a provenance as unlikely as Macpherson's *Ossian* (see *The Sobieski Stuarts* by H. Beveridge, 1909).

You can keep to the east side of Strathglass on the small road down to Cannich, but if you cross back to the A831, stop off at the Holy Well of St Ignatius, beside the road at **Glassburn**, where there is an intriguing old headstone in a modern cairn, with engravings referring to St Columba (563), St Bean (1015), and St Margaret (1070), as well as to Pope Leo XIII. At **Cannich**, 17 miles southwest of Beauly, the A831 returns eastwards through beautiful Glen Urquhart to Loch Ness (*see* pp.132–3). Three miles to the southeast (2 miles by foot), the **Corrimony Cairn** is a Stone- and Bronze-Age burial chamber, its passage still roofed, surrounded by a stone circle. The Glass meets up with the Cannich and the Affric at Canich, with two more glens that, like Strath Farrar, should be explored on foot. The scenery is gentler than that of the western Highlands but just as beautiful. Steep, pine-clad rocks rise from peaty lochs in moss-green valleys where gnarled old trees are encrusted with silvery lichens. If you have time to explore only one glen, then **Affric** is the most beautiful, though there's no guarantee of solitude. Drive to the car park 2 miles before Affric Lodge and leave your car. Take the track past the lodge – the path north of the loch is more scenic. At its western end, follow the river to Alltbeithe, about 10 miles from the car park, where there is a youth hostel. Ten miles or so further on is Loch Duich on the west coast.

Muir of Ord and Contin

Muir of Ord lies north of Beauly on the A862. Muirs (moors) provided large areas of unfenced land for the assembling of cattle and sheep, and this one, being at the confluence of several routes, was the largest tryst in the north of the country in the 19th century – beasts were shod at Muir of Ord for the hard surfaces of the routes to the southern markets. Little of the colour and bustle of the straggling village that grew up to serve the needs of the drovers survives here however. Quite a few chambered cairns and ancient remains can be found in the vicinity, but on the whole the agricultural landscape is tame and unremarkable. **Gilchrist**, or Kilchrist, on the outskirts of Muir of Ord, witnessed a nasty scene in 1603 when the Macdonells of Glengarry locked some Mackenzies in the parish church and torched them.

Contin, about 8 miles northwest on the A835, on the west side of the River Blackwater, has an old coaching inn from which passengers used to depart on the tortuous journey west to Poolewe and Ullapool after the roads were built in the 18th century. Telford built the first bridge here, later swept away by flood water. Dealers came from England to the Contin Horse Fair to buy sturdy Highland ponies for work in the coal mines – fair days were festive occasions, drawing people from far afield to jostle and gossip over braziers amongst the peddlers' stalls and animal pens.

Strathpeffer

Before going west, visit Strathpeffer, 2 miles northeast on the A834, a famous spa town until the First World War. The springs were used as early as 1770, and visitors, including foreign royalty, came to take the sulphur and chalybeate waters. In 1819 Dr Thomas Morrison pronounced these the most efficacious in Britain; they were analysed and found to contain more hydrogen than any other. The small Pump Room was built in 1859, and villas, hotels and hospitals sprung up around it. It has recently been restored and is open to the public, with free water tasting – hold your nose! The Spa Pavilion is to be restored as a centre for performing arts. After the First World War the spa's popularity declined, though Strathpeffer remained a holiday resort. Lying in a sheltered dip in wooded hills with houses and hotels rising in neat terraces from its heart, the town is now a holiday centre whose gently refined atmosphere has won it the title 'Harrogate of the North', with a preponderance of coach tours.

In the **Old Victorian Station**, there is a **Craft Centre** with craftsmen at work, and the **Highland Museum of Childhood** (*open April–Oct Mon–Sat 10–5, Sun 2–5; July–Aug 10–7*). Here is a splendid display of artefacts celebrating Highland childhood in the past, with a shop and tearoom. There are **Highland Games** in August with all the traditional events, such as tossing the caber, putting the shot, piping and dancing, and drinking. The village is dormant in the winter.

The **Eagle Stone** stands 3ft tall on a hillock to the east of the town, reached by a well-signed lane near Eaglestone House. It is a Pictish symbol stone with an engraved eagle and a horseshoe and was the subject of one of the Brahan Seer's prophecies (*see* 'Seers, Sorcerers and Superstition', pp.27–8). If the stone should fall three times, he said, then ships would tie up to it. Setting aside a mighty tidal wave, this seems improbable at first, but the seer had uncanny prescience. It is said that the stone has already fallen twice (it's now cemented into place) and that on the second occasion the Cromarty Firth flooded up to the old county buildings in Dingwall. The stone is only 4 miles to the west and the River Peffery runs very close by on its way to the firth, though way down in the valley.

A couple of miles due east of the symbol stone – along the ridge called *Druim Chat*, meaning 'cat's back' – there is a well-preserved vitrified fort, **Knockfarrel**, one in a line of three great Pictish defence sites, the other two being at Craig Phadraig in Inverness and Ord Hill in Kessock. You can see the foundations clearly – a vast place, 810ft (250m) across, believed to have been a stronghold of Fingal and his warriors.

More fact than legend was the clan battle between the Macdonalds and the Mackenzies in 1429 at Kinellan, just southwest of Strathpeffer. Margaret Macdonald, daughter of the Lord of the Isles, had been sent to the 6th Chief of the Mackenzies to be his wife, though they had not met. When she arrived she was found to be blind in one eye, so her furious bridegroom-to-be returned her to her family accompanied by a groom, a horse and a dog, all blind in one eye. The Macdonalds swiftly sought their revenge for such an insult, but they lost the battle.

Climbing **Ben Wyvis**, the great bulk to the north of Strathpeffer, takes about 3 hours. Start from the bridge over the Allt a' Bhealaich Mhoir near Garbat on the A835 Dingwall–Ullapool road. A signed path goes to the summit. Bear left above the forest and up the west ridge of An Cabar. This takes you to the extraordinary Glas Leathad Mor, a soft carpet of moss stretching for about 1½ miles to the summit. It is wonderful walking, on some of the most unusual mountain terrain in Scotland.

Back in Contin, head west on the A835 a couple of miles to the **Rogie Falls**, well signposted and only a short walk from the car park. You won't be alone here but it is usually possible to find a reasonably secluded spot for a picnic amongst the birches, rowans and gnarled oaks, with bracken, heather and mossy crags for carpet and table. There is a suspension bridge over the river where you can, with luck, watch salmon trying to leap the falls: they often reach astonishing heights. There is a salmon ladder at the side for the ones that don't manage.

Easter Ross

Dingwall North to Ardgay

Dingwall

At the junction of several main routes on the southwestern corner of the Cromarty Firth, Dingwall's name is derived from the Norse *thing* (parliament or council) and *volle* (place). For Queen Victoria, who stopped here several times in her royal train, it was set 'in a glen, with hills rising above it, extremely pretty and it reminds me of Switzerland [her ultimate accolade].' Pretty isn't quite the right word for Dingwall today. It is a Highland market town, with an early 18th-century town house and tollbooth and an ancient mercat cross. It is possible that Macbeth was born here in the castle that once stood in Castle Street, of which only a handful of stones remain. Robert the Bruce's wife is said to have been a prisoner here during his exile, and it was the hereditary home of the Earls of Ross in the 13th and 14th centuries. It is hard to believe that Dingwall was a thriving port before the waterway at the mouth of the River Peffery silted up – cutting off deep-water access to the Cromarty Firth. The canal at the end of Ferry Road was built by Telford in an attempt to cut through the encroaching mud flats. It was always an important livestock market and even today you may hear a few exchanges in Gaelic around the market square on Wednesdays. The **Dingwall Highland Gathering** is in July.

Spare a moment to read the war memorial in the Station Square, in the form of an intricate rustic cross. It was first erected in Fontaine Notre Dame in France by members of the Seaforth Highlanders, in honour of their comrades who fell at the Battle of Cambrai. The original remained in France for six years, its inscription composed by the villagers: '*Mort Pour La Patrie, 4ème Les Seaforth Highlanders, Honneur aux Hommes, Mobilisés dans ce village pour la Bataille de Cambrai 1917.*' In 1924 the Seaforth Reunion Club brought the cross home to Scottish soil, and thus it stands today, its wood recently replaced but the inscription original.

The **Town House** (*open Easter–Sept; adm*) is a museum with a special exhibition about General Sir Hector Macdonald (1853–1903). Known as 'Fighting Mac', Hector was a brave, tragic man who rose from the ranks to become a Major General – almost unheard of in those days. He distinguished himself through many acts of conspicuous bravery, until the Battle of Omdurman, in 1898, when he and 'his black brigade performed prodigies of valour' and won the day. Fêted as a public hero, with honours of all kinds lavished upon him, he attained the rank of Major General KCB and was finally posted to Ceylon. While there, 'grave charges affecting his moral character were made against him'. It is almost certain that these charges were totally unfounded – being a man of the people, he treated his servants and house boys as members of the family, unlike many others in his position. It was expected that his court martial in 1903 would result in a complete acquittal but he shot himself before it could take place. Deeply shocked by this appalling smear against their beloved Hero of Omdurman, the local people erected an impressive monument to him on Mitchell Hill, a battlemented tower that is a landmark for miles.

Where to Stay

Kinkell House, Easter Kinkell, near Dingwall, t (01349) 861 270, www.kinkellhousehotel. co.uk (*expensive–moderate*). Very comfortable.

Kiltearn House, by Evanton, t (01349) 830 617, www.kiltearn.co.uk (*moderate*). A comfortable, peaceful guesthouse.

Novar Arms Hotel, Evanton, t (01349) 830 210, www.novararms.com (*moderate*). A good choice: a former coaching inn dating from 1850, but fairly modern in style inside; 18 rooms and a restaurant.

Tulloch Castle Hotel, Dingwall, t (01349) 861 325, www.swallowhotels.com (*moderate*). Warm welcome; good value, friendly staff.

Black Rock Bunkhouse/Hostel, Evanton, t (01349) 830 917, www.blackrockscotland. co.uk (*budget*). Good value, with camping grounds, linen hire, a pub close by, and a bus stop. *Open April–Oct.*

Dingwall to Ardgay

The surprising Indian temple on the hill above **Evanton**, known as the **Fyrish Monument**, is a folly erected by General Sir Hector Munro (1726–1805) as a philanthropic gesture to provide work for the unemployed in the area. It is modelled on the gateway to Negapatam, an Indian town captured by Sir Hector in 1781. Although it is clearly seen from the road, it is much more fun close up, and not an exacting climb.

Because it is potentially dangerous, **Black Rock Gorge** at Evanton, 6 miles north of Dingwall on the back road, isn't signposted. Go through the village and take the left turn just after the bridge. Take the third track to the left about 1½ miles down Glen Glass, and you will find a magnificent 2-mile chasm, with sheer sides up to 200ft deep and so narrow that in places it would almost be possible to jump across. At this point it might be wise to chain and padlock your children and dogs. The River Glass tumbles on its way far below and you could catch the quick flash of a water sprite, darting through the mossy chasm in the sparkling air.

If you are going northwest and don't want to explore the Tain Peninsula, by far the most scenic route from the south is on the A836, starting a couple of miles on from Evanton. This road goes up over the windswept, heathery moors and then zigzags down through dramatic ravines to the Dornoch Firth. Stop at the Stone Viewpoint, at Struie, about 10 miles up the road, for panoramic views. There is a view indicator and a board explaining the glacial action that created this lovely land- and seascape.

The Tain Peninsula

Although the exploitation of North Sea oil has inevitably changed the character of the hammerhead peninsula jutting eastwards between Nigg Bay and Tain, it has enough attractions to make it worthy of attention. A two-car ferry (**t** *(01862) 871 255; daily from May–Sept*) runs between Nigg and Cromarty.

The A9 bypasses **Invergordon**, 14 miles northeast of Dingwall, and unless you have a reason to stop off, don't bother. It is a busy industrial centre on the western tip of Nigg Bay, dominated by the surrealistic constructions built for the oil industry. The Cromarty Firth is one of the finest deep-water anchorages in the world and is now one of the most important European centres for the repair and maintenance of the exploration rigs. Although not a town to visit for an outing, there is something curiously striking about some of the giant skeletons whose fragile-looking girders are built to withstand the full force of a North Sea gale.

Don't let the A9 sweep you past the B9165 turning to **Fearn**, off to the east in the midst of rich farmland, where cottages with pretty gardens are grouped around a green. Fearn Abbey was founded in the 13th century and its restored nave and choir are still used as the parish church. The first martyr of the Scottish Reformation, Patrick Hamilton (1498–1528), was titular abbot here. He was of royal descent through an illegitimate granddaughter of James II, and educated in Paris and Louvain, where he came under the influence of Lutheran theology. Converted to

Protestantism, he married and returned to St Andrews where he was arrested and tried for heresy by Archbishop James Beaton. He was burnt at the stake in St Andrews in 1528 (there is an impression of his face on the stone wall nearby, left there when his soul flew out of the flames). This martyrdom was one of the sparks that kindled the Scottish Reformation.

Portmahomack, about 7 miles north of Fearn on the B9165, sprawls upwards around a sheltered harbour. The **Tarbat Discovery Centre**, in Tarbatness Road (*open Mar–Dec*) is an old church focused on local archaeology and a major current dig. At **Tarbat Ness**, on the northern tip of the peninsula, one of the highest lighthouses in Britain warns ships of the dangerous sandbanks threatening the entrance to the Dornoch Firth. The Norsemen called them Gizzen Briggs and were among their earliest victims. The views are stupendous and there are sometimes seals basking on the rocks below. You can walk for miles along the shore or on the red sandstone clifftops. At **Shandwick**, about 10 miles down the east coast, people have found interesting fossils in the bay and its caves. The 9ft (3m) stone cross-slab above the village was erected in memory of one of three Norse princes who were shipwrecked on a reef here, while chasing an Earl of Ross who had abused his wife – their sister.

Tain

Tain, on the south side of the Dornoch Firth, 11 miles north of Invergordon, takes its name, like Dingwall, from the Norse word *thing* – a meeting place or parliament. Of

Shopping

Anta Pottery, Fearn, t (01862) 832477, *www.anta.co.uk*. A factory outlet with inexpensive seconds and amazing bargains. *Open Mon–Sat 9–5.*

Aldie Water Mill, Tain, t (01862) 893 786. A working pottery shop in a restored mill, with an above average craft shop. *Open daily 10–5, seasonally; ring for dates.*

Highland Fine Cheeses Factory, Knockbreck, Tain. Demonstrations and samples. *Open during working hours.*

Where to Stay and Eat

Glenmorangie House, Cadboll, Fearn, t (01862) 871 671, *www.glenmorangie.com* (*expensive*). The best place to stay in the area.

Morangie House Hotel, Tain, t (01862) 892 281, *www.swallow-hotels.com* (*expensive*). Very comfortable: 26 individually styled rooms in a Victorian mansion in its own grounds. Well prepared and reasonably-priced food.

Mansfield Castle, Tain, t (01862) 892 052, *www.swallowhotels.com* (*expensive–moderate*). Baronial-style Victorian country house in nice grounds near eight decent golf courses. Good food.

Cadboll Cottage, Fearn, t (01862) 871 572, *mounta33@aol.com* (*budget*). An attractive Victorian farmhouse run as a Wolsey Lodge – warm and friendly with excellent dinners.

Golfview House, 13 Knockbreck Road, Tain, t (01862) 892 856, *www.golf-view.co.uk* (*budget*). Friendly B&B.

Brambles Tea Room, Tain. Serves delicious home-baked goodies and has a gift shop.

Falls of Shin Coffee Shop, Falls of Shin, near Lairg. Excellent, unfussy food.

Grants, Tain. The ovens in this bakery are over 100 years old and still in use.

The Oyster Catcher, Portmahomack, t (01862) 871 560. Splendid café with murals and a great atmosphere. *Open Tues–Sun all year except Feb daily 11–6 and 7–8.30.*

Tomich Tea Room, on the A9 near Alness. A good stop-off for tea or coffee. Excellent baking and lunches, and a gift shop.

more historic than aesthetic interest, it has a pleasant east-coast sturdiness, its red-sandstone buildings sheltered by hills to the west as they gaze across the Dornoch Firth and its acres of sand flats at low tide.

Malcolm Canmore granted it royal status in the 11th century, probably because St Duthus, or Duthac, was born here in about 1000. He died in Ireland towards the end of the century and his remains were brought back here to be interred in St Duthus Chapel, now an overgrown ruin in the cemetery, between the 18-hole golf course and the sea. It was built on the site of his birth as a 'prayer cell', with a resident hermit guarding the sacred relics, which were believed to work miracles. Hundreds, maybe thousands, of people made pilgrimages here.

Like other sacred places, this was a place of sanctuary for fugitives. Elizabeth de Burgh, wife of Robert the Bruce; his daughter by his first wife, Marjory, who was to become mother to Robert II; and Isabella Countess of Buchan, whose family, the Macduffs, held the hereditary right to crown the kings of Alba, together took refuge here when fleeing to Orkney while Bruce was in exile. The sacred right of sanctuary was violated by the Earl of Ross, who took them prisoner and handed them over to the English in 1307 – an act Scotland did not forget. The chapel was torched by a smuggler, McNeill of Creich, in 1427, to destroy an enemy he had chased inside.

St Duthus Collegiate Church was built in 1360 on the site of an earlier church, traces of which can be seen in the chapterhouse. It is now a showplace and memorial, no longer used for worship. After the chapel was burnt, the relics of St Duthus were brought here (they disappeared in 1560) and this became the focus for pilgrims. Among them was James IV, seeking absolution for having been instrumental in his father's death. He made the pilgrimage every year for 20 years, but not entirely from religious fervour: he liked to keep in touch with his people all over Scotland and had established his favourite mistress, Janet Kennedy, in Darnaway Castle in Morayshire. Look out particularly for the stained-glass windows showing Malcolm Canmore and Queen Margaret bestowing a royal charter on the town; and an assembly of the Scottish parliament adopting John Knox's Confessions of Faith in 1560.

Tain and District Museum (*open Easter–Sept Mon–Sat; donation box*), in Castle Brae off the High Street, was founded as an exhibition for the visit of the Queen Mother in 1966 and became permanent. It has relics, manuscripts, photographs, archaeological remains and 18th- and 19th-century displays of social history. There is also information on St Duthus and on the patronage of James IV. **Tain Through Time** (*t (01862) 894 089, www.tainmuseum.org.uk; open daily mid-Mar–Oct 10–6; closed Nov–mid-Mar; adm*) offers a 'sound and light' show, guides in costume, audiovisual shows, live acting, artefacts and documents, all giving an excellent interpretation of Tain and its history. There is also an audio tour of the town's historic sites. The **Tolbooth** is 16th century, rebuilt in 1707, the year of the Act of Union. It is a striking building with a tall, castellated keep, a conical spire and angle turrets. Its bell is the original curfew bell of 1616.

North of the town is the **Glenmorangie Distillery**, with a new Visitor Centre (*t (01862) 892 477, www.glenmorangie.com; open all year for guided tours*), founded in 1843. The A9 takes you a couple of miles west from Tain and then sweeps across a grand causeway-bridge over the Dornoch Firth, considerably shortening the distance north. The route to the west is the A836, past Bonar Bridge along the southern shore of the Dornoch Firth.

Ardgay to Lairg

✓ Croick Church

Turn left at Ardgay (pronounced Ardguy, as in Fawkes) 14 miles west of Tain, just before Bonar Bridge at the head of the firth and you won't regret a 10-mile detour up Strath Carron, a wide valley bordered by hills, bracken and lichen-hung birches. Little Croick Church lies at the end in a walled churchyard surrounded by a scattering of wind-bent trees in a pocket of desolate moorland – one of the most poignant places in Scotland. Nowhere tells the story of the Clearances so eloquently. In the spring of 1845, families who had been evicted from their crofts in Glencalvie by the Duke of Sutherland's agents, had nowhere to go. They camped here in an improvised shelter against the outside church wall, made from rugs and plaids stretched over poles. The memorials they scratched on the diamond panes of this simple kirk can still be read today: 'Glencalvie people was in the church here May 24 1845...' 'Glencalvie people the wicked generation...' Inside, the kirk is plain, with unadorned walls, an iron stove, benches and table and a big pulpit. An interesting display board shows an assortment of contemporary newspaper cuttings from *The Times*. You can walk on up the track from the end of the road, for miles into the hills.

Bonar Bridge and Around

Bonar Bridge, about 5 miles beyond Struie and a mile north of Ardgay, is so called after the bridge that spans the Kyle of Sutherland, a replacement of Thomas Telford's, built in 1813. Once a staging post on the A9, when this was the only route north, it is now a backwater hoping for tourists. In the 14th century an iron foundry was established here which consumed all the timber in the area in its rapacious smelters. James IV ordered more trees to be planted, some of which can still be seen among the ubiquitous pines of the Forestry Commission. A ferry bridged the Kyle until a tragedy in 1809 when too many passengers were allowed to board the ferry, against the wishes of the sheriff, Mr MacCulloch. It was a calm night, but the boat was unevenly laden and it capsized, drowning over 70 people, including the sheriff.

The Kyle of Sutherland separates Easter Ross from Sutherland: the River Shin runs into it from the north and the lovely Oykel runs in from the rugged hills in the

Where to Stay and Eat

Oykel Bridge Hotel, Rosehall, near Lairg, t (01549) 441 218 (*expensive–moderate*). A charming and pretty place by the river with a secluded, colourful garden. Caters mainly for fishermen. Delicious locally produced food – convenient and comfortable base for local activities.

Mrs Munro, Corvost, Ardgay, on the road to Croick Church, t (01863) 755 317 (*budget*). In a somewhat ramshackle farm steading. Not many frills (there are no *en-suite* rooms), but a warm welcome and excellent meals.

northwest. After the rather tame landscape of the Black Isle and the Tain Peninsula, you are back in truly Highland scenery, with walks and climbs all around and not too many people other than fishermen. The roads aren't crowded, and once you step away from them you can walk for miles and not see a soul.

About a mile past Ardgay, heading up the west side of the Kyle of Sutherland, turn left up a track to the site of the Battle of Carbisdale in 1650. You can also get to it past the school further on in Culrain. This was one of Charles II of England's least honourable legacies. He had encouraged James Graham, 1st Marquis of Montrose, to go to Scotland to try to win the Crown for him without having to sign the Covenant. Montrose, who had previously been a Covenanter himself, gathered up a little army and was defeated here at Carbisdale on 27 April. He escaped and was given refuge by Macleod of Assynt, but was then betrayed – opinions differ as to by whom – captured and taken to Edinburgh. But Charles had by now signed the Covenant and found it expedient not to intervene when his loyal subject was condemned to death and hanged at the Mercat Cross in May.

The massive neogothic pile that towers over the road just to the north is **Carbisdale Castle**, nothing to do with Montrose, but an early 20th-century peace offering to the dowager Duchess of Sutherland after an ugly battle with her stepchildren over her husband's will, which landed her with a six-week jail sentence. It is now a youth hostel with a difference (*t 0870 004 1109, www.syha.org.uk*). Gracious slumming here – and you don't have to earn your keep.

Lairg is a road junction with the railway close by, not particularly exciting but a useful centre for fishing holidays and for stocking up the picnic box. The **Ferrycroft Countryside Centre**, at Lairg (*t (01549) 402 160; open April–Oct daily 10–5*), has displays of the local natural history and archaeology, as well as the history of the woodlands and man in the northern Highlands. It is also the Ranger base and Tourist Information Centre. The southeast end of Loch Shin straddles the River Shin, serving several outlying crofting communities as well as tourists. It is also the sheep market for the area. Not far down the Shin, the **Falls of Shin** are impressive but too popular, with a car park, café and gift shop.

The A839 goes west from Lairg to Inchnadamph on Loch Assynt and the northwest. It joins up with the A837 from Invershin, a prettier route through Strath Oykell. Just after the roads join, turn north up Glen Cassley to look at the impressive waterfall, with an old graveyard below. Overenthusiastic planting of conifers all around here spoils what must once have been glorious open views.

Back to the A9 causeway over the Dornoch Firth, Dornoch (*see pp.181–2*) lies out on the northeastern side of the firth, bypassed by the main road.

Sutherland and Caithness

13

Sutherland and Caithness

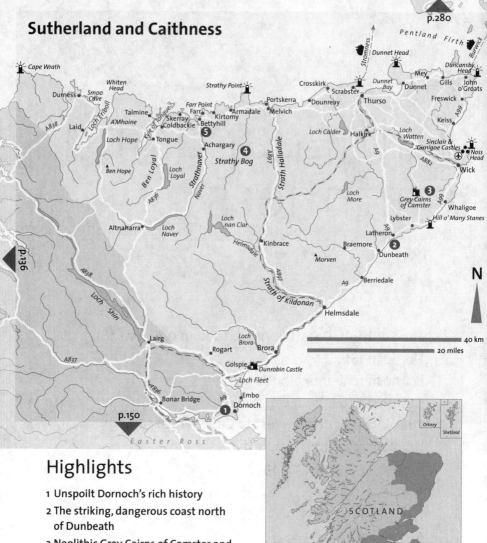

Highlights

1 Unspoilt Dornoch's rich history
2 The striking, dangerous coast north of Dunbeath
3 Neolithic Grey Cairns of Camster and nearby magical hamlet of Whaligoe
4 The melancholy and fragile ecosystem of Strathy Bog in the Flow Country
5 Bettyhill's Strathnaver Museum

Sutherland was named by the Vikings as the land to the south of Caithness – an indication of the degree to which the two northern counties of Scotland were colonized by the Norsemen in the past. As you go north you will notice fewer Gaelic-derived names and more with Nordic origins. In the last couple of centuries, the fortunes of many of the villages and small towns along the coast rose and fell with the herring industry. The settlements along this coast reflect the hardship of the lives of the people who lived there, with little sign of frivolous embellishment.

Nevertheless, many of the harbours are attractive, if somewhat changed from the days when they were packed out with fishing boats. The Flow Country is the name given to the 150,000 acres of peatlands in Caithness and Sutherland. If you have time, explore these great tracts of wasteland along the glens of the rivers that run down to the sea from the south. This distinctive landscape is awesome in a melancholy way and certainly not unattractive when the sun shines.

The Southern Coast: Dornoch to John o' Groats

Dornoch

Dornoch, a Royal Burgh, is delightfully unexpected. Tucked away above the Dornoch Firth, it has hung on to an old-world dignity and managed to remain unspoilt in spite of the new road bridge. A higgledy-piggledy town with an attractive central square, it is a holiday resort and a golfing centre. On the same latitude as Hudson Bay and Alaska, it has the most northerly first-class golf course in the world and many say it is the finest in Scotland – monks from St Andrews played on its links in medieval times.

Excavations have dated settlements in the area at least as far back as 1000 BC. There is thought to have been a community of Celtic monks long before David I referred to a monastery here in 1140. Dornoch claims to be the place where the last witch in Scotland was burned a barrel in 1727, and there is a Witch's Stone to commemorate the occasion in a private garden in Carnaig Street. Some say Janet Horne was convicted of having turned her daughter into a pony and ridden her to a witches' meeting where she had arranged for the Devil to shoe her. During her trial she

Tourist Information

Dornoch: The Square, t (01862) 810 555. *Open all year.*

Where to Stay and Eat

Dornoch Castle Hotel, Dornoch, t (01862) 810 216, *www.dornochcastlehotel.com* (*expensive*). 16th-century bishop's palace. Traditional, characterful rooms – great food, good cellar, nice garden. *Open April–Oct.*

Royal Golf Hotel, First Tee, Dornoch, t (01862) 810 283, *www.swallowhotels.com* (*expensive*). Splendid views, good food and friendly.

Skibo Castle, near Dornoch, t (01862) 894 600, *www.carnegieclub.co.uk* (*expensive*). Private sports club and hotel, hosted Madonna's wedding to Guy Ritchie.

Fourpenny Cottage, Skelbo, t (01862) 810 159, *www.homepages.tesco.net/~fourpenny* (*moderate*). B&B.

Highfield House, Evelix Road, Dornoch, t (01862) 810 909, *www.highfieldhouse.co.uk* (*moderate*). Comfortable B&B.

2 Quail Restaurant and Rooms, t (01862) 811 811, *www.2quail.com* (*moderate*) Small and relaxed, with memorable food and comfortable rooms. *Must book for the restaurant.*

Eagle Hotel, Castle St, Dornoch, t (01862) 810 008, *www.eagle-dornoch.co.uk* (*budget*). Recently refurbished, peaceful and cosy – typical of Dornoch itself. With a couple of family rooms.

Trevose Guest House, Dornoch, t (01862) 810 269, *trevose@amserve.net* (*budget*). Attractive old stone cottage with a colourful garden, looking on to the beautiful Cathedral Square. *Open Mar–Oct.*

misquoted the Lord's Prayer in Gaelic, thus signing her own death warrant. She was tarred, feathered and burnt to death; history doesn't relate what happened to her daughter – the pony.

The Town

Dornoch Cathedral dates from 1224. St Gilbert of Moray (or Moravia as it was called in Latin) was Bishop of Caithness in 1222. Worried by the murders of two of his predecessors, he decided to move his seat into an area where he could look for protection from his kinsman, the Earl of Sutherland. The cathedral he built must be the most cosy in the country: small and cruciform, with a remarkable inner glow from colourful windows that illuminate its mellow raw-stone walls. Gilbert died in 1245, the last Scotsman to be canonized before the Reformation. The remains of a number of Earls of Sutherland, from 1248 to 1766, lie in the transept. In 1924, to celebrate its 700th anniversary, much of the Victorian work was stripped away to reveal the original 13th-century stonework and thus it stands today as the main parish church.

A gift shop with gallery, stands opposite the cathedral where the old Town Jail used to be. Dornoch is flanked by miles of clean sand, ideal for holidays today but not so good for the evicted crofters of the 19th century who, during the Clearances, were moved here and expected to farm the infertile dune land. Small wonder many had to emigrate. There is an exhibition of Dornoch's history at **Historylinks** (*t* (01862) 811 275, *www.historylinks.org.uk; open Easter week daily 10–4, May Mon–Fri 10–4, June–Sept daily 10–4, Oct–Easter Wed–Fri 10–4*), in the Meadows.

Dornoch to Dunbeath

Embo, 3 miles north of Dornoch along the sands, was one of the villages set up during the Clearances to house crofters displaced from their homes by the Duke of Sutherland. The cottages of the original hamlet were built in 1830, their gable ends facing the sea; the area is now a gigantic caravan park and holiday resort. There are two Stone Age burial chambers dating from 2000 BC at the entrance to the caravan site. When they were excavated it was discovered that two later cist tombs had been built into the originals. A battle was fought near here against the Danes during which Sir Richard de Moravia, the brother of the founder of Dornoch Cathedral, was killed.

On a grassy mound on the shore of Loch Fleet, a couple of miles further north, stands the scant ruin of 14th-century **Skelbo Castle**. It was here, in an earlier wooden castle in 1290, that emissaries of Edward I waited to greet the little Princess Margaret, Maid of Norway, whose marriage to Edward's son was to solve the problem of sovereignty in Scotland. It was here, however, that they also heard of the child's death, caused by seasickness on the voyage. This triggered off the Scottish Wars of Independence and Edward's ruthless 'hammering' of the Scots.

The A9 hugs the coast through a string of towns and villages, each with an 'east coast' austerity and the uncompromising stoicism that characterizes the inhabitants of this harsh climate. Whenever you can, dive west and discover the bleak majesty of

Shopping

Capaldi's Ice Cream Shop, Brora. A family business that has produced exceptional ice cream for the Highlands since the 1920s.

Hunters of Brora, outskirts of Brora, t (01408) 623 500. Their tweed is famous throughout the world, with large quantities of cloth, yarn and rugs exported mainly to America. *Open Mon–Fri 9–5.30, Sat 9–5.*

Where to Stay and Eat

Royal Marine Hotel, Golf Road, Brora, t (01408) 621 252, *www.highlandescape hotels.com* (*expensive*). Country house hotel affiliated to the Links Hotel. With leisure club, indoor swimming pool and conference rooms.

The Factor's House, Berriedale, t (01593) 751 280 (*moderate*). Wolsey Lodge in a family house on a sporting estate, 300ft above the sea: comfortable and friendly, with good food using plenty of local ingredients.

Navidale House Hotel, Helmsdale, t (01431) 821 258, (*moderate*). Splendid clifftop country house and fishing hotel overlooking the sea and with a reputation for good seafood.

St Callan's Manse, Rogart, t (01408) 641 363, *www.miltonbankcottages.co.uk* (*moderate*). Friendly, relaxed, hospitable guesthouse, built for the minister of the adjacent kirk and standing in 60 acres of grounds.

Glenaveron Guest House, Golf Road, Brora, t (01408) 621 601, *www.glenaveron.co.uk* (*budget*). Non-smoking B&B.

Rogart Railway Carriage, Rogart Station, t (01408) 641 343, *www.sleeperzzz.com* (*budget*). Unusual hostel based in former sleeper trains in Rogart Station (eight 2-berth compartments).

Sutherland Arms, Golspie, t (01408) 633 234, *www.sutherlandarmshotel.com* (*budget*). Former coaching inn: very good value with a friendly atmosphere.

Tigh Fada, 18 Golf Road, Brora, t (01408) 621 332, *www.tighfada.fsnet.co.uk* (*budget*). Another non-smoking B&B.

La Mirage, opposite Timespan Heritage Centre near Helmsdale, t (01431) 821 615 (*inexpensive*). Worth getting a snack here to see the Barbara Cartlandesque décor.

this forsaken land, with its poignant memorials to a time when today's tumbled ruins were townships teeming with life. It is bleak and, in its own way, beautiful.

Golspie

Golspie, 9 miles north of Dornoch, is the farming centre for the area and has a good golf course. Its 17th-century St Andrew's Church has a splendid old canopied pulpit, fine panelled walls and carvings. You cannot forget the Clearances around here – one of the main perpetrators, the first Duke of Sutherland, lived nearby at Dunrobin Castle. A 30ft-high red-sandstone statue, depicting him as a hero draped in a toga, towers over the landscape from its 70ft plinth, high on Ben Vraggie (*Beinn a'Bhragaidh*) to the west of Golspie, his back to the lands he cleared of people. This statue has been the cause of much dispute recently; some would like to see it torn down and smashed – the Highland Clearances being an emotive subject (*see* **Topics**, p.21). It was, in fact, the Duke of Sutherland's wife who authorized the atrocities perpetrated by his agents. By the 1820s the Sutherland estates covered one and a half million acres, 'an area unequalled in the British Empire'. The first Duke was blamed for his harshness to crofters, but praised for sponsoring many social improvements in the area. The truth lies somewhere in the middle and the blame rests mainly with his unscrupulous agents, who were given a free hand to implement 'improvements' to the estate. Climb to the top of Ben Vraggie and read the statue's inscription. It was erected a year after the Duke's death, in 1834, and its fulsome eulogy to a 'judicious, kind and liberal landlord...' is somewhat ironic.

Dunrobin Castle

Dunrobin Castle (*t (01480) 633 177; open April–Oct Mon–Sat 10.30–4.30, Sun 12–4.30; adm*) stands on a natural terrace overlooking the sea, a mile north of Golspie. Built as a great square keep in 1275 by Robert, Earl of Sutherland, on the site of an ancient broch, it was redesigned and extensively rebuilt in the romantic Gothic style between 1845 and 1850, by Sir Charles Barry, who also designed the Houses of Parliament in London. Queen Victoria stayed here in 1872; the description in her Highland Journal is worth reading. This huge extravaganza rises above formal gardens, its towers and turrets a flamboyant pastiche of French and Scottish architecture. Many of the rooms reflect the hand of the architect Sir Robert Lorimer, a leading light in the Scottish Arts and Crafts movement, who made quite a few improvements during the First World War. The castle contains some fine paintings, including two Canalettos, magnificent furniture, tapestries and other heirlooms. A summerhouse in the park contains a museum, with archaeological exhibits, Victoriana, crafts and natural history including a zoo's worth of stuffed animals. There is a café/restaurant in the castle.

Brora

Five miles up the coast from Golspie, **Brora** is a tourist resort and small industrial town with some of the best salmon fishing in the country. Its older part on the south side of the river dates mainly from the 18th century. An important port as early as the 16th century, there is little to see of the harbour now, due to silting. The *Statistical Account of 1793* records that 'the sea and even the very shore here abounds with excellent fish'. It was from here that the first emigrants to New Zealand left the north of Scotland. Brora was at one time well known for its brickmaking industry. The **Brora Heritage Centre** (*t (01408) 623 500; open June–Sept Mon–Sat 10.30–5.30,*) is particularly good, giving an excellent and informative history of the area. The district is littered with hill forts and Pictish brochs, the best being 3 miles north between the road and the sea, with domed chambers. Two headless skeletons were excavated from the site in 1880.

If you take the minor road west out of Brora, you get a good look at Sutherland's unique landscape. The road follows the river, past Loch Brora, where you will probably pass frustrated salmon fishermen in season, and down Dunrobin Glen back to Golspie. There are several good tracks north across the moors from this road.

Helmsdale

Helmsdale, 10 miles north of Brora, is a fishing and holiday town where the main road and railway part company. You have to search for the remains of 15th-century Helmsdale Castle, on a plateau above the natural harbour. It was within these innocent-looking walls in 1567 that Isobel Sinclair poisoned the Earl and Countess of Sutherland, so that her son might inherit the earldom. The plot failed, though, because her son drank the poison by mistake and died with them. The castle was rebuilt in the early 19th century by the Duke of Sutherland – him on the Monument. It was he who, having evicted the crofters from his lands, tried to make amends by resettling them. Helmsdale was devised as a fishing/farming community, the crofters being divided into those who would work the smallholdings attached to the village and those who would fish. Few of the families had any knowledge of the sea or the tradition of fishing, so fishermen from such established fishing ports as Fraserburgh were encouraged to move here to set an example. The east coast herring boom was just starting and the Duke provided an extensive harbour and well-equipped curing sheds, the best on this coast, and boats came from all over the country – upwards of 200 packed into the harbour. The life of fishermen in those days was a hard one, vividly depicted in the novels of Neil Gunn. The *New Statistical Account* has an interesting description of a typical day during July, August and September when the herring were running. The boats usually left between five and seven o'clock in the afternoon and shot their nets about dusk. Thus they drifted, until about three o'clock in the morning, when all hands hauled in the nets over the stern and disengaged the fish from the meshes. Returning to shore, they landed the catch for the women to gut and pack into barrels with salt. Then they spread their nets out to dry, and returned to their homes for refreshment and a few hours' rest before starting again. This went on for five nights a week, every week; sometimes they got no sleep at all.

There was a bad slump at the end of the 19th century when the local fishermen found they couldn't compete with the larger boats and the advanced gear of their competitors, but they recovered in the 1930s. Today the harbour has a resident fleet and the town's major industry is processing lobster, crab, scallop and prawn.

Timespan Heritage Centre (*t (01431) 821 327; open April–Sept Mon–Sat 10–5, Sun 12–5; July–Aug till 6; last admission 1 hour before closing; call for out of season opening times; adm*), signed off the main road into the village, traces the history of man in the Kildonan area from the stone circles, cairns and brochs of prehistory, through to the present day. Imaginative film and animated tableaux are very effective, though young children might find some of the displays scary. There is a café.

Even if you don't want a meal, find room for a snack so you can look in at **La Mirage**, opposite Timespan (*see* 'Where to Stay and Eat', p.183). The lady in charge, a Barbara Cartland fan, has created a sort of 'Cartlandesque' boudoir from which to run her pink café, with a fake palm tree in the middle and acres of photographs of celebrities – delightfully incongruous in this down-to-earth seaport.

Around Helmsdale

The River Helmsdale, one of the most renowned salmon rivers in Scotland, flows through the Strath of Kildonan, erstwhile territory of Clan Gunn. Its population in 1811 was 1,574; 20 years later it had fallen to 257. Gold has occasionally been found in burns that feed the Helmsdale, giving rise to periodic gold fever. **Baile an Or** (gold field), about 8 miles up the glen from Helmsdale, grew into a gold-rush shanty town after a good yield from the Kildonan Burn in 1869, but great expectations yielded little lasting treasure. You will find details in the Timespan Heritage Centre (*see* above).

The **Ord of Caithness** is the coastal pass from Sutherland into Caithness. Before the road was improved it was one of the most nerve-racking drives in the country, with seaward precipices so terrifying that 'whenever any of the landed proprietors entered the county, a troop of their tenants assembled on the border and drew the carriage themselves over the hill, a distance of 2 miles, that nothing might be trusted in such a scene to the discretion of quadrupeds'. The Rev Donald Sage, wrote a fascinating memoir in 1825, *Memorabilia Domestica*, which describes this area in detail, including first-hand experiences of the Highland Clearances.

They say that no superstitious Sinclair – the clan of the Earl of Caithness – has crossed the Ord on a Monday, since that Monday in 1513 when the Earl led his men this way to fight for James IV at Flodden, from which not one of them returned. There is a broch at Ousdale, a couple of miles beyond the Ord, where the A9 runs inland for a while. Take the track to the old hamlet of **Badbea**, 2 miles east on the cliffs. Crofters from Ousdale took refuge here during the Clearances and stories are told of the beasts and children having to be tethered to prevent them being blown into the sea.

Dunbeath to John o' Groats

Dunbeath to Wick

Dunbeath, 6 miles to the north of Berriedale, was another of the east-coast ports that shared in the herring boom. The local laird built the harbour in 1800 and by the middle of the century there were about 90 boats based here. The writer Neil Gunn was born here in 1891 in a house built by his seaman father. Several of his books reflect his strong association with this area: *Morning Tide*; *The Silver Darlings*; and *Highland River*, a brilliant portrayal of life around Dunbeath Water. **Dunbeath Heritage Centre** (*www.dunbeath-heritage.org.uk; open April–Oct 10–5*), in the Old School, tells about him and about local history. With 14th-century origins, spectacular **Dunbeath Castle** is visible from the road on a steep rock south of the harbour. Though captured by Montrose in 1650, it was occupied for centuries, almost uninterrupted, by Sinclairs. The Dunbeath Highland Games are held in July.

Tourist Information

John o' Groats: County Road, t (01955) 611 373. *Open April–Oct.*

Where to Stay and Eat

Dunbeath Hotel, Dunbeath, t (01593) 731 208 (*moderate*). Excellent base, in a traditional-style building and good food. All rooms are *en suite*.

Norseman Hotel, Riverside, Wick, t (01955) 603 344, *www.swallow-hotels.com* (*budget*). Large and not that remarkable to look at, but right on the water, centrally located and with a friendly atmosphere.

Queen's Hotel, 16 Francis Street, Wick, t (01955) 602 992 (*budget*). Solid and respectable, a former manse on the A9 at the entrance to town. Most rooms are *en suite*.

Seaview Hotel, John O'Groats, t (01955) 611 220, *www.johnogroats-seaviewhotel.co.uk* (*budget*). Plain building with few frills but good views. Dogs welcome. The restaurant serves local fish and farm produce.

Wellington Guest House, High Street, Wick, t (01955) 603 287, *www.visitscotland.com* (*budget*). In the heart of things, lively and with good hospitality.

The **Clan Gunn Museum and Heritage Centre** (*t (01593) 741 700; open June–Sept Mon–Sat 11–1 and 2–4; July–Aug as before, inc Sun 2–4; adm*) is at **Latheron**, 3 miles beyond Dunbeath, in a converted 18th-century church. It tells the story of this ancient clan from its Norse origins, illustrating its links with America before Columbus. The churchyard has a small hut which was used as a watch house against grave robbers. It was customary for someone to keep watch for 14 days after a funeral to prevent body snatching.

Christianity is believed to have been brought to Latheron by St Ninian early in the 5th century. The ruined pre-Reformation chapel of St Mary has doors less than 4ft high. In 1699 the minister was suspended by the Presbytery when he admitted that he had not administered the sacraments or catechized anyone for 16 years and that he had danced, or as he put it, 'gone up and down the room' at a wedding. In 1734 the minister was suspended for nine months because he 'slit a man's ear for stealing'. From here up to Clyth Ness the coast is strikingly picturesque, with high cliffs and rocky ledges sticking out into the sea – quite dangerous. The name of some of the coves – the Whaler, the Frenchman – are grim reminders of ships that foundered here in days gone by. **North Shore Pottery Mill**, at Mill of Forse, near Latheron, is a working pottery and shop in the restored mill.

The A9 runs due north from here to Thurso across desolate moorland. A considerable length of this road was laid out in one day in the 18th century, under the command of a local laird, Sir John Sinclair. He used every able man and beast and stone in the district. About 6 miles up the road is the **Achavanich Standing Stone Circle**, a ritual site in the form of a truncated oval, thought to have once contained up to 60 stones. Less than a mile to the west is **Rangag Broch**, dating from 150 BC.

In **Lybster**, 4 miles north of Latheron, turn off the broad thoroughfare, flanked by sturdy, dignified houses, and go down to the harbour, scooped out of rock to provide a perfect haven for the large fishing fleet that plied the waters here in the 19th century. For centuries this district was the most sparsely populated part of Latheron parish, inhabited by only a small number of scattered crofters.

In 1810 the local laird built a wooden pier within the small creek at the mouth of the Reisgill Burn to allow his tenants to supplement their income by fishing. The project was successful and the pier was replaced in 1833 with the present stone one. The harbour is very attractive, with steep grassy banks forming a sheltered bowl, covered with primroses in spring. By 1840, Lybster was the third-largest fishing station in Scotland, with upwards of 200 boats working out of the harbour until the slump in the herring industry towards the end of the century. Many men resorted to their crofts and endured such hardship they were forced to emigrate. The fleet is now reduced to a few lobster boats and a number of pleasure craft, but the atmosphere is still very much that of a fishing community. **Lybster Harbour Visitor Centre** (*t (01593) 721 520; open April–Oct daily 10–8*), focuses on local birdlife, the history of the herring industry and boat building. There is a coffee shop and yacht facilities. There is also an **Art Gallery** (*open June–Sept*), with work by local artists, pottery and glass work.

About a mile east of Lybster, on the A99, take the minor road north up the Clyth Burn, signed to **Grey Cairns of Camster**, about 5 miles over the moor. In this remote spot, easy to miss in the mist if there aren't cars already parked there, are two spectacular restored Neolithic monuments, including what has been described as the most outstanding, long horned cairn in the country, at 200ft (61m), and dating to about 3800 BC. On the right are two beehive-shaped chambers, incorporated at a later date into the huge elongated mound of piled stones with horns at either end. The corbelled, dry-stone roofs cover the hidden chambers which you can crawl into through very low narrow tunnels – not for the claustrophobic. The other chamber is on the left: a single, smoothly rounded cairn with an entrance tunnel. Human and animal remains were excavated and it is intriguing to ponder on what sort of men these were. The climate was milder and better in those days and the soil more fertile, enabling those early farmers to cultivate wheat and raise cattle and sheep.

A couple of miles to the east, up a short road signed off the A99, the **Hill o'Many Stanes** is an early Bronze Age site which has puzzled archaeologists for years. What seems to be small standing stones randomly dotted over the heather, is in fact a ribbed fan, each rib containing about eight or more stones, numbering some 200 in all, and thought once to have been about 600. It could have been a ritual site for burials, like other henges, or some form of astronomical calculator for calculating the farming cycle. Whatever its purpose, it is eerie to stand on this lonely, windswept moor trying to picture those early settlers, once surprisingly numerous in this northern corner of the British Isles.

About 8 miles north on the A99 from Lybster, past a church on a sharp bend, you come into the unsigned hamlet of **Whaligoe**. A staggered crossroads has a left turn marked to an alpine nursery. Almost opposite, flanked by a telephone kiosk and a letterbox, a small road goes past a row of terraced cottages to a house with a high stone wall, where you can park. A flight of 365 recently restored stone steps zigzags steeply down the cliff to the old harbour, long gone but once used by fishing fleets to moor and unload their catches among the cheerful bustle and banter of the fishermen and the teams of women working at the gutting. Fishermen used these steps to get to their boats, and lives were lost in their use. This is a magical place now, the deep cleft in the sheer cliffs providing a sheltered bay with ink-dark water, wild flowers and no people. In some places, to secure their boats from being dashed to pieces against the rocks in storms and high tides, the fishermen hung them by ropes on hooks fixed in the rock – they were safely suspended until the weather improved.

Wick

Certainly Wick in itself possesses no beauty: bare grey shores, grim grey houses, grim grey sea; not even the greenness of a tree... In Wick I have never heard anyone greet his neighbour with the usual 'Fine day' or 'Good morning'. Both come shaking their heads, and both say, 'Breezy, breezy!' And such is the atrocious climate that the remark is almost invariably justified by the fact. The streets are full of highland fishers, lubberly, stupid, inconceivably lazy and heavy to move. You bruise against them, tumble over them, elbow them against the wall – and all to no purpose; they will not budge; and you are forced to leave the pavement every step.

So wrote Robert Louis Stevenson to his mother in 1868. By contrast, Elin Burritt, an American traveller, wrote in 1864, that it was 'a brave little city by the Norse Sea, which may not only be called the Wick but the candle of Northern Scotland... the great metropolis of Fishdom.'

Wick, so called from the Viking word *vik* meaning 'bay or creek', is a substantially built seaport and tourist centre, stretching round the sweep of Wick Bay, 15 miles northeast of Lybster. There is a harbour, airport and railway terminal. Norse pirates were drawn to Wick by the shelter of its bay at the mouth of the river and by the magnet of the rich farmland beckoning from the west. Created a Royal Burgh in 1589, it had the exclusive right to trade abroad, being closer to Europe than Thurso, which had the better harbour. It was only properly developed in the 19th century by the British Fisheries Society. It is difficult to believe now that 1,122 herring boats once plied from the complex of three harbour basins before the decline of the herring stock. At the height of the boom, 3,800 fishermen were employed and about 4,000 people had related jobs such as curing. None of the boats was more than 30ft long, all undecked and unprotected against wind and waves. The sight of the fleet putting to sea in the late afternoon was memorable.

In 1845 the *New Statistical Account* took a grimmer look at the fishing boom: 'The herring fishing has increased wealth, but also wickedness. No care is taken of the 10,000 young strangers of both sexes who are crowded together with the inhabitants within the narrow limits of Wick during the six weeks of the fishery, when they are exposed to drink and every other temptation...There is great consumption of spirits, there being 22 public houses in Wick and 23 in Pulteneytown... Seminaries of Satan and Balial.' If the fishing was successful, the report continues, not less than 500 gallons of whisky were consumed in a day. Wick today is a shadow of its former self, but white-fish trawlers still use the harbour. On the morning of 19 August 1848 a gale from the southeast struck Wick just as the fleet was heading homewards. Forty-one boats were lost, most of them within sight of the harbour.

The **Heritage Museum** (*open June–Sept Mon–Sat 10–5*) near the harbour, tells the fishing story of Wick, with a good collection of fishing gear. When the herring industry declined, On the north side of the town, in the Airport Industrial Estate, visitors can watch craftsmen fashioning molten glass, shaping it and engraving it. It is interesting that in this land so full of echoes of Norse occupation, the designs of the glass are distinctively Scandinavian.

Around Wick

To the south of the town, perched on a peninsula between two precipitous cliffs, with a ditch protecting it from the mainland, **Old Wick Castle** was probably the resort of St Rognvald and other Norse dignitaries when they visited the mainland from Orkney. (Rognvald made a pact with God that he would build a great cathedral in honour of his uncle, St Magnus, if he should win the Earldom on Orkney, and St Magnus Cathedral in Kirkwall was the result.) Known to seamen as the 'Auld Man o'Wick', this three-storey ruin had no water supply and so was unable to withstand long sieges. It was abandoned in the 16th century.

Take time to walk along the cliffs and appreciate the spectacularly shaped rocks. **Brig o' Trams** is a natural rock arch, and there is splendid rock sculpture at **Noss Head**, a glorious 3-mile walk north to the lighthouse. From the point, it is less than half a mile west to **Sinclair** and **Girnigoe Castles**, the dramatic ruins of two separate castles on a precipitous promontory looking north over Sinclair's Bay. As you walk across a field to reach them, they seem to grow out of the horizontally layered cliff. The Sinclairs lived in the two castles as one dwelling, constantly attacked by ambitious rivals. Ghosts lurk in the walls: in 1570 the 4th Earl, suspecting his son of plotting to kill him, imprisoned him in the dungeons for seven years till he died of 'famine and vermine'. This is quite a dangerous spot, so harness your children.

The great sandy sweep of Sinclair's Bay leads north along a coastline believed to be among the earliest inhabited in Scotland. Excavations have revealed that Middle Stone Age man existed here in large numbers on the fertile hinterland, living a primitive life long after more advanced cultures – New Stone Age and Iron Age – were flourishing in other parts of the country.

Lyth Arts Centre (*t (01955) 641 270; open July and Aug daily; adm*), about 4 miles inland, off the A99 halfway round the bay, is an unexpected venture in a Victorian village school in the middle of nowhere. During the two months of the year they are open, they exhibit the work of artists and performers from many countries, some of great merit, and there is a permanent collection of Scottish work. Live performances are presented from April to September: drama, dance and all types of music, and there is a café.

On the northern point of the bay, at **Keiss**, a tall slender tower on top of the cliff is all that remains of **Keiss Castle**, home of William Sinclair, founder of the first Baptist church in Scotland. A couple of miles further on, the scant ruin of 12th-century **Bucholie Castle** was the stronghold of Sweyn Aslefson, a Norse pirate featured in the old Norse sagas.

A 10th-century Viking settlement is still in the process of being excavated a mile further on at **Freswick**. **Northlands Viking Centre**, at Auckengill (*open June–Sept daily 10–4*), tells the whole Norse story.

John o' Groats

John o' Groats, loosely accepted as Britain's northeastern extremity (actually at Duncansby Head, a couple of miles east), is linked diagonally to Land's End, 876 miles away (also not technically Britain's southwestern extremity). It is a bleak, scattered village, washed by the Pentland Firth – an awe-inspiring vista on the edge of the world. But it has to be said that John o' Groats itself is often a disappointment to tourists – little more than an uninspiring coach and car park, a few ugly buildings containing souvenirs, snacks and woollens, a rather overpriced 'craft community', and a flat, dreary landscape, though the **Tourist Information Centre** is good.

The small settlement got its curious name from a Dutchman, Jan de Groot, who established a ferry link with the newly acquired islands of Orkney in 1496, under the rule of James IV. It is said Jan charged such extortionate rates for his ferry that magistrates ordered him to fix the fare at four pence – a silver coin called a 'groat'.

There is a **Last House Museum** (*open all year*), with local history, including photographs of local shipwrecks, and a **Journeys End Exhibition** (*open Easter–Oct*), with an audiovisual presentation. **Wildlife Cruises** (*t (01955) 611 353; daily in summer, weather permitting, starts at 2.30, lasts 1½ hours*) run from John o'Groats. You may see puffins, Arctic skuas, storm petrels, seals and lots more. They also run tours to Orkney.

Duncansby Head

Duncansby Head is Scotland's real northeastern corner, a couple of miles east of John o' Groats, and much more satisfying. You can drive out to the lighthouse and then walk along the cliffs to see dramatic stacks and rock formations. Many different sea birds throng the headland, and in clear weather the only limit to the view over the Pentland Firth is the keenness of your eye. The 12-knot tide rip here is a notorious hazard to shipping: over 400 wrecks have been recorded in the last 150 years. Away from the blemishes of tourism, the coastline is perfect for those who like wild and lonely places, birds and wild flowers, and exhilarating extremes of weather.

The Northern Coast: West to Cape Wrath

This is an edge-of-the-world highway. The blanket bog to the south has been a bone of contention between conservationists and foresters. The distinctive peatland is a fragile, living surface of floating peat with heather and sedges growing over a carpet of sphagnum mosses, supporting an amazing concentration of rare wildlife. Forestry tycoons have already 'reclaimed' 16 per cent of the Flow Country, proud to have made productive use of such a 'dreary wasteland'. Conservationists argue this is Europe's largest bog, as well as the oldest and least disturbed blanket bog in the world. Its depth, up to 20ft, and age, mean that it holds within its soggy bosom important data for meteorological historians. Threatened victims among its population include 55 species of birds related to Arctic tundra, including 70 per cent of Britain's greenshanks, meadow pipits, red-throated divers, peregrines and merlins. Among the many plants which could be lost to the forests is the rare insect-eating sundew.

Very different and equally rewarding are the side-tracks to the north off the A836, each one unfolding a new, wild view of the Pentland Firth. Spare a thought for the Roman fleet of Agricola, which supplied the advancing legions as they tried to conquer Scotland. They battled their way round from the east coast and triumphantly reported that Britain was indeed an island.

John o' Groats to Thurso

Castle of Mey (*t (01847) 851473, www.castleofmey.org.uk; open 10.30–4, mid-May–late Sept, but may close for certain periods; adm*), 7 miles west of John o' Groats, was built around the middle of the 16th century for the 4th Earl of Caithness and remained in the family until 1889. It was bought and restored in 1956 by one of Britain's best-loved public figures, Queen Elizabeth, the Queen Mother, for whom it was a holiday retreat until her death, at the age of nearly 102, on 30 March 2002. Turrets of the castle can be glimpsed from the road, sheltered by trees at the end of no-entry drives.

Dunnet Head, 9 miles further on, is the most northerly point of Scotland's mainland, a sheer promontory of red sandstone, with a lighthouse 300ft (91m) above the sea. Walking out to the point (although it is possible to drive), you're surrounded by dozens of species of colourful wild flowers. There are puffins here – endearing birds with their comic tuxedo garb and vivid striped beaks, burrowing in the turf. The village of Dunnet is a scattering of houses on the vast sweep of Dunnet Bay.

Signed on the way towards the point is **Mary Ann's Cottage** (*open June–Sept Tues–Sun 2–4.30; adm*). Mary Ann Calder lived here until she moved to a nursing home at the age of 93 in 1990, and the cottage and croft have been preserved as they were when worked by Mary Ann and her husband James and by their predecessors, going back 150 years. The buildings reveal the past, pre-improvement community system of crofting and show how more modern concepts replaced the old.

The tower of the white church behind the hotel, with its saddle-backed roof, dates from the 14th century, a pre-Reformation survivor that confirms the comforting continuity of a place that seems to have changed little over the years. The fishing is good around here, in sea, river and loch. A halibut weighing 210lbs (93kg) was caught here with rod and line in 1975. Intrepid surfers also brave the waves.

Thurso

The name of Thurso, 20 miles west of John o' Groats, stems from the Norse *Thorsa* meaning River of the God Thor, and the town is perhaps more interesting as a flag on the Scottish map than as a tourist attraction. It used to be the main trading port for Scandinavia and was granted the status Burgh of Barony in 1633, which gave it the right to trade within Scotland. As an important Viking stronghold, it reached its zenith in the 11th century under Thorfinn, who defeated King Duncan's nephew in 1040 in a mighty battle here. In 1158 the body of murdered Earl Rognvald was brought here, probably to a chapel on the site of St Peter's Church. It is now the largest town north of Inverness, with elegant 18th-century houses built of brown sandstone around a central square, and a long, narrow harbour. Sir John Sinclair of Ulster, related to the Sinclair Earls of Caithness, was born in Thurso Castle in 1754 and was instrumental in the building of the present town. He was a noted agriculturist and a keen 'improver', and was one of the few landlords in this area who saw the enormous potential of

Cheviot sheep and yet desired nothing more than the protection of his tenants. He was also a prime mover in the publication of James Macpherson's Ossianic collection in 1765 – inspiring Samuel Johnson's contempt.

St Peter's Church, near the harbour, dates from the 12th or 13th century, and stands on the site of the chapel where Earl Rognvald's murdered body was brought. Most of what survives dates from the 16th and later centuries – some of the original stone can be seen in the curious choir. The church was used for worship until 1862. **Thurso Castle**, the Victorian Gothic ruin on the east side of the river, was built for Sir John Sinclair in 1872 and lived in by Sinclairs until it was demolished in 1952.

Harald Tower, just over a mile along the coast to the northeast, was built in 1780 to replace a previously demolished chapel which had served as a burial place for the Sinclairs and contained the grave of Harald, Earl of Caithness, a mighty warlord who ruled over half Caithness and Orkney and was killed in battle nearby in 1196.

Thurso to Cape Wrath

Scrabster, a mile to the northwest of Thurso along the bay, is the terminal for the car ferry to Stromness in Orkney, now run by North Link ferries (*www.northlinkferries. co.uk; three times daily Mon–Fri, twice daily at weekends*). It is an invigorating nearly 2-hour trip on a fine day. It is likely that Scrabster was a powerful Viking stronghold in the 12th century. A castle was built to house the bishop in 1223, and remained the bishop's palace until the abolition of episcopacy.

At Crosskirk, overlooking Crosskirk Bay, 5 miles or so west of Thurso, signed off the main road, **St Mary's Chapel** is about half a mile's walk across turf on low cliffs. This simple little roofless kirk dates from the 12th century, its chancel containing three Gunn memorials accessed from the nave by a small doorway. Remote and peaceful in a walled churchyard, the place has a timeless serenity.

The **Dounreay Nuclear Power Station**, 7 miles on along the cliffs, was established in 1954, bringing prosperity to Thurso, with a workforce of 2,000. Its closure in 1994 brought hardship to many of the local workers, and relief to the anti-nuclear brigade. Work is now in progress to 'decommission' the three reactors and associated plant, a £2.7 billion operation ensuring local employment until 2036; meanwhile non-nuclear activities for the plant are being investigated. An exhibition (*t (01847) 802121; open May–Sept daily*) gives an insight into Dounreay's role in British science.

About 6 miles west, the A897 branches off south back to Helmsdale through Strath Halladale and Strath of Kildonan. Continue west along the main road a few miles and turn north to **Strathy Point** where the sea has carved a series of fabulous arches and caverns in the cliffs.

The coast from here to Bettyhill is wonderfully diverse, with sheltered sandy beaches and sea-eroded cliffs. On Farr Point, **Borve Castle** stands in ruins, a former stronghold of the Clan Mackay, destroyed by the Earl of Sutherland in 1515.

Bettyhill on the shore of Torrisdale Bay is said by some to be named after a local woman Betty Cnocan, who kept an inn at the hilltop, rather than after the Duchess of

Tourist Information

Bettyhill: Clachan, **t** (01641) 521 342. *Open April–Sept.*
Durness Tourist Information Centre, **t** (01971) 511 259.

Where to Stay and Eat

Altnaharra Hotel, Altnaharra, **t** (01549) 411 222, *www.altnaharra.com* (*moderate*). A real Highland hotel, catering for fishermen since 1800 – comfortable, with good food.
Ben Loyal Hotel, Tongue, **t** (01847) 611 216, *www.benloyalhotel.co.uk* (*moderate*). Comfortable and prettily furnished, with relaxed and friendly owners.
Borgie Lodge Hotel, Skerray, **t** (01641) 521 332, *www.borgielodgehotel.co.uk* (*moderate*). 19th-century house in a secluded glen. The owners have fishing rights on local rivers and the hotel's 20 hill lochs.
Cape Wrath Hotel, Kyle of Durness, Durness, **t** (01971) 511 212, *www.capewrath.com* (*moderate*). Built in 1820 as a sporting lodge. Well equipped, old-fashioned and comfortable, and good home cooking. Fishing by arrangement.
Forss Country House Hotel, west of Scrabster, **t** (01847) 861 201/2, *www.forsscountryhouse.*

co.uk (*moderate*). A very special place to stay: built in 1810 in 20 acres only 100 yards from falls of the River Forss. First-class food and well over 100 malt whiskies. As well as the spacious, elegant rooms there are lodges for extra privacy and flexibility.
Melvich Hotel, Melvich, **t** (01641) 531 206, *www.smoothhound.co.uk/hotels/ melvich.html* (*moderate*). Very comfortable country house hotel with peat fires and friendly staff. With its own brown trout lochs and access to salmon fishing.
Sheiling Guest House, Melvich, **t** (01641) 531 256, *www.b-and-b-scotland.co.uk/sheiling. htm* (*moderate*). Comfortable and friendly, with good views and excellent breakfasts.
Tongue Hotel, Tongue, **t** (01847) 611 206, *www.tonguehotel.co.uk* (*moderate*). The nicest place to stay in Tongue, with Victorian charm and style. Built in 1880 as a hunting lodge, it lies at the foot of Ben Loyal overlooking the Kyle of Tongue.
Cloisters, Church Holme, Talmine, **t** (01847) 601 286, *www.cloistertal.demon.co.uk* (*budget*). Delightful B&B, great setting.
Port-Na-Con, near Durness, **t** (01971) 511 367, (*budget*). Very comfortable guesthouse. Good food, especially seafood.
The Old Nick Tea Room, next to the Strathnaver Museum in Bettyhill. A welcome if unsophisticated place for a snack.

Sutherland, who cleared the people of Strathnaver to Bettyhill, telling them to rebuild their lives by fishing and cultivating wind-torn land on the infertile coast.

Strathnaver Museum (**t** *(01641) 521 330; open April–31 Oct Mon–Sat, ring for winter visits; adm*) is housed in what was once the large church of the parish of Farr. If you only have the time and inclination for one museum in the far north, let it be this one. The story of the Clearances is poignantly told by children, on simple posters, in a building in which it is likely the minister may have read out eviction notices to his congregation. There is a lot else to see, including old photographs, a bothy room with a box bed, and a Clan MacKay room. In a description of the Battle of Druim na Coup in 1431, when the MacKays cut down their Sutherland rivals to a man, the sad end came when Angus Dhu MacKay came back to survey the scene of his victory and was killed by the arrow of the last dying Sutherland. Also in the museum is an exhibition about Rob Donn, or Doun, born of humble origins in Strathmore in 1715, and illiterate, who became one of Scotland's leading Gaelic poets. Next door is a tearoom (*see* above), a Tourist Information Centre, and a craft shop.

To get some idea of how those crofting families must have suffered, go through the village and take the little road south signed to **Achanlochy** by the bridge over the

River Naver. About a mile along there is a cairn in a gravel pit with Achanlochy written on it. Walk up the slope to the site of one of the cleared hamlets, well explained on an information board. From this hillock you can picture how it would have been, living in Strathnaver before 1819. Bettyhill is referred to in Gaelic as *am blàran odhar* – the grey place, or the little dun-coloured field – in contrast to the lush, green, sheltered land of the Strath from which its people were evicted.

Also along this road, before Achanlochy up on the left, is a remarkable Neolithic burial cairn, a great mound of tumbled stones 75 yards long. One of the three burial chambers, now unroofed, is easy to get into and you can see the construction method, with huge stone slabs set vertically with flat-laid dry-stone walling. The B873 runs south through Strathnaver where many croft houses went up in flames during those troubled times, and where people died of exposure, huddled against the ruins of their homes. **Invernaver National Nature Reserve**, around the mouth of the River Naver, has the finest collection of mountain and coastal plants in the north. Among the rarer birds that breed here are greenshank, ring ouzel and twite. On the edge of the reserve, on a plateau, is the remains of a Neolithic community, **Baile Marghair**.

Tongue to Whiten Head

Tongue, about 10 miles on from Bettyhill, is on the eastern shore of the **Kyle of Tongue**. When Borve Castle, along the coast, was destroyed by the Gordons of Sutherland in 1554, the Mackays adopted Tongue as their stronghold. Here they remained until Donald Mackay espoused the cause of Charles I and republican troops garrisoned the town. **Coldbackie Bay**, on the northeastern side of the Kyle is lovely for bathing and picnics, with clean sand, dunes and birds.

A new mansion, the **House of Tongue**, was built in 1678, with a wing added by a later Mackay, 3rd Lord Reay, who also built the first road fit for a horse-drawn carriage in this area, to take him to church. This is the house on the shore to the east of the causeway, with an impressive steading. The Clan Mackay was not so loyal to the Stuarts a century later. When a sloop called the *Prince Charles* – formerly HMS *Hazard*, captured by the Jacobites – was on its way to Inverness carrying French gold to boost the Prince's funds in March 1746, it was spotted by some naval ships and chased up the coast and into the Pentland Firth. Hoping to evade the English by sailing into the shallow Kyle of Tongue, it foundered on a sandbank. In the ensuing battle the *Prince Charles* was destroyed. The crew escaped hoping to carry the gold overland to Inverness but anti-Jacobite Mackays followed, captured them and locked them in the boathouse that still stands near House of Tongue. Sensing their imminent defeat, the fugitives threw the gold into a loch but most of it was recovered (Prince Charles sent 1,500 of his men north to collect the gold, thus significantly depleting his army for the fateful battle at Culloden). Stories are still told of the occasional piece of gold turning up – one piece supposedly emerged firmly wedged into a cow's hoof.

The name Tongue is Norse and the ruin of **Castle Varrich** which stares down on the village from a rocky hill was a Norse stronghold in the 11th century. Nothing much is known about it, but it is a nice walk from the village, with a profusion of wild flowers, including gentians, in season and good views of the Kyle. On the way, you pass a series of reed beds, an ingenious 'green' method of purifying and disposing of sewage, explained on information boards. The road crosses the middle of the Kyle on a causeway and at low tide the whole long, shallow inlet seems to be drying out. Go out on the narrow road up the west side of the Kyle, to more spectacular coastal scenery, sandy bays, weird-shaped rocks, fishing hamlets and remote clifftop walks. **Portvasgo**, almost at the end of the road, is one of the few places where you can find the very rare *Primula scotica*, which nestles in the sheep-cropped turf on the cliffs.

There are good walks out along the coast to **Whiten Head** – or An Ceann Geal – at the tip of the peninsula between Tongue and Loch Eriboll, with caves under the cliffs where Atlantic grey seals play. This peninsula – called A'Mhoine – is a wilderness of moor, rock and hill, beautiful in sunshine, but awesome in storm.

If you want a good day's walk, head up either **Ben Hope** (a Munro) or **Ben Loyal**. Hope is quicker, about 5 hours and not too challenging, but it needs good navigation. Start at the cowshed a couple of miles south of the head of Loch Hope, where a path goes up the bank of a burn. There is a choice of ascents: the northern one, up the main burn, has a tricky bit, with an alternative path through the gully if you can't face it. There are wonderful views from the top, with Strath More laid out below you and the Pentland Firth lashing away to the north. Ben Loyal takes longer, about 7 hours, and is best done from the north, where there is a path and you can miss the bog that spoils the shorter approach from the east. Begin at the start of a private road to Ribigill Farm, 1½ miles south of Tongue on the old road. The farm track goes south over the moor to Cunside Cottage (near which is a chambered cairn called Jeremy's Grave, marked on the map as *Uaigh Dhiarmaid*). The track becomes a path and takes you up the burn where you climb steep turf and heather to reach the first summit and, if you have the energy, the others beyond. It's fairly obvious once you start.

Loch Hope and Loch Eriboll

A couple of miles before you reach Loch Eriboll on the A838, a very minor road runs south down **Loch Hope** towards Altnaharra and the road southwards. Ten miles down, on the Strathmore River, there is the ruin of a broch – **Dun Dornaigil** – well placed to guard the glen and provide shelter in times of attack. You can't go inside but there is an impressive large triangular lintel above the doorway.

Loch Eriboll runs parallel with the Kyle of Tongue, a deep sea loch running some 10 miles inland and the subject of one of the prophesies of the Brahan Seer early in the 17th century. He named Loch Eriboll as a place where a war would end one day. In 1945, at the end of the Second World War, German submarines came into the loch to surrender. Servicemen stationed here during the war to protect convoys passing through the Pentland Firth nicknamed it Loch 'Orrible. After the First World War, land on the west side of the loch was allocated to the repatriated heroes to give them a chance to start a new life. One look at the inhospitable landscape will explain why they were less than delighted with the munificence of this gesture.

There are the remains of several ancient settlements around here. About a mile north of Laid School on the west side of the loch, there is a complete and untouched souterrain, with curved steps leading to a round chamber. You need a torch for this earth house, which floods after heavy rain. Look for two cairns in a bracken-infested lay-by on the right just past a fish farm in a bay; it is towards the loch from here.

Smoo Cave is signposted from the road just before Durness, down a steep, stepped path, with a grassy slope opposite festooned with the names of visitors of all nationalities, picked out in pebbles on the turf. The vast limestone cavern has three compartments formed by continuous erosion. The outer chamber is 200ft (61m) long and 120ft (37m) high, its glistening, floodlit walls hung with ferns and lichen, with holes in the roof and access to the inner chamber over a bridge. Here the Alt Smoo River thunders down from the cliffs into the cave in an awe-inspiring 70ft waterfall which fills the cave with spray. You can get into the third chamber by boat when there isn't too much water. Walter Scott came here in 1814 and wrote one of the best descriptions of it in his diary.

Durness to Cape Wrath

Durness, 6 miles west of Loch Eriboll, is the gateway to Cape Wrath, the top left-hand corner of Scotland. Perched on the coast, built to withstand the fury of the elements, it is a small reprovisioning base for exploring this area and has an excellent **Tourist Information Centre** (*see* 'Tourist Information', p.194). It was a Pictish settlement in about 400 BC and has been farmland ever since, bought by the Sutherlands in 1829. When attempts were made to clear it in 1841, over 300 crofters protested vociferously until troops of the 53rd Regiment were ordered to move in from Edinburgh. Some of the land was cleared, but Durine and Sangomore were reprieved, giving inspiration to others who had hitherto accepted their fate. There are crofting communities all around, with the Kyle of Durness cutting off road access to the Cape (*seasonal tourist information, t (01971) 511 259*).

Balnakeil Craft Village (*mostly open from Easter and closed by end of Oct; some shops closed Sun*) is in a ghastly former Ministry of Defence Early Warning Station camp along the road heading west from Durness to the golf course. It is a 'community co-operative of crafts' where a group, mostly of incomers, sell their predictable, not always home-made stuff. 'For Sale' notices seem numerous, and 'Gone out – back in an hour' suggests little trade. A rather depressing place but there are a couple of coffee shops and if you persevere you may even find bargains.

Durness Old Church, not far on along the same road, dates from 1619. It is an ivy-clad, roofless shell on the site of at least two older churches. Just inside the entrance on the left is a recessed tomb dated 1623 and well preserved. Among the elaborate carvings both on it and on a plaque above are a skull and crossbones with the hopeful inscription 'Memento Mori'. The epitaph reads: 'Donald Macmurchow hier lyis lo, vas il to his freind, var to his fo. True to his maister in veird and vo' (*var* – worse, *veird* – prosperity). This is said to be the grave of a notorious highwayman, who hoped to buy his way into the afterlife by making substantial contributions to the building of the church and his tomb. One of the previous churches on this site appears in records in the Vatican as having contributed to one of the Crusades in the 12th century.

In the kirkyard there is a monument to Rob Donn, born in 1715 and one of the greatest Gaelic poets, whose work has been compared to that of Burns. Of humble origins, he was illiterate, but Gaelic poetry was an oral art and he had the gift. Cattle drover and notorious poacher, he composed and recited his poetry for all occasions. Although Gaelic poetry loses its lyrical magic in translation, much of his was translated and endures today. He wrote about ordinary people living ordinary lives and was always invited to celebrations – if he was not, he composed rude comments in verses which spread like wildfire.

The Summer Palace for the bishops of Caithness was where the substantial Balnakeil Farmhouse now stands, opposite the church. One of the best walks in the area begins here, out round the bay to *Fair Aird* – Far Out Head – through dunes and over springy turf, carpeted with wild flowers in spring, where you might also see puffins. The far end of the bay is good for hardy swimmers. Further on round the corner, the Durness Golf Course is the most northerly in mainland Britain with perhaps the most glorious surroundings. One hole includes a shot 'over the Atlantic' and the club rule is that players give way to anglers on Loch Lanlish.

Cape Wrath

A ferry runs across the Kyle of Durness in the summer, weather and conditions permitting (*t (01971) 511 376*), and connects with a minibus out to the cape (*t (01971) 511 287/343*). Officially, it runs from 9.30am and makes about eight trips a day, but as it can't run at low tide the timetable is flexible; the round trip takes about 2 hours.

The Clo Mor Cliffs are the highest in Britain – 523ft (161m) high, with veins of rich pink pegmatite running through the gneiss. The lighthouse on the point was built by Robert Louis Stevenson's father. It is an outlandish place – compelling in its end-of-the-world, wild loneliness – and a paradise for ornithologists. (The name Wrath – pronounced Raath – comes not from the often furious seas around the cape, but from the Viking word *hvarf*, which means 'turning point'.)

To the north lies the island of North Rona, with Stack Skerry and Skule Skerry further east. Turn your back on the great fort-like lighthouse and look across the bleak moor – the Parbh – that stretches away to the south. Wolves once roamed here in great numbers: an eerie thought as the mist comes creeping in over the desolate wasteland and you look around to make sure the minibus hasn't left without you. You can walk on round the coast to Sandwood Bay, only about 6 miles as the crow flies but over difficult, slow terrain with several rivers to be forded, taking up to 6½ hours, with no track. It is then 4½ miles further to the nearest road. Sandwood is lovely and worth visiting (*see p.148*), but you are better off walking up from the Kinlochbervie end and retracing your steps (9 miles round trip).

The Islands of the Clyde

14

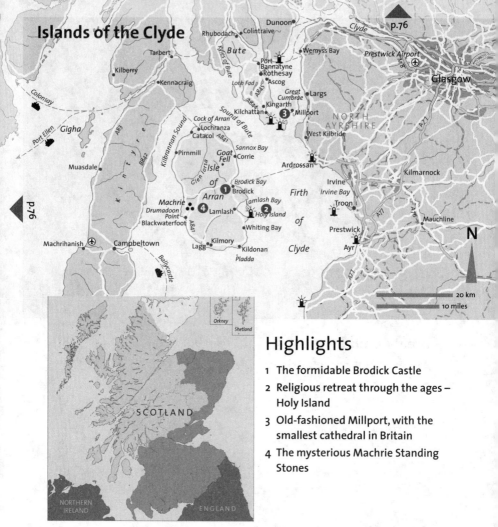

Islands of the Clyde

Highlights

1 The formidable Brodick Castle
2 Religious retreat through the ages – Holy Island
3 Old-fashioned Millport, with the smallest cathedral in Britain
4 The mysterious Machrie Standing Stones

Great Cumbrae

Although it wouldn't thank you for saying so, Great Cumbrae is so close to the Ayrshire mainland that it hardly counts as an island. The island is less than 4 miles in length and 2 miles wide, with a 12-mile coastal road round it – ideal for cycling. The highest point is 416ft (127m). Because of its proximity to Glasgow, many go to Cumbrae in the summer, so don't expect isolation; the beaches are packed on a fine day. Water sports are popular and the Scottish National Watersports Centre, based in Largs, caters for all kinds of aquatic activities. Windsurfing is good off Millport beach.

Millport has a wonderfully old-fashioned seafront holiday atmosphere. It straggles around a wide bay looking south across the Tan to Little Cumbrae, which was maintained as a deer forest by Robert II and Robert III, who both used the now-ruined 14th-century castle as their royal residence. The Victorian Gothic Episcopal collegiate

Getting There

The roll-on, roll-off ferry runs every 15 minutes from Largs, taking just a few minutes.

Tourist Information

Millport: **t** 0845 225 5121, *www.ayrshire-arran.com*. Open Easter–Oct.

Where to Stay and Eat

Ambler Guest House, Millport, **t** (01475) 530 532, *amblergh@easynet.co.uk* (*moderate*). A family-run, modern house on the seafront.

College of the Holy Spirit, College Street, Millport, **t** (01475) 530 353, *www.scotland. anglican.org/retreats* (*moderate*). Guest/retreat house attached to the cathedral.

Millerston House, Millport, **t** (01475) 530 480 (*moderate*). Another good B&B.

The Royal George Hotel, Millport, **t** (01475) 530 301 (*moderate*). In a fine position overlooking the bay.

Mrs McLuckie, Millport, **t** (01324) 551 570 (*£125–510 pw*). Six self-catering seafront flats in a house built in 1794 (sleeps 2–10).

The Ritz Café, Millport. Wonderful, 1950s-style place, run since 1906. They have won awards for their ice cream.

church, consecrated in 1876 as the Cathedral of the Isles, is the smallest cathedral in Britain, seating 100 people. Its founder, George Frederick Boyle, later the Earl of Glasgow, was involved in the Oxford Movement in the late 1840s and the cathedral was his attempt to revive the Episcopal Church in Scotland, complete with 'bells and smells'. The accompanying theological college was closed in 1885 and its buildings are now a retreat centre and holiday accommodation (*see* above).

Arran and Holy Island

The miracle of Arran – Gaelic for 'peaked island' – is that it has clung to its character despite the thousands of holiday makers attracted every year by its beauty. It is slightly larger than the Isle of Wight, about 20 miles across and 56 miles in circumference. Often described as 'Scotland in miniature', it is divided in two by the Highland Line that splits the mainland from northeast to southwest. The northern half is rough and hilly, its highest hill being the granite Goat Fell; the southern half is gentler. Because of the complexity of its geology, Arran is a popular place for university field studies. Although hotels, guesthouses and chalet settlements ring the island, it is possible to roam inland for miles and feel surprisingly remote.

Arran was inhabited by Neolithic farmers, as its ancient stones and burial cairns prove. The Irish Scots settled in the early 6th century, making Arran part of the Kingdom of Dalriada. The Vikings sacked it in 797 and it was claimed by Magnus Barelegs in 1098. Somerled, Lord of the Isles, of Norse descent, annexed Arran and it became part of the Kingdom of Scotland in the Treaty of Perth in 1266. In the 1650s it was occupied by Cromwellian troops who were massacred for their pains. The Clearances took their toll in the 19th century when enclosed sheep farms drove out one third of the population and killed off Gaelic culture.

The main village and ferry terminal is Brodick (Norse *Breidr vic* – broad bay) with a population of about 1,000. The other ferry terminal is at Lochranza in the north of the island, with crossings to Claonaig. There is so much to do here that it would be easier

Getting There

Ferries run between Ardrossan and Brodick (with train connections to Glasgow Central) about 6 times a day, 4 times on Sundays, taking 55 minutes. Ten sailings a day run between Claonaig and Lochranza, taking half an hour, with bus links to Brodick; t (01475) 650 100/000. For **Holy Isle Ferry Service**, ring t (01770) 600 998/600 349. These numbers also cover self-drive boat hire for angling, fishing trips and charters.

Tourist Information

Brodick: The Pier, t (01292) 678 100, *www.ayrshire-arran.com*.

Shopping

Arran Aromatics, a mile north of Brodick, t (01770) 302 595. Natural body-care products. *Open daily 9.30–5.30.*
Arran Provisions, the Old Mill, Lamlash. Arran's unique blends of preserves, and a Dunlop cheese made at the Creamery in Kilmory.

Sports and Activities

Flying Fever, 2 Coastguard House, Kildonan, t (01770) 820 292. Hang-gliding and paragliding, with cheap accommodation.
Brodick Boat and Bicycle Hire, t (01770) 302 868, t 840 255, or t 302 272.

Where to Stay

Kilmichael Country House Hotel, Brodick, t (01770) 302 219, *www.kilmichael.com* (*expensive*). Attractive house – the winner of various de luxe awards, with excellent food (open to non-staying guests).

Auchrannie Country House Hotel, Brodick, t (01770) 302 234, *www.auchrannie.co.uk* (*moderate*). Mansion in 10 acres, with a grand leisure complex. One of the best places to eat, in the bistro bar or dining room.
Kinloch Hotel, overlooking the sea at Blackwaterfoot, t (01770) 860 444, *www.bw-kinlochhotel.co.uk* (*moderate*). A comfortable modern eyesore with good food, indoor pool, solarium, sauna and squash court.
The Lagg Hotel, Lagg, t (01770) 870 255, *www.lagghotel.com* (*moderate*). An 18th-century coaching inn on the river with pleasant terraced gardens, nice atmosphere and reasonable food.
Royal Arran Hotel, Whiting Bay, t 700 286, *www.royalarran.co.uk*. (*moderate*). A turn-of-the-20th-century sandstone home, with very reasonable and comfortable rooms and plenty of character. If you're (very) lucky you might spot dolphins leaping in the bay.
Catacol Bay Hotel, on the shore at Catacol, t (01770) 830 231 (*budget*). Fairly basic, but with exceptional food. Live music, and a week-long folk festival in early June. More like a family home than a hotel.
Corrie Hotel, Corrie, t (01770) 810 273 (*budget*). Beside the sea, very good value and easy-going – lively bar frequented by locals.

Eating Out

Kilmichael Hotel (*see* 'Where to Stay') (*expensive*). A good choice for a special dinner.
Brodick Bar, Brodick (*moderate*). A large and lively eatery, with the accent on fresh produce.
Creelers, Home Farm, a mile north of Brodick, t (01770) 302 810 (*moderate*). Memorable seafood. Book ahead. *Only open mid-Mar–Oct*.

to list what is not available. There is every kind of water sport, as well as golf, riding, pony trekking, tennis, squash, bowling and – of course – walking and climbing. Time spent bird watching will reward you with sightings of rare species, and the island's flora and fauna are diverse. The best way to explore the island is by bicycle.

Brodick

The resort of Brodick is a large village with plenty of hotels and other accommodation. It spreads around the great sandy sweep of Brodick Bay, overlooked by Brodick Castle with the hills in the background. Old Brodick is below the castle, while New Brodick developed during the 19th century as increasing tonnages meant that new facilities would be needed to cope with the new steamers in the Clyde. The **Isle of Arran Heritage Centre** (*open April–Oct daily 10–4.30; adm*) is in an 18th-century croft-farm at Rosaburn on the edge of Brodick, with smithy, cottage and stable block. There is plenty of splendid nostalgia here.

Arran Chocolate Factory (*t (01770) 302 595*) and **Arran Brewery Company** (*t (01770) 302 353*), both in Brodick, are good for a rainy day.

Brodick Castle

www.nts.org.uk; open 1 April (or Good Friday if earlier)–31 Oct daily 11–4.30, last adm 4pm; 1 July–31 Aug daily 11–5, last adm 4.30; reception centre and shop 10–5; restaurant 11–5; garden and country park all year daily 9.30–sunset; adm.

Maintained by the National Trust for Scotland, this castle stands high on the north side of the bay. In 1503 James IV gave it, with the Earldom of Arran, to his cousin James, Lord Hamilton. There was probably once a Viking fort on the site, and remains of previous strongholds may be incorporated into the present castle, which occupies a good strategic position. 'Bruce's Room' and the link with Robert the Bruce must be a reconstruction, as the castle was completely demolished in 1455 and again in 1544.

The rather splendid red sandstone fortress is a mixture of Scottish Baronial and Gothic Revival: tall and formidable, set in gorgeous gardens. The oldest section visible from outside is the gaunt east tower, built in 1588 by the 2nd Earl of Arran, guardian to Mary, Queen of Scots. Cromwell's troops occupied the castle following the execution of the 1st Duke of Hamilton, and the death in battle of his heir, the 2nd Duke, and were responsible for extensive fortification and extensions. The 10th Duke was largely responsible for the castle's appearance today, planned by James Gillespie Graham in the mid-19th century.

The interior is neo-Jacobean (1840s) and contains a lot of treasures, including all that is left of the fabulous collection of William Beckford of Fonthill, in Wiltshire, who spent his vast fortune and energy collecting objects from all over the world. His daughter, Susan Euphemia, married the 10th Duke of Hamilton. A good guidebook gives details of the objects on display, and the gardens are exotic enough to appear in *Vathek* – Beckford's masterpiece of oriental extravagance.

Sheltered by the mild Gulf Stream climate, the gardens were rescued by the Duchess of Montrose, daughter of the 12th Duke who inherited the castle in 1895, with the help of her son-in-law (JPT Boscawen of Tresco Abbey, which is why many of the trees and plants came from Tresco); the gardens support fine rhododendrons. Beyond, the surrounding Country Park is also in the care of the National Trust for Scotland and encompasses wild-flower meadows, waterfalls and woodland walks.

Around the Island

The road round the island only loses the sea occasionally, while the String Road cuts through the middle from Brodick to Blackwaterfoot. Another road – the Ross Road – cuts through Glen Scorrodale from Lamlash to Lagg Inn.

Goat Fell (2,866ft/874m) north of Brodick, which dominates Arran, is best attacked on a clear day. There are a number of ways up, and the view from the top makes it worthwhile. Some say the name comes from *geit-fjall*, Norse for goat mountain, others that it was *gaoith bheinn* – Gaelic for windy mountain. Whichever is correct, you won't see goats, though you might see golden eagles gliding on air currents in a corrie below you, and you will certainly feel the wind. One way is to start opposite the car park at Cladach on the north side of Brodick Bay. You can't miss the well-signed stony track, which turns into a path through woods, heads up the glen of the Cnoacan Burn and traverses the moorland to the eastern ridge of Goat Fell. Here it joins another path, from Corrie, and goes quite steeply up to the top. If you start from Corrie, it's a bit quicker. Allow about 5 hours there and back.

Corrie is about 6 miles north of Brodick, with white cottages, trim colourful gardens, a harbour, quay and beach – a picturesque village popular with artists. There are plenty of nice walks up into the glens, which cut into the hinterland like spokes of a wheel. **Glen Sannox**, a couple of miles north, hides some delightful, secret places where heather, lichens, mosses and alpine willow grow, as well as rare flowers. The **Fallen Rocks**, a couple of miles along a coastal track, are thought to be the relics of a landslip in the Palaeozoic Age, which sent these massive boulders, some as big as houses, tumbling to the beach. Rock climbers like this area, and Sannox also has a nine-hole golf course, and a **pony-trekking centre** (*t* (01770) 810 222).

Lochranza, possibly from loch of the *chaoruinn* (rowan), lies 2 miles southwest of the northern headland, Cock of Arran, and is the chief settlement at the north end of the island. **Lochranza Castle** is a romantic, 13th-century, three-storey L-plan ruin on the tidal flats, backed by the hills, with a pit prison in the vaulted basement. It is said to have been a staging post for Robert the Bruce in 1307 when he was returning from his encounter with the spider on Rathlin Island, to liberate Scotland from the clutches of Edward II. The **Isle of Arran Distillery** (*t* (01770) 830 264, *www.arranwhisky.com; open March–Oct 10–6*) is 'Scotland's Newest Distillery'. Heading south from Lochranza down the west side of the island, the road clings to the sea with hills tumbling down almost to the beach.

Steep-sided **Glen Catocol** runs inland up into the hills through beech, oak and larch, chestnut and fir, on carpets of vivid green ferns. **Thunderguy**, 5 miles south of Lochranza, gets its strange name from *tor-na-gaoith* – hill of the wind. Two miles further south, **Pirnmill** is derived from the bobbin mill (now converted into holiday flats) that was here in the days when linen was an important industry on the island. **Glen Iorsa** runs northeast through marshy bog land, hemmed in by barren hills. The southwest corner of the island is rich in prehistoric remains. These include **Auchgallon Stone Circle**, 15 red sandstone blocks which once encircled a cairn; the **Farm Road Stone Circle**, close by; the **Machrie Standing Stones**, slim, primeval monoliths whose purpose is still unknown; and the **Kilmory Cairns**, at Lagg Inn.

It was at **King's Caves** at Drumadoon, **Blackwaterfoot**, that Robert the Bruce is said to have sheltered when returning to free Scotland from the English. Legend brings the 3rd-century warrior-poet, Fingal (Fionn) MacCumhail here, father of Ossian and leader of the Feinn, who feature in the old sagas. There are rock carvings of animals and typical Pictish hunting scenes in the caves. A lovely 10-mile drive (or walk) goes up Glen Scorrodale from **Sliddery**, along Sliddery Water to Lamlash Bay.

Kildonan, 6 miles east of Sliddery, is a sprawling farming village with two hotels, a sandy beach and **Kildonan Castle**, a ruined keep on a rocky plateau protected by a precipitous cliff on the seaward side and a ravine on the north. There are views from here of **Pladda Island Lighthouse** and **Ailsa Craig**, which rises like an iceberg 13 miles out to sea. Look for a colony of Atlantic grey seals along the shore towards Bennan Head to the west. Unafraid and curious, they come quite close to the shore to inspect passers-by. The mysterious carcass of a large sea creature, discovered here in 1981, baffled experts for some time until it was identified, with great disappointment, as a gigantic basking shark. Before the headland, a winding path used by smugglers in the 18th century hugs the cliffs and leads to the road above.

Whiting Bay, 5 miles north of Kildonan, is a popular holiday village. Here, shops and hotels jostle with holiday cottages along the waterfront. There is a craft shop which specializes in leather, pottery and woodcarving, and there is an 18-hole golf course with splendid views across the Firth of Clyde to the Ayrshire hills. **Glen Ashdale Falls** are signposted from the south end of the village, up a steep, wooded glen to where crystal water cascades down on to glistening rocks. The **Giant's Graves** (signposted) is a stone circle traditionally associated with Fionn MacCumhail.

Lamlash, 3 miles south of Brodick on Lamlash Bay, which is almost blocked at the mouth by Holy Island, completes the circular tour of the island. The bay provides a wonderfully safe anchorage, now a yachtsman's haven, and has given shelter to many an important traveller. King Haakon and his fleet took refuge here before their defeat in the Battle of Largs in 1263, and in 1548 the ship carrying five-year-old Mary, Queen of Scots to France from Dumbarton sheltered here. Lamlash has annual sea angling competitions, renowned throughout Scotland.

Holy Island

Holy Island (*www.holyisland.org*), a mile offshore, provides excellent shelter for the bay. An Early Christian and medieval monastery was established here. The 6th-century St Molaise went into retreat in a cave on the western shore at the base of Mullach Mor. Viking inscriptions in the cave are said to date from the 13th century, graffiti scratched by King Haakon's fleet while they waited for the weather. It was the same bad weather that was to prove their undoing, for the Scots deliberately kept them waiting for their battle until they were completely demoralized by seasickness. There is the ruin of a 14th-century monastery and a chapel on the island, as well as the ghost of a farmer's wife, murdered by her husband after she had presented him with his fifteenth daughter. The Buddhist monks from Samye Ling, in Eskdalemuir in the Borders, bought the island in 1992, and have developed it into a retreat and meditation centre (*for further details call **t** (01770) 601 100*).

Bute

Bute is another holiday island too close to the mainland for seclusion, though it does have the odd lonely corner, mostly in the northwest. It is 15 miles long and from 3 to 5 miles wide, with the Highland Line almost cutting it in two across Loch Fad.

Rothesay is the main town with bright lights and tourist traps, a little run-down though great efforts are being made to revive it. Its Victorian public lavatories are a sight in themselves. The **Kyles of Bute** are the narrow straits separating the island

Getting There

A roll-on, roll-off car ferry runs frequently from Wemyss Bay to Rothesay, taking half an hour. There is also a ferry from Colintraive in Argyll (**Caledonian MacBrayne, t** (01475) 650 100, *www.calmac.co.uk*), taking five minutes to cross the Kyles of Bute to Rhubodach, where the drovers used to swim their cattle across. Planes fly from Glasgow.

Tourist Information

Rothesay: 15 Victoria Street, *www.rothesay-scotland.com*.

Events and Activities

There is plenty of organized jollity in the summer: a **Jazz Festival** in May, a **Folk Festival** in July and the **Bute Highland Games** in August. There are angling competitions, a bowling tournament, three golf courses, tennis, riding, fishing and water sports.

Where to Stay and Eat

Ardmory House Hotel and Restaurant, Ardmory Road, Ardbeg, **t** (01700) 502 346 (*moderate*). Overlooks the Clyde, with a restaurant open to non-residents.

Ardyne Private Hotel, 38 Mountstuart Road, Rothesay, **t** (01700) 502 052, *www.rothesay. scotland.com* (*moderate*). On the seafront, with spectacular views. A good family base.

Cannon House Hotel, Battery Place, Rothesay, **t** (01700) 502 819, *http://cannonhousehotel. co.uk* (*moderate*). Pretty Georgian town house with views over the bay and good food. Sailing available.

Kingarth Hotel and Restaurant, Kingarth, **t** (01700) 831 662, *www.kingarthhotel.com* (*moderate*). A comfortable, country inn-style hotel by Kilchattan Bay, with good food.

St Blane's Hotel, Kilchattan Bay, **t** (01700) 831 224, *www.stblaneshotel.com* (*moderate*). On the water's edge, with six moorings and a courtesy bus. Pets welcome.

Bayview Hotel, Rothesay, **t** (01700) 505 411 (*budget*). Looks over Rothesay Bay; cheerful, and a 10-minute walk from the pier.

The Commodore, 12 Battery Place, Rothesay, **t** (01700) 502 178, *www.commodorebute.com* (*budget*). On the seafront near the town centre: an attractive building with comfortable well-equipped bedrooms and free coarse fishing. Small, modernized self-catering cottage in the grounds.

Mrs Watson, Ascog House, Ascog, on the coast southeast of Rothesay, near Mount Stuart House, **t** (01700) 503 372 (*budget*). One of the best B&Bs, in a 250-year-old farmhouse, secluded and very friendly, with log fires.

New Farm, Mount Stuart, **t** (01700) 831 646 (*budget*). Delightfully cosy little cottage, with home-baked bread, traditional Scottish breakfasts and dinners cooked with home-grown herbs and vegetables.

Ardencraig House, High Craigmore, Rothesay, **t** (01700) 505 077, *www.ardencraig.org.uk* (*moderate*). Newly done up Palladian mansion with 5 luxury self-catering apartments (sleeping 2–6) and 7 chalets in the grounds (sleeping 4–6).

Kames Castle, Port Bannatyne, **t** (01700) 504 500, *www.kames-castle.co.uk*. 6 self-catering Victorian cottages in a private estate on Kames Bay (sleeps 2–9).

West End, Gallowgate, Rothesay, **t** (01700) 503 596 (*inexpensive*). Award-winning fish-and-chip restaurant.

from the mainland in the northwest and northeast. Sailors are at an advantage, having access to a number of secret bays populated only by seals and sea birds. There is plenty to do in Bute, especially for the gregarious: swimming, sailing, golf, bird-watching, walking, cycling and nightlife.

Rothesay

Bute Museum (open April–Sept Mon–Sat 10.30–4.30, Sun 2.30–4.30; Oct–Mar Tues–Sat 2.30–4.30) covers the island's history, archaeology and natural history. The **Winter Garden** is a Grade-A listed building, built on to an existing bandstand in 1924. Its circular cast-iron and glass structure with a domed roof has been restored and is a multipurpose building with a cinema and restaurant. **St Mary's Chapel** is a smattering of ruins in the grounds of Rothesay's High Kirk. It was the medieval parish church and served as a cathedral of the Isles in the 17th century. One of the tombs is thought to be that of Marjory, first wife of Walter the High Steward, father of Robert II and founder of the Stewart/Stuart dynasty.

Rothesay Castle (open April–Sept daily 9.30–6.30; Oct–Mar Mon–Sat 9.30–4.30 exc Thurs pm and Fri, Sun open 2–4.30; adm) is one of the finest surviving medieval castles in Scotland, with origins thought to go back to 1098. It was the seat of the Marquesses of Bute (see 'Mount Stuart', below), an almost circular 'castle of enclosure' with high curtain walls and drum towers, surrounded by a moat. It's hard to understand why it was built where it is. Nineteenth-century experts dismissed its strategic position as 'wretchedly deficient', arguing that it showed 'very little in favour of the military knowledge that erected it – even the gate is neither flanked nor machicolated'. It was captured by Vikings despite defenders pouring molten lead and pitch on them from the battlements. King Haakon occupied it before the Battle of Largs. Robert the Bruce captured it in 1313 and it was his great-great-grandson who was first created Duke of Rothesay, a title held by the present Prince of Wales. The castle was used as a headquarters when both James IV and James V tried with little success to subdue the arrogant Lords of the Isles. Cromwell battered it badly during the Civil War and it was burned by Argyll during the Monmouth Rebellion in 1685. It remained a ruin until restoration began in the 19th century.

Mount Stuart

Mount Stuart (t (01700) 503 877, www.mountstuart.com; house open May–Sept by guided tour only, grounds 10–6; winter by prior arrangment; adm), 5 miles south of Rothesay, only opened to the public in 1995, so it has not yet become as familiar as many other stately homes. It is a remarkable monument to what money, determination and persistence can achieve. John Patrick Crichton-Stuart, born at Mount Stuart in 1847, inherited the title 3rd Marquess of Bute six months later, together with 110,000 acres and one of the largest private fortunes of the time. He converted to Catholicism when he was 21 and was the inspiration for Disraeli's Lothair, in which a wealthy nobleman juggles the merits of Catholicism and Anglicanism. The Butes were of royal descent, from Robert II, whose son John Stewart became Keeper of Rothesay Castle and was granted lands on the island.

The first house at Mount Stuart was built in 1719 and was gradually decaying when the 3rd Marquess came of age in 1869. He started with repairs, vitally needed because of extensive dry rot, and then made plans for rebuilding. He spent more than £2,000 a year, no mean sum in those days, until 1877 when a fire gutted the central block. This gave him the excuse he needed to stop tinkering and build a new house, and in 1878 the architect Robert Rowand Anderson finally drew up the designs for him.

Lord Bute took a very active interest in the progress of his new venture; many of the papers, letters and plans survive, both at Mount Stuart and in Edinburgh University Library. It was a long-drawn-out procedure, with orders and counter-orders, and Lord Bute overseeing every step. When his architect once commiserated with him over a delay, he replied: 'Why should I hurry over what is my chief pleasure? I have comparatively little interest in a thing after it is finished.' Money was no object: when choosing between marble and granite for some pillars, on being told granite would cost £20,000 more, he remarked: 'true, but that's not the point. The question is which will look best.' Completed in 1891, the hall was a triumph, with 12 windows illustrating the constellations filling the room with rich, flickering colour and showing off the Gothic elevations of green, white, buff and grey Italian marble. Lord Bute was an enthusiastic Wagnerian and it could be that he was influenced by the rich contrasts of scenery in *Parsifal*, which deeply moved him. Much remained to be done when he died in 1900 and although further drawings were commissioned and schemes discussed, nothing more came of them until, by his widow's death in 1932, the house was seen as a liability. In 1920 the 4th Marquess had advertised it for sale 'conditional to its complete demolition and removal by the Purchaser. Suitable for re-erection as a Hotel-Hydro, Restaurant, Casino or Public Building, etc'. Fortunately no one showed an interest and the house survived until John, the 6th Marquess, began full-scale renovation and restoration in 1983. Ten years later he died, and his family decided that as it had been his intention to open the house to the public, they should honour his wishes. Hence the chance to enjoy this magnificent creation today.

There are 300 acres of designed landscape and 18th-century woodland, created by the 3rd Earl between 1725 and 1778. A major project is under way in a large octagonal glass pavilion in the kitchen garden, an attempt to create a 'microcosm' of mountain and rainforest from Borneo and Papua New Guinea. There is a gift shop and tearoom, and an adventure play area with a huge doll's playhouse.

Other Sights

St Blane's Chapel, on the southern peninsula, just off the road, is a roofless 12th-century ruin with a carved Romanesque chancel arch, dedicated to St Blane, who was born on Bute in the 6th century and founded a monastery close by. **Ascog Hall Fernery and Garden**, at Ascog, is a splendid sunken Victorian Fern House, fully restored in 1986, brimming with subtropical species. **Kames Castle** (private self-catering accommodation, clearly seen from the road between Port Bannatyne and Ettrick Bay; *see* p.206) dates back to the 14th century, with a house added in 1799. The home of the Bannatyne family, it passed to a nephew, Henry Home, later Lord Kames, in 1780 and later to the Earls of Bute.

The Inner Hebrides and the Small Isles

15

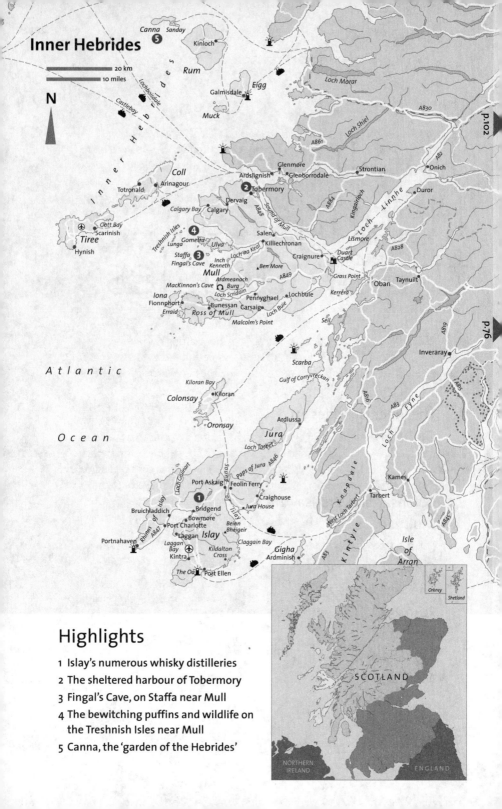

Inner Hebrides

20 km
10 miles

N

Atlantic

Ocean

Highlights

1 Islay's numerous whisky distilleries
2 The sheltered harbour of Tobermory
3 Fingal's Cave, on Staffa near Mull
4 The bewitching puffins and wildlife on
  the Treshnish Isles near Mull
5 Canna, the 'garden of the Hebrides'

The Inner Hebrides

Gigha

Pronounced with a hard 'g' at the beginning and a silent 'g' in the middle – Ge'a – Gigha's name is said to come from *Gudey* – Norse for God's Isle – and indeed this subtropical island is an earthly Garden of Eden. On the other hand, the name could come from the Norse *gja-ey* – cleft island. Although it is only 56 miles from Glasgow and 3 miles from the mainland, this low-lying, fertile piece of land, 7 miles long by a mile wide, has managed to retain its island character. It is firmly on the tourist map, but even that has not broken its magic spell.

Visiting the Island

Gigha has had at least 14 owners over the past 200 years, and accordingly the inhabitants have been dependent on the whims of landlords who often looked on the island as a business venture or a tycoon's toy. Gigha has now opted for community ownership which means that with a generous injection of public money the inhabitants have bought the island for a song. As with other crofting community trusts, there are already problems: the big house is up for sale and there are plans to sell off plots of land to incomers to try and pay off some of the huge debts accrued in the buyout. Time alone will tell.

Meanwhile you are as likely to be sold your groceries with a strong English accent as with the soft west Highland lilt. What the perpetrators of these communal buyouts seem to forget, when they talk about 'returning the land to the people' is that in the days before 'white settlers' the land never belonged to 'the people'. Some of the landowners may have been harsh but a great many of them had considerable knowledge of land management and the means to implement it. Perhaps the most influential of the incoming lairds in the 'good old days' was Colonel Sir James Horlick, whose malted beverages made him a fortune. He bought Gigha in 1944 and lived there till his death in 1972, indulging his passion for gardening.

Getting There

Flights go from Glasgow to Campbeltown; taxis from there take you 25 miles to the Tayinloan ferry terminus. Or **drive** to Tayinloan, leave your car and hire a bicycle for the one road on the island. The **ferry**, Caledonian MacBrayne, **t** (01475) 650 100, takes cars (20mins), hourly in the summer, less in winter.

Tourist Information

Campbeltown: West Highland and Islands Tourist Board, The Pier, **t** 0845 225 5121.

Where to Stay and Eat

The Gigha Hotel, t (01583) 505 254, *www.gigha. org.uk* (*moderate*). The perfect honeymoon retreat, in an original 1789 inn. Not grand, but with a cosy lounge and cheerful bar in which to pick up local gossip. In a lovely position with good food; they will arrange golf and skippered boat hire for sea angling or trips round the island. The hotel also has 6 self-catering cottages.

Post Office House, t (01583) 505 251, *www.gighastores.co.uk (budget)*. Guesthouse accommodation and a self-catering cottage.

Achamore Gardens (*open daily all year dawn–dusk; adm*) was the result. Thanks to the balmy Gulf Stream, as well as the acidic soil, the already established trees and, of course, the Horlick fortune, these 50 acres are a riot of rhododendrons, azaleas and camellias in early summer, along with many rarer exotic plants, shrubs and trees. The **Achamore creamery**, recently revived and supplied by local Ayrshire cattle, produces a very good cheese; previously, the milk – some half a million gallons a year – had to be sent off to Campbeltown every day. There is also a fish farm on the estate.

The village is **Ardminish**, where everything happens. Perhaps the most celebrated of Gigha's 120 residents is Seumas McSporran, a sturdy figure with a genial smile almost as wide as his face. He has lived here for all but two years of his life and until he retired, held some 14 or 15 jobs. 'I had to consult a list to keep up to date with them.' They included shopkeeper, bicycle hirer, gas agent, sub-postmaster, postman, registrar, Pearl Assurance agent, coastguard, special constable, fireman, ambulance driver, taxi driver and undertaker. He had a uniform or outfit to go with each job. His shop, a family concern, stocks everything you might need, and they can also get things from the mainland for you (*t (01583) 505 251; see* 'Where to Stay and Eat', above).

The ruined medieval parish church is at **Kilchattan**, with intricately carved late medieval grave slabs in the burial ground. Nearby is the 'ogham stone', brought from Ireland in pre-Christian times, with an indecipherable inscription on it. There are quite a few archaeological sites: cairns, standing stones, forts and duns. A Viking grave was found in 1849 at East Tarbert Bay, in which was a set of ornate portable scales with decorated pans and weights. King Haakon stopped off here on his way to defeat at the Battle of Largs, probably sheltering from the awful weather which made his men so seasick that they hadn't a chance against the hardy locals.

Islay

Islay (pronounced Eyela), 15 miles off the west coast of Argyll and only 23 miles north of Northern Ireland, is the most southerly of the Inner Hebrides, and one of the largest at 25 miles long and 19 miles across – 246 square miles. Its landscape is varied, from hilly moorland traversed by burns, to sheltered woods and fertile farmland, with a rugged coastline giving way to open sweeps of beach. A favourite holiday island for bird watchers, naturalists, photographers and artists, it also has much to interest archaeologists, having been inhabited since Neolithic times. Excellent trout and salmon fishing can be found on the rivers Duich and Sorn and on well-stocked lochs such as Gorm, Torrabus and Ballygrant. Boats can be hired locally for sea fishing. Warmed by the Gulf Stream, miles of sandy beaches offer swimming and sunbathing, and the surf is sometimes good. The 18-hole golf course at Machrie is well known.

Perhaps best known for its distinctive peaty malt whisky, Islay has a number of distilleries, such as Laphroaig, Lagavulin, Ardbeg and Bowmore, that scent the air with the pungent smell of smouldering peat. Now and then islanders tangle with conservationists who insist that the special Duich Moss peat, essential for the flavour

Getting There

Ferries cross from Kennacraig to Port Askaig (2 hours), and from Kennacraig to Port Ellen (just over 2 hours). Western Ferries, t (01496) 840 681. **Flights** go from Campbeltown and Glasgow, British Airways, t 0845 222 111.

Tourist Information

Bowmore: The Square, t (01496) 810 254. *Open all year.*
Campbeltown: The Pier, t (01586) 552 056. *Open all year.*

Events and Activities

The 2-week Islay **Folk Festival** is at the end of May/early June, t (01496) 302 413.
There are plenty of distilleries on the island:
Ardbeg Distillery, Port Ellen. Visitor centre, tour and café. *Open all year Mon–Fri 10–5, weekends also June–Sept; adm.*
Bowmore. Claims to be the oldest distillery on Islay. Tour and dram. *Open all year; adm.*
Bunnahabhainn, Port Askaig. Home of Black Bottle Scotch Whisky. Visitor Centre, tour, shop and dram. *Open all year Mon–Fri; adm.*
Caol Ila Distillery Visitor Centre, Port Askaig, t (01496) 302 760. Tours and tasting, shop. *Open by appt only; adm.*
Lagavulin Distillery, Port Ellen, t (01496) 302 400. *Open all year Mon–Fri by appt; adm.*

Where to Stay

What you may miss in glamour here, you will certainly gain in Highland hospitality.
Bridgend Hotel, Bridgend, t (01496) 810 212, *www.bridgend-hotel.com (moderate)*. At the head of Loch Indaal; with a nice garden.
Harbour Inn, Bowmore, t (01496) 810 330, *harbour@harbour-inn.co.uk (moderate)*. Overlooking Loch Indaal, and good value. Very good food. *Book ahead.*

Kilchoman House by Bruichladdich, t (01496) 850 382, *kilchomancottages.co.uk (moderate)*. Six self-catering cottages in 40 acres of farmland near a sandy beach. Separate restaurant with very good food. *Book in advance.*
Kilmeny Farmhouse, Ballygrant, t (01496) 840 668, *www.kilmeny.co.uk (moderate)*. Cosy 5-star guesthouse with good views, de luxe awards and excellent food.
Port Askaig Hotel, Port Askaig, t (01496) 840 245 *(moderate)*. On the Sound of Islay with good views of Jura.
Port Charlotte Hotel, Port Charlotte, t (01496) 850 360, *www.portcharlottehotel.co.uk (moderate)*. Victorian hotel on the main street with a conservatory and a garden going down on to the sandy beach.
Ballygrant Inn, Ballygrant, t (01496) 840 277, *www.ballygrant-inn.co.uk (budget)*. Comfortable, family-run place in 2½ acres of woodland. The food is good and the rooms are cosy with log stoves.
The Kennels, Ballygrant, t (01496) 840 237 *(budget)*. Located some way off the main road in quiet woodland – home-baked hospitality.
The Old Granary, Kintra Farm, t (01496) 302 051 *(budget)*. Converted barn serving good basic food. Camp site, a hostel and B&B in the farmhouse; also has self-catering cottages. *Open May–Aug.*

Eating Out

The following are all in the *moderate* category:
Ballygrant Inn, Ballygrant. *See* 'Where to Stay'. Reasonable pub meals.
Croft Kitchen, Port Charlotte, t (01496) 850 230. Coffee/gift shop by day and restaurant by night. *Booking essential. Open Mar–Oct.*
Harbour Inn. *See* 'Where to Stay'.
Kilchoman House. *See* 'Where to Stay'.
The Machrie, Port Ellen, t (01496) 302 310. Good food and not too expensive.
Port Charlotte Hotel. *See* 'Where to Stay'.

of Islay whisky, should be preserved for Greenland white-fronted geese. The distilleries welcome visitors (*see* 'Events and Activities', above). Apart from whisky, agriculture is the main industry. Tourism is a growth industry with 45,000 summer visitors coming in on the ferries and 11,000 by air. So far they haven't managed to spoil the island. In 1831 the population was 15,000; it now stands at 4,000.

Historically, Islay was the administrative capital of the Lords of the Isles, and therefore of prime importance until the forfeiture of the Lordship in 1493. There was a military and naval base at Dunivaig on the south coast and the civil headquarters were on two small islands on Loch Finlaggan. These were the centres of power for an administration which, at its zenith in the early 15th century, ruled all the islands off the west coast and almost the entire western seaboard from Cape Wrath to the Mull of Kintyre. Martin Martin, whose *Description of the Western Isles of Scotland*, published in 1703, encouraged Dr Johnson to make his tour, describes 'Ila' in great detail, and it doesn't seem to have changed all that much in the intervening 300 years.

Visiting the Island

Port Ellen is the ferry arrival point at the south end of the island; its distillery, built in 1815, dominates the skyline above Leodamus Bay, but is now no longer in operation. It's an attractive little place with terraced houses round the harbour and a laid-back atmosphere. A road runs round the coast northeastwards for about 10 miles and then gives way to a track. Three familiar names grace this road – Laphroaig, Lagavulin and Ardbeg, all distilleries – and an amusing story is told about them. John Campbell of Ardmore, a relative of the laird and previous Chamberlain to the Duke of Inveraray, died in 1860 and his body was returned to Islay for burial in the family plot at Kildalton. It was carried, as was the custom, in relays along the road, with frequent stops to rest along the way. With the three distilleries so handy it was easy to get flasks refilled for toasts to the deceased and for refreshment. When the cortege reached the cemetery they realised they were without the coffin. Hurrying back, they discovered it lying peacefully on the road between Lagavulin and Ardbeg.

Dunyvaig Castle is the 14th-century ruin on the cliff 3½ miles to the east of Port Ellen. It was the stronghold of the Macdonalds of Islay when the Lords of the Isles were dominant and considered themselves above the authority of the crown. They had an excellent vantage point here from which to keep an eye on invaders from the south. Dunyvaig was their military and naval headquarters.

Kildalton Cross, beside ruined Kildalton Chapel, about 4 miles on up the road, is an important survival of Celtic art: an early-Christian wheel cross over 7ft high, probably dating from the 9th century, carved from a single block of locally quarried stone. It's the finest example of its kind outside Iona, and its carvings look incredibly fresh after nearly 2,000 years. Somehow it escaped the Viking raids which so devastated the Celtic Church in the west. In the 1890s the remains of a Viking ritual killing were also found under the cross. There was an Early Christian chapel and a monastery here, too, before the present Kildalton Chapel was built by the Lords of the Isles in the 14th century. It is roofless but substantial, with some late-medieval grave slabs inside.

Claggain Bay, a couple of miles north of the Kildalton Cross and chapel, is sandy, with rocky pools, against a backdrop of **Beinn Bheigeir**, the highest hill on the island, standing at 1,612ft (496m). The road peters out after Claggain Bay but there are lovely walks further on along the coast, or west into the hinterland.

The **Oa Peninsula** (pronounced 'Oh'), 5 miles southwest of Port Ellen, was the rugged haunt of smugglers and illicit whisky distillers, who made cunning use of its sheer cliffs honeycombed with caves. The only road goes down to the Mull in the southwest; otherwise most of it is accessible only by foot – good bird-watching here. The American Monument – an obelisk in memory of two American ships which sank here at the end of the First World War – is signed off the road to the Mull of Oa, about a mile's walk uphill. The setting is spectacular, and if you brave it in a storm you can understand how the ships were wrecked. **Machrie**, on Laggan Bay northwest of the Oa, has a well-known 18-hole golf course on the machair, and the airport. The River Laggan runs into the north of the bay and Martin Martin records: 'I was told by the Natives that the Brion of Ila, a famous Judge, is, according to his own Desire, buried standing on the Brink of the River Laggan; having in his right Hand a Spear, such as they use to dart at the Salmon.'

Bowmore, about 9 miles north of Port Ellen, was the old capital and administrative centre of the island, built by Daniel Campbell the Younger in 1768 on the site of monastic lands. It is one of the earliest of Scotland's planned villages, introduced by wealthy 'improvers' in the 18th century. A delightful feature of the village is the **round church**, built as the parish church in 1769. It is of Italian design and so shaped to deprive the devil of any corners in which to lurk. Bowmore Distillery claims to be the oldest legal distillery on Islay and is still privately owned (*see* p.213).

The **Rhinns of Islay** projects westwards like a great hammer head with wonderful walks, views and excellent fishing. **Port Charlotte** is a pretty village halfway down the southeastern edge of the hammer with a **Museum of Islay Life** (*open Easter–Oct Mon–Sat 10–5, Sun 2–5; adm*), in a converted church. There are quite good displays here on local history, as well as the usual array of traditional artefacts and some 16th-century carved stones. The **Islay Natural History Trust** (*t (01496) 850 288; open April–Oct Sun–Fri 10–3; ring for times; adm*) is an excellent wildlife information and field centre which is good for all ages and very hands-on, with guided tours.

Ellister, south of Port Charlotte, is a wildfowl sanctuary, and **Loch Gruinart** to the north is an RSPB reserve. Here, in 1598, at the head of the loch, was fought the Battle of Traigh Gruinart – one of the last great clan battles, between the Macleans of Duart and the Macdonalds. The Macleans had invaded Islay intending to capture the castle of Gorm, in Loch Gorm, but the Macdonalds defeated them, slaying 380 of the 400 who landed, including the Maclean chief. From **Portnahaven**, at the southwest tip of the Rhinns, the green coast of Ireland is only spitting distance away. The **Cultroon Stone Circle**, of which only three are still standing, is by the road to Kilchiaran.

Inland from the head of Loch Indaal, **Loch Finlaggan**, with its ruins on an islet, was the administrative capital of the Lords of the Isles. It is difficult to picture how it must have been in those medieval days, looking at its peaceful isolation now. Here, the 14 members of the Council of the Isles met on the small *Eilean na Comhairle* – Council Isle – at Finlaggan. On Eilean Mor, linked to the Council Isle by a causeway, there are the remains of a chapel and over 20 buildings, many of which date from the time of the Lordship. Writing nearly 300 years ago, Martin Martin writes of Loch Finlaggan and the Court of the great Mack-Donald, where he had his residence, his house and chapel, while his guards, called *Lucht-taeh*, 'kept Guard on the lake-side nearest to the Isle'. He tells of how the Judge got an eleventh share of any sum in debate. And he tells of 'a big Stone of seven Foot square, in which there was a deep Impression made to receive the Feet of Mack-Donald; for he was crown'd King of the Isles standing in this Stone, and swore that he would continue his Vassals in the possession of their lands, and do exact Justice to all his Subjects' (*see* Dunadd Fort, pp.91–2). He then describes the anointing by the Bishop of Argyll and seven priests, and all the ritual of kingmaking. The 14 chiefs summoned to the council meetings came from all over the Kingdom of the Isles, many in coracles, each with his 'tail' – henchmen from the clan. They were proud men, settling their disputes and problems independently of the Scottish Parliament, usually with wisdom and justice, and often bloodshed. There is no doubt that, in spite of the efforts of the Crown to undermine their strength, the Lords of the Isles ruled with effect. There is a visitor centre here (*open April–Oct – ask at the Bowmore Tourist Information Centre*), illustrating some of the intriguing history of those times and displaying archaeological remains unearthed by recent digs.

Port Askaig is a ferry terminal for the mainland and for Jura. It is a ramshackle little place in a steep-sided bay with views across the Sound of Islay to Jura. The hinterland to the north and west is a network of rivers and burns, virtually without roads.

Jura

Just off the northeast coast of Islay, Jura has very little tourist accommodation and is far less frequented, though more beautiful – some 27 miles long, 5 to 6 miles wide and sparsely populated. Silver and white sandy beaches give way to rugged shingle, teeming with wildfowl. Loch Tarbert almost cuts Jura in two from the west. The three Paps (or 'bosoms') of Jura rear up at the south end of the island – the highest is 2,576ft (793m). Their distinctive outlines are as familiar to sailors as the Cuillins of Skye, and serve as a landmark for miles. A single-track road runs south from the ferry and then some way up the east coast. Most of the island is only accessible on foot. The west coast – private land – has some amazing caves, some of which have

Getting There

There is no direct link with the mainland. A **car ferry** runs frequently from Port Askaig on Islay to Feolin on Jura, a 10-minute crossing; fewer ferries on Sundays.

Tourist Information

Campbeltown: The Pier, **t** 0845 225 5121, *www.visitscottishheartlands.com*.

Where to Stay and Eat

Exploration Jura, t (07899) 912 116 (*moderate*). Accommodation in a house or bunkhouse – guided hill-walking tours or Land-Rover tours available. *April–Oct*.

Jura Hotel, Craighouse, **t** (01496) 820 243, *www.jurahotel.co.uk* (*moderate*). The only hotel, but all you could wish for: relaxed, friendly, in a lovely setting and with good local food. *Often fully booked*.

been adapted for temporary use by shepherds, and, in recent years, by a young woman artist.

Wild and rugged, Jura is famous for its red deer, some 5,000 of them, which are keenly stalked by the owners and guests of the sporting estates of which the island is comprised. Martin Martin recorded in the 18th century that 'the hills ordinarily have about three hundred Deer grazing on them, which are not to be hunted by any, without the Steward's Licence.' The name Jura comes from the Norse word *dyr-ey* – deer island – though Martin Martin was told by 'natives' that it comes from Dih and Rah – two Norse brothers who fought and killed each other and whose ashes are buried in urns under two 7ft stones 60 yards apart at Knock-Cronm.

One hundred and fifty years ago Jura had about 1,000 inhabitants; now there are less than 200. With only one hotel and limited bed and breakfast accommodation, tourism is mainly geared towards day visitors from Islay. The sportsmen who pay large sums for their pursuits aren't too keen on seeing hikers either. Most of the locals work on their crofts, or for the Forestry Commission as estate workers, or in the distillery.

History

In the 19th century Jura was the stepping stone for drovers taking cattle from Islay and Colonsay to the mainland markets, with two to three thousand head of cattle crossing every year. Archaeological remains show that Jura was inhabited as long ago as 7000 BC. There is a Neolithic burial cairn south of Strone Farm and no fewer than seven Bronze Age standing stone sites in the southeast. Of the several Iron Age forts and duns, the best is An Dunan, on Lowlandman's Bay. Martin Martin recorded that this island was the most 'wholesome' place in all Scotland, due to its position, the height of its hills and 'by the fresh Breezes of Wind that come from 'em to purify the air'. The inhabitants, he said, were less prone to: 'Gout, Agues, Sciatica, Convulsions, Vapours, Palsies, Surfeits, Lethargies, Megrims, Consumptions, Rickets, Pains of the Stomach or Coughs.' Apparently, few women died in childbirth. He was told of one man, Gillouir Mack-Crain, who lived 180 years. The natives were 'very well proportioned, being generally black of Complexion, and free from bodily Imperfections'.

The Island

One of Jura's most infamous features is the **Corryvreckan Whirlpool**, in the strait between its northern point and Scarba. Notorious to west-coast sailors, it can be both lion and lamb. Flood tides meet around a steep pyramid rock, 15ft below the surface, causing the whirlpool, whose noise has been heard up to 10 miles away. Roaring like an express train, its mighty maw has been known to suck down whole boats, but at slack tide it can be approached by sea, its satin-smooth water ruffled by tiny eddies that pull gently at a boat without harm.

In May 1946 George Orwell, born Eric Blair, rented Barnhill, an abandoned farmhouse at the end of a 5-mile, heavily rutted track from Ardlussa where his landlady Margaret Fletcher lived. Over a period of summer visits, he wrote *Nineteen Eighty-Four* here, fighting the tuberculosis that was to kill him, and was contented in his rather morose way. He was a competent boatman, but on one occasion he misread the tide table and capsized in the Corryvreckan with his three-year-old adopted son Richard and a couple of friends. Miraculously, no one was drowned and they were rescued, unscathed, from a rock by some lobster fishermen.

Craighouse, the only village, on the southeast coast looking out across the Sound of Jura to Knapdale and Kintyre, has the island's only hotel and the distillery.

Jura House Gardens is an oasis on the southern shore (*open all year; adm*). Its large walled garden was established in the middle of the 19th century to exploit the natural features and beauty of the area; thanks to the mild climate exotic Australasian plants are grown. Everything is organically produced, and there is an attractive walk through woodland to the shore at Ardfin.

Colonsay and Oronsay

These two tiny islands, joined at low tide, lie 10 miles west of Jura, 25 miles from the mainland. **Colonsay** is about 8 miles long and up to 3 miles across, while **Oronsay** is little more than 2 miles in any direction. To the west, way out to sea, the only thing between here and Canada is Dubh Artach Lighthouse. The landscape is made up of craggy hills, woods and a rocky coastline broken by silver sands.

The name Colonsay comes from St Columba who landed here on his way to Scotland from Ireland. Legend has it that when he could still see the land from which he had been exiled, he pressed on to Iona – whether from repugnance or homesickness is not related. (It is also said that he banished snakes from the two islands, as he did on Iona.) The Gaelic name is *Eilean Tarsuing* – cross-lying island, which indeed it is.

Getting There

Ferry Information: Caledonian MacBrayne, Gourock, t 08705 650 000. There are three boats a week from and to Oban (2¼ hours), and a sailing from Kennacraig via Islay, allowing a 6-hour day visit. A tour bus meets this boat and takes visitors round the island (*April–Sept Wed*).

Tourist Information

Oban: Argyll Square, t 0845 225 5121, *www.visitscottishheartlands.com. Open all year.*

Shopping

Virago, Colonsay, adjacent to the Colonsay hotel. An interesting bookshop with new and second-hand books on Scottish and West Highland themes. They can often get out-of-print books for you. Also sells coffee and crafts.

Where to Stay and Eat

The Isle of Colonsay Hotel, Kiloran, t (01951) 200 316 (*expensive–moderate*). Small, family-run and friendly, with excellent food using local ingredients whenever possible. They also have self-catering chalets and run wildflower courses.

Mr and Mrs Lawson, Seaview, Colonsay, t (01951) 200 315. A very well-run, comfortable and welcoming guesthouse (*moderate*). They also have a self-catering studio flat (sleeps 2), as well as two cottages (£200–£600 pw).

The Colonsay Estate, Colonsay, t (01951) 200 312 (*ring for prices*). Self-catering in a number of first-rate houses.

Oronsay's name might stem from St Oran, a disciple of St Columba, or from the Norse *orfiris-ey* – ebb-tide island, though it is when the tide ebbs that it stops being an island. The strand linking the two can submerge rapidly in the flood tide, so be warned – you have about 3 hours either side of low tide. Colonsay seems to have a little of every type of landscape: machair, woodland, cultivated woodland, both rocky and sandy beaches, cliffs, moorland and pasture.

Around the Islands

Kiloran Bay, in the northwest of Colonsay, is probably the most unspoilt beach in all the islands. After a strong westerly wind there are rollers good enough for surfing, though it can be dangerous. Both islands have higher than average sunshine, comparable with Tiree which holds the record for Scotland, and the annual rainfall is half that of the Argyll mainland. Frost and snow are rare. Over 500 species of wild flowers can be found including rare purple orchids, sea samphire, marsh helleborine, a burnet rose unique to Colonsay and the very rare orchid, *Spiranthes romanzoffiana*. Bluebells and primroses bloom in spring, wild irises flower in damp corners, harebells nod on the sand dunes, and purple thrift clings to the rocks. Over 150 bird species have been recorded. Wild goats flourish at Balnahard and on Oronsay, thought to be descended from survivors of a wreck of the Spanish Armada in 1588, carried on the ship to provide provisions for the fleet. If you are lucky you may see otters.

Archaeological remains point to early settlement on both islands. On Colonsay, Fingal's Limpet Hammers are standing stones at Kilchattan; Dun Eibhinn, behind Scalasaig, is an Iron Age fort, later occupied by the MacDuffies or MacFies of Colonsay until they were deposed as the ruling families by the MacNeills in 1701. There are Mesolithic sites at Loch Staosnaig, locally known as Queen's Bay.

Oronsay has Mesolithic shell mounds dating from before 4000 BC, giving one of the earliest records of human settlement in Scotland. Dun Domhnuill is an Iron Age fort on top of a rocky mound, well sited for defence. The stabilized ruins of Oronsay Priory and cloisters date from 1330–50, founded by Augustinian monks under the patronage of the Lords of the Isles; masonry within the circular wall which encloses the ruins dates from the 6th century. Here, until about 1500, was one of the workshops where the monks produced the intricately carved grave-slabs and crosses that can be found all over the Highlands and Islands. The Oronsay Cross is a good example, and there are about 30 other carved stones within the Prior's House dating from the 15th and 16th centuries. There is a prostrate sanctuary cross halfway over the Strand.

In 1841 these two islands had a population of 979; now it is about 100, and they have become a holiday haven away from it all. Although self-catering cottages are fast outnumbering those of residents, they have not yet spoiled the tranquillity.

Colonsay House, sheltered niche in woodland north of Loch Fada, was built by Malcolm MacNeill in 1722, probably with the stones of Kiloran Abbey, which once stood here; enlarged in the 18th century, it is now holiday flats. The estate was bought in 1904 by Donald Smith, Lord Strathcona and Mount Royal, a Forres man who made his fortune in Canada. He used the natural contours, rocks and streams to create the attractive gardens which you are allowed to visit.

According to Martin Martin, when the 'natives' of Colonsay went across to the Priory, it was their custom to make a tour 'sunways' about the church before they 'entered upon any kind of business.' While he was here, his landlord borrowed a Bible from him in order to fan the face of a sick relative with the holy pages. Three doses of this treatment appear to have cured the patient. There is a primitive and challenging 18-hole golf course on the west coast.

Mull

Mull – 'Isle of the Cool, High Bends' – is the second largest of the Inner Hebrides after Skye, and merits a whole book to itself. Shaped like a caricature of the British Isles, its southwestern peninsula kicks skittishly upwards. Encircled by 300 miles of

Getting There and Around

Caledonian MacBrayne, t 08705 650 000, run frequent **car ferries**: Oban–Craignure (40mins); Oban–Tobermory (2 hours), Lochaline–Fishnish (15 mins Kilchoan–Tobermory (30 mins). Ask about the 'Rover' and 'Multi-stop' tickets – cheaper for island-hopping.

Charter flights can be arranged from Glasgow. You can hire **cars** easily. Most roads are single track with passing places.

Inter-island cruises, Dervaig, t (01688) 400 264 or Turus Mara, t (01688) 400 242. High-speed charter boats to Staffa, the Treshnish Isles, Coll, Eigg and Muck. You need to be well prepared for quick weather changes and bring seasickness pills: the slow Atlantic swell can disturb even hardened mariners. You might see whales and dolphins however.

Tourist Information

Craignure: The Pier, t 08707 200 600. *Open all year.*
Tobermory: Main Street, t 08707 200 625. *Open April–Oct.*
Oban: Argyll Square, 08707 200 630. *Open all year.*

Events and Activities

Mull Experience, t (01680) 812 309/421. Coach tours to Duart Castle, Torosay Castle and Gardens and Mull Railway – includes entrance fees and ferry (Oban–Craignure).
Island Encounter Wildlife Safaris, at Aros, t (01680) 300 441.
Isle of Mull Land Rover Wildlife Expeditions, Tobermory, t (01688) 302 044, *www.scotlandwildlife.com*. From Ulva House Hotel (*see below*). Daily expeditions with lunch, to see otters, eagles etc. *All year.*
Drama Festival: March
Music Festival: April
Tobermory Highland Games (and **Children's Highland Games**): July
West Highland Yachting Week: early August
Salen Show: including a dog show, August
Car Rally: October
Wet- or dry-fly trout fishing: available in Mishnish Lochs, Loch Tor and Loch Frisa. Licences, tackle and bait can be obtained from **Brown's Ironmongers**, Tobermory High Street, or the **National Forestry Commission** office at the south end of Loch Frisa.

Where to Stay and Eat

Druimard Country House, Dervaig, t (01688) 400 345, *www.druimard.co.uk* (*expensive*). Victorian country house hotel, select and luxurious with excellent food and service, close to the theatre.
Glengorm Castle, near Tobermory, t (01688) 302 321, *www.glengormcastle.co.uk* (*expensive*). Luxury B&B in Victorian castle with spectacular views. Not cheap, but worth it.

rugged coastline, it is deeply cut by lochs, with many wooded hills and secret corners, some easily reached by coastal roads, others only on foot. Mull's western seaboard is sprinkled with islands: Iona, Inch Kenneth, Ulva, Staffa and, further west, the Treshnish Isles with Coll and Tiree beyond. There are plenty of boat trips to the islands and some of the hotels charter their own boats. In addition, local men will take you fishing or sightseeing, which is by far the most fun way to get about. The whole coast is a sailor's paradise: Loch Na Keal, Loch Scridain, Loch Buie and Loch Spelve are deep sea lochs which penetrate far inland and provide sheltered anchorages. The hinterland is a mass of hills dominated by **Ben More** (3,169ft/966m) in the west, its scree-covered flanks the result of a volcano which exploded some 60 million years ago.

Students come from far afield to study the interesting geology, and archaeologists come to study the large number of prehistoric sites. There are some fine castles and

The Western Isles Hotel, Tobermory, t (01688) 302 012, *www.mullhotel.com* (*expensive–moderate*). Massive Victorian pile, with great Highland hospitality, stunning views and old-world charm. Large conservatory overlooks the harbour, with great food.

Ardachy House Hotel, Uisken, t (01681) 700 505, *www.ardachy.co.uk* (*moderate*). Small and cosy, overlooking the sands of Ardalanish. Dinner by arrangement.

Craignure Inn, Craignure, t (01680) 812 305, *www.craignure-inn.co.uk* (*moderate*). A friendly 17th-century inn on the water, renowned for its lively bar.

Druimnacroish Country House Hotel, Dervaig, t (01688) 400 274, *www.druimnacroish.co.uk* (*moderate*). A converted water mill with country-house atmosphere and good service. Nicely furnished, pretty bedrooms.

Highland Cottage, Breadalbane Street, Tobermory, t (01688) 302 030, *www.highlandcottage.co.uk* (*moderate*). Stylish little hotel with excellent food.

Pennyghael Hotel, Pennyghael, t (01681) 704 288, *www.pennyghaelhotel.com* (*moderate*). In a spectacular setting by the loch, informal and family-run, with good home cooking.

Tiroran House, north shore of Loch Scridain, t (01681) 705 232, *www.tiroran.com* (*moderate*). Remote and enchanting Wolsey Lodge. Cosy and hospitable, with a nice garden and good food.

Tobermory Hotel, Tobermory, t (01688) 302 091, *www.thetobermoryhotel.com* (*moderate*). On the waterfront and a characterful place.

Ulva House Hotel, Strongarbh, Tobermory, t (01688) 302 044, *www.ulva-house.co.uk* (*moderate*). A characterful Victorian house, overlooking the sea, very cosy and good food. They run wildlife expeditions (*see* 'Events and Activities').

Ardbeg House Hotel, Dervaig, t (01688) 400 254 (*budget*). A Victorian country house in a nice setting, cosy and full of character.

Bellachroy Hotel, Dervaig, t (01688) 400 314, *www.bellachroyhotel.co.uk* (*budget*). Dates from the 16th century when it was a droving inn. Cheap, cheerful, and very friendly.

Calgary Hotel and Dovecote Restaurant, Calgary, t (01688) 400 256, *www.calgary.co.uk* (*budget*). Good food – you can stay too.

Mishnish, Tobermory, t (01688) 302 009 (*budget*). Excellent pub, with great lively atmosphere and good-value rooms.

Killiechronan Estate, Killiechronan, t (01786) 462 519, *www.selfcatering-mull.com*. An old farmhouse and outbuildings converted into self-catering holiday cottages at the head of Loch Na Keal. Salmon-fishing and pony-trekking facilities are on offer on the estate itself.

The Garden Barn, Tobermory, t (01688) 302 235 (*inexpensive*). Part of the farm where they make Mull cheddar: you can get good farmhouse food here. *Ring for open times*.

The Puffer Aground, Salen, t (01680) 300 389 (*inexpensive*). Good café.

Red Bay Cottage, Fionnphort, t (01681) 700 396 (*inexpensive*). Cosy home cooking with an emphasis on steaks.

an ancient pilgrim track across the Ross of Mull, used by pilgrims to Iona. Johnson and Boswell came to Mull during their tour of the Hebrides. Johnson lamented the lack of trees, attributing this to local idleness, but applauded the French wine he was given.

In 1821 the population was 10,600. Until fairly recently, there was a steady decline, but it now seems to have stabilized at about 2,400; with fishing, farming, tourism and building to employ them, fewer young people are leaving for the mainland, and there are many English and mainland Scottish incomers arriving for the island's insular peace and beauty. There is not always perfect harmony between the 'white settlers' and the 'natives', however.

There are more red deer than people: over 3,000 roam the island, and smaller fallow deer can be seen in the woods around Gruline and Salen. Polecats, weasels, stoats, mink, feral ferrets and otters also share the island. Wild white goats can be seen from Grass Point down to the Ross of Mull.

Tobermory

Tobermory – 'the Well of St Mary', and 'Balamory' of TV fame – is an unexpected gem, with one of the most sheltered harbours in Scotland tucked in behind a headland. Founded as a fishing village in 1789 on the site of an earlier Christian settlement, tall Georgian houses line the harbour, washed in strong poster-paint colours, with long, narrow windows and gabled dormers. You won't find too many tartan souvenirs here: stacks of lobster creels, business-like tackle shops and pubs show where priorities lie. Some people who live in remote Morvern and Ardnamurchan on the mainland go across to Tobermory to do their shopping, it being their nearest metropolis.

Mull Museum (*open Easter–mid-Oct Mon–Fri 10–4, Sat 10–1; adm*), in an old baker's shop, is a concession to one of Mull's main industries – tourism. Here you can get a good overview of the history of the island, and of the wrecked galleon *Florencia*, part of the Spanish Armada and still a focus of interest today. The ship sought shelter here in a storm in 1588. Always hospitable, the islanders treated the Spaniards with courtesy, restocking their stores and entertaining them in grand style. But Scotsmen are thrifty as well as hospitable, and when rumours spread that the *Florencia* was about to depart without having paid its dues, a local man, Donald Maclean, went aboard to remonstrate. He was locked up in the ship's cell but managed to escape. In retaliation he blew up the ship, together with the hoard of gold and treasure it was alleged to have been carrying. So far only a few coins and cannon have been rescued, but the search continues. Divers should note that the wreck is protected and it is forbidden to dive in its area. Tobermory's nine-hole golf course is owned by the Western Isles Hotel (*see* p.221) – the spectacular views down the Sound of Mull are apt to distract players, however. Mull's only **distillery** with tours is in Tobermory (*open Easter–Oct 10–5*). **An Tobar** (*open Mar–Dec*), in Argyll Terrace, is an arts centre and gallery. It has exhibitions, music, workshops, talks and coffee sessions round the fire.

West from Tobermory via Ardmeanach Peninsula

West from Tobermory, the B8073 passes the three-in-one Mishnish Lochs where there is good trout fishing. Snake Pass, beyond the last one, is the home of many adders and the start of a nice walk out to Loch Frisa. On the hill down into Dervaig there is a cemetery at Kilmore, with some of the oldest gravestones on Mull. Film buffs may recognize this as one of the locations for *Where Eight Bells Toll*.

Mull Little Theatre (*t* *(01688) 302 673, www.mulltheatre.com*), in Dervaig, 5 miles from Tobermory, featured in the *Guinness Book of Records* as the smallest professional theatre in Britain, with 37 seats, but it has recently lost that accolade by providing six extra seats. Six times a week from Easter to October, two or more actors from visiting professional companies stage really excellent and varied productions which should be booked well in advance. Amateur productions are staged in the winter.

The **Old Byre Heritage Centre**, a mile beyond Dervaig (*open Easter–mid-Oct daily; adm*) is a typical crofting museum with tableaux showing life at the time of the Clearances, including a half-hour video, shown hourly from 10.30am.

The west coast road gives views out to the scattering of islands that enhance the wonderful seascapes, especially when seen against a setting sun. There are good sandy beaches; **Calgary Bay** is particularly notable. Calgary was once a prosperous crofting community, but its people were evicted and made their way across the Atlantic, trekked across Canada and established a town in the Northwest Territory in 1884. Nostalgic and homesick, they called their new town after their old home.

Boats run from Dervaig or Ulva to the **Treshnish Isles** and to **Staffa** when the weather is fair. A new landing stage on Staffa makes access easier in rough weather, and some cruises allow you an hour ashore. You can go into **Fingal's Cave** by boat, or walk into it along a platform around its edge. This huge, cathedral-like cavern is made up of columns of basalt, similar in geology to Ireland's Giant's Causeway, some hexagonal, truncated at different levels like organ pipes. The formation inspired Mendelssohn in 1829 to write the *Hebrides* overture.

During Queen Victoria's cruise of the west coast, her royal yacht anchored off Staffa and the royal party were rowed into the cave in an open rowing boat: 'the effect was splendid, like a great entrance into a vaulted hall: it looked almost awful as we entered and the barge heaved up and down on the swell of the sea. It is very high, but not longer than 227 feet, and narrower than I expected, being only 40 feet wide. The sea is immensely deep in the cave. The rocks, under water, were all colours – pink, blue, and green – which had a most beautiful effect. It was the first time the British standard with a Queen of Britain, and her husband and children, had ever entered Fingal's Cave, and the men gave three cheers, which sounded very impressive there.'

Cruises which include **Lunga** in the Treshnish Isles are especially good during the nesting season – however, if you linger too long over the bewitching puffins at the start, you may never see the rest of the island. They sit about, scratching, chatting to each other and popping in and out of their burrows, an arm's length from you, but there are also kittiwakes, razorbills, shags and guillemots, and lots of black rabbits.

The island of **Ulva** will be familiar to anyone who knows the poem *Lord Ullin's Daughter*, which tells the sad tale of her eloping to join her lover, 'The Chief of Ulva's Isle', and of how she drowned in the ferry as she fled her father's wrath. Lord Ullin stands helpless on the shore:

'Come back! Come back!' he cried in grief,
Across the stormy water,
'And I'll forgive your Highland chief,
My daughter! Oh, my daughter!'
'Twas vain: the loud waves lashed the shore
Return or aid preventing.
The waters wild went o'er his child,
And he was left lamenting.
'Lord Ullin's Daughter' by Thomas Campbell (1777–1844)

On a calm day these waters look innocent enough, but Lord Ullin's daughter was not the only one to perish here. Among many others was 'the young Laird of Col' who, having treated Dr Johnson to warm Highland hospitality in 1773, perished in the passage between Ulva and Inch Kenneth a year later. A ferry runs all day in summer (*t (01688) 500 226*). Ulva has a **Heritage Centre** (*open Easter–mid-Oct Mon–Fri 9–5 and Sun June–Aug; adm*) in a restored thatched croft house. Try the oysters and Guinness in its licensed tearoom. Nearby, Eas Forss is a waterfall that cascades over the cliff into a pool and then under a rock, arching into the sea 10 miles from Ulva ferry. You can also walk across a causeway to the even smaller island of **Gometra**, where there is a very secure natural harbour, a haven for sailors caught in a storm. The walks and views all down the west coast are good. Much of the coastline is columnar basalt with sandy bays and rocky coves, sea birds and abundant wildflowers.

The best way to climb **Ben More** (3,450ft/1,050m) is from the southern shore of Loch na Keal, from the bridge over the Abhainn na h-Uamha. You more or less follow your nose across the moor and up, reaching An Gearna first and then on up the steeper slope of Ben More, where it's truly magnificent. To make a round trip, go on across to A' Chioch and then down the Abhainn na h-Gearna which has lovely pools and waterfalls to cool yourself in and a 'natural' bridge.

Where the B8035 turns south, inland across the Ardmeanach Peninsula, look out across the entrance to Loch na Keal to **Inch Kenneth**, named after one of St Columba's followers. It served Iona as a granary and was the burial place for Highland chiefs when the weather was too wild for the crossing to Iona. A ruined chapel and a number of carved slabs and crosses remain. Johnson and Boswell were here in 1773 as guests of Sir Allan Maclean and his two daughters, one of whom was to marry young Col, who was on his way to see her when he drowned the following year. Dr Johnson was pleasantly surprised by the civilized conditions of the Maclean household in comparison to some of his other Highland experiences. Boswell found some human bones here which he buried in a shallow grave, applauded by Johnson who could not assist because of his squeamish nature. The island was bought by Lord Redesdale, father of the Mitford sisters, and Unity Mitford took refuge here after her association with Hitler and the Nazis. The rather strange, elongated appearance of the present house is the result of their 'improvements'.

The southwestern end of Mull's **Ardmeanach Peninsula** is owned by the National Trust for Scotland. Leave the B8035 where it turns southeast and take the track to

Balmeanach Farm. A path from here goes out to the cliffs and, after less than a mile, descends steeply on to the beach. **MacKinnon's Cave** is most impressive, stretching back hundreds of yards, and may be the one visited by Johnson. His escort forgot to take a flare and had to go and find one: be warned – and don't go in on a rising tide. You can walk right round the coast from here, but it is quite a hike.

Alternatively take the track from the southeastern corner of the peninsular back west to **Burgh**, on the headland. **MacCulloch's Tree** is signposted. John MacCulloch was the naturalist and geologist who discovered the tree in 1819. Sixty million years ago, between sporadic outbursts of lava and in a warm, humid climate, soils developed here and supported a substantial flora of oak, hazel, maidenhair and magnolia trees. This one had been overwhelmed by lava and is still vertical, about 40ft high and 6ft wide. Most of the trunk was replaced by lava, so that what you see today is really just a cast of the tree. Sadly, though well protected now, what little remained of the actual tree was mostly removed by fossil collectors, but the thought of its antiquity is awesome.

The scenery is gentler on the **Ross of Mull**, the island's southwestern headland. Almost attached to its tip, the tidal island of **Erraid** is where, in Robert Louis Stevenson's *Kidnapped*, David Balfour and Alan Breck were shipwrecked before setting off to witness the Appin Murder (*see* p.107). Stevenson's uncle looked after lighthouses in this area. The island is now inhabited by members of the Findhorn Foundation, who sometimes seem to find communicating with non-members difficult.

Uisken on the south coast, reached by the road from Bunessan, is a lovely beach with lonely crofts, mostly ruined – another victim of the Clearances. **Bunessan** has the Isle of Mull Wine Company, which makes Isle of Mull Vermouth and 'The Mull Riveter' – a blend of their own vermouth and bitters with vodka. Here also is the **Isle of Mull Angora Rabbit Farm** (*t (01681) 700 507; open Easter–Oct Sun–Fri 11–5; adm*), where there are clipping and spinning demonstrations, an angora shop, tea and snacks.

At **Pennyghael** on the northeast shore of the peninsula, head south through Glen Leidle to **Carsaig**, a lovely spot with a massive, beautifully constructed old pier, no longer used by ferries. There is an interesting old laird's house (privately owned) and the Inniemore School of Painting, a residential summer painting school established in 1967 in a Victorian lodge. Leave your car here and walk the 3 miles southwest along the coast to Malcolm's Point. Here are the **Carsaig Arches**, a famous geological freak which left a natural jagged archway carved through the rock.

From the head of Loch Scridain the A849 goes back inland to the east coast through Glen More. About 17 miles on from Bunessan, take the track south to Lochbuie, about 4 miles, for a lovely walk along Loch Airdeglais through Gleann Chaiginn Mhoir. Or you can drive, crossing the bridge over the Lussa River at Ardura, and running along past Loch Spelve and Loch Uisg. Moy Castle, the ruin at the head of Loch Buie, was the ancestral home of the MacLaines of Lochbuie. It was later replaced by an elegant Georgian mansion which still stands nearby. There are several caves along the western shore of Loch Buie, one of which is called Lord Lovat's Cave, though no one seems to know the story behind this.

Duart Castle

Duart Castle (*open April daily 11–4, May–mid-Oct daily 10.30–6; adm*) is about 5 miles northeast of the head of Loch Spelve, an impressive fortress on a headland guarding the approach to the Sound of Mull and clearly seen from the Oban ferry as it passes Lady's Rock, off Lismore Lighthouse at the head of Loch Linnhe. In the 16th century a Maclaine of Lochbuie, disenchanted by his wife, tethered her to this rock. Taking pity on her, some passing fishermen released her and she fled to her father, Campbell of Inveraray. This irate chief invited the Maclaine to stay on the pretext of commiserating with him on the loss of his wife. After dinner the 'deceased' wife confronted her husband and her relatives set about him with broadswords. Home of the 28th chief of the Clan Maclean, the castle dates from the 12th century and is one of the oldest inhabited castles in Scotland. The massive enclosure would have contained timber buildings, to which has been added a great tower house and later works. Probably built by descendants of Somerled, it passed to the Lords of the Isles and then by marriage, around 1367, to the Macleans. It was besieged by Campbells in 1691 and garrisoned by Commonwealth forces until the Restoration, when it was restored to the Macleans. But their Stuart sympathies led to its forfeiture and it became a government barracks from 1741 to 1748. It was then allowed to rot until it was bought back in 1911 and restored by the then Maclean chief, Sir Fitzroy, a gallant Hussar Colonel who had ridden with the Light Brigade in the Crimea. He died at the age of 100, affectionately known as 'Old Man A Hundred'.

As well as the keep, visitors can see the cell where prisoners from the Spanish galleon *Florencia* were held after it had been sunk in Tobermory in 1588 by Donald Maclean. There are relics of the Maclean family in the main hall, with many of the gifts presented to the late Chief during his world tours – he was, among other things Chief Scout and Lord Chamberlain. There is also an exhibition of scouting throughout the Commonwealth, in the old staff rooms at the top of the castle.

Just south of Duart, the road to **Grass Point**, on Loch Don, was the old drovers' road for cattle and sheep from the Outer Isles bound for mainland markets. It was also the landing point for pilgrims going to Iona. The seal on one of the rocks round the bay is of rather a different species – it was the handiwork of the sculptor, poet and writer, the late Lionel Leslie. First cousin of Winston Churchill, he and his wife Barbara came to live in the old drovers' inn here after the Second World War, building it up from a ruin with their own hands. Boatloads of visitors came over from Oban in the summer to have tea, buy local crafts and listen to the sculptor's fascinating stories. Even in his mid-eighties his wit was as sharp as the stone he could no longer see to carve. There were also bas-reliefs of a deer, an eagle, fighting swans and horses on the walls of a roofless byre beside the house, in lasting memory of a great artist and a great man. (The house has now been done up for holiday lets.)

Duart Bay to Salen

Torosay Castle (*open mid-April–Oct daily 10.30–5; gardens open all year; adm*) is a mile west as the crow flies across Duart Bay. Designed in 1856 by David Bryce, with all the Scottish Baronial embellishments so beloved by the Victorians, it has 11 acres of terraced Italian-style gardens with a statue walk and water garden laid out by Sir Robert Lorimer. Although the castle has none of the history of Duart, its endearing informality and random collections make it a fun visit. As well as wildlife paintings by Thorburn, Landseer and Peter Scott, and portraits by Poynter, de Lazlo, Sargent and Carlos Sancha, there is a wealth of memorabilia belonging to the Guthries, who own the castle. There are numerous hunting trophies including the enormous head of a prehistoric Irish elk, archives, a library and huge family scrapbooks going back 100 years. In the high season boats run from Oban direct to Torosay. A **miniature railway** (*open Easter–mid-Oct; adm*) runs the mile and a half from Craignure Pier to the castle – the only passenger train service in the Hebrides, a 260mm gauge.

The roofless, ruined church by the cemetery at **Salen** is unlikely to be restored. A wicked Maclean of Duart was buried here many years ago with the consequence that the roof blew off. Three times they put it back and three times it blew away, unable to settle over the remains of such a villain. The 1st-century statue of the Virgin Mary that used to be in this church has sadly been stolen. **Aros Castle**, just across Salen Bay, dates from the 14th century and was one of the strongholds of the Lords of the Isles.

Iona

An I mo chridhe, I mo grîdh
An îte guth manaich bidh geum bî
Ach mun tig an saoghal gu cruch
Bidh I mar a bha

In Iona of my heart, Iona of my love,
In the place of monks' voices will be lowing of cattle
But ere the world shall come to an end
Iona shall be as it was.

St Columba's Prophecy

Getting There

The passenger ferry from Fionnphort on Mull takes 5 minutes. **Gordon Grant Tours**, t (01631) 562 842, offers a Sacred Isles Tour in summer, from Oban via Staffa to Iona, with 2½ hours on Iona before the return journey.

Where to Stay and Eat

Argyll Hotel, Iona, t (01681) 700 334, www.argyllhoteliona.co.uk (*moderate*). On the water, built in 1868, with cosy en-suite rooms, though some baths are so small you have to ablute in sections. Excellent food.

St Columba Hotel, Iona, t (01681) 700 304, www.stcolumba-hotel.co.uk (*expensive–moderate*). On rising ground next to the abbey, north of the village, half a mile from the jetty, plenty of mod cons; some rooms have sea views.

The Abbey, Iona, t (01681) 700 404 (*budget*). Pretty spartan – monkish food and no licence. Visitors are expected to take part in the day-to-day activities of the community. They also run week-long courses. *Full board Mar–Dec.*

Finlay Ross, the souvenir shop on Iona, t (01681) 700 334, www.finlayrossiona.co.uk (*budget*). Does good B&B and bicycle hire.

No one can visit Mull without making a pilgrimage to the 'cradle of Christianity', though St Ninian was spreading the word nearly 150 years before St Columba founded his church on Iona in 563.

History

Columba, whose name comes from the Gaelic *Colum Cille* meaning 'Dove of the Church', was born in Donegal in Ireland in AD 521, of royal descent. He was exiled, possibly for having indulged in a spot of plagiarism while transcribing a rare text belonging to his mentor, and may even have been excommunicated. Although Iona claims to have been his first landfall, there are several other places on the western seaboard with similar claims. Given the inhospitability of the Atlantic and the small, probably leaky boat crammed with a dozen monks, it is most unlikely that they sailed directly across from Derry to Iona. Their most likely route would have been within the lee of Islay and Jura, and the chances are that they stopped off several times, to shelter, to take on provisions, and maybe even to explore. Eventually, however, they did land on Iona, and stayed – some say because it was the first place from which Columba could no longer see Ireland.

Here was a man born to lead and fight with all the romantic dreams and ideals of a Celt; a man steeped in religious learning, burning with missionary zeal, banished from his beloved homeland, leaving scandal and disgrace in his wake. His biographer, St Adamnan, was ninth Abbot of Iona some 80 years after Columba's death, and he seems to have viewed his subject through rose-tinted spectacles. With only apocryphal evidence, we have to draw on our imaginations to try to see the man through what he created and what he left behind. Archaeological excavations revealed occupation by farming communities as far back as 3500 BC, and a formation of standing stones on Mull are thought to be waymarks for pilgrims to Iona, indicating a site of pre-Christian worship or ritual. One of Columba's great strengths was that he was tolerant of the pagan rituals that had preceded him. Those first converts hedged their bets, as can be seen on ancient crosses that combine Christian symbols with pagan, and Columba was careful with his new brood until he had established confidence in his One God and was able to lay down rules for living a godly life.

Iona was a productive island, surrounded by waters full of fish, strategically situated on the sea routes between Ireland and Scotland and along the west coast. The monks grew crops, mainly barley, on the machair where the soil was a fertile mix of peat and sand. They raised cattle and poultry and lived off bread, eggs, fish, meat and dairy products. They used seals for oil, skins and food, and were skilled craftsmen with metal, glass, wood and leather. They slept in single cells in a timber monastery and ate communally in a refectory. It was a simple, hard-working life combining the daily struggle to exist with their vocational life of prayer, study and evangelism. They spoke Latin and Gaelic, chanted psalms, copied and illuminated manuscripts.

Paganism was not their only enemy. The voracious Vikings were a constant menace, raiding, pillaging and murdering, until, in 807, the Abbot and his monks escaped to Kells in Ireland, leaving a tiny community behind to keep the faith alive.

Iona was by now a renowned Holy Island and an important burial place for kings: 48 Scottish, 8 Norwegian and 4 Irish rulers are traditionally believed to be interred here. Among the Scottish kings were Kenneth Macalpine, Macbeth and Duncan, whom he murdered. Over the centuries, in spite of the Vikings, the various buildings were consolidated. In 1200 Reginald, son of Somerled, Lord of the Isles, founded a Benedictine community, and in 1507 the abbey church became the cathedral for the bishopric of the Isles. The Reformation brought to an end the monastic life founded by Columba, and Protestantism seems to have been adopted without too much of a struggle of conscience. Plainchant no longer rose from the cloisters and the cathedral fell into disrepair; spiritual needs were supplied by a series of ministers, disrupted now and then by secret visits from deposed Catholic priests; secular life went on the same. In the 1630s attempts were made to restore the Cathedral of the Isles, in conjunction with Charles I's hopes to reintroduce Catholic elements into the new church, but by the end of the 18th century the monastic buildings were ruinous.

The potato famine of 1846 took its toll, and in 1847, 98 people, one-fifth of the community, emigrated. The remaining islanders managed to keep going and by the end of that century Iona a popular destination for day-trippers in yachts and steamers, and for holiday-makers. The locals were not slow to see the potential profit from pious pilgrims and tourism – the sale of guidebooks, souvenirs and craftwork proliferated. In 1899 the Iona Cathedral Trust was founded and repair work began, proceeding spasmodically as funds were raised, and the first service was held in the partly restored cathedral. Once this and its satellite buildings were more or less functioning, thoughts turned to the monastic ruins.

In 1938 George Macleod, a Presbyterian socialist who had renounced an inherited title (later to accept one bestowed by the State), settled a new community on the island and began rebuilding the monastery. He believed that the church needed to get closer to the lives of ordinary people and that practical and spiritual work in a community would be good training for people with vocations for public service. Thus the Iona Community was born. Few in the community spoke Gaelic; they were not Gaels and had no cultural ties with their adopted home. There could never be full integration, although the natural courtesy of the islanders forbade outward animosity towards the zealous incomers.

Visiting the Island

When Johnson and Boswell came here in 1773, Johnson was deeply moved by the atmosphere: 'that man is little to be envied whose piety would not grow warmer among the ruins of Iona'. Today he may have felt differently. Opinions differ: for some, the sanctity of the restored abbey has been erased by the zeal of Iona Abbey Limited, and they find it hard to kneel and say a prayer among the hugging and hand-holding and happy-clappery of the community, despite its commendable focus on worldwide issues. Instead they find their peace in St Oran's Chapel and in the *Reilig Odhráin* – the ancient burial ground – and in the remoter parts of the island. Mammon rules within the precincts, and even a ferryman has been known to ram a visiting boat innocently trespassing on his commercial berth. But with under three hours, day visitors haven't time to disrupt the real Iona. When the last boat leaves at about 5.30pm, the native islanders emerge and get on with their real lives.

There is a well-stocked, licensed Spar shop selling delicious home-made bread, run by a local family, who also run the only pub and an excellent restaurant. There is an up-market craft shop; a tourist trap souvenir shop called Finlay Ross, which sells good books; and a marvellous little pottery with pieces that mirror the exceptional colours of the Iona land and sea. There is also a tiny bookshop with a tiny doorway, across the road from the Columba Hotel, selling, when it is open which isn't often, everything from rare books to tatty paperbacks. **Iona Heritage Centre** (*open April–Oct Mon–Sat 10.30–4.30; adm*) is in Telford Manse, with local history, a small shop and a café.

Iona is special, in spite of all the trappings and communal bonhomie. Walk away from the designer Holy Place and climb the small hill, Dun I, to the north of the abbey. Look down on the restored buildings where so much attention has been paid to the fabric that they forgot to restore the Holy Spirit; on the postcard and booklet stalls; on the trails of people with strap-hung cameras, chattering and munching. Listen and you may catch a faint echo of ironic laughter and feel a charismatic presence beside you. St Columba was known to have had a well-developed sense of humour.

Coll and Tiree

Coll and Tiree, less than 11 miles off the northwest of Mull, are low-lying islands which look barren from the sea until you step ashore and discover green fields surrounded by an almost continuous string of deserted white beaches, home to lots of different sea birds, seals and otters. Strong winds, very shallow soil and free-ranging sheep keep them treeless, hence the deceptively barren look from afar. Because there are no proper hills to attract rain clouds, these islands have an exceptionally high record of sunshine, but for the same reason there is little shelter from the persistent and battering wind. A number of the old-style cottages survive, with rounded corners to withstand the gales, and humpy thatched or tar-felted roofs.

Coll

Coll is an endearing fish shape, 13 miles long and 3 miles wide, with a population of about 150, down from as many as 1,450 before the Clearances. The low terrain is surrounded by wonderful sandy beaches, azure water and rocky coves, backed by machair strewn with wild flowers in spring. Johnson and Boswell spent some days on Coll, as bad weather forced them to seek shelter here en route to Mull from Skye. Dr Johnson, recovering from seasickness, was glad to make a landfall anywhere. Later, he remarked: 'it would require great resignation to live in one of these islands if you were shut up here, your thoughts would torment you: you would think of Edinburgh or London and that you could not be there.' By the fifth day of their enforced stay, he said: 'I want to be on the mainland and go on with existence. This is a waste of life.'

Two standing stones at **Totronald** called *Na Sgeulachan* – the Tellers of Tales – are thought to be part of a pagan temple, and traces of prehistoric forts and duns scatter the island. During the Norse occupation of the islands, Coll was the headquarters of Earl Gilli, brother-in-law to Sigurd, ruler of Orkney and the Hebrides in 1000. By the end of the 13th century it belonged to the MacDougalls of Lorne, from whom it was taken by Robert the Bruce. It passed to a second son of the Macleans of Duart in the early 1400s and remained in their ownership until 1856, when Hugh, last Maclean laird of Coll, was forced to sell his estates to pay for his extravagant lifestyle. It was bought by John Stuart of Glenbuckie, factor to the Duke of Argyll, and his ruthlessly efficient farming methods resulted in mass emigration to Canada and Australia by the unfortunate crofters unable to afford his inflated rents. Traces of their abandoned croft houses can still be seen at the northern end of the island. The population includes quite a few incomers and holiday-home owners.

The island is known for its trout-filled lochs. Sea fishing is also good, and local fishermen will take visitors out in their boats. Walking, cycling, swimming, bird watching, botany and relaxation are the chief occupations for visitors. There is a nine-hole golf course at **Arinagour**. This village has the main concentration of Coll's population, a trim place which lies around the western shore of Loch Eatharna, with little cottages and gardens. **Breachacha Castle**, at the southern end of the island, is now used as the headquarters for an adventure training school. The later (new) castle dates from 1750 and was described by Dr Johnson as 'a tradesman's box' and by Boswell as 'a neat gentleman's house'. It was heightened and baronialized in the

Getting There and Around

There is a **boat** from Oban (daily exc Thurs and Sun), 3 hours to Coll, 4½ hours to Tiree. Boats also run from Tobermory, **Caledonian MacBrayne, t** 08705 650 000. There are one to two **flights** to Tiree from Glasgow (*daily except Sun*), and from Barra (*Tues–Thurs*). You can hire a **car** to meet you at the ferry or hire a **bicycle**, the best way to get about, but for the wind.

Tourist Information

Local knowledge is far the best, but for practical information:
Oban: Argyll Square, **t** 08705 200 630, *www.visitscottishheartlands.com.*

Where to Stay

Isle of Coll Hotel, at the head of Arinagour Bay Coll, **t** (01879) 230 334, *www.collhotel.com* (*moderate*). Has a jolly, Hebridean atmosphere.
Kirkapol House, Gott Bay, Tiree, **t** (01879) 220 729, *www.kirkapoltiree.co.uk* (*moderate*).

Converted Victorian church on the beach. Great character and very friendly.
Scarinish Hotel, Gott Bay, Tiree, **t** (01879) 220 308, *www.tireescarinishhotel.com* (*moderate*). A pleasant base.
Tigh-na-Mara, looking over Arinagour bay, Coll, **t** (01879) 230 354 (*moderate*). A modern guesthouse.
Tiree Lodge Hotel, Gott Bay, Tiree, **t** (01879) 220 353 (*moderate–budget*). Originally a hunting lodge. Self-catering accommodation available in a converted coach house.
Tigh Solas, Arinagour, Coll, **t** (01879) 230 333, *tigh.solas@virgin.net* (*moderate–budget*). Modern bungalow offering B&B – very friendly.
Achamore, near Arinagour, Coll, **t** (01879) 230 430, *jim@achamore.freeserve.co.uk* (*budget*). Comfortable, with a fine setting.
Arinagour, Arinagour, Coll, **t** (01879) 230 373 for B&B, **t** 230 339 for self-catering (*budget*). Self-catering chalet and three flats, as well as a house, bungalow and bothy for B&B.
Lighthouse View, Scarinish, Tiree, **t** (0141) 778 1405 (£200–290 pw) Sleeps 6 (*early booking essential*).

mid-19th century but is now almost beyond hope of restoration. Coll's economy depends mainly on farming, fishing and tourism. A small factory in Arinagour makes a range of herbal skin-care products.

Tiree

Tiree, southwest of Coll, is about 12 miles long, 7 miles at its widest, dwindling to less than a mile at its narrowest. The resident population of about 800 (4,450 before the Clearances) swells almost to 19th-century proportions during the tourist season. Much more fertile than Coll, its name comes from *Tir-iodh* – Land of Corn – dating from the days when it supplied corn to Iona. It is so low and flat that it has the Gaelic nickname *Tir fo Thuinn* – Land Below the Waves. The highest hill, **Ben Hynish**, is a 480ft (148m) pimple, topped with a prominent 'golf ball' radar station for tracking aircraft. Tiree shares with Coll a reputation for glorious beaches, abundant wild flowers and birds, as well as a high average of sunshine. This, with its magnificent Atlantic rollers, has earned it the title 'Hawaii of the North'. Windsurfers come from all over Britain to compete in Tiree where the clean, gently sloping beaches are first rate in all directions of wind. **Wave Classic** is a major event every October, during which world-class windsurfing can be watched. There is a nine-hole golf course, popular with the island's phenomenal population of hares. **Sandaig Museum** (*open June–Sept Mon–Fri 2–4*) is in a restored thatched cottage, with exhibits of island life.

A standing stone near Balinoe is thought to have been part of a Druid temple. Many of the island names are Viking in origin, from the 400 years of Norse occupation (*c.* 890–1266). Among the many ancient remains scattered over Tiree is **Dun Mor Broch** on Vaul Bay on the north coast. A well-preserved ruin, it is one of the tall, hollow towers probably built for refuge from Norse and other invaders. It is 30ft (9m) in diameter, its walls as much as 13ft (4m) thick. **Gott Bay** is a 3½-mile crescent of sand, backed by rich machair carpeted with wild flowers. The ferry docks at **Scarinish**, the main township on Gott Bay, and there are a number of crofting townships dotted around, many with restored thatched cottages. **Hynish**, in the south, has a small dry dock, flooded by an elaborate system of fresh water from springs. **Skerryvore Lighthouse Museum** (*open daylight hours*), in the old signal tower at Hynish, tells the story of the construction of the famous Skerryvore Lighthouse, visible through a telescope, built by the father of Robert Louis Stevenson. There is a young people's outdoor training centre based in the lighthouse cottages. On the north shore of Balephetrish, *Clach a' Choire* – Stone of the Corrie – is a large, granite boulder perched on a rocky base, a relic from the Ice Age. Decorated with intriguing prehistoric carvings, the boulder is known locally as the Ringing Stone because of the metallic note it produces when struck. It is said when *Clach a' Choire* shatters, Tiree will sink below the waves.

Views are marvellous all round the coast, especially those eastwards to the Treshnish Islands, with the aircraft-carrier-shaped *Bac Mor* – The Dutchman's Cap. One of the best places to see the birdlife is under the sheer cliffs below Carnan Mor in the south. Look for the distinctive greenstone on the beaches, found also in Iona.

The Small Isles

Rum

Rum is an island shaped like a squashed diamond, rising to a series of peaks; an unmistakable landmark for sailors, 8 miles west of Sleat in Skye. The peaks of the Rum Cuillins reach 2,000ft (610m) and contain some semiprecious stones as well as rocks similar to those found on the moon. These hills are the first to be hit by Atlantic depressions which deposit an annual rainfall of 90 inches. Inhabited since the Mesolithic Age, Rum was later held by the Clanranald Macdonalds until the 15th century. They exchanged it for Maclean of Coll's 'great galley' which turned out to have rotten timbers. The population of over 400 was reduced to one family in 1826 to make way for one sheep farm of 8,000 sheep. It was bought by the 2nd Marquess of Salisbury in 1845, deer were introduced and it became a private sporting estate. It was bought in 1879 by John Bullough, a self-made Lancashire textile machinery manufacturer, and his son George built Kinloch House. The organization now known as Scottish Natural Heritage acquired it from his widow in 1957 and it is now an 'outdoor laboratory' dedicated to discovering how the Hebrides can best support their wildlife.

The name Rum is thought to come from the Greek *rhombos*, referring to its rhomboid shape. The 'h' that sometimes creeps into its spelling was added by the Bulloughs, hoping to give the name a Gaelic flavour, not realizing that 'r' is never aspirated in Gaelic. (Some say that another reason for the 'h' was George Bullough's

Getting There

Caledonian MacBrayne, t 08705 650 000, runs a service to all four islands, not every day and not on Sundays. Ring for timetables.
Murdo Grant, t (01687) 450 224, *www.arisaig.co.uk*. Regular cruises from Arisaig (6 a week to Eigg; less frequent to Muck and Rum). Fast boat, with a bar – takes 130 people. He will also charter. *May–Sept.*

Tourist Information

Visit Scotland, t 0845 225 5121. Eigg website: *www.isleofeigg.org.*

Where to Stay and Eat

Kinloch Castle, Rum, **t** (01687) 462 037, *kinlochcastle@snh.gov.uk* (*moderate–budget*). Hostel-style accommodation, with faded grandeur as well as dormitories. The dormitory section is in the old servants' quarters, and there is a canteen-style restaurant.

Eigg's inhabitants juggle with tourism, private enterprise, public subsidy and a desire to get away from it all. Contact Sue Kirk, **t** (01687) 482 405, who can organize or recommend accommodation.
The Glebe Barn, at Cleadale, Eigg, **t** (01687) 482 417, *glebebarneigg@compuserve.com* (*budget*). Offers 24 beds.
An Laimhrig, Eigg, **t** (01687) 482 468. A craft shop/tearoom – also does evening meals.
Canna Guest House, Canna, apply to 5 Charlotte Square, Edinburgh, EH2 4DU, **t** (0131) 243 9300 (*ring for prices*). A National Trust for Scotland property – members get priority. There is no shop on the island.
Muck Estate Office, Muck, **t** (01687) 462 365. Can arrange self-catering cottages and camping. There is a craft shop/tearoom **t** 462 362/990, with good home baking, and craft courses.

wish to disassociate his island from the alcoholic drink.) Rum's chief interest is its wildlife, and special permission must be obtained from the Scottish Natural Heritage warden to visit most places.

The half-wild golden-brown ponies are said to be descended from survivors of a Spanish galleon, part of the Armada, which was wrecked off these coasts in 1588. There are also wild goats, golden eagles, plenty of red deer and a prodigious colony of Manx shearwaters which nest in underground burrows in the south of the island. There are also rare alpine plants.

The red sandstone castle that looks across the bay is **Kinloch Castle**, built in 1901 by the Bulloughs. It is said they offered extra wages to employees to work in kilts, despite the fact that Rum is notorious for its midges. The castle is now a hotel/hostel (*see* 'Where to Stay and Eat', above). It has the atmosphere of a baronial seat and most of the original furnishings survive intact, if a little jaded. One of its features is the extremely rare electric 'orchestrarian', a Heath Robinson contraption tucked under the stairs, whose parts represent a full orchestra, activated by a vast library of preset cylinders each programmed with a well-known tune. All the working components can be seen in action in a huge glass chamber in the hall. The conducted tours of this amazing time warp are well worth doing. The guide is full of amusing gossip about past visitors, including Edward VII in amorous pursuit of the mistress of the house.

Eigg

The poet Hugh MacDiarmid wrote: 'if I have to choose among the Hebrides, I choose Eigg.' However, that fiery Scottish nationalist might not have said the same today.

Seven miles off Morar on the mainland, 7 miles by 5 in dimensions, Eigg is shaped like an upturned boat or a crouching lion, its name derived from the Gaelic for 'notch', referring to the deep divide between the massive Sgurr in the south, and the rest of the island. In 1844 Hugh Miller (*see* Cromarty, pp.157–9) came to the island with John Swanson, the Free Kirk minister for the Small Isles. Swanson was preaching and Miller had gone along for the ride with his geologist's implements. To his surprise, he discovered that the Sgurr of Eigg, 'a veritable Giant's Causeway, columnar from end to end, rested on the fossilized remains of a prostrate forest'. This was at a time when his deep religious convictions were battling with his study of fossils, which led to doubts about the credibility of the creation story in the Bible.

Eigg is a magical isle surrounded by clear, sparkling water. Its recent history of bitter politics has not detracted one bit from its beauty, though there is a rather run-down feeling about the place. Settled since prehistoric times, it has remains going back to Iron Age forts, a 6th-century Christian church, Viking burial mounds and the site of a Macdonald burial ground. This was a base for the Lords of the Isles and their Clanranald descendants, who were not above acts of piracy in the surrounding seas.

In 1828 the debt-ridden Clanranalds sold Eigg, along with most of their other territories in the western Highlands and Islands. The new owner, Hugh MacPherson, was a professor of archaeology, and there followed a succession of industrial tycoons, one of whom created an Italianate lodge and garden in the late 1920s. Because of its great beauty and comparative remoteness, Eigg has always attracted 'white settlers'. Its decline from a true Hebridean island was no different to that of any other: incoming Victorians clearing out the people and using it for sport.

In recent decades the story of the island's ownership has become something of a soap opera. English incomers and escapers from the mainland now outnumber the islanders, who have mostly been too courteous to protest against what became a state of open warfare with the proprietors. The penultimate landlord, a flamboyant philanthropist, was loathed by the incomers with no justification whatsoever. They transformed him into a symbol of the cruel 'laird'. A priceless vintage car he had imported was torched and a vindictive war waged on Schellenberg by the media. Eventually he sold up and departed, to be replaced by a fire-eating German artist known as Maruma. The absentee Maruma turned out to be full of empty promises and financially unsound.

The community's determination to become masters of their own destiny strengthened, and they have now bought the island for themselves, with the help of generous donations and the pledge of considerable sums of public money. A new ferry terminal was completed in 2004, allowing cars access to the island for the first time in its history (although there are restrictions on the amount and type of traffic allowed to disembark). A year later, islanders were granted lottery funding to create a 24-hour electricity supply using renewable energy. At present, public subsidies support a couple of basket makers, someone whittling sticks, a few artists and tillers of soil and some rather prickly drawers of the dole. One thing is sure: Eigg has no place in the *Gaidhealtachd* – Gaeldom – today.

Walking up around the bay from the little harbour in the southeast, you come upon the ancient burial ground at Kildonan Church. This is the resting place of the Macdonalds of Clanranald, whose chieftain owned Eigg until the 1820s. A broken Celtic cross, a scattering of gravestones and a roofless ruin are all that remain.

An aura of tragedy still hangs over *Uamh Fhraing*, a cave southwest of the pier, easily reached by a path from Galmisdale – take a torch. In 1577 some Macleods were forced to shelter from a storm on Eigg. Owing to constant feuding over disputed land, the Macdonalds were not welcoming. The Macleods left and returned later to take revenge. The Macdonalds took shelter in this cave and the landing party found only an old woman, whose life they spared. But as they were putting out to sea they saw a scout, sent from the cave to see if they had gone. They rushed back, found the cave and lit a fire at its mouth, suffocating all 398 inhabitants – the entire population of the island. Sir Walter Scott is said to have found bones here in 1814 and taken a souvenir away with him. Several reliable people have seen ghosts in the vicinity.

Palm trees and flame trees thrive on the almost subtropical climate of the garden surrounding the lodge. The 'Musical Sands' on the Bay of Laig are well worth a visit, so called because they make a curious keening sound in certain conditions. Cattle wander on the beach and the views across to Rum are glorious on a clear day. A craft shop/tearoom here does light lunches and evening meals.

Canna

Sometimes called the Garden of the Hebrides, Canna lies less than 5 miles off the west coast of Rum and is actually two islands, joined to Sanday in the southeast by a causeway. Together, they are shaped like a hand gun, measuring 5 miles by 1 mile, with a grassy plateau sloping in stepped terraces down to the sea, sliced off by cliffs to the north. The highest point is only 690ft (212m) above sea level. Magnetic Hill (458ft/141m) in the north, is so called because of its magnetic rock that can distort the true readings of a ship's compass. Martin Martin put this to the test: 'I laid the Compas on the stony Ground near it, and the Needle went often round with great Swiftness, and instead of settling towards the North, as usual, it settled here due East.'

Canna was an Early Christian settlement, and there are still the remains of a Celtic nunnery with one of the three oldest Celtic church structures identified in Scotland. The island was part of the land attached to the Benedictine monastery of Iona, and has a weathered cross and a well, said to have curative powers. The Clanranald Macdonalds held the island until debts forced them to sell to Hector MacNeill in the 1820s. He evicted 200 islanders, in arrears with their rent after the decline of the kelp industry. A family of Glasgow shipbuilders called Thom bought it in 1881; they built the pier and Tighard House. In 1938 the island was bought by the late John Lorne Campbell and his wife Margaret Fay Shaw. They were both learned scholars of Gaelic literature and music and they built up an impressive archive which they shared hospitably with any interested visitor. They instigated agricultural improvements and planted woodland; having no heirs, they gave the island to the National Trust for Scotland in 1981. An application to the Heritage Lottery Fund to help with the creation of a centre for Gaelic culture and learning was successful and Dr Fay Shaw, a tiny nonogenarian with an impressive intellect, died not long ago. The library incorporates the largest collection of Gaelic folk songs and tales ever made and complete sets of all the relevant reference books; meanwhile, a tiny fragile Hebridean community survives here, but only just.

Muck

About 7 miles south of Rum, Muck is the smallest of the Small Isles, its name derived from the Gaelic *muc mara* – sea pig or porpoise. It is a pretty little green island with lovely sandy beaches. The Macleans of Ardnamurchan owned the island until the end of the 18th century, the last laird running into debt due to an overextended family and his excesses during his post as Deputy Lieutenant of the Tower of London. The Clanranald Macdonalds rescued him, in return for Muck, which they had to sell off in their turn to pay off their own debts. Poverty in the 19th century drove many of the islanders to emigrate. A sea captain called Thomas Swinburne bought it in 1854, developed the fishing, introduced sheep, built Gallanach House and sold it in 1879 to Lawrence Thompson MacEwan, who already owned Eigg. He introduced cows and exported cheese. His heir, William MacEwan, planted the first trees in 1922 and created a model island unit, carried on today by his son Lawrence and 25 residents.

Skye

16

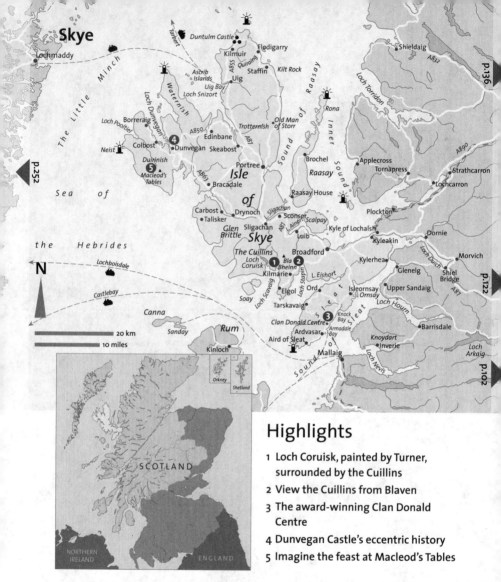

Skye

Tarbert · Duntulm Castle
Lochmaddy
Flodigarry
Kilmuir
Quiraing
Shieldaig
A855
Ascrib · Staffin · Kilt Rock
Islands · Uig
Uig Bay
Loch Snizort
A832
Waternish
Loch Dunvegan
Loch Torridon
Borreraig
Loch Poolie!
Rona
Trotternish
Old Man
Colbost · A850 · Edinbane
of Storr
Neist · Dunvegan · Skeabost
Applecross
Duirinish · Portree
Brochel · Tornapress
Strathcarron
Macleod's · Isle · Raasay
Tables · Bracadale
Lochcarron
Sea · of
of · Raasay House
Plockton
Carbost · Drynoch
Skye
Sligachan
Talisker · Sconser
Glen · Sligachan · Ainort · Scalpay
Dornie
Brittle · Skye · Luib · Kyle of Lochalsh
the · Hebrides
Morvich
Broadford
Kyleakin
N
The Cullins
Loch · Bla
Kylerhea
Glenelg · Shiel
Lochboisdale
Coruisk · Bheinn
Bridge
Kilmarie · L. Eishort
Castlebay
Elgol · Ord · Isleornsay · Upper Sandaig
Ornsay
Soay · Loch Hourn
Canna · Tarskavaig
Knock
Rum · Clan Donald Centre · Bay · Barrisdale
20 km
Sanday · Ardvasar · Armadale
Knoydart
10 miles
Aird of Sleat · Bay · Inverie
Kinloch · Mallaig
Loch
Arkaig
Orkney
Shetland

SCOTLAND

NORTHERN
IRELAND · ENGLAND

Highlights

1 Loch Coruisk, painted by Turner, surrounded by the Cuillins
2 View the Cuillins from Blaven
3 The award-winning Clan Donald Centre
4 Dunvegan Castle's eccentric history
5 Imagine the feast at Macleod's Tables

Skye is *An t-Eilean Sgiatheanach* – the Winged Island – *sgiath* meaning 'wing' in Gaelic, referring to the winged promontories of Trotternish in the northeast and Duirinish and Waternish in the northwest. On the map Skye looks more like a great, misshapen lobster claw than a flying bird, its pincers being its lumpy peninsulas separated by fjord-like inlets, surrounded by many islands. Its silhouette is dominated by the Cuillins, a massive range of black, pointed peaks, and by Macleod's Tables, the two, distinctive flat-topped hills further north.

The island contains extraordinary volcanic features such as the Quiraing and the Old Man of Storr. Among archaeological sites testifying to prehistoric settlements are two particularly fine examples of brochs: Dun Ardtreck, near Carbost, and Dun Beag, just west of Bracadale, both well built with square-sided facing stones.

Skye is one of the most popular of the Western Isles; though tourism has had a significant impact on it, it has not yet spoiled it. The opening in 1995 of the new government-sponsored and privately funded road bridge between Kyle of Lochalsh and Kyleakin has improved communications dramatically, but not without a great public furore. Surprisingly, this elegant half-mile link, the longest single-span bridge outside Australia, does not actually detract much from the scenery.

Off the main roads, there are still rural communities relatively untouched by the influx of rucksacks and campers. Gaelic is no longer the first language, though it is still spoken and road signs are bilingual. Spirited attempts are being made to revive the old language, and *Sabhal Mor Ostaig*, the Gaelic College in Sleat, is flourishing. Gaelic playgroups are opening all over the island and Gaelic folk music and other elements of the culture are experiencing an incredible revival. The influx of non-Gaelic speaking 'white settlers' seems to be fashioning a kind of 'designer Gaeldom' however, which may be romantic, but is not the *Gaidhealtachd* in its old guise.

Portree, the chief village on the island, is lively and expanding, particularly in summer. There is an excellent range of cultural activities, traditional music, Highland Games, and some good accommodation and eating places.

During Bonnie Prince Charlie's escape after Culloden, he hid on Skye, having arrived from the Outer Isles disguised as Flora Macdonald's maid, and it was from Skye that he escaped back to the mainland and exile in France. The island is dotted with caves that he is said to have hidden in, rocks that he sat on, huts that he sheltered in and several places where he bid his faithful subjects goodbye.

The Battle of the Braes and the Glendale Martyrs

The Clearances took their toll in Skye as elsewhere: 30,000 people are thought to have emigrated from the island between 1840 and 1888. The Battle of the Braes in 1882, and the consequent protest of the 'Glendale Martyrs', were very largely responsible for the Crofters' Holdings Act (*see* p.24), which established security of tenure at a fair, controlled rent, and is still effective today. The battle was a protest by the people of several townships of the Braes, south of Portree, against their landlord, Lord Macdonald, for depriving them of essential grazing land. Encouraged by other rent strikes, and by the successful Irish Land Act of 1881, they withheld their rents, tore up the resulting eviction orders and attacked the unfortunate officers commanded to serve them. Fifty Glasgow policemen were drafted in, baton charges were met with hails of stones, and arrests were made. No one was killed but a great deal of public interest was aroused.

Meanwhile, encouraged by the Braes men, those of Glendale and Husabost near Dunvegan followed suit. The authorities, sensing a revolutionary situation and with lessons learned from Ireland, were anxious to appease. The token arrest of five Glendale men was made. They spent two months in prison and emerged as triumphant heroes, known ever since as the Glendale Martyrs. Gladstone hastily set up the Napier Commission, many of whose commissioners, such as Donald Cameron of Lochiel and Sir Kenneth Mackenzie of Gairloch, were sympathetic to the crofters' cause. Their thorough and shocking report resulted in the Crofters' Holdings Act.

Getting There and Around

The free Skye Bridge crosses from the mainland at Kyle of Lochalsh to Kyleakin on Skye; a daily **ferry** service Mallaig–Armadale (½hr – essential to book); and a limited, summer service Glenelg–Kylerhea. Caledonian MacBrayne, **t** (01475) 650 100 run a regular ferry service between Uig and the Outer Isles.

Trains run from Inverness to Kyle of Lochalsh – one of the most scenic routes in Britain. Even better is the West Highland Line, Glasgow–Mallaig, connecting with the ferry to Armadale.

On the island, there is a limited **bus** service, and you can hire cars in Broadford and Portree. Skyeways, **t** (01599) 534 477, *www.skyeways. co.uk*, operate buses serving Kyle of Lochalsh, Broadford, Shiel Bridge and Glenelg. Broadford has a 24-hour petrol station.

Tourist Information

Portree *(open all year)*, **Broadford** *(open March–Sept)* and **Dunvegan Lochside**: **t** 0845 225 5121.

Events and Activities

Portree: Skye Week, in June, has every sort of Scottish entertainment.

The Portree Show takes place in July; the Skye Highland Games in early August; the Portree Folk Festival in mid-August; and the Portree Fiddlers' Rally in September.

The **Gathering Hall**, Portree. Lively Friday night 'gatherings' – good place for a 'crack'.

Shopping

Edinbane Pottery, at the head of Loch Greshornish, *www.edinbane-pottery.co.uk* *(open daily Easter–Oct)*. A workshop and gallery specializing in wood-fired and salt-glazed pottery.

North West Fishermen, Portree, down by the pier. Fishing tackle, flies and fishing permits.

Skye Batiks, Portree and Armadale.

Skyeskyns, on Loch Bay, *www.skyeskyns.co.uk*. A working tannery where you can buy a good range of fleeces and leather goods.

The Skye Woollen Mill, Portree. Often has excellent cashmere and lambswool products at reduced prices and there's a coffee shop.

Where to Stay and Eat

Corry Lodge, Liveras, Broadford, **t** (01471) 822 235, *www.corrylodge.co.uk* *(expensive)*. Up-market guesthouse with dinner by arrangement, in a charming, comfortable 18th-century house with sea views and nice grounds. Excellent food.

Hotel Eilean Iarmain, Isleornsay, Sleat Peninsula, **t** (01471) 833 332, *www.eilean iarmain.co.uk* *(expensive)*. Traditional 'Highland' right on the water with good views. Excellent food in the restaurant and the bar.

Kinloch Lodge Hotel, northeast corner of the Sleat Peninsula overlooking Loch na Dal, **t** (01471) 833 214, *www.kinloch-lodge.co.uk* *(expensive)*. Former tacksman's house converted into a Macdonald lodge in the 1870s. Now the home of Lord Macdonald, who is the High Chief of Clan Macdonald, and Lady Macdonald, a well-known gourmet

Sleat Peninsula to Portree

Kyleakin and the Sleat Peninsula

Kyleakin, until the Skye Bridge opened in 1995 a busy ferry terminus with lots of visitors hanging about, is now something of a backwater: a cluster of unremarkable buildings and a large, useful slipway. The small harbour is overlooked by **Castle Maol** (or Moil, or Dunnakyne), a jagged double-toothed fragment of a ruin on a knoll; familiar from postcards. This 12th-century relic was once a Mackinnon stronghold. Kyleakin and Dunakin are said to be so named after King Haakon, who sheltered here with his fleet while on his way south. The **Bright Water Visitor Centre**, on the Pier at cookery writer. An attractive, white building, with marvellous views. Everything served here is home-made. Family portraits and antiques add an ancestral touch to the cosy atmosphere.

Skeabost House Hotel, Skeabost, **t** (01470) 532 202, *www.skeabostcountryhouse.com* (*expensive–moderate*). Large, comfortable Victorian lodge, built in 1870. Offers salmon fishing and very decent lunches.

Ardvasar Hotel, Ardvasar, **t** (01471) 844 223, *www.ardvasarhotel.com* (*moderate*). Nice old hotel, simple and reasonably priced. *Open Mar–Dec.*

Bosville Hotel, Portree, **t** (01478) 612 846, *www.macleodhotels.co.uk/bosville/* (*moderate*). Friendly and comfortable. Its **Chandlery Seafood Restaurant** has views over the harbour.

Churchton House, Raasay, **t** (01478) 660 260 (*moderate*). Guesthouse with a friendly atmosphere.

Dunollie Hotel, Broadford, **t** (01471) 822 253, (*moderate*). In the middle of Broadford, large establishment with cheerful staff and atmosphere.

Duntulm Castle Hotel, gloriously situated near the castle, **t** (01470) 552 213, *www.duntulm castle.co.uk* (*moderate*). Also has five self-catering cottages, all with wonderful sea views, ranging from cosy chalet to luxury bungalow (sleeps 4–8).

Ferry Inn, Uig, **t** (01470) 542 242, *www.ferryinn. co.uk* (*moderate*). A bit cheaper but equally as friendly as Uig Hotel (*see* below).

Flodigarry Country House Hotel, Flodigarry, **t** (01470) 552 203, *www.flodigarry.co.uk* (*moderate*). 19th-century shooting lodge in secluded grounds beneath the Quiraing, with views to the mainland. Has a billiard room, cosy bedrooms, a bar and a splendid conservatory.

Isle of Raasay Hotel, Raasay, **t** (01478) 660 222, *www.isleofraasayhotel.co.uk* (*moderate*). Good value. *Open all year.*

Kinlochfollart, by Dunvegan, **t** (01470) 521 470, *www.klfskye.co.uk* (*moderate*). Restored former manse on the shores of Loch Dunvegan, run as a Wolsey Lodge with an informal, relaxed family atmosphere. Its good home cooking uses local ingredients.

Lyndale House, Edinbane, **t** (01470) 582 329, *www.lyndale.net* (*moderate*). A 300-year-old ex-tacksman's house for B&B, in a lovely position. Very comfortable and friendly, with a private sitting room.

Rosedale Hotel, Beaumont Crescent, Portree, **t** (01478) 613 131, *www.rosedalehotelskye. co.uk* (*moderate*). Comfortable and serves good food.

Royal Hotel, Bank Street, Portree, **t** (01478) 612 525, *www.royal-hotel-skye.com* (*moderate*). Not quite what it was in the days when Prince Charles took his leave of Flora Macdonald in one of its parlours, but some of the atmosphere of history clings to the walls of the older part.

The Tables Hotel and Restaurant, near Macleod's Tables, **t** (01470) 521 404, *www.tables-hotel.co.uk* (*moderate*). Small, friendly hotel with panoramic views. Has a self-catering cottage at Waternish.

Uig Hotel, on the hill overlooking Uig Bay and the ferry terminal, Uig, **t** (01470) 542 205, *www.uighotel.com* (*moderate*). Old, friendly coaching inn with character, comfortable rooms. Good breakfasts, a useful stopover for an early ferry.

Kyleakin (**t** *(01599) 530 040, www.eileanban.org; open May–Nov; phone for times*), tells about lighthouses and the Vikings, and allows you to pry into the private lives of seals and birds, as well as the otters on Eilean Ban (*see* 'Kyle of Lochalsh', pp.137). The new bridge whips you westward; after 2 miles a turning left leads over moorland, through Glen Arroch to Kylerhea, pronounced Kyle-ray, where the ferry runs to Glenelg.

A couple of miles past this turning, the A851 leads south to the **Sleat Peninsula**, formerly Macdonald territory. **Isleornsay** overlooks the Sound of Sleat on the peninsula's east coast, reached across 9 miles of heather-carpeted moor. Once the commercial centre for the island, called *Eilean Iarmain*, this attractive group of buildings includes a hotel, shop, small art gallery, ceilidh hall, whisky centre and the

Viewfield House Hotel, on the outskirts of Portree, t (01478) 612 217, www.viewfield house.com (moderate). Victorian country villa in 20 acres of garden and woodland. It retains very much the atmosphere of a relaxing, comfortable family establishment, surrounded by pictures, furniture and heirlooms, many of them there since the house was built.

White Heather Hotel, Kyleakin, t (01599) 534 577, www.whiteheatherhotel.co.uk (moderate). Right on the harbour, run by a local family, with all the islanders' warmth and friendliness.

Sligachan Hotel, at the head of Loch Sligachan, t (01478) 650 204, www.sligachan.co.uk (moderate–budget). Famous hotel popular with anyone planning to climb the Cuillins, as well as with fishermen. Splendidly easy-going and traditional. The hotel knows how to pamper people who come in cold and hungry.

The Isles Inn, Somerled Square, Portree, t (01478) 612 129 (budget). Central and friendly.

The Kings Haven, Portree, t (01478) 612 290 (budget). Restored Georgian house overlooking the harbour. Comfortable, with relaxed atmosphere.

Mrs Flora Cumming, Eilean Dubh, Edinbane, t (01470) 582 218 (budget). One of the best B&Bs in Skye. Like going to stay with an old friend – you'll be reluctant to leave.

Mrs B. La Trobe, Fiordhem, Ord, Sleat, t (01471) 855 226, www.fiordhem.co.uk (budget). One of the best B&Bs on Skye, where the sea laps below the dining room, which has picture windows looking west to the setting sun. Magnificent Highland hospitality.

Non-residents can dine here: take your own wine. Two holiday cottages, too.

Mrs Mackay, Raasay, t (01478) 660 207, osgaig@lineone.net (budget). B&B with evening meals. Open all year.

The Skye Picture House, Broadford, t (01471) 822 531, www.skyepicturehouse.co.uk (budget). Guesthouse with fine sea views.

Gedintailor, Braes, south of Portree, contact Mrs J.D. Bengough, White Lodge, Church Street, Sidbury, Devon, EX10 0SB, t (01395) 597 214. One of Skye's best self-catering houses: a cosy converted croft house, looking across to Raasay and the mainland. A much-loved home to the owners, containing all the comfy extras of family life (sleeps 6–7).

Neist Point Lighthouse, Neist Point, t (01470) 511 200. Unmanned these days and with cottages available for holiday lets.

The Three Chimneys and House Over-By, by Colbost, t (01470) 511 258, www.threechim-neys.co.uk (expensive). First-class restaurant, worth every penny. Six luxurious rooms.

Harlosh House, 5 miles south of Dunvegan, t (01470) 521 367 (moderate). Supper to a very high standard, especially the seafood.

The Lower Deck, Portree harbour, t (01478) 613 611 (inexpensive). Delicious seafood. Open April–Oct 11am–10pm.

Macleod's Tables Restaurant Bistro, near Macleod's Tables, t (01470) 521 310 (inexpensive). Licensed – serves everything from snacks to full meals. Ring for evening bookings. With holiday cottages available all year, Estate Office, t (01470) 521 206.

Seagull Restaurant, southeast of Broadford on the main road (inexpensive). Good place to eat, and popular with the locals. Open April–Oct 5–10pm and for Sunday lunch.

old sea-flushing lavatory – now a dovecote. There's a lighthouse and a ruined chapel, dedicated to the Columban monk Oran, on the Isle of Ornsay, just offshore.

Sabhal Mor Ostaig – big barn of Ostaig – is the Gaelic college, in a former Macdonald home farm near Isleornay. Founded by Iain Noble, it runs successful courses on the Gaelic language, music and culture. **Castle Camus** or **Knock Castle**, 3 miles further on, overlooking Knock Bay, is an overgrown ruin, once held by the Macdonalds on condition they were always ready to receive the king or one of his representatives. A *glaisrig* haunts this ruin – a female sprite who accepts libations of milk.

Armadale Castle, another 3 miles south, was built by James Gillespie Graham in 1815, incorporating an earlier mansion, with additions by David Bryce in 1856. Gutted, partly demolished, and left as a 'sculptured ruin', it stands today as a centrepiece for the lovely restored gardens. The **Museum of the Isles** (*t (01471) 844 305/227, www.clan donald.com; open end April–Oct 9.30–5.30; adm; grounds open all year*) incorporates the **Clan Donald Centre** and the history of the Lords of the Isles. The museum is first class – imaginative, innovative and visually satisfying. The former coach house and stable block has won awards for its restoration and conversion into a well-stocked book and gift shop, along with an excellent restaurant.

Armadale Pier, the ferry terminal for the summer boat to Mallaig, is unexpectedly well served for such an end-of-the-road place. There is a seafood takeaway, a craft shop, a batik shop and **Sleat Trading** – a smart tourist trap with a good selection of out-of-print books relating to Scotland. The road continues for another 5 miles to **Aird of Sleat** with glorious views across the sound. A couple of miles' walk takes you to the lighthouse on the southern tip of the peninsula, where there is a sandy beach and more good views. Returning on the same road, the narrow, twisting lane to the west, a mile north of Armadale, runs 5 miles through woodland and moor, past lochans and mossy glades among silver birches, out to the west coast of Sleat.

Tiny settlements cluster round coves and sandy beaches. **Dunsgaith Castle**, about 2 miles north of Tarskavaig, is one of the oldest fortified headlands in the Hebrides, the Macdonalds' home until the late 16th century. Little remains now except stacks of stones on a rock 40ft (12m) high, overlooking Loch Eishort. Celtic legend tells of Scathach the Wise, Queen of Skye in the Dark Ages, who held court here and preached the arts of peace and war to Cuchullin, an Ossianic hero. Cuchullin went back to Ireland to practise his newly learned arts, leaving his beautiful, impregnated wife Bragela weeping in vain at Dunsgaith on 'The Isle of Mist'.

Another 2 miles north at **Ord**, the views to the Cuillins across Loch Eishort and southwest to the Isle of Rum are magnificent. It is 15 miles to **Broadford**, the track rejoining the main road a couple of miles short of Isleornsay. This straggling settlement is a busy, useful place on a crossroads. There is also, somewhat incongruously, **Skye Serpentarium** (*www.skyeserpentarium.org.uk; open Easter–Oct daily; adm*), a collection of smaller reptiles, and a home to abandoned or illegally imported reptiles. There are 'handling sessions'.

Fourteen miles to the southwest is **Elgol**, a scattered village with more splendid views. From here you can get a boat across Loch Scavaig to **Loch Coruisk** (*coire uish –* cauldron of water), one of Skye's special places, painted by Turner and a popular destination for Victorian tourist steamers. The ***Bella Jane*** (*t 0800 731 3089, www.bella jane.co.uk; weather permitting; must book ahead*) makes a single trip for walkers and all-day return trips. There is time to walk across the ice-smooth rocks to the long, deep and dark inland loch, reaching northwestwards into the foothills of the Cuillins, which fence it round with steep, uncompromising security. In the evening the sun goes down behind the hills, sending up great shafts of colour refracted by the proximity of the hills.

For the energetic, another route to Coruisk is along the Camasunary track, which starts at Kilmarie, about 3 miles before Elgol. It is a relatively easy walk, taking a good two hours over stony ground through bracken and heather with just one tricky bit known as 'The Bad Step'. It is from this Camasunary track that non-serious climbers should climb *Bla Bheinn* – **Blaven** – considered by some to be the finest mountain in Skye, partly because of its wonderful view to the other Cuillin peaks, as well as of the whole area. It is a 6–7 hour walk/climb, and though you need a map the way is simple. You cross the moor on the track from just south of Kilmarie until you get to the cairn above Camasunary, where you take the right fork across the hillside to the foot of the ridge. Another cairn, on a rock, marks the path up the ridge to the top.

Those exploring by boat should put into the perfect natural harbour on the island of **Soay**, off the entrance to Loch Scavaig. The remains of a primitive shark factory can be seen on the quay, established after the Second World War by the author Gavin Maxwell. His book, *Harpoon at a Venture*, is a compelling read about the days when sharks and whales were so plentiful in the Minch that at times the water seemed to be black with them. The factory folded after a few years due to financial difficulties.

Continuing north from Broadford, the road follows the east coast, looping around long inlets, up and down hills. In a thatched cottage at **Luib**, 7 miles northwest on Loch Ainort, there is a Folk Museum (*open April–Oct daily; adm*) with an 'on the trail of Bonnie Prince Charlie' exhibition. From Luib, there is an easy 4-mile walk due south following the river along Strath Mor between the peaks of the red Cuillins to the 'Black Cuillin' – Blaven.

The Cuillins

Cú Chulainn was a Celtic hero who according to tradition visited Skye from Ireland to learn martial arts and from whom the name for the Cuillins was thought to have derived. Other derivations include *cuilionn*, a Celtic word for 'wilderness' and a Nordic word, *kjollen*, meaning 'keel-shaped ridge'.

The Cuillins attract serious mountaineers from afar and should only be tackled by people who know what they are doing: they have claimed many lives over the years and make no concessions to ill-equipped amateurs. The Red Cuillins to the east are weathered and eroded into symmetrical cones, while the tougher, rougher Black Cuillins have withstood erosion and, according to geologist John MacCulloch, writing in 1824, have 'a nutmeg-grater-like surface in contact with which the human body may almost defy the laws of gravity'. (MacCulloch didn't manage to climb the Cuillins, partly perhaps because he tried to do so on a horse.) The main semicircular ridge, with spurs intersected by deep and often sheer corries, includes some 20 Munros. Surrounded by the sound of cascading water, these hills reign supreme, looking as if they have been dragged upwards from the earth by their Creator.

The road north up the east coast, 9 miles from Sligachan to Portree, runs through empty Glen Varragil: bleak moorland forestry plantations, rivers and burns. Just south of Portree the B883 road goes out to **Braes**, overlooking the Sound of Raasay, scene of the Battle of the Braes (*see* p.239), and home of the late Gaelic poet Sorley MacLean.

Portree

Portree is a busy little tourist resort, lively and attractive, built round a natural harbour with houses rising steeply from the water's edge, neat and brightly painted.

The name is derived from *Port righ* – King's Port – after a visit by James V during a Hebridean tour in 1540. During the summer, bus excursions run from the town to many of Skye's beauty spots. Coming into Portree from the south you pass **Aros Experience** (*www.aros.co.uk; open daily 9 till late; adm to exhibition*), which takes you through graphic representations of the Jacobite rising – it is one of the best of these many ventures. There is also a chance to hear Gaelic concerts here – ask at the desk for details.

It was in a room in what is now the **Royal Hotel** in Portree that Prince Charles (a.k.a. Betty Burke) took his leave of Flora Macdonald. He repaid her the half-crown she had lent him, gave her a miniature of himself, and declared: 'For all that has happened, I hope, Madam, we shall meet in St James yet.' He bowed, kissed her hand and departed – a fugitive with a bundle of clean shirts, a wrapped-up chicken, a bottle of whisky and a bottle of brandy tied at his waist, and a £30,000 reward on his head.

North of Portree

Trotternish

Geographically part of the Quiraing, or Trotternish Ridge, the **Old Man of Storr**, about 7 miles north of Portree, is another of those landmarks familiar from postcards. The easiest route is through the forest along maintained paths, rather than up the steep grassy slopes to the south. At over 180ft (55m) high and 40ft (12m) in diameter, the Old Man is the tallest of a group of mighty towers and pinnacles of basaltic rock, a great weathered stack, undercut and pointed at the top like a giant fir cone. In 1891, a hoard of treasure was unearthed on the shore below; silver neck rings, brooches, bracelets and beaten ingots, along with 10th-century coins, some from Samarkand. It is believed they were hidden there by a Norseman, who presumably came to an untimely end. They are in the Antiquities section of the Royal Museum of Scotland, in Edinburgh. There is good trout fishing in the **Storr Lochs**, from bank or boat.

The road twists up the east coast of Trotternish with staggering views; to the south lie the Cuillins and to the west, the Quiraing ridge. Stop at the car park at **Loch Mealt**, 7 miles north of the Old Man of Storr. The loch here drains in a sheer 300ft (92m) white cascade, plummeting into the cobalt sea. **Kilt Rock**, north of Loch Mealt, is so called because of its vertical basalt columns, on horizontal stripes of grey and white oolite, much like the pleats and pattern of a kilt.

The **Quiraing** is 2 miles west of Staffin. Park by the burial ground or in the lay-by at the top of the hill and approach it across the moor. The last bit is quite a scramble up scree, through a narrow gorge flanked by great pillars of basaltic rock, like a surreal Gothic cathedral. At the top is a plateau of emerald-green grass, as big as a football pitch; a magical place with panoramic views. Cattle were driven up here for safety during raids in the old days – they must have been as nimble as mountain goats.

Flodigarry, about 3 miles north of Staffin, is where Flora Macdonald lived for eight years, after her marriage to Captain Allan Macdonald of Kingsburgh in 1751. Six of her seven children were born in the pretty cottage which is now an annexe to the hotel.

Duntulm Castle is a jagged ruin less than 5 miles to the west. The castle, with a water gate, stands in an easily defended position on a precipitous cliff; today it is much eroded and at risk of further collapse. It became the stronghold of the Macdonalds of Sleat from the 16th century under the authority of James VI, during his attempts to discipline the Hebridean chiefs. Sir Donald Gorm Macdonald was ordered to maintain his fortress in good condition, to restrict his household to six gentlemen, to limit his consumption of wine to four tuns (1,008 gallons) a year and to produce three of his kinsmen annually as surety for his good behaviour. The family left the castle after a nursemaid carelessly dropped the chief's infant son into the sea whilst holding him out of a window to look at the boats. She was punished for her carelessness by being cast adrift in an open boat full of holes.

A story is told of Hugh Macdonald, the heir of another chief, who hired a hit man to speed up his inheritance. Unfortunately his written instructions got muddled and the assassin received an invitation to dinner, while the instructions for the murder were delivered to the chief. Hugh found himself incarcerated in the vaults of the castle he had coveted with only salt beef to eat and nothing to drink. It is said that many years later a skeleton was unearthed here, clutching an empty water pitcher.

One of Scotland's most popular heroines, Flora Macdonald, is buried below a large, white Celtic cross in the windswept churchyard at **Kilmuir**, a couple of miles further south. The cross replaces the original, which was a victim of souvenir hunters. Dr Johnson visited her during his Hebridean tour in 1773, and described her as 'a woman of middle stature, soft features, gentle manners and elegant presence'. This is admirably portrayed in Alan Ramsay's painting of her, which shows a woman with large eyes and a calm, fine-boned face of classic Scottish beauty. They say her shroud is the sheet on which Prince Charles slept when he was hidden at Kingsburgh House.

As is well known, Flora smuggled the Prince, disguised as her maid Betty Burke, from Loch Uskavagh in Benbecula to Skye, and was instrumental in ensuring his safe sojourn until his departure from Portree. It was a brave venture and he was no easy conspirator, striding about, hitching up his skirts and presenting his unshaven cheek for the embrace of his hostess at Kingsburgh. For her act of courage Flora was briefly imprisoned. She then lived with her family in North Carolina for some years before returning to Skye for the last decade of her life, dying at the age of 68. From the churchyard you can look westwards across the entrance of Loch Snizort, where Flora and the Prince approached Skye on their daring voyage from the Outer Isles.

The **Skye Museum of Island Life** (*open April–Oct Mon–Sat; adm*) is close to the churchyard, and one of the best of its kind. Two thatched cottages and a byre have been restored and a number of new buildings constructed, to show life in a mid-19th-century crofting township, complete with the usual domestic artefacts and some interesting documents and photographs. The land stretching away to the south is known as the Granary of Skye and was once a loch until drained in the 19th century.

Ruinous **Monkstadt House**, 4 miles south of Kilmuir, succeeded Duntulm as the Macdonald seat before they built Armadale Castle. A plain 18th-century laird's house, it was the home, in 1746, of Sir Alexander Macdonald, who supported the Hanoverian cause. Flora and the Prince landed here while the house was occupied by Hanoverian troops, but fortunately Macdonald was away ingratiating himself with the Duke of Cumberland in Fort Augustus and they were met by his wife Lady Margaret, who was a staunch Jacobite. The Prince hid in the grounds where he was served by Macdonald of Kingsburgh who brought him food and wine under the noses of the redcoats.

Sir Alexander is reputed to have shipped Highlanders to the Caribbean as slaves. In fact, he seems to have been reasonably honest, if naive, and only sanctioned the removal of undesirables, such as thieves, from his lands. It is said that Macleod of Dunvegan was much more deeply and dishonourably involved in this nasty practice.

Uig Bay, 3 miles to the south, lies at the foot of a green amphitheatre of hills, a long pier cutting across it like an out-flung arm. The village of Uig is busy with ferry traffic at certain times of the day, for this is the terminal for the ferry to the Outer Isles. If you are lucky, one of the fishing boats that use the pier may have berthed with a load of scampi and may agree to sell you a bagful, scooped up from a great pile on its deck. Boil these for just a few moments and eat them while still warm, accompanied by a slice of locally baked brown bread from the village shop.

Waternish

At Borve, 11 miles south of Uig, take the right turn (west) to **Skeabost**, at the head of **Loch Snizort Beag**. Below the bypassed stone bridge, the river branches round an island, now reached by a timber footbridge. This was the site of an ancient Christian settlement, probably founded by St Columba whose name it bears. It was the burial ground for the Bishops of the Isles, from at least 1079 to 1498. The small cruciform church dates from the 13th century and the 16th-century mortuary chapel is said to contain the remains of 28 Nicolson chiefs. There are some important medieval gravestones carved with effigies; information plaques give some of the site's history.

At **Trumpan** is the consolidated ruin of Cille Chonain, a church with an unholy history. In 1597, when the Macleods were attending a service here, they were attacked by their bitter enemies, the Clanranald Macdonalds from South Uist, who set fire to the church and burnt virtually the entire congregation. One woman, cutting off a breast in order to escape through a narrow slit-window, managed to get away and warn the remainder of the Macleod clan, who arrived with their Fairy Flag and massacred the Macdonalds as they returned to their boats. No wonder, really, that exasperated monarchs like James VI kept trying to subdue the clans.

From the road south towards Dunvegan, the outline of **Macleod's Tables** dominates the horizon. It is said that when Alasdair Macleod went to the court of King James V at Holyrood in Edinburgh in the 16th century, he was asked somewhat patronizingly whether he was impressed by the grandeur of the palace. He replied that he saw nothing to compare for grandeur with his own domain in Skye. When the King then visited Skye in 1540, Macleod gave an open-air banquet for him on the lower of the two 'tables', lit by his kilted clansmen each holding aloft a flaming torch. 'My family candlesticks', he told the King, with a casual sweep of his hand.

Dunvegan

Dunvegan Castle (*t (01470) 521 206, www.dunvegancastle.com; open summer 10–5.30; winter 11–4; boat trips, shops and restaurant summer only; adm*), 5 miles southwest of the Fairy Bridge, is the seat, since about 1200, of the Macleods, who can trace their lineage back 30 generations to Norse origins. Standing on a rock, this massive castle's Georgian and Victorian additions do little to soften its austere appearance. Johnson and Boswell came to stay, and the doctor slept in the 15th-century Fairy Tower. Sir Walter Scott stayed in the same room in 1814. One of the castle many family heirlooms is Rory Mor's Horn, shown to Dr Johnson: 'an ox's horn, hollowed so as to hold perhaps two quarts, which the heir of Macleod was expected to swallow at one draught, as a test of his manhood, before he was permitted to bear arms, or could claim a seat among the men.' This initiation rite is still practised, the quantity to be quaffed being a bottle and a half of claret: the present chief managed to down his in 1 minute 57 seconds in 1965.

Displayed above a marquetry table is the castle's *pièce de résistance*: the **Fairy Flag**, a frail scrap of faded and worn silk, shot with gold thread and marked with crimson 'elf spots'. Legend tells of the Macleod who fell in love with a fairy, hundreds of years ago. The lovers were forced to part (at the Fairy Bridge, to the north) and the fairy left the flag as a coverlet for their child. This flag had the power to save the Macleod Clan from destruction three times, but only if waved in a genuine crisis. It has been used twice so far – once during a famine caused by cattle plague. Less romantically, it was subjected to modern tests that dated it to between AD 400 and AD 700 and suggested Middle Eastern origins; perhaps an early Macleod went on one of the Crusades. The Gardens are both formal and informal, with attractive walks.

Boat cruises run from the jetty below the castle to the little islands where seals bask on the rocks. In August the Gala Day and the Dunvegan Show are held here. There is a craft shop in the former Factors House near the pier. A few miles past the castle you can see seal colonies and swans, and, at Claigan, a path leads to lovely coral beaches.

Duirinish

The Duirinish Peninsula, topped by Macleod's Tables, stretches away west of Loch Dunvegan. Macleod's Maidens, only visible if you walk or go by sea, are off the southern tip 8 miles south of Dunvegan. These three basalt stacks are named after the wife and daughters of a Macleod, who drowned here in a shipwreck. Despite the Tourist Route signs, the peninsula is not awash with picnic sites and caravans yet. At **Colbost** there is another Folk Museum (*open Easter–Oct Mon–Sat; adm*), a restored 'black house', complete with peat fire in the middle of the room. There is also an illicit whisky still, once common all over the Highlands, though this one is certainly not an original. Three miles to the west at Glendale – home of the Martyrs (*see* p.239) – is an old water mill by the shore with a thatched roof. This road is of particular interest to piping enthusiasts. The **MacCrimmon Piping Heritage Centre** at Borreraig is a tribute to the MacCrimmons, hereditary pipers to the Macleods of Dunvegan and leading pipers and pipe teachers through the 17th and 18th centuries. One of them, Padruig

Og, founded a piping school here which closed in about 1770, its scant remains marked by a cairn on the headland. The **Piping Museum**, in the old school (*t (01470) 511 316; open at varying times all year, Tues–Sun*), gives piping tuition; you can also hear wonderful recordings of *piobaireachd*. The **Toy Museum**, at Glendale (*open Mon–Sat 10–6*) has a good collection of old toys.

Carry on west round Loch Pooltiel, with its sheltered anchorage, and then to Neist Point, the most westerly point on Skye. Park at the top if you want to walk down to the lighthouse – unmanned, and now self-catering holiday lets (*see* p.242).

About 8 miles south on the main road from Dunvegan, look carefully up to the left as you drop down into Bracadale. **Dun Beag** (always accessible) is one of the best brochs in Skye. It seems to grow out of the hillside and would be easy to miss though only a few minutes' climb away, over springy turf and stones. Once 40–50ft (12–15m) high, this 2,000-year-old relic was used as a refuge by farmers, herdsmen and their families. Its double walls were braced by a honeycomb of chambers and galleries with cells in which the people took refuge, linked by passages and stairways. The animals would have been driven into the inner enclosure; there are also traces of outbuildings.

A detour west from Drynoch takes you to **Talisker**, home of Skye's malt whisky, with tours on weekdays. Johnson and Boswell stayed at Talisker House, at the foot of Preshal Mor, home of Colonel Macleod who had been granted indefinite leave due to 'this time of universal peace' (Napoleon being barely 4 years old). Johnson found Talisker rather gloomy: 'Talisker is the place beyond all that I have seen, from which the gay and the jovial seem utterly excluded: and from where the hermit might expect to grow old in meditation, without possibility of disturbance or interruption. It is situated very near the sea, but upon a coast where no vessel lands but when it is driven by a tempest on the rocks.' Johnson also recorded the sad story of the young man who lost his dog in the night and found only its carcass in the morning with two replete eagles close by. This is a good base for exploring the Cuillins and there is a camp site and a hostel here.

Raasay

The island of Raasay, reached by ferry from Sconser (*t (01478) 660 226; daily except Sundays*), is 13 miles long and about 3 miles at its widest, with the smaller island of Rona just off its northern shore and the lump of Scalpay to the south. Within the lee of the Skye and Applecross hills, it is sheltered and relatively fertile, and was one of the hiding places of the fugitive Prince Charles who spent a couple of days and a night in a 'mean, low hut' here, in a downpour, in July 1746.

Dr Johnson visited the island during his tour of the Hebrides with the faithful Boswell and was lavishly entertained at **Raasay House**, 'a neat, modern fabrick', built by his hosts the Macleods out of the shell of the old house that was ravaged in 1746. They were greeted on the lawn in front of the house by a large number of visiting gentry, having negotiated a difficult landing stage which Johnson decided had been deliberately kept thus in order to deter invaders. The Macleods had three sons and ten daughters and the visitors were entertained with dancing and 'Erse' songs. Amazingly, 'six and thirty people sat down to two tables in the same room for supper'. Allowing for the large family, their tutor and guests, this still points to a considerable household. Johnson was delighted with the 'general air of festivity, nor did ever fairies trip with greater alacrity. More gentleness of manners, or a more pleasing appearance of domestick society, is not found in the most polished countries.' As their stay on the island continued, however, he found the lack of intellectual stimulation irksome and was impatient to get on with his tour. Boswell recorded that, though Macleod of Raasay's lands didn't yield much revenue, he was such a good landlord that 'in the present rage for emigration, not a man has left his estate'. A hundred fighting men had left Raasay to join Prince Charles' army and 'all but about fourteen' returned home. In retribution for their loyalty to the Jacobite cause, the island suffered badly.

About a month after Culloden a party of sailors, marines and militia, under a Lieutenant Dalrymple, methodically burned and pillaged everything in sight, including the laird's house and most of the other houses on the island, and wantonly slaughtered all the animals they could find. The sight of these depredations greatly distressed Prince Charles and he swore that one day he would have the burnt turf cottages replaced with proper stone houses. Having arrived at dawn, he departed on the evening of the following day, deciding that Raasay had nothing to offer as a place of refuge. With dogged determination, the islanders managed to rebuild their lives and recover their former existence until the salt tax was imposed, preventing the export of fish – their main livelihood.

In 1843 the last resident chief became bankrupt and was forced to sell up and emigrate to Tasmania. From then on the island passed through the hands of a succession of self-interested owners wanting a sporting estate. It was eventually compulsorily purchased in 1979 for £135,000 from a Dr Green, who had paid less than £8,000 for it. He was an absentee landlord who let the place fall into wrack and ruin. Raasay House, almost beyond hope, was rescued and is now the **Raasay Outdoor Centre** (*t (01478) 660 266, www.raasayoutdoorcentre.co.uk; open April–Oct*) for outdoor pursuits. There are one-day and week-long residential courses and a good licensed café and restaurant.

Castle Brochel – *Caisteal Bhrochail* – (always accessible) is a ruin on a rock on the eastern shore overlooking a bay with the hills of Torridon massing on the eastern horizon. It was once the stronghold of the Macleods of Raasay and the danger notices are fully justified. Boswell, exploring this ruin, discovered that it contained a privy – a convenience that was sadly lacking in Raasay House where they were staying. He pointed this out to their host: 'You take very good care of one end of a man, but not of the other'.

There are two carved crosses within easy walking distance of Raasay House and a ruined medieval chapel dedicated to St Moluag of Lismore, standing beside an 18th-century chapel in an enclosed burial ground. There are the remains of a broch at Dun Borodale. A nice walk up the Inverarish Burn takes you to the flat-topped, volcano-like Dun Caan, upon which Boswell and his companions danced a Highland Fling while he was being shown the island on a 24-mile hike.

The Outer Hebrides

17

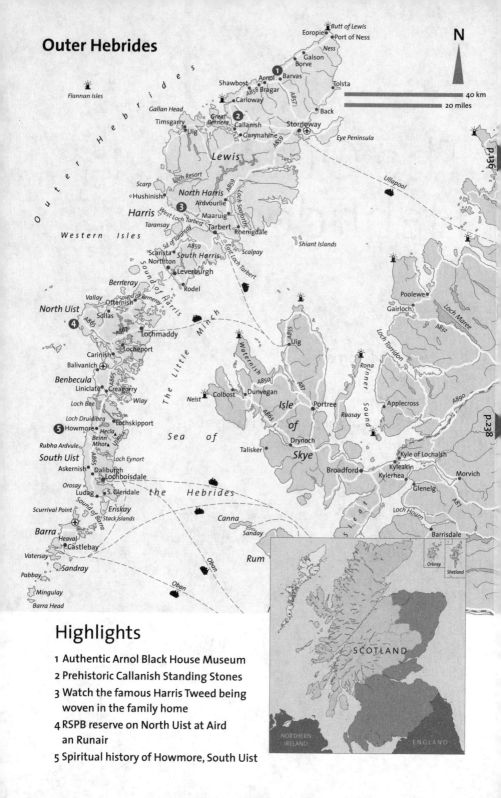

Outer Hebrides

N

40 km
20 miles

Flannan Isles

Outer Hebrides

Butt of Lewis
Eoropie · Port of Ness
Ness
Galson
Borve
Shawbost · Arnol · Barvas
Bragar
A858
Carloway
Tolsta
A857
Timsgarry · Great Bernera · Callanish
Gallan Head
Uig · Garynahine
Back
Stornoway
Lewis
Eye Peninsula

Loch Resort
A859
Scarp
Hushinish · North Harris
Harris · Ardvourlie
Taransay · Maaruig
West Loch Tarbet
Loch Seaforth
Tarbert · Rhenigdale
Western Isles
Sd of Taransay
A859
Scarista · South Harris · Scalpay
Northton · East Loch Tarbert
Leverburgh
Rodel
Shiant Islands

Sound of Bernera
Berneray
Vallay · Otternish
North Uist · Sollas
A865
A865
Lochmaddy
Carinish · Locheport
Balivanich
Benbecula · Liniclate · Creagorry
Loch Bee · Wiay
Loch Druidibeg · Lochskipport
Howmore · Hecla
Rubha Ardvule · Beinn Mhor
South Uist · Loch Eynort
Askernish · Daliburgh
Orosay · Lochboisdale
Ludag · S. Glendale
Scurrival Point
Eriskay · Stack Islands
Barra
Heaval · Castlebay
Vatersay · Sandray
Pabbay
Mingulay
Barra Head

Ullapool

Waternish
A855
Uig
Rona
Poolewe
Gairloch
Loch Maree
A832
Loch Torridon
Inner Sound
Applecross
A890
A850
Neist · Colbost · Dunvegan
A863
Portree
Raasay
The Little Minch
Isle of Skye
Talisker · Drynoch
Kyle of Lochalsh
Broadford · Kyleakin
Kylerhea · Morvich
Glenelg
A87
Loch Hourn
Barrisdale

Sea of
Canna
Sanday
the Hebrides
Rum
Oban
Oban

SCOTLAND

Orkney · Shetland

NORTHERN IRELAND · *ENGLAND*

Highlights

1 Authentic Arnol Black House Museum
2 Prehistoric Callanish Standing Stones
3 Watch the famous Harris Tweed being woven in the family home
4 RSPB reserve on North Uist at Aird an Runair
5 Spiritual history of Howmore, South Uist

Of all Scotland's islands, the Outer Isles seem to evoke the deepest nostalgia, and their exiles suffer the strongest pangs of homesickness. The distinctive tang of peat smoke, the Gaelic, the wild flowers on the machair, the cry of the curlew, the fundamental faith, the humour – these and many other characteristics cast an unbreakable spell. The Outer Hebrides run about 130 miles from the Butt of Lewis in the north to Barra Head in the south. The main islands include Lewis and Harris, Berneray, North Uist, Benbecula, South Uist, Eriskay and Barra. About 29,000 people live here – mostly bilingual Gaels. An aerial photograph reveals a land broken up by a vast number of lochs and lochans, which once provided waterways throughout the islands. The climate is unpredictable. Gaelic still lives, and some road signs are in Gaelic – the Western Isles Tourist Board has published an excellent booklet with all the names in both English and Gaelic. The tourist brochures show white beaches, aquamarine seas and azure skies. It can be like this, but even when the gale-force winds invade, these islands are still marvellous.

Lewis (*Leódhas*) and Harris (*Na Hearadh*)

Lewis and Harris are joined to form the largest and most northerly land mass in the Outer Hebrides – Siamese twins with two separate identities. Lewis, the northern two-thirds of this island, has mountains in the southwest, undulating moor in the middle, hundreds of lochs – especially in the southeast – green fertile croftland and

Getting There

By Sea
Caledonian MacBrayne, The Ferry Terminal, Gourock, PA19 1QP, t (08705) 650 000, *www.calmac.co.uk*, runs ferries to the Outer Isles, and some of the inter-island services. Ask about Island Hopscotch, and Island Rover fares. Apply from the Comhairle, t (01851) 703 773, or from local tourist information centres. Timings vary day to day and are seasonal:
Ullapool–Stornoway, Lewis (2½hrs);
Uig on Skye–Tarbert, Harris (1½hrs);
Uig on Skye–Lochmaddy, North Uist (1½hrs);
Oban/Mallaig–Lochboisdale, South Uist/ Castlebay, Barra (Oban–Castlebay 5hrs, Mallaig–Castlebay 3½hrs);
Otternish/Newton Ferry, North Uist–Leverburgh on Harris (1hr).
Tay gram, from Aberdeen, are setting up a rival service, Ullapool–Stornoway.

By Air
British Airways Express, St Andrew's Drive, Glasgow Airport, Paisley, PA3 2TG, t 0870 850 9850, *www.ba.com*: Glasgow/Inverness–Stornoway (*up to three times daily*). Glasgow–Barra/Benbecula.
Highland Airways, t 0845 450 2245, *www.highlandairways.co.uk*, run inter-island flights between Stornoway, Benbecula and Barra, and Inverness–Stornoway.

By Rail
Trains go to Oban, Mallaig and Kyle. For Ullapool, go to Inverness by train and link with a bus. National rail enquiries, t 08457 48 49 50, *www.nationalrail.co.uk*.

By Road
Scottish Citylink Coaches, t 0875 50 50 50, *www.citylink.co.uk*, and **Skye-ways Express Coaches**, t (01599) 534 328, run services to Ullapool, Uig, Oban and Mallaig which all connect where possible with ferries. Public transport on the islands is excellent, operated through local garages and supplemented by the Post Bus Service. A car is essential for random exploring, however, and can be hired locally.

many fine beaches. Aline Lodge, at the head of Loch Seaforth, marks the boundary between the two lands. Harris is divided into north and south by a narrow isthmus at Tarbert (*Tairbeart*), between East and West Loch Tarbert. North Harris has outstanding mountain scenery and the west coast of South Harris has machair and vast white sandy beaches. The east coast of South Harris is a complete contrast, with a rugged, rocky landscape cut by numerous inlets studded with rocks and islands. Although geographically one island, Lewis and Harris are effectively divided by the high range of hills along their border, the moors of Lewis giving way to the hills of Harris, dominated by Clisham, the highest mountain in the Western Isles at 2,600ft (800m). These hills and their glens are certainly impressive and offer wonderful walks.

History

The early history of Lewis includes that of Harris. The first settlers were thought to be a Mediterranean race, megalithic Stone Age or early Bronze Age, who colonized the west of Britain by sea (and built the Callanish Standing Stones) in the 2nd millennium BC. Then came migrating Celts from central Europe in about 500 BC who built brochs, of which Carloway is a prime example. Norse invaders in the 9th century are thought to have married into island families and given their blood to the original clans: the Morrisons, Nicolsons and MacAulays. But it was the Macleods, also reputed to have been of Norse descent, who dominated much of Lewis' history, and it was between two Macleod brothers that Lewis and Harris were divided at an unknown date: Torquil Macleod got Lewis and Tormod, Harris.

In 1598 James VI agreed a contract with some Lowland 'Gentlemen Adventurers', who, in return for financial rewards, were to invade Lewis and teach its people 'religion and humanity by deporting them or exterminating them'. These men sailed for Stornoway and took the castle, but the Macleods were too strong for them and after several attempts to gain supremacy the Lowlanders were forced to withdraw. In 1607, after a third colonizing attempt was made, Stornoway was granted status as a Burgh of Barony. Lord Kintail, Chief of the Clan MacKenzie, now bought the right to Lewis from the 'Gentlemen Adventurers', and there ensued a battle for power between the MacKenzies and the Macleods which, after a major struggle, the MacKenzies finally won – in 1623 the MacKenzie chief was created Earl of Seaforth. Cromwell, who had a grudge against the Earl of Seaforth, destroyed Stornoway Castle in 1653.

After Culloden in 1746, Prince Charles hoped to find a boat in Stornoway to take him back to France. The local reverend found out and led a party of armed men to the island of Scalpay where the Prince was hiding, but was sternly repulsed by the Prince's host, Donald Campbell, who, though no Jacobite, was deeply aware of the obligations of Highland hospitality. When the islanders heard of Prince Charles' presence, however, they did not wish to tangle with the government, despite being sympathetic to his cause. They indicated that, although they would not betray him, they would prefer him not to linger. They refused to lend him a boat or even a pilot and he was forced to retreat south to the Uists and Benbecula.

In 1844 the Mackenzies sold Lewis to Sir James Matheson who built Lews Castle overlooking Stornoway and tried to create a viable economy including an unsuccessful attempt to extract tar from peat. His activities included afforestation, new houses, gas and water works and an improved harbour in Stornoway. He tried to help his tenants after the potato famine in 1845 by providing work on road and quay building, drainage and land improvement. He established a regular shipping service to the mainland and was responsible for the building of about 150 miles of roads.

Lord Leverhulme, founder of Lever Brothers, bought Lewis and Harris in 1918 and spent close to a million pounds trying to redeem the islanders from poverty and create wealth through enterprise and the exploitation of the natural resources of the sea. He financed fishing boats, a cannery and ice factory, roads, bridges and even a light railway. He created a chain of retail fish shops – MacFisheries – with the ambition of controlling the fishing industry from sea to plate. Stornoway was to become the main town of the West Highlands – the 'Venice of the North'.

But there was a strong desire by islanders returning from the First World War to control their own lands, particularly as there was land settlement taking place elsewhere in the Highlands. They preferred the idea of possessing their own crofts. Land raids began in 1919. After much legal wrangling and financial difficulties, Lord Leverhulme was forced to withdraw his interests from Lewis. This brought about drastic unemployment and hardship and the emigration of over a thousand men to America. He turned his attention to Harris and transformed the small village of Obbe into a busy harbour town, renamed Leverburgh, with a number of ambitious projects for public works. With his death in 1925, Leverburgh reverted to the sleepy village it is today. A small ferry terminal with the unfinished remains of Leverhulme's enterprises gives it a slightly scruffy appearance.

The economy of the two islands is based on crofting, fishing and Harris Tweed, supplemented by increasing investment in tourism. Under the Harris Tweed Act, the cloth is only 'Harris Tweed' if it has been handwoven by the islanders in their homes on the islands and finished on the islands, and it must comply with the quality requirements in the regulations which apply to the famous Orb trademark. Controversial plans to form huge quarries in the hills for infill rock have been refused permission and, after a lengthy appeal, plans have been withdrawn for good, to the relief of many inhabitants.

The islanders speak different Gaelic dialects. Local children are brought up speaking Gaelic at home, but English is more and more the language of the playground at school and at social events. Gaelic is having a bit of a renaissance at the moment and is playing a more important part in education.

Lewis (*Leódhas*)

Lewis has some spectacular prehistoric remains including the 4,000-year-old Standing Stones at Callanish, and 2,000-year-old Carloway Broch. Since the 1843 Disruption, the people of Lewis have been staunch members of the Free Church, and nowhere else have the 'Wee Frees' exerted more influence.

Tourist Information

Western Isles Tourist Board, 26 Cromwell Street, Stornoway, Isle of Lewis, HS1 2DD, t (01851) 703 088, *www.visithebrides.com*. *Open all year.*

Where to Stay and Eat

The Royal Hotel, Stornoway, t (01851) 706 600, *www.calahotels.com* (*moderate*). Probably the best hotel in Stornoway. Old-fashioned and friendly. More modern and under the same consortium are: **Cabarfeidh Hotel**, t (01851) 702 604; **Caladh Inn**, t (01851) 702 740.

Angus and Catherine MacIver, Whitehaven, Loch Street, Barvas, t (01851) 840 253 (*moderate–budget*). A truly Hebridean welcome.

Baile-Na-Cille, Timsgarry, t (01851) 672 242, *www.bailenacille.com* (*moderate–budget*). Overlooking Uig Sands and one of the nicest places to stay. Easy, friendly hospitality in a family-run converted 18th-century manse. Set menu dinners of good home cooking served at friendly communal tables.

Doune Braes Hotel, Carloway, t (01851) 643 252, *www.doune-braes.co.uk* (*moderate–budget*). Provides a reliably warm welcome.

Eshcol Guest House, Callanish, t (01851) 621 357, *www.eshcol.com* (*moderate–budget*). Superb views, and the Standing Stones in the background. Highly recommended for its food, friendliness and dependability.

Galson Farm Guest House, South Galson, t (01851) 850 492, *www.galsonfarm.co.uk* (*moderate–budget*). Restored 18th-century farmhouse B&B with sea views and a good bunkhouse. Dinner by arrangement.

Hebridean Guest House, Bayhead Street, Stornoway, t (01851) 702 268, *www.hebridean guesthouse.co.uk* (*moderate–budget*). Overlooks golf course; comfy and friendly.

Mrs Margaret Fraser, Seaside Villa, Back, t (01851) 820 208, *www.seasidevilla.co.uk* (*moderate–budget*). Cosy B&B cottage overlooking the picturesque bay. Excellent home cooking. *Open Mar–Oct.*

Mrs C. Mackay, Blackburn, 109 Newmarket, Stornoway, t (01851) 705 232 (*moderate–budget*). Welcoming, with good breakfasts.

Park Guest House, James Street, Stornoway, t (01851) 702 485 (*moderate–budget*). Nice to stay in, with excellent food.

Gearrannan Black House Village, t (01851) 643 416, *www.gearrannan.com*. Three converted black houses for self-catering. *Available all year* (sleeps 2, 5 and 16).

Bonaventure, Aird, Uig, t (01851) 672 474, *www.bonaventurelewis.co.uk* (*expensive–moderate*). An unexpected French/Scottish restaurant with fantastic food, stunning views and great atmosphere; also has bedrooms. *Closed Sun and Mon.*

Tigh Mealros, Garynahine, t (01851) 621 333 (*moderate–inexpensive*). Very good eating place with excellent seafood. BYOB.

The Copper Kettle, Dalbeg (signed off the main road), t (01851) 710 592 (*moderate–inexpensive*). Tearoom with home baking, and an unexpected haven of a restaurant (with sunset views). *Book for evening meals.*

Black House Café, near Callanish Standing Stones (*inexpensive*). Cosy tearoom with home baking, tweed, woollens and souvenirs.

Stornoway

Stornoway (*Steòrnabhagh*), the only town in the Outer Isles, is where 8,000 of Lewis's population of 20,159 live. It houses the headquarters of the Western Isles Council – *Comhairle nan Eilean* – which struggles to bolster Gaelic culture. Stornoway is the terminal for Caledonian MacBrayne's ferry service to Ullapool, and its airport links the island with Barra, Inverness, Benbecula and Glasgow. In the 16th century it was an historic Burgh and a flourishing trading centre, but the 20th century did it few architectural favours. It's a sturdy, unglamorous town with adequate shops for basic needs, a swimming pool and golf course, a college, a museum and a small, go-ahead Arts Centre. When Lord Leverhulme was forced to give up his attempts to boost the economy of Lewis, he offered to give the island to the people, but, much as they valued land ownership, pride forced the islanders to refuse his gift. Stornoway Town Council, however, accepted the land of the Stornoway Parish, including croft land, the town itself, Lews Castle and grounds. The Stornoway Trust was formed, and administered by elected trustees so that the crofters are at the same time their own landlords and tenants of the Trust. After some teething problems, the grounds have been revitalized with public walks and a college has been built on the policies. There are plans for restoration of the old castle which meanwhile stands empty, staring gloomily down on the town. Below it, the main focus of the town is the busy harbour with fishing boats and all the clutter of the waterfront.

Western Isles Museum – *Museum nan Eilean (www.cne-siar.gov.uk/museum; open April–Oct Mon–Sat; Sept–Mar Mon–Fri)*, at the top of Francis Street, has collections that focus on the social history of the Western Isles. To get full benefit here you must be prepared to spend time reading the many wall hangings, nicely displayed but rather indigestible if you have limited time. There are plenty of hands-on activities, workshops and activity days.

The award-winning **An Lanntair Art Gallery** *(www.lanntair.com; open Mon–Sat)* is in an impressive new building on the corner of Francis Street. Lively and popular, the gallery's exhibitions are changed monthly, with music events, and an emphasis on aspects of Gaelic culture. There is also a café and gallery shop. The **Lewis Loom Centre** (*t (01851) 704 500, www.lewisloomcentre.co.uk; open Mon–Sat 10–5; adm*), in an old grain store overlooking the inner harbour in Bayhead, leads you through the traditional methods of carding, spinning, warping and waulking, all by hand, with plant-dyed wools and weaving (*guided tour, 30–40mins*). There is also a shop.

Beyond Stornoway

Three miles south of town on the edge of **Arnish Moor**, a cairn commemorates the night Prince Charles spent here while trying to negotiate for a boat for his escape. When Donald Macleod, one of his three companions, went ahead into Stornoway to make enquiries, he found a number of nervous, armed Mackenzies who had heard that the Prince was arriving with an army of 500 Highlanders.

East of Stornoway, past the airport, a narrow neck of land connects **Point** (*an Rubha*) to the rest of Lewis. It is also called the Eye (or *Ui*) Peninsula, after a Norse word meaning narrow ford or isthmus. The 14th-century **St Columba's Church**, at the western end of Point, is the burial ground of the Macleod chiefs. There are some fine carvings in the church, last used in 1828, and now threatened by erosion from the sea.

North of Stornoway, **Back** (*am Bac*) and **North Tolsta** (*Tolastadh*) have fertile croft land, steep cliffs and large expanses of white beach, unique for the east coast of the Western Isles. At the end of the road is Lord Leverhulme's 'bridge to nowhere', the beginning of the road he hoped to build between Tolsta and Ness to complete the coastal road. The **Butt of Lewis** (*Rubha Robhanais*), a bleak headland on the northern tip of the island, 27 miles from Stornoway by road, is a bird watcher's dreamland.

The **Ness** (*Nis*) district just to the south has a hotel and the **Ness Heritage Centre** (*t (01851) 810 377; open in summer*), a good little museum with interesting stuff on

The Wreck of the *Iolaire*

On New Year's Eve 1918 a troop ship, *Iolaire*, left Kyle of Lochalsh with 284 naval ratings on board, returning to their homes on Lewis after the First World War. A gale blew up from the south in the small hours of New Year's Day. The Iolaire hit Holm Rock at the entrance to Stornoway harbour and sank; 205 men died, affecting almost every family on the island. Most of the 79 survivors owed their lives to John Macleod who jumped into the sea with a heaving line and swam ashore with it. Anchoring himself to rocks on the beach, he pulled a hawser across from the ship, giving the survivors a hand-hold along which to guide themselves to the beach.

display, as well as tea, coffee and home baking. **Harbour View Gallery**, at Port of Ness, has contemporary watercolours and local scenes. **Taigh Dhonnachaidh** is Ness's arts centre and the area also boasts a thriving football and social club. There are good beaches here, particularly the one near the harbour at Port Ness. On the road out to the lighthouse, the old *feannagan*, or inappropriately named 'lazy beds', can be seen clearly, an old and difficult method of agriculture practised throughout the islands until relatively recently and still sometimes in evidence.

There was nothing lazy about the hard work that went into digging these strips and fertilizing them with seaweed carted laboriously from the shore in heavy creels.

At **Eoropie** (*Eoropaidh*), the hamlet southwest of the lighthouse, is the restored 12th-century **St Moluag's Chapel**, known as *Teamphull Mholuidh* and built on the site of an Early Christian chapel. The key for this charming little place is obtainable from the shop. Episcopal services are held occasionally and there is a strong feeling of the simple, uncomplicated faith that keeps such a remote church alive. About 10 miles down the A857, the 20ft (12m) monolith, the **Trushel Stone** (*Clach an Truiseil*), is the largest single stone in Scotland, a relic from prehistoric settlers. There is a primal aura around this site, as there is at the burial cairn within a stone circle surrounded by bleak moorland at **Steinacleit**, about a mile away.

Arnol, about 8 miles further on, has the **Arnol Black House Museum** (*t (01851) 710 395, www.historic-scotland.gov.uk; open April–Sept daily, Oct–March Mon–Wed and Sat; adm*) in an authentic, restored black house dating from 1870 and inhabited by a local family until 1964. It is perhaps the best example of its kind, particularly if you can persuade the curator to turn off the electric lighting so that it is seen as it was when occupied. The original furniture, made mostly from driftwood, has been preserved and a peat fire burns all day on the floor in the middle of the main room, with no hole in the roof to allow the smoke to escape. It has a large enclosure for animals at one end, a living room and a sizable bedroom with box beds, as well as extensive storerooms.

At **Bragar**, little more than a mile beyond Arnol, look for a gateway, set back and at right angles to the road, topped by the massive jaw bone of an 85ft (26m) blue whale that was washed ashore in the bay in 1920, the harpoon that killed it still embedded in the bone. So impressive was the corpse that a blacksmith in Stornoway was commissioned to create this archway, which soon became a landmark.

Shawbost Folk Museum (*open April–Sept Mon–Sat; donation box*), in a converted church, is a couple of miles further on and very easy to miss. It stands beside the school and in front of a factory-type building. Started by local schoolchildren, the museum is a splendidly random collection of artefacts, most of them donated by locals. The exhibits are laid out on tables, reminiscent of the white elephant stall at a village fête, with delightfully naive handwritten labels.

Don't miss **L for Leather**, just beyond the museum on the same side of the road, a small cottage identified by piles of netting and buoys in the garden and the name painted on the gable end. Pick your way round to the door and discover Kenny Stephen, who always welcomes visitors for a yarn in his flower-bedecked workshop, surrounded by the bags and belts he used to create with leather collected from all over the world. **Shawbost Norse Mill and Kiln** (*always accessible*) is signed not far beyond Shawbost to the right, with a car park and short walk over a brae. These two small thatched buildings illustrate how barley was processed into meal at a time when this was a crucial part of crofting life. The buildings were restored with assistance from local schoolchildren who helped to set up the museum.

Between Shawbost and Carloway (*Carlabhagh*) there are two good sheltered beaches at **Dalbeg** (*Dail Beag*) and **Dalmore** (*Dail Mor*), down two turnings off the A857. In **Carloway**, 5 miles southwest of Shawbost, drive to the end of Gearrannan road. Just round the corner a cobbled road twists down to a cluster of traditional black houses – the **Gearrannan Black House Village** (*www.gearrannan.com*) – restored by the Gearrannan Trust and now a popular attraction. One is the Gatliff Trust Hostel, one is an amenity centre and four are set up for self-catering, sleeping 2–16 (*see* 'Where to Stay and Eat').

Carloway Broch (*always accessible*), a couple of miles beyond the village, is the best-preserved broch in the Hebrides. Part of its circular double-thickness dry-stone wall rises to about 30ft (9m), close to its original height, with a honeycomb of galleries and stairs in the cavity. These 2,000-year-old brochs, of which the ruins of hundreds lie scattered around Scotland's coastline, are thought to have been refuges for communities from invaders. The one small entrance in the tapered structure was easy to defend. There is a good **visitor centre** here (*open May–Sept Mon–Sat 10–5*).

Callanish Standing Stones

Callanish (*Calanais*) Standing Stones (*always accessible*) are well signposted, about 6 miles south of Carloway overlooking Loch Roag. A path leads up from the car park to the stones. There are no real restrictions to access, although visitors are encouraged to look at the stones from an encircling path. Erected about 4,000 years ago, they rank in importance with Stonehenge, and form one of the most complete prehistoric sites in Britain. The 47 surviving stones are said to depict a 'Celtic wheel-cross' with a burial cairn at the centre, approached from the north and south by avenues of pillars. Traces of cremated bones were found in the cairn. The central pillar casts its shadow along the entrance passage into the grave only at sunset on the days of the equinox. Speculation about their purpose favours some sort of astrological observatory, though they are also thought to be linked to rituals that included human sacrifice. Whatever their true function, the atmosphere here is primal.

Beyond the car park, a mini **Museum and Visitor Centre** (*t (01851) 621 422; open April–Sept Mon–Sat 10–7; Oct–Mar Mon–Sat 10–4; adm*) has an audiovisual show and displays of information about the site, as well as a scant, predictable souvenir shop and a good café. The building, designed to be out of sight from the stones, is very modern in concept, rather like a child's kit-construction of a jumbo-sized 'traditional' island dwelling.

Far more atmospheric and very easy to miss, because the tourist signs point you to the Historic Scotland-owned Visitor Centre, is the authentic-looking converted **Black House Café** and gift shop diagonally opposite the stones (*see* 'Where to Stay and Eat'). You can reach it on foot from the main car park, after you have made a visit to see the stones, or you could drive round to it on a badly signed road about half a mile north of the main turning.

On a clear day the **Flannan Islands Lighthouse** can be seen some 15 miles out to sea to the west. On 15 December 1900 a passing ship signalled that the Flannan light wasn't working. A supply boat was already on its way there, on a routine trip, but was delayed for a further 11 days by stormy weather. By the time it arrived, all three of the lighthouse-keepers had vanished without trace. As in case of the mysteriously deserted ship the *Marie Celeste*, a meal was laid on the table; nothing except an overturned chair indicated alarm.

Southwest of Callanish

After Callanish the B8011 branches southwest at **Garynahine** (*Gearraidh Na H-Aibhne*) for **Great Bernera** (*Bearnaraigh*) and **Uig**. The island of Bernera is reached by a 'bridge over the Atlantic' built in 1953. The men of Bernera were agitators in the period leading to the 1886 crofters' revolt, when they marched with their grievances to the landlord, Sir James Matheson, in his castle in Stornoway. **Bosta Iron Age House** (*t (01851) 612 331; open April–Sept Mon–Fri 12–4*), at Bernera, is a replica Iron Age house and museum, built close to where archaeologists excavated the real thing. The community centres at both Bernera and Uig serve coffee, tea and home baking. **Bosta Beach** on the northern tip is well worth a visit. Go on down the B8011 and explore the district around Uig, which has some of the most beautiful scenery in the islands. At **Valtos** there is an **outdoor centre**, for rock-climbing, abseiling, archery etc. While in this area, it would be tragic to miss a visit to **Bonaventure** (*see* 'Where to Stay and Eat', p.256).

The **Lewis Chessmen**, made of walrus ivory and of 12th-century Norse origin, were dug up (by a cow they say) in 1831 in the sands of **Ardroil** (*Eadar Dha Fhadhail*), just south of Gallan Head. Nuns from the Benedictine convent at Brenish are thought to have buried them here. Replicas can be bought all over the islands. The original chessmen are divided between the British Museum and the Museum of Scotland. This is grand walking country.

Heading south from Stornoway the road runs through the 'Lochs' area, and a detour east on the B8060 leads down to Lemreway (*Leumrabhagh*). The land here is split by deep sea lochs and lochans surrounded by heathery hills.

Harris (*Na Hearadh*)

The boundary between Harris and Lewis runs between Loch Resort and Loch Seaforth, with Harris itself being further split into north and south by the narrow isthmus at Tarbert, between West and East Loch Tarbert. This relatively small 'island' contains a kaleidoscopic variety of scenery: mountains, moorland, lunar rockscapes, sandy beaches, and myriad rocky or sandy inlets backed by heather-strewn crags.

History

The early history of Harris (population about 2,200) is similar to that of Lewis, until the one landmass was divided between two Macleod sons. The Macleods held Harris for 500 years, with fewer battles for supremacy than were fought in Lewis. Around the time of the 1745 Rising, the chief, Norman Macleod, bankrupt by gambling and improvidence, raised the rents of his impoverished tenants. His grandson, General Norman Macleod, who inherited the property in 1772 together with a vast debt, sold it to his kinsman Captain Alexander Macleod of Berneray in 1779. Captain Alexander was an enlightened landlord. He imported east-coast fishermen to teach the islanders, lent money for boats and equipment, and provided cottages and land, rent free. He established a spinning factory, built a school, an inn and several roads. In 1834 his grandson sold Harris to the Earl of Dunmore who later sold North Harris to the Scotts. The Earl's mother, the Dowager Countess of Dunmore, is said to have been the founder of the Harris Tweed industry. She bought a length of the island-created tweed in 1842 and introduced it to her aristocratic friends. Harris Tweed soon became the 'in' thing for sportsmen, their wives and gamekeepers all over the country.

When Lord Leverhulme, who had bought Lewis and Harris in 1918, pulled out of Lewis in 1923 he concentrated on developing Obbe as a fishing station, renaming it Leverburgh. He bought a Norwegian whaling station at Bunavoneadar, built a spinning mill and started on an ambitious road-building programme. Although his schemes had far more support from the islanders than they had in Lewis, none flourished and they died with him in 1925. The estates and various developments were subsequently sold for a fraction of the amount Leverhulme had invested in them. Today, Harris's economy, like that of Lewis, is based on fishing, tweed and, increasingly, tourism and information technology.

Visiting Harris

Tarbert (*An Tairbeart*) is the main village, at the head of East Loch Tarbert, with the Tourist Information Centre, a few shops – mostly souvenirs – and the ferry port linking Harris with Uig on Skye. It is an attractive, down-to-earth place; a good base for fishermen. There is a good tearoom by the pier (*see* p.262).

Scalpay (*Scalpaigh*), the island at the entrance to East Loch Tarbert and accessible by causeway, was where the fugitive Prince Charles stayed for four days with his three companions, as guests of the tenant Donald Campbell, hoping to arrange a boat from Stornoway. Campbell's house stood where the Free Church Manse stands today.

Tourist Information

Harris: Pier Road, Tarbert, **t** (01859) 502 011. *Open all year.*

Where to Stay and Eat

Rodel Hotel, Rodel, **t** (01859) 520 210, *www.rodelhotel.com* (*expensive*). Overlooking the harbour. Has been restored to its former excellent standard of comfort and Highland hospitality.

Scarista House, just off the road at Scarista, **t** (01859) 550 238, *www.scaristahouse.com* (*expensive*). Comfortable Georgian manse overlooking 3 miles of glorious sandy beach, with peat fires, antique furniture, a good library, and a fine reputation. Excellent set-menu dinner, with extensive wine list. Non-residents can eat here (*must book*). Two self-catering cottages in the grounds (*£345–650 pw; sleeps 2–6*).

Allan Cottage Guest House, Tarbert, **t** (01859) 502 146 (*moderate*). A splendid place, once the Harris telephone exchange, now a cosy guesthouse with very good food.

Carminish Guest House, Strond, Leverburgh, **t** (01859) 520 400, *www.carminish.com* (*moderate*). Modern house in a fine situation with views over the Carminish Islands and the Sound of Harris. An ideal base to explore the glorious southwestern corner of Harris. Good food and friendly owners.

Harris Hotel, in Tarbert, **t** (01859) 502 154, *www.harrishotel.com* (*moderate*). Large by island standards, sprawling and easy-going. Not all rooms are *en suite* but it's cosy and welcoming.

Am Bothan Bunkhouse, Leverburgh, **t** (01859) 520 251, *www.ambothan.com* (*budget*). A unique bunkhouse, with its own special brand of hospitality. There's a dormitory with futons, family bunkrooms, cosy living rooms and views across the Sound of Harris. It was designed and built by its enterprising owner, Ruaridh Beaton, a yachtsman who also designs and builds boats.

Mrs Corinne Miller, Minchview House, Tarbert, **t** (01859) 502 140 (*budget*). Friendly B&B with views from each room across the Minch to Skye. *Open April–Oct.*

Mrs Christina Morrison, Dunard, Tarbert, **t** (01859) 502 340/493 (*budget*). A 19th-century house with 21st-century comfort and a great welcome.

Mrs Flora Morrison, Tigh na Mara, East Tarbert, **t** (01859) 502 270 (*budget*). Modern, really good B&B with lovely views, and dinner if wanted – spotlessly clean, 5 minutes' walk from the ferry. Home baking and hearty meals.

Reinigeadal Hostel, North Harris, *www.gatliff.org.uk* (*budget*). One of four independent 'Gatliff' hostels in the Hebrides, this is in a wonderfully remote old croft. No phone or reservations – just turn up.

Angus Macleod, overlooks Tarbert and East Loch Larbert, **t** (01859) 502 364, *www.macleodmotel.com*. Four well-equipped, tastefully furnished modern self-catering cottages (sleeping 4–6).

Mrs Margaret Mackay, 4 West Tarbert, **t** (01859) 502 361. Cottage overlooking the sea (sleeps 5).

Scaladale Centre, Ardvourlie, **t** (01859) 502 502, *www.scaladale.co.uk*. A newly built self-catering complex attached to a youth centre (sleeps up to 28).

The Anchorage, Leverburgh, **t** (01859) 520 225, by the pier (*moderate–inexpensive*). Serves meals and has lively themed evenings.

First Fruits Tea Room, in Pier Road Cottage, Tarbert (*inexpensive*). Has delicious meals and snacks in traditional surroundings. Excellent teas.

The footpath east from the Tarbert–Scalpay road was until recently the only access by land to the small village of Rhenigidale (*Reinigeadal*). The new road down from Maaruig makes life easier for this small community, which includes a youth hostel. When weather permits, boat cruises run from Tarbert to the **Shiant Islands**, 12 miles to the east, wild and cliff-lined with a natural sea arch and a huge colony of puffins as well as other sea birds. Compton Mackenzie did some of his writing here. The Shiants are overrun by a colony of black rats, virtually extinct elsewhere.

The road to Stornoway from Tarbert runs through heather-carpeted hills sliced by burns, and bleak moorland. The B887 goes west off the A859 to **Bunavoneadar** (*Bun Abhainn Eadarra*), where you can see the remains of the Norwegian whaling station Lord Leverhulme tried unsuccessfully to regenerate. Whales were plentiful in these waters but, as with Gavin Maxwell's shark fishery on Soay, there were insurmountable problems. About 8 miles further on, salmon jostle in the sea waiting to jump up the falls where **Loch Leosaidh** disgorges down a series of rock slabs into the sea below **Amhuinnsuidhe Castle** (pronounced approximately 'Aven-soyr' or 'Aven-soy-rr'). If you are lucky you will see the fish making their heroic leaps from pool to pool in the journey to their spawning grounds. The road runs right past the front door of the castle just beyond the falls. There is a lovely walk starting up the track to the power station just before you come down to the salmon leap and castle. Park at the power station and walk up the track to the dam, round the reservoir and the loch beyond into a dramatic 'hidden' glen.

Hushinish (*Huisinis*), 6 miles on from the castle, has a sheltered sandy beach at the head of the bay. The island of **Scarp**, a lump of sheer rock north of Hushinish Point, is best known as the recipient of a very advanced method of postal delivery in 1934 – the dream-child of the German rocket scientist Gerhardt Zucher. Mail and emergency medicines were to be fired at it from a rocket. A special stamp was issued, coveted by philatelists, and the first rocket was launched with 30,000 letters. Alas, it exploded, destroying the mail and the dream. A film has been made about this 'rocket project'.

The island of Taransay at the mouth of West Loch Tarbert, is familiar to TV fans, as the stage for *Castaway 2000*. A handful of volunteers from all walks of life, were dumped on the island – last inhabited in 1974 – to see if they could be self-sufficient for a year. It was not exactly pioneering: they were provided with 'pools' of livestock and a great deal else, and were rescued every time anyone felt a sniffle coming on, but it provided great amusement to the viewing public and to those who sneaked in by boat with illicit contraband, and heard the less publicized stories. The 'rocket project' film was also shot here. Two of the pods are now used as an artists' retreat, **Outside the Box** (*t (01436) 850 123, otbcovepark@aol.com*).

The east-coast route down South Harris, called the Golden Road, is a tortuous single track through a bleak, stony landscape enhanced by wonderful remote rocky inlets and the clustered cottages of small communities. Tiny parcels of land were painstakingly cultivated and nurtured here by people evicted from the fertile west coast, expected to try and make a living from fishing. Many of their descendants are weavers and, around **Plocrapool** (*Plocrabol*), there are a number of places where you can watch them weaving Harris Tweed on looms in their houses. A reasonably priced tweed and woollens shop is signed off the road in Plocrapool.

St Clement's Church (*always accessible*), at Rodel (*Roghadal*) on the northern headland of Loch Rodel, is the finest pre-Reformation church in the Western Isles. Frequently restored, it was recently repaired by Historic Scotland, though some of the walls and the greater part of the tower are original. Of the two medieval tombs inside, the most magnificent is that of Alasdair Crottach, the Macleod chief from Dunvegan who entertained James V on MacLeod's Tables (*see* p.247) and died in 1548. A pointed surround and a recessed arch behind the recumbent stone effigy are decorated with elaborate carvings, unrivalled in the Hebrides. Walk round the outside to the east face of the tower. There is a worn carving of St Clement above the window and below him, to the right, a *sheila-na-gig* – a 'fallen angel' woman with flowing hair and skirts lifted to display her private parts, a common device originating from Ireland, thought to distract the evil spirits that followed worshippers into church. Some hideous public lavatories nearby blight this wonderful building, however.

The attractive, secluded 18th-century harbour at Rodel is overlooked by the **Rodel Hotel**, built by Captain Alexander Macleod in 1785 when he returned rich from India and bought Harris.

Leverburgh and Around

Leverburgh (*An T-ob/Tob*), on the south coast about 3 miles northwest of Rodel, was developed from the small settlement of Obbe by Lord Leverhulme. It isn't much of a place to linger in now: a few rather dismal souvenir and bookshops, a café above the general store and, somewhat surprisingly, a smart beautician, complete with hanging baskets of dried flowers on lamp posts. The ferry to North Uist runs from here.

Northwest, at Northton (*Taobh Tuath*), **Seallam** is an excellent **Genealogy Research and Visitor Centre** (*t (01859) 520 258, www.seallam.com*), with a fascinating exhibition on the Western Isles. You could spend hours in this place without noticing there is also a café and shop. Nearby in the Old Schoolhouse, Bill Lawson is a fountain of knowledge on local genealogy and history, and he runs guided walks (*see* 'Tracing Your Ancestors', pp.43–4). **MacGillivray Centre**, at the end of the Northton Road, is an unmanned interpretation centre, focussed on W. MacGillivray the ornithologist, and local flora and fauna. Wonderful sandy beaches fringe the west coast, including **Luskintyre Beach** (*Losgaintir*), one of the most beautiful you could ever hope to find. Park at the end of the road and walk on round the dunes to the north.

Isles South of the Sound of Harris

Berneray (*Eilean Bhearnaraigh*) and North Uist (*Uibhist a Tuath*)

The small, peaceful island of Berneray lies to the south of Harris, just off the northern shore of North Uist, and accessible by a causeway from Otternish in North Uist. About 8 miles in circumference with a population of about 130, engaged mainly in crofting, lobster fishing and knitting, it is low-lying with 3 miles of sandy beach on the west coast. The name comes from the Norse, Bjorn's Isle. The houses at **Ruisgarry**, a conservation area, still have their thatched roofs, and there are plans for restoration;

Getting There

The main village in North Uist is Lochmaddy, the terminal for **car ferries** from Uig on Skye and Tarbert on Harris. A car ferry also runs from Newtonferry (Otternish) to Leverburgh on Harris. Balivanich Airport across the causeway on Benbecula provides an **air link** with Glasgow, Stornoway and Barra.

Tourist Information

North Uist: Pier Road, Lochmaddy, t (01876) 500 321. *Open early April–mid-Oct.*

Sports and Activities

Uist Outdoor Centre, near Lochmaddy, t (01876) 500 480, *www.uistoutdoorcentre. co.uk.* Adventure training establishment for subaqua diving, water sports, climbing, walking, wildlife watching, environmental and field studies. Bunkroom accommodation.

Where to Stay and Eat

Carinish Inn, Carinish, North Uist, t (01876) 580 673 (*moderate*). A modern and comfortable place to stay.

Langass Lodge Hotel, overlooks Loch Langass, North Uist, t (01876) 580 285, *www. langasslodge.co.uk* (*moderate*). Converted shooting lodge – a cosy, remote and peaceful haven, with first-class food.

Lochmaddy Hotel, Lochmaddy, North Uist, t (01876) 500 331, *www.lochmaddyhotel. co.uk* (*moderate*). Comfortable, old-established fishing hotel, with good food.

Temple View Hotel, Carinish, North Uist, t (01876) 580 676, *www.templeviewhotel. com* (*moderate*). Traditional, hospitable island house.

Berneray Hostel, Berneray, *www.gatliff.org.uk* (*budget*). One of four independent 'Gatliff' hostels in the Hebrides. Two converted black houses (sleeps 16). No reservations: just turn up. A wonderful base for walkers.

Donald MacKillip, Burnside Croft, Berneray, t (01876) 540 235 (*budget*). Owner will share his crofting activities if desired.

Mrs Mary Ann Macdonald, Sollas, North Uist, t (01876) 560 208 (*budget*). A wonderful hostess for this B&B, and a renowned knitter of socks.

Mrs Alina Morrison, Lochmaddy, North Uist, t (01876) 500 275/324 (*budget*). B&B by the ferry terminal.

Mrs Norma Shepherd, Struan House, Sollas, North Uist, t (01876) 560 282 (*budget*). Modern house with glorious views and 4-star treatment.

Sealladh Traigh, Claddach Kirkibost, North Uist, t (01876) 580 248 (*budget*). A modern, welcoming guesthouse overlooking the sea, with good home cooking.

Mr Angus Dingwall, Lochmaddy, North Uist, t (01876) 500 391. Modernized holiday cottages – nice views (sleep 4–6).

Mr Peter and Mrs Morag Murray, Bayhead, North Uist, t (01876) 510 379. Self-catering (sleeps 4).

Mrs MacAskill, Morven, Berneray, t (01876) 540 230. Modern, well-equipped self-catering croft house – sea views (sleeps 8).

Alasdair Seale, near Lochmaddy, North Uist, t (0131) 447 9911. Self-catering in two cottages (sleep 6–7).

two are now a cosy hostel. For some years the Prince of Wales retreated here, playing at crofting.

The island of North Uist, between Harris and Benbecula (to which it is linked by a causeway), is about 17 miles long and 13 miles wide. It encompasses a great deal of water – so much so that half the total area is submerged. Wild peat moors and myriad lochs and lochans cover the island's eastern side and centre, while to the north and west there is farm land, with some splendid sandy beaches. Loch Eport almost cuts the island in two from the east. Grimsay is the tidal island in the southeast, linked to both North Uist and Benbecula by causeway and a centre for the fishing industry, mainly lobster.

History

Prehistoric remains tell of ancient settlers, and the Nordic colonists bequeathed many Norse place names – Uist is derived from the Norse *I-vist*, an abode or in-dwelling. The Macdonalds of Sleat, descendants of Somerled, held the island from 1495 until 1855. The early 19th-century kelp boom encouraged more settlers than the poor land could support; by the time the market slumped the population had risen to 5,000. This slump, and the subsequent clearance of the land by Lord Macdonald, forced over 1,000 islanders from their lands and caused violent confrontation between crofters and the police. The island is now owned by the Granville family. The population is about 1,800, with an economy based on crofting and fishing – mainly for shellfish – fish farming, tweed, knitwear and tourism. The island is firmly Presbyterian, in contrast to the strong Catholicism of the south.

Lochmaddy

Lochmaddy (*Loch na Madadh*) is the island port, a sprawling village with a sheltered harbour, busy when the boats come in. Some say the three rocks at the harbour entrance look like crouching dogs – the port's name comes from the Gaelic for dog, *madadh* – but you need a good imagination to see it. There is a museum and arts centre, near the pier in the former inn – **Taigh Chearsabhagh** (*www.taigh-chear sabhagh.org; open Mon–Sat 10–5; adm*), with exhibitions of local history and activity workshops, a shop and café. The **Tourist Information Centre** is beside the harbour. Walk out to the **'Sea-Sky'** chamber (*always accessible*) at **Sponish**, close by. In a small stone beehive there is an intriguing camera obscura aimed at the sea and sky.

Around the Island

A road circles the island through a series of crofting and fishing townships. Peat bogs flank the road with rows of neatly stacked peat bricks waiting to be transported to the houses. About 3 miles west of Lochmaddy there are three standing stones on the slope of **Blashaval** (*Blathaisbhal*). These are the 'Three False Men', said to be three men from Skye who were turned to stone by a witch as punishment for deserting their wives; another explanation is that they represent three spies who were caught and buried alive. Five miles west of Lochmaddy, a small road goes north to **Newton Ferry** (*Port Nan Long*). In a loch on the right of this road is a well-preserved fortress, **Dun-an-Sticir**, occupied as late as 1601 by Hugh Macdonald, descendant of the Macdonalds of Sleat. Back on the circular road, **Eilean-an-Tighe** is a rocky islet in Loch-nan-Geireann, 2 miles west. It was the site of a Neolithic potters' workshop, the oldest to be excavated in western Europe. The pottery found here was of a very high quality, and there was so much of it that the factory must have supplied a large area.

In **Sollas** (*Solas*), 3 miles west, a medieval settlement is being excavated. This district was also the scene of one of the episodes of the Clearances. In 1849 Lord Macdonald, 4th Baron of the Isles, was faced with debts of around £200,000. He decided to evict some 600 crofters from the overcrowded, uneconomic area around Sollas. There were some unfortunate and much publicized skirmishes with the sheriff's officers and the police. The crofters were forced to give in, but there was a three-year delay before they were shipped off to Canada – in a frigate carrying smallpox germs below decks.

Vallay (*Bhalaigh*), pronounced Varlie, is a tidal island at the entrance to a wide shallow bay running north and west from Sollas. The ruin of a large Edwardian house stands sadly crumbling above the sand, once the home of Erskine Beveridge, the famous naturalist and archaeologist. There are also the remains of the earlier house and outbuildings built in 1727 and home of the Macdonalds of Vallay, one of whom became the Senator of British Columbia, as well as a litter of antiquities – duns, standing stones and chapel ruins. You can walk out to Vallay at low tide but watch out for the flood tide; it fills the channels fast, cutting off the unwary. The road south across the moor from here is called the Committee Road, built in the 19th century as a famine relief scheme, to provide a short cut to the west coast.

Scolpaig Tower, on a small island in Loch Scolpaig just off the road about 3 miles to the west, is a 'folly' built in the 19th century from the ruins of a dun. At **Hosta**, about 4 miles on round the coast, a footpath leads 2 miles east across the moor to a chambered cairn on **Clettraval**, built when birchwood copses grew here. Later, an Iron Age fort was built over it, and pottery excavated here was found to be the same as that made in the workshop at Eilean-an-Tighe. At **Balranald** (*Baile Raghaill*), stretching out to the most westerly tip of the island at **Aird an Runair**, there is an RSPB reserve, supporting one of the highest densities of breeding waders in Britain. Altogether 183 species of bird have been recorded on the reserve. Visitors are asked to report to the RSPB cottage on arrival.

Unival is a hill north of the road, 6 miles southeast of Huna. Walk across the moor up its eastern flank, on the west side of Loch Huna, to a chambered burial cairn with a small cist. A couple of miles further down, the road forks south to the right and northeast to the left. The left-hand road completes the circuit of the island. Two miles along this road back to Lochmaddy, a track to the right is signposted to Langass Lodge Hotel. Park at the hotel and take the footpath up behind it, a 10-minute walk up through heather, bracken and bog myrtle. On the hillside is an oval of standing stones – **Pobull Fhinn**, Finn's People. This is a memorable prehistoric site, its mysticism enhanced by its remoteness.

Less than a mile northeast on the main road, **Barpa Langass** is a large man-made mound of stones shaped like a squashed beehive. This well-preserved chambered burial cairn is the tomb of a chieftain, thought to date from about 1000 BC. Visitors are asked not to crawl through the tunnel into the cairn, both for their own safety and for the preservation of the site. Great stone slabs line the interior and there are traces of where other cells may have led off the main chamber. From here it is about 6 miles on to Lochmaddy. Going back southwest to the fork, **Carinish** (*Carinis*), where there are some interesting remains, is 2 miles down the road to the south.

Teampull-na-Trionaid (Trinity Temple) is a ruin on top of a knoll on the Carinish promontory at the southern end of the island. This church was founded by Beathag (Beatrice), daughter of Somerled, Lord of the Isles, in about 1203 on the site of an earlier church, and was regarded as an important seat of learning for priests in medieval times, similar to the one on Iona. There are interesting gravestones here.

The last battle to be fought in Scotland using just swords and bows and arrows was the Battle of Carinish, in 1601 between the Macdonalds of North Uist and the Macleods of Harris, thought to be due to a Macdonald divorcing his Macleod wife and sending her home. The Macleods descended on Carinish in a frenzy of rage and all but two of them were killed in the battle that ensued. *Feith-na-Fala* (The Field of Blood) marks the site of the battle, just north of the Carinish Inn.

Benbecula (*Beinn Na Faoghla*)

Benbecula, derived from the Gaelic *beinn a'bhfaodhla* – mountain of the fords – is about 5 miles long by 8 miles wide, linked to the south of North Uist by a succession of causeways. The low-tide route across North Ford is dangerous; locals tell hair-raising stories of quicksands. Rueval, a rounded hillock, gives a good view of the otherwise flat, waterlogged island. The airport at **Balivanich** has air links to Glasgow, Stornoway and Barra. The population of about 1,800 is dominated by army personnel and their dependants, who are stationed at Balivanich to work on the missile range in South Uist. The base has been considerably reduced these days. The Presbyterianism of the north and the Catholicism of the south meet in Benbecula in roughly equal strength, and without animosity.

The history of the island is that of its neighbours, recorded in a few prehistoric remains and predominantly Norse place names. It was part of the patrimony of the Macdonalds of Clanranald from the 13th century until 1838 when they were forced to sell their lands to pay impatient creditors. Colonel Gordon of Cluny bought the island, together with South Uist, Eriskay and Barra, and his family owned it for just over a

Shopping and Activities

D. MacGillivray and Co, Balivanich, opposite the cone-shaped water tank at the airport, **t** (01870) 602 525. Unpretentious building concealing an Aladdin's cave of tweed and woollen products and an excellent selection of new and second-hand books.

Macleans of Benbecula Bakery. Their famous shortbread and cookies are sold in gift boxes under the Scottish Parliament brand name. There is a 9-hole **golf course**, a mile north of Balivanich on the B892.

Where to Stay and Eat

Dark Island Hotel, Liniclate, **t** (01870) 603 030, *www.isleshotelgroup.co.uk* (*moderate*). A good central base, with 42 rooms; the food features local game and crab.

Isle of Benbecula House Hotel, Creagorry, **t** (01870) 602 024, *www.isleshotelgroup. co.uk* (*moderate*). By the sea, with 20 comfortable rooms, Gaelic-speaking staff; the meals feature good use of local produce.

Mrs Gretta Campbell, 5 Torlum, Borve, **t** (01870) 602 685 (*moderate*). Guesthouse.

Mrs Esther MacDonald, Gramsdale, **t** (01870) 602 536 (*moderate*). Thatched self-catering croft house (sleeps 2–4).

Mrs Morag Macintosh, overlooking South Ford, **t** (01870) 602 239. Well-equipped self-catering house (sleeps 8).

Stepping Stones, Balivanich, **t** (01870) 603 377 (*moderate–inexpensive*). Restaurant/café, run by chef brothers, who make the most of local ingredients.

hundred years, during which time many people were ruthlessly cleared from their homes and sent abroad. The northern part of the island was then sold to the Air Ministry and the remainder to a London businessman. It is now owned by South Uist Estates.

At **Nunton**, 2 miles south of Balivanich, there is a ruined 14th-century chapel which belonged to a nunnery whose inmates were brutally massacred when the building was destroyed during the Reformation. Stones from the nunnery are said to have been used to build the large farmhouse by the road, the 18th-century former home of the Macdonalds of Clanranald, Nunton. This L-plan building succeeded Ormiclate Castle on South Uist as Clanranald's residence after the Benbecula branch of these Macdonalds inherited the chieftainship. The Nunton Steadings have been converted to offices, with a history section open to the public on Sunday afternoons. **Borve Castle**, a gaunt ruined keep 4 miles south of Balivanich, was another Clanranald stronghold and scene of many a bloody skirmish. The scant remains of the castle chapel, a 15th–16th-century centre for Gaelic culture, can still be seen nearby.

In 1988 a new secondary school and community centre was built at **Liniclate** (*Lionacleit*) at the southern end of the island, serving children throughout the islands, some of whom previously had to board on the mainland for their education. Open to the public, one of the rare bones of contention between Presbyterians and Catholics was over its Sunday opening (*see* **Topics**, pp.26–7). There is a museum, swimming pool, library and restaurant, and good ceilidhs and events in the theatre in the summer.

Wiay (*Fuidhaigh Wiay*), an island off the southeast tip of Benbecula, is a bird sanctuary for a variety of wildfowl including snipe, duck, geese and swans. It was from **Rossinish** on Benbecula's northeast corner that Prince Charles sailed 'over the sea to Skye' disguised as gawky Betty Burke, the servant of Flora Macdonald.

South Uist (*Uibhist a Deas*)

A straight causeway links Benbecula with South Uist, less than half a mile across South Ford. At low tide here there is usually at least one figure stooped over the sand, scooping up the cockles that lurk just below the surface. South Uist is about 20 miles long and 8 miles wide – a land area of 141 square miles, with hills and long sea lochs to the east and silvery shell-sand and machair to the west. The peat bog and moorland is studded by more than 190 freshwater lochs with excellent fishing. Beinn Mhor, less than halfway down in the east, is the highest peak at 2,034ft (626m).

The island suffered badly from the Clearances in the 19th century, at the hands of Colonel Gordon of Cluny (*see* 'Benbecula', above). The present population of about 2,200 inhabits crofting townships scattered throughout the island, linked by a network of one-track lanes radiating from the main, north–south road which varies from single track to short stretches of EU-funded double-track carriageway. These random lengths of fast highway terminate abruptly, often without obvious warning, and can be extremely dangerous. Since the mid-20th century the economy has been dominated by the army missile range on the northwestern corner of the island.

Tourist Information

South Uist: Pier Road, Lochboisdale, **t** (01878) 700 286. *Open Easter–Sept.*

Shopping

Jewellery workshop and gift shop, Lochdar, near the causeway to Benbecula.

Salar Fish Farm Shop and Smokehouse, Loch Carnan, **t** (01870) 610 324. Delicious smoked salmon and much more. Good for presents.

Where to Stay and Eat

Borrodale Hotel, Daliburgh, **t** (01878) 700 444, *www.isleshotelgroup.co.uk* (*moderate*). Busy and cheerful, with mostly *en-suite* rooms. Will arrange free golf, and it's a good place to hear live Scottish music. *Open all year.*

Orasay Inn, near Loch Carnan, **t** (01870) 610 298, *www.witb.co.uk/links/orasayinn.htm* (*moderate*). Small, modern and comfortable, with good food.

Angler's Retreat, Lochdar, **t** (01870) 610 325, *www.anglersretreat.net* (*moderate– budget*). Small, friendly, modern B&B on a croft. Dinner available. *Open Mar–Dec.*

Clan Ranald, Garryhallie, north of Daliburgh, **t** (01878) 700 263, *www.clan-ranald.co.uk* (*moderate–budget*). Comfortable guesthouse where you can be sure of a warm welcome.

Lochboisdale Hotel, South Uist harbour, **t** (01878) 700 332, *www.lochboisdale.com* (*moderate–budget*). Victorian fishing hotel with extensive fishing rights and sea views.

Mrs Flora MacInnes, Sealladh Mara, in South Lochboisdale, **t** (01878) 700 580 (*moderate– budget*). One of the best B&B houses on the island, overlooking the loch – comfortable, with warm hospitality.

Pollachar Inn (*Pol A Charra*), 5 miles south of Daliburgh, **t** (01878) 700 215, *www. pollacharin.co.uk* (*moderate–budget*). Comfortable and convivial, overlooking one of the best views in Scotland.

The Shieling, Garryhallie, **t** (01878) 700 504 (*moderate–budget*). Next door to Clan Ranald; equally friendly and cosy.

Boisdale House, South Lochboisdale, contact Victoria Hayes, **t** (020) 7582 2418. Delightful self-catering family house on south shore of Loch Boisdale; 7 bedrooms, (sleeps 13), 3 bathrooms, large sitting room, TV room, indoor games room (*£1,000–£2,000pw*). A self-contained 1-bedroom flat sleeps 2.

Mrs Marion Campbell, Eriskay, **t** (01878) 720 274/720 236. A chalet with two bedrooms (sleeps 4) for self catering (*£200pw*).

Tobha Mor, Howmore (Gatliff Trust) (*budget*), *www.gatliff.org.uk*. Renovated black house, run as an independent hostel (sleeps 17). No telephone, no bookings: just turn up.

Am Politician, at Baile, **t** (01878) 720 246 (*moderate–inexpensive*). The only bar on the island, serving good seafood meals.

South to Beinn Mhor

A roadside shrine to the Virgin Mary, just south of the causeway from Benbecula, is a reminder that you are on the threshold of the Catholic south. The first road to the east, a mile south of the causeway, goes out 2 miles to **Loch Carnan**, a beautiful fjord-like sea loch with a pier for large boats. Three miles to the south, the main road becomes a causeway and crosses **Loch Bee**, one of the largest swan reserves in Britain. The area of marshland to the east is a nature reserve, the breeding ground of many wildfowl. The hill just south of Loch Bee is another named Rueval, crested by the futuristic-looking army Range Head. Rocket targets can sometimes be seen (and heard) off the west coast. Rising from Rueval's western slope is a white granite statue of **Our Lady of the Isles**, carved by Hew Lorimer. The purity of the Madonna holding her child enshrines the islanders' deep faith. It was erected by the community in 1957.

The next road east runs 4 miles out to **Loch Skipport** (*Loch Sgioport*), another fjord-like sea loch where there is a deep-water anchorage, a salmon farm and the skeleton of a pier which used to be the principal ferry stop for the island. The **Loch Druidibeg National Nature Reserve**, just to the south, provides an ideal habitat for many species of waterfowl. Less than 2 miles further south on the main road, beyond the road west to **Drimisdale** (*Dreumasdal*), there is a small loch with an island and a ruined castle. A submerged causeway runs out to the island. Beware! Some of its wobbly stones have been known to topple the unwary into the dark peaty water of the loch. The ruin was once **Caisteal Bheagram**, a 16th-century keep that was a Clanranald stronghold. Some years ago the present Captain of Clanranald tried to map out the original layout of the castle and discovered that its ruins cover almost all the island.

Howmore

A mile south, a side road runs west a mile to **Howmore** (*Tobha Mor*), the most important religious site in the Outer Hebrides, with a history that goes back over a thousand years. There was probably a monastery and a collegiate church here in medieval times. Substantial fragments of two churches, dedicated to Mary and Columba, and three chapels survive. The *Book of Clanranald*, compiled by the MacMhuirichs, the hereditary poets and genealogists to the Clanranalds, records that several members of the ruling family of Clanranald were buried here between 1500 and 1700, and a number of gravestones and wheel-cross monuments adorn the enclosure (some modern). One of the surviving chapels is called *Caibeal Chlann 'ic Ailean* – Clanranald's Chapel – built in 1574 for the Clanranald chief, Iain Muideartach, who 'left funds to erect a chapel at Howmore where his body was buried'. It was from this chapel that the Clanranald Stone disappeared in 1990, a heavy armorial panel bearing the arms of Clanranald. Dating from the 16th-century, it was lying on the ground near the ruins and was stolen by two young men who coveted it for their London flat. Five years later one of the young men died, some say cursed by the stone's removal, and his father discovered it propped up in his son's living room. It has since been returned to the small museum at Kildonan (*see* p.272). A network of one-track roads and tracks west of the main road meander through the machair, linking small townships and isolated dwellings – some lead across dunes to the beach.

Ormiclate Castle, or *Ormacleit*, a couple of miles south of Howmore, between the main road and the sea, is a roofless shell attached to a late-18th-century restored farmhouse. The castle, finished in 1707, was built by Allan Macdonald of Clanranald, whose wife Penelope had spurned their humble dwelling, declaring that 'even her father's hens were better housed'. Eight years later, Ormiclate was burnt down, on the eve of the Battle of Sheriffmuir in which the chief was killed (*see* Castle Tioram, p.117–18).

Beinn Mhor and Loch Eynort

Hecla (1,988ft/606m) and **Beinn Mhor** (2,034ft/620m) rise to the east of the main road, from which they can be approached over a wasteland of bog. The summits can be dangerous in high winds, especially the sharp serrated edge of Beinn Mhor, with vertiginous drops off the east side. East of Hecla is **Usinish lighthouse**, no longer manned. When the writer Gavin Maxwell was trying to make a go of shark fishing, the lighthouse keeper here was an enthusiastic informant as to when there were sharks in the area. **Nicolson's Leap**, just south of Usinish Point, is said to be the place where a Nicolson leapt the 50ft (15m) chasm on to the rock stack, escaping revenge from a Clanranald chief. Having been found in bed with Clanranald's wife, Nicolson took their baby son hostage, then tried to bargain from the top of the stack. When he failed to do a deal, they say he leapt into the sea, still holding the baby in his arms.

To the south, **Loch Eynort** (*Loch Aineoirt*) is another sea loch. This is a good starting point for walks over the remote moorland between Lochs Eynort and Skipport. Beinn Mhor can also be reached from here, as can Ben Corodale, about 4 miles northeast of the end of the road. This wild country north of Loch Eynort, among the hills and glens surrounding Beinn Mhor and Hecla, was where Prince Charles took refuge for a while in a shieling, hiding in a cave when discovery seemed likely. The cave is not the easily visible one above a group of ruined houses by a burn. The true one is difficult to find, up on the rock face. This whole area is only accessible on foot or by boat. It was off this bit of coast, in 1980, that Hercules the Bear, famous star of TV adverts, went missing during a recreational swim with his owner. He evaded capture for three weeks, dwindling to a fraction of his normal weight, being too domesticated to cope with life in the wild. He recovered, and eventually died of old age.

South to Lochboisdale

Bornish, west of the main road about a mile south of the Loch Eynort turning, is a straggle of dwellings with a church. Gaunt and rectangular on the outside, this charming church has a raw, unfaced stone interior with a large crucifix against a rich red cloth behind the altar as the focal point. The road runs out west to **Rubha Ardvule**, surrounded by slabs of flat rock – a good viewpoint, particularly during Atlantic gales. Archaeologists have excavated Dun Vulan, which you can see to the left.

Kildonan Museum (*t (01878) 710 343; open June–Sept daily; adm*), beside the main road a couple of miles to the south, has been restored and extended with a Lottery grant and public funding. Housed within an extension of the old Kildonan school, the museum contains displays ranging from archaeological finds to crafts, local artefacts, photographs and history. A café and some attractive landscaping enhance this imaginative project. The archaeological department of Sheffield University has been working on the island for many years and their research is frequently featured.

Half a mile south, a road west is signed to Milton (*Gearraidh Bhailteas*) where a cairn marks **Flora Macdonald's birthplace** (she was born in 1722). Flora's father was a Clanranald tacksman. She was tending her brother's cattle at a shieling about 3 miles from here when the Prince was brought to her in need of help. **Askernish** (*Aisgernis*), a mile south, has a nine-hole golf course on the machair where players dodge sheep and plovers' nests among the dunes. The South Uist Games take place on the golf course in July, usually followed by a dance or a concert in the church hall. Everyone on the island turns out for the event. As well as piping, dancing and all the traditional sports, there are jovial gatherings of spectators among the parked cars and in the beer tent.

Daliburgh (*Dalabrog*) is a village on the crossroads west of Lochboisdale. A road to the west leads to the Catholic parish church of St Peter's, a large, simple building dating from the 1860s, weathered and unadorned, the priest's house attached. This is the living heart of the island, filled to capacity for Sunday Mass and well attended throughout the week. The Church of Scotland kirk and manse stand prominently on the crossroads. Northwest of St Peter's lies what must be one of the most beautiful, remote burial grounds in the country, on the machair's edge overlooking the Atlantic.

The road east from Daliburgh goes 3 miles to the port of **Lochboisdale** (*Loch Baghasdail*). The village is at its busiest when the Caledonian MacBrayne ferries are arriving or departing, turning the quay into a bustling place with a babble of Gaelic voices. A few visiting yachts anchor in the two small bays either side of the pier in the summer. Looming over Loch Boisdale's northern shore is Ben Kenneth (*Beinn Ruigh Choinnich*). There is a challenging race to its summit every year for the young men of the area, who may take whichever route they choose. It has been known for a competitor to start by diving off the pier – travelling 'as the crow flies'!

South Lochboisdale to Eriskay

A mile south of Daliburgh, a small road runs about 2 miles west to Kilpheder (*Cille Pheadair*), from where a track leads out to the machair and an Iron Age Pictish wheel house. This communal dwelling with a central hearth had elaborate drainage systems and storage places sunken deep into the floor. Two miles south of Daliburgh, a road runs east for 2 miles through **South Lochboisdale** (*Taobh A Deas Loch Baghasdail*). From the parking bay at the end of the road, a map is needed to follow a faint track over hills and moor, along Lochs Kerrsinish, Marulaig and Moreef, a total of 5 miles southwest to **Bun Struth**, a loch joined to the sea by a narrow passage of sheer rock, surrounded by hills. It is inaccessible except by boat or on foot, inhabited only by sheep, birds and the ghosts of the people who once lived in the now-ruined croft houses that lie scattered over the area. When the tide is out, the loch is higher than the sea, draining over a shelf of rock in the entrance passage, marooning boats until the next tide, which swirls in fast (and is tricky to navigate). Golden eagles can sometimes be seen gliding on the air currents to the north of Loch Marulaig.

All of the southeastern foot of the island is good walking country; sheep tracks serve as paths, the best route chosen by observation of the boggy terrain ahead. Views from the summits of the hills are spectacular; however, when Skye looks so close you could almost touch it, and when its rocks glint, it usually means rain.

The road out to the west, opposite that to South Lochboisdale, leads to a white shell-sand beach with the gloomy remains of a once-flourishing seaweed factory. A few years ago any islander could cut seaweed – a laborious job – and sell it to this factory, where it was processed into alginates for use in a large number of products ranging from soap to beer and cosmetics. Now, any seaweed that is harvested is collected in lorries and shipped to factories on the mainland. If you see a small boat chugging at snail's pace through the water with a vast, dark patch behind it, it is towing a floating island of seaweed. The white beach runs for miles in great sweeps of sand where keen eyes will spot tiny pink cowrie shells. The wide fringe of machair is famous for its carpet of wild flowers in the summer. Opposite the seaweed factory there is a small conical island called **Orosay**, accessible at low tide, with good views.

The road south climbs to the bizarrely set, modernist wedge-shaped church at **Garrynamonie** (*Gearraidh Na Monadh*), built in 1963 and designed by a priest from Barra, Father Calum McNeil. Here, you can hear Mass in Gaelic. Opposite the church was the old schoolhouse (now demolished) where Fredrick Rea, a young Englishman, was sent as headmaster at the end of the 19th century, the first Catholic schoolmaster for at least a century. He spoke no Gaelic. The students acted as his interpreters and each child arrived at school carrying peat for the fire, often having walked several miles in bare feet. His recently reprinted book, *A School in South Uist*, tells of his life here.

Ludag is a couple of miles east along the south coast. A sandy bay beyond, at South Glendale, dries out at low tide and is a good place for cockles, and the sheltered, turf-covered rocks around make it an excellent picnic spot. Southeast of Glendale, along the rocky shore and below the water, lies part of the wreck of the *Politician*, immortalized as the *Cabinet Minister* by Compton Mackenzie in his book *Whisky Galore*. The true story was only slightly embroidered in the novel. The ship was carrying 20,000 cases of whisky to America in 1941 at a time when whisky was scarce on the islands. Magnetic minerals in the rocks distorted the compass readings and she went off course, riding over Hartamul, the rock at the entrance to the Sound of Eriskay and finishing up against the cliff. The islanders made a valiant attempt to 'rescue' the whisky, thwarted by the bureaucracy of the Customs and Excise Department, and not a few families still own a much-valued 'Polly Bottle'. Stories are told, with a twinkle and a knowing shake of the head, of animals reeling down the road, and of bottles dug up on the machair that had been buried for years.

South Uist is littered with places where Prince Charles is said to have sheltered. He certainly hid for a time in the jagged ruined castle on **Calvay Island**, at the entrance to Loch Boisdale, clearly seen from the ferry.

Eriskay (*Eiriosgaigh*)

From the Norse *Eiriks-ey* – Eric's Island – Eriskay is a mere 2½ by 1½ miles in size with a community of about 200, largely Catholic. The MacNeils of Barra owned it until 1758 when they sold it to the Macdonalds of Clanranald. When Colonel Gordon of Cluny bought it in 1838, with South Uist, Barra and Benbecula, he offered some of the Uist crofters holdings in Eriskay where the land was too poor even for sheep. With the choice between this meagre allotment and emigration, many of them chose the former and managed to subsist on scant crops and potatoes grown in lazy beds. The main occupations today are fishing and crofting. Eriskay ponies are the last survivors of a small, native Scottish breed used to carry seaweed and peat, and are sadly almost extinct. The island has invented its own unique pattern for hand-knitted sweaters.

Visiting the Island

The new causeway links Ludag in South Uist with **Haun** (*Haunn*), a smiling village of white cottages with roofs of bright blue, pink, green and red, sheltered by hills. St

Michael's Church, perched high above the harbour, is the heart of the community, built in 1903 by Father Allan MacDonald, who wrote down the folklore and many of the songs of the Hebrides, and was a distinguished poet and scholar. The plinth of the altar is the prow of a lifeboat, the focal point for a community whose existence has always been influenced by the sea. The ship's bell outside the church was rescued from the **Derfflinger**, one of the German fleet that sank in Scapa Flow in 1919.

Just beyond the village on the western shore there is a crescent of sand called Prince Charlie's Bay. This was where the prince landed from France on 23 July 1745 and where he spent his first night on Scottish soil. The black house he stayed in was pulled down in 1902. Its smoky interior drove him out into the fresh air several times during the night. The pink convolvulus called Prince Charlie's rose, in the machair round the bay, is said to have been introduced here from a seed dropped from his shoe, though it can now be found elsewhere on the mainland. Ben Scrien is the highest hill – 610ft (186m). The Stack Islands lie just off the southern tip of Eriskay, only accessible by boat; there is a rocky creek on the east side of the main island that offers safe shelter in calm weather. From here it is a scramble up the precipitous cliff to the Weaver's Castle at the top. A notorious Macneil lived here, much feared as a wrecker and pirate. He built the castle as a stronghold, and stole a girl from a shieling in South Uist to be his wife and the mother of a large number of sure-footed children.

Barra (*Barraigh*)

Barra, 4 miles south of South Uist at the nearest point, is partly fringed by a number of smaller islands, known as the Bishops' Isles, including Vatersay, Sandray, Pabbay and Mingulay to its south, all of which were once inhabited. Eight miles long by 4–5 miles wide, Barra is encircled by a 12-mile road with an arm running north to the airport and Scurrival Point. It has a predominantly Catholic population of about 1,300.

Beaches and machair, croft land and a hilly interior make up this compact haven of an island, which took its name from St Barr (Finbarr) of Cork who converted its people to Christianity. The seascapes have inspired many artists, writers and musicians. The history of the island echoes that of the other islands, told by its prehistoric remains, Norse names and a medieval castle. When it was bought by Colonel Gordon of Cluny in 1838, he offered to sell it to the government as a penal colony. His offer was turned down. Later, the Clearances led to massive emigration.

Castlebay

No one arriving by ferry forgets their first sight of **Castlebay** (*Bagh A Chaisteil*). **Kisimul Castle** (*t (01871) 810 313; open Easter–Oct daily 9.30–6.30; adm*) stands on a rock in the middle of the harbour. Some claim that it dates from 1060 and is one of Scotland's oldest castles, but there is no firm evidence that it existed before the 15th century. It is most romantic when silhouetted against a half-dark sky on a summer night. The Macneils acquired the castle as a reward for fighting with Robert the Bruce at Bannockburn. The clan was famous for its lawlessness, piracy and arrogance. A

Tourist Information

Barra: Main Street, Castlebay, **t** (01871) 810 336, *www.isleofbarra.com*. *Open Easter–mid-Oct.*

Where to Stay

Castlebay Hotel, Castlebay, **t** (01871) 810 223, *wwww.castlebay-hotel.co.uk* (*moderate*). Comfy and good value.

Craigard Hotel, Castlebay, **t** (01871) 810 200, *www.isleofbarra.com/craigard.html* (*moderate*). Smaller but also good.

Isle of Barra Hotel, Tangasdale Beach, **t** (01871) 810 383, *www.isleofbarra.com/iob.html* (*moderate*). Modern and in a glorious setting on the beach.

Tigh-Na-Mara, Castlebay, **t** (01871) 810 304 (*moderate*). Two minutes' walk from the ferry, with *en-suite* bedrooms, TV and tea-making facilities, and many pictures of the Prince of Wales, who paid a visit here.

Aros Cottage, North Bay, **t** (01871) 840 355, *www.isleofbarra.com/aros.html* (*budget*). A modern bungalow B&B.

Faire Mhaoldonaich, overlooking Castlebay, **t** (01871) 810 441, *www.isleofbarra.com/fm.html* (*budget*). A comfortable B&B.

Grianamul, Castlebay, **t** (01871) 810 416, *www.isleofbarra.com/grianamul.html* (*budget*). Near the ferry terminal; a friendly B&B; also self-catering.

Sea Breezes, Bruernish, Northbay, **t** (01871) 890 384, *www.isleofbarra.com/seabreezes.html*. Two well-equipped modern houses (each sleeps 4–8).

Northbay House, Balnabodach, **t** (01871) 890 255, *www.barraholidays.co.uk*. Self-catering in a former school (sleeps 4). Also does B&B (*budget*). No smoking throughout.

---

clansman from Barra is said to have declared, 'The reason there was no Macneil on Noah's Ark is that the Macneil had a boat of his own.' Traditionally, a Macneil clansman used to scale the tower daily and proclaim: 'Macneil has dined: Kings, Princes and others of the Earth may now dine.'

Martin Martin tried to gain admittance to the castle during his visit to Barra but the Macneil and his wife were away and their retainers refused to let him in, being 'very apprehensive of some Design I might have in viewing the Fort, and thereby to expose it to the Conquest of a foreign Power; of which I suppose there was no great cause of fear.' Kisimul was virtually destroyed by fire at the end of the 18th century and remained in ruins until the 45th Macneil chief, returning from his adopted homeland in America in 1937, bought it and restored it. The castle was taken over from the present Macneil, who lives abroad, by Historic Scotland, for the price of a bottle of his favourite whisky.

Neat shops and houses line the road that climbs from the harbour in Castlebay, overlooked by Heaval, Barra's highest hill (1,260ft/388m). High on Heaval's southern shoulder stands a statue of the Blessed Virgin, her child on her shoulder, holding a star. This sculpture was carved from Carrara marble and erected in 1954 to celebrate the Marian Year, and in memory of the 58 men from Barra who died in the Second World War, mostly in the Atlantic convoys. This and the large Catholic church, Our Lady, Star of the Sea, which also overlooks Castlebay, are symbols of the deep faith of the people of these islands. Martin Martin had another disappointment when he tried to see a wooden statue of St Barr, kept on the altar of one of the churches. The locals hid it whenever he tried to view it, 'lest I might take occasion to ridicule their Superstition, as some Protestants have done formerly'.

Around the Island

The Isle of **Vatersay** (*Bhatarsaigh*), just off the south coast of Barra, has a population of about 70. Until 1990, cattle destined for the market had to swim across the Sound of Vatersay to meet the ferry in Barra, but when a prize bull, Bernie, was drowned in 1986, the outcry forced the government's hand and a long-awaited causeway was built. The other islands, now uninhabited, are only accessible by private boat.

Two miles west from Castlebay, the standing stones beside the road past the Isle of Barra Hotel are said to mark the grave of a Norse pirate. **Dun Bharpa** is a large chambered cairn surrounded by standing stones, on the eastern side of Beinn Mhartainn, reached from the end of the road through Craigston.

On the eastern side of the peninsula at the north end of the island, the 2 square miles of white cockleshell strand is **Traigh Mhor**, where the plane touches down on the firm sand when the tide permits. The house, called **Suidheachan**, overlooking this impressive strand was built in 1935 for Compton Mackenzie, the writer who settled in Barra in 1928 and caught the spirit of the Hebrides more perceptively than most. He attracted a lively community of writers and Gaelic scholars and is buried in the graveyard at Eoligarry (*Eolaigearraidh*), just to the north. Here among the roofed ruins of a chapel are burial slabs said to have arrived from Iona as ballast in an ancient galley. This is **Cille Bharra** (St Barr), Barra's most important historic site, founded in the 7th century, but with the ruins of three medieval buildings dating from the 12th century. The stones in the chapel include a replica of one from the 10th–11th century. The original, discovered in 1865, is in the Museum of Scotland in Edinburgh.

Another well-known name in the cemetery is that of John MacPherson, better known to lovers of Gaeldom as 'The Coddy', who died here on his native island in 1955. *Tales from Barra*, recorded in both Gaelic and English, is a collection of folk tales told by the Coddy in his inimitable voice – a delight for exiled Scots all over the world. A grassy mound is all that remains of Eoligarry House, a three-storey Georgian house built by the Macneils after Kisimul Castle burned down in 1795 and was subsequently lived in by the MacGillivrays. Boats (*t (01871) 810 223*) run from Castlebay in the summer to the island of **Mingulay**, deserted since 1912 but enchanting, with a sandy beach and sad ruins, including a graveyard. The famous Mingulay Boat Song – a ceilidh favourite – tells of the women waiting at the harbour 'since break of day' for their fishermen who never return.

St Kilda

St Kilda, consisting of four islands and a few great rock stacks, is the most westerly of the British Isles apart from Rockall. The National Trust for Scotland owns this lonely archipelago, partly occupied by a small detachment of gunners who man a missile-tracking station, with a nature reserve managed by Scottish Natural Heritage.

The main island, on which the people used to live, is called **Hirta**, possibly derived from the old Norse for shepherd – *hirt*. The origin of the name St Kilda is disputed – there was no saint of that name. Kilda may have come from Hirta, which the islanders

Tourist Information

www.kilda.org.uk
There are a number of **cruises** to St Kilda but passengers are only able to land when weather permits, which isn't very often.

The best approach is via the NTS, **t** (0131) 243 9300, *www.nts.org.uk*, who may be able to arrange for you to join a working party. Private yachts are frequently unable to find safe shelter for long enough to anchor and go ashore.

actually pronounced Hilta. Essential reading for anyone planning a visit is *The Life and Death of St Kilda* by Tom Steel, and *An Island called Hirta* by Mary Harman. Recent archaeological work uncovered an ancient stone building thought to date from the Bronze Age, and it is thought that further research may reveal occupation for up to 3,500 years. There is the site of a pre-Viking settlement at Glen Bay but no written record until a visit by Dean Monro in 1549, who described 'a simple, poor people, scarse learnit in aney religion'. About 150 years later Martin Martin wrote of a population 'happier than the generality of mankind, as being the almost only people in the world who feel the swetness of true liberty'. He spoke too soon: subsequent history is one of decline brought about by isolation in a world increasingly obsessed by centralization and conformity. A small, patriarchal, strongly Presbyterian society subsisted, paying rent to their landlords, the Macleods of Harris and Dunvegan, with meat, feathers and oil from sea birds. (Martin Martin calculated that 180 islanders ate about 226,000 birds each year.) Pulpit-thumping ministers held them in an iron grip, regulating their lives and driving them to the kirk on pain of everlasting damnation, often to the detriment of essential work on the land. They were frequently cut off by storms. Except for 1727, when a smallpox epidemic increased the death rate, the population of about 200 in the 18th and 19th centuries remained fairly constant, kept in check by puerperal fever. The men were the Parliament, meeting daily to discuss the day's work, often using up precious daylight hours in their lengthy debate.

In 1834 the first tourist boat landed on Hirta. The introduction of money and visitors from the 'sophisticated' mainland reduced the islanders' self-reliance and made them dissatisfied: many of the younger ones left to seek their fortunes on the mainland. In 1930 the few remaining able-bodied members of the community, attracted by the lure of the outside world and dragged down by continuous hardship, persuaded the older ones to evacuate to the mainland.

Some of the houses at Village Bay have been preserved, as have their *cleits* – beehive-shaped cells of rough stone that served as larders and storerooms. The careful design of these *cleits* allowed air and wind to circulate inside and preserve the meat of the sea birds; it also kept clothes and gear dry.

A visit to this gale-torn outpost fills one with a curious melancholy, that a community could have existed here for so long, beset by worries, and then ultimately sail away and abandon its roots forever.

The Northern Isles

18

Northern Isles

40 km

20 miles

N

Muckle Flugga
Haroldswick
Baltasound
Unst
Yell
Fetlar
Ronas Hill
Esha Ness
Hillswick
Sullom
Toft
Out Skerries
Brae
Whalsay
Papa Stour
Mainland
Sandness
Shetland
Walls
Whiteness
Scalloway
Lerwick
Isle of Noss
Bressay
Sandwick
Mousa Broch
St Ninian's Isle ④
Jarlshof
Sumburgh
Sumburgh Head

A t l a n t i c

O c e a n

Foula

Fair Isle

N o r t h

S e a

Papa Westray
North Ronaldsay
Westray
Rousay
Sanday
Eday
Egilsay
Stronsay
Brough of Birsay
Birsay
Gurness Broch
Wyre
Skara Brae
Dounby
Balfour
Shapinsay
Mainland
② Maeshowe
Ring of Brodgar
Stenness
Kirkwall
Orkney
Stromness
① Scapa Flow
Old Man of Hoy
Rackwick
Lamb Holm
③
Hoy
Burray
St Margaret's Hope
South Ronaldsay
Pentland Firth
Burwick
Dunnet Head
Duncansby Head
Scrabster
John o'Groats

p.180

Orkney
Shetland
SCOTLAND
NORTHERN IRELAND
ENGLAND

Highlights

1 Wreck-diving at Scapa Flow, Orkney
2 Stone-Age burial cairn, Maeshowe, Orkney
3 Italian Chapel on Lamb Holm, Orkney
4 Mousa Broch, Shetland

Although separated by 60 miles or so of wild ocean, and very different in character, Orkney and Shetland have a common history and tend to be bracketed together. Norsemen called them the 'Nordereys' (Northern Isles). Orkney, on old red sandstone, has fertile farmland, while Shetland has poorer soil and relies on the sea. The poet Hugh MacDiarmid wrote: 'It is indeed impossible to eke out a decent living in Shetland by crofting alone. That is the difference between Orkney and Shetland: the Orcadian is a farmer with a boat, the Shetlander is a fisherman with a croft.'

Both groups – about 70 Orkney islands and 100 Shetland islands – were inhabited in the Stone Age. The Picts colonized them in the 1st century AD and were subjected to continual harassment from the Vikings for centuries, until the Norse King Harald Harfagri annexed them in 875. When Harald succeeded to the throne of Norway in about 860, large parts of his kingdom didn't recognize the authority of the Crown. Harald was in love with a Princess Gyda, daughter of one of the rebel 'kings', and she refused to marry him until he had conquered all Norway. He vowed that he would not cut his hair or his beard until he had done this. He claimed his bride 10 years later.

All the dispossessed jarls, or minor kings, took refuge in Orkney and Shetland and proceeded to harass Norway with wild Viking raids. King Harald, exasperated, collected up a fleet and sailed down to put an end to their antics. He landed at what is now Haroldswick in Unst, Shetland, and declared all the islands to be a 'Jarldom'. The Norse occupation of these islands is recorded in romantic, stirring sagas, handed down over the centuries. The *Orkneyinga Saga* is one of the best known.

By the 13th century, although still ultimately under Norse rule, the islands were presided over by Scots earls. It wasn't until Princess Margaret of Norway and Denmark became betrothed to James III of Scotland in 1468, that her father, King Christian I, pledged the islands to Scotland as part of her dowry. They were formally annexed in 1472 and ever since then they have been part of Scotland.

Norse place names still predominate, and the people of these northern islands are a blend of Norse and Scots, very different in character to the dreamy Celts of the Hebrides. They are extremely friendly, extrovert and stolid, industrious and mainly Presbyterian. Their accents are singsong; the old 'Norn' language (partly old Norse, partly Icelandic) disappeared during the 18th century although some phrases have remained, and when the islanders talk among themselves they use many words more akin to Norwegian than English.

The coming of the oil boom struck hard at established roots, bringing innovations that were not always popular, and making Shetland relatively rich compared to the rest of Scotland. On the whole, however, the islanders have managed to retain their old way of life and things have settled down.

Orkney

Orkney lies 6 miles off the north coast of Scotland, separated from the mainland by the Pentland Firth with its notoriously treacherous fast tides. On the same latitude as St Petersburg, the island group extends 53 miles from north to south and about

Getting There

British Regional Airways, t 0870 850 9850, *www.ba.com*, operates Aberdeen–Orkney.
Loganair, t (01856) 872 494, operates all the others (from Edinburgh, Glasgow, Inverness and Wick), with connections from London, Birmingham and Manchester. There is also a service from Shetland to Orkney (*Mon–Sat*). There is a short 'Airbridge' flight from Wick to Kirkwall and inter-island services.
Northlink Orkney and Shetland Ferries, t 0845 6000 449, *www.northlinkferries. co.uk*, run Aberdeen–Lerwick (12hrs), Aberdeen–Kirkwall (6hrs–7hrs 15 mins), Kirkwall–Lerwick (5hr 30 mins–7hr 45 mins) and Scrabster–Stromness (1hr 30 mins).
John o' Groats Ferries, t (01955) 611 353, *www.jogferry.co.uk*, John o' Groats–Burwick, South Ronaldsay (40–45mins). Passengers and bicycles only (*1 May–30 Sept daily*).
Pentland Ferries, t (01856) 831 226, *www. pentlandferries.co.uk*, car and passenger service, Gills Bay (mainland)–St Margaret's Hope. Special winter rates.
There are **rail** links, **t** 08457 48 49 50 (national rail enquiries), to Thurso, Aberdeen, or Wick for flight/ferry connections.
Scottish Citylink, t 08705 50 50 50, *www.citylink.co.uk*. Coaches to the various ferries and airports from major UK cities, sometimes with overnight stops in Glasgow, Edinburgh or Inverness.
The Orkney Bus, t (01955) 611 353. Inverness and Kirkwall, via the John o' Groats ferry, *www.jogferry.co.uk* (*1 May–7 Sept daily*).

Tourist Information

Orkney Tourist Board: 6 Broad Street, Kirkwall, KW15 1NX, **t** (01856) 872 856, *www. visitorkney.com*.
Stromness: t (01856) 850 716.

Events

St Magnus Festival in Kirkwall, towards the end of June, is a week of music, drama and art, attracting companies from many countries. Book well in advance, both for performances and for accommodation. For two weeks in July there is a **Craftsmen's Guild** in Kirkwall, with local craftwork. Stromness has a **Folk Festival** in May and a **Shopping Week** in July.

Where to Stay and Eat

Balfour Castle, Shapinsay, **t** (01856) 711 282, *www.balfourcastle.co.uk* (*expensive–moderate*). Run as a private hotel for up to 12 people – complete with turrets, towers and battlements. Much of the interior is unchanged from when it was created by 30 Italian craftsmen more than 150 years ago. Great, informal hospitality in a family home. *See also p.290.*
Ayre Hotel, on the harbour front, Kirkwall, **t** (01856) 873 001, *www.ayrehotel.co.uk* (*moderate*). It's 200 years old and a good place to stay if you want to be in Kirkwall. Some rooms overlook the sea.
Cleaton House, Cleaton, Westray, **t** (01857) 677 508, *www.cleatonhouse.co.uk* (*moderate*). Attractive Victorian manse, now a small, comfortable hotel, with lovely views, friendly staff and good food.
Foveran Hotel, St Ola, Kirkwall, **t** (01856) 872 389, *www.foveranhotel.co.uk* (*moderate*). Only 2 miles out of Kirkwall, with stunning views of Scapa Flow. Built in Scandinavian style in 34 acres, very peaceful. Excellent menu – particularly the seafood. The hosts will advise on where to explore.
Kirkwall Hotel, overlooking the Kirkwall harbour, **t** (01856) 872 232, *www.kirkwall hotel.com* (*moderate*). Large, French-roofed stone building of 1890. Comfortable, with a good restaurant.

23 miles from west to east. Oslo is closer than London. Nineteen of the 70 islands are inhabited. Orkney means 'seal islands', the *ey* being Norse for islands: no one talks of 'the Orkneys', just Orkney. First impressions are of emerald green plateaux of turf above sheer rock cliffs and sandy beaches washed by sparkling sea; fertile farmland with large farmhouses, many producing Orkney cheese, and more cattle than sheep.

Standing Stones Hotel, on the shore of Loch Stenness, t (01856) 850 449, *www.standing stoneshotel.co.uk* (*moderate*). Fishing hotel in a lovely position, congenial and comfortable despite the 'modern' décor.

Stromness Hotel, Stromness, t (01856) 850 298, *www.stromnesshotel.com* (*moderate*). Your safest bet: traditional stone-built hotel overlooking the harbour. Handy for the ferry, with good food.

Taversoe Inn, Rousay, t (01856) 821 325 (*moderate*). Has glorious views.

West End Hotel, Main Street, Kirkwall, t (01856) 872 368, *www.orkneyisles. co.uk/westendhotel* (*moderate*). Small hotel with character, built in 1824. Good local atmosphere in the lounge bar.

Mrs Anderson, Rickla, Sandwick, t (01756) 761 575, *www.rickla.com* (*moderate–budget*). First-class B&B, peaceful and welcoming.

Mrs Forsyth, 21 Willowburn Road, Kirkwall, t (01856) 874 020 (*moderate–budget*). Cosy B&B.

Barony Hotel, Birsay, t (01856) 721 327, *www.baronyhotel.com* (*budget*). Orkney's oldest fishing hotel is a fairly inexpensive and friendly place to stay.

The Belsair, Sanday, t (01857) 600 206, *joy@sanday.quista.net* (*budget*).

Beltane Guest House, Papa Westray, t (01857) 644 267 (*budget*). Converted terraced cottages. Small, cosy, very friendly and they will collect you from the boat or plane. Good food, with the community shop next door.

Ferry Inn, John Street, Stromness, t (01856) 850 280, *www.ferryinn.com* (*budget*). Unpretentious, with strong nautical flavour.

Kettletoft Hotel, Sanday, t (01857) 600 217 (*budget*). Small family-run hotel in village.

Mrs Flett, Sanday, t (01857) 600 467 (*budget*). B&B. A comfortable guesthouse.

Mrs Strachan, Sinclair View, 5 Franklin Road, Stromness, t (01856) 850 199 (*budget*). Comfortable B&B – you will be well looked after.

Mrs Wallace, Shapinsay, t (01856) 711 256, *jean@girnigoe.net* (*budget*). Cosy B&B and good dinner.

The Observatory Guest House, North Ronaldsay, t (01857) 633 200, *www.nrbo. f2s.com* (*budget*). Stay in solar- and wind-powered accommodation.

The Robertsons, Mill of Eyrland, Stenness, t (01856) 850 136, *www.millofeyrland.co.uk* (*budget*). B&B in a comfortable converted water mill with a lovely garden. The two-room Hopper Suite is for up to 5 people.

Mrs Currie, 1 Dundas Crescent, Kirkwall, t (01856) 873 541, *brandyquoy@ netscapeonline.co.uk*. Self-catering house in a walled garden overlooking the Earl's Palace (sleeps 6).

Mrs Francis, Outbrecks, Stenness, t (01856) 851 223, *www.outbreakscottages-orkney.co.uk*. Six charming old self-catering Orkney stone cottages with wonderful views (sleeps 4–5).

Mr Gray, St Ola, Kirkwall, t (01856) 874 590, *www.orkneyholidays.com*. Two self-catering flats (sleeps 4).

Ms Rae, Rousay, t (01856) 821 252. Self-catering semi-detached house (sleeps 3).

Mrs Thomson, Sanday, t (01857) 600 339. Self-catering farmhouse on a working farm with lovely views (sleeps 6).

Mrs Towrie, Sanday, t (01857) 600 347. Modern self-catering bungalow (sleeps 6).

Mr Work, Kirkwall, t (01856) 873 235. Self-catering cottage and stables (sleeps 4).

Old Kirk, Skara Brae, Sandwick, t (01856) 771 570. Self-catering in a splendid setting (sleeps 8).

Creel Inn and Restaurant, Front Road, St Margaret's Hope, South Ronaldsay, t (01856) 831 311, *www.thecreel.co.uk* (*moderate*). Some of the finest food in Orkney, and you can stay here as well.

The Hamnavoe Restaurant, Graham Street, Stromness (*moderate*), t (01856) 850 606. Delicious and imaginative food, especially the seafood, with an open fire.

Inland there is more wild heathland. Apart from Hoy, nothing is higher than 900ft (278m). A great dome of clear sky sheds an ethereal greenish light, and sunsets in May and June are fantastic; at midsummer the sun is above the horizon for 18 hours – it is possible to read a book outside all night. This midsummer twilight is called 'Grimlins' from the Norse word *grimla*, to glimmer or twinkle.

Bird-watching is almost compulsive. One in six of all sea birds breeding in Britain nests in Orkney. The long-eared owl, its 'ears' elongated feathers, is an endearing resident. Its low, moaning hoot is an eerie sound at night. Short-eared owls hunt by day over the moors; there are also red-throated divers, razorbills and puffins.

For **botanists** the wild flowers are a joy: tiny *Primula scotica*, a survivor from the last Ice Age; grass-of-Parnassus, whose honey-scented white flowers litter the marshland; bog pimpernel, oyster plant, bog asphodel and many, many more. For general **naturalists** there is the unique Orkney vole to look out for, a sweet little round ball of fur. There are otters – in fact, Kirkwall must be just about the only town to display a red triangular road sign reading: 'Otters Crossing 100yds'.

Fishermen leave Orkney with enough fishing stories to keep them happy till they return. Brown trout are the best in Britain and fishing is free, thanks to Norse law. Sea angling is also good. **Water sports** enthusiasts will find perfect waters for **subaqua** diving, especially wreck-diving around Scapa Flow. There are also more prehistoric remains than anywhere else in Scotland, some in a remarkable state of preservation: brochs, standing stones, burial cairns – an average of three sites per square mile.

It is beyond the scope of this book to describe each of the many hundreds of historic sites and antiquities that pepper Orkney: the Orkney Tourist Board in Kirkwall has a good selection of guides, including *The Orkney Guide Book*, *The History of Orkney* and *Ancient Monuments of Orkney*, as well as booklets on specific sites.

Mainland Orkney

When an Orcadian talks of the Mainland, he means Mainland Orkney – the big island. (The mainland of Scotland is 'the sooth'.)

Kirkwall

Kirkwall is the capital of Orkney and one of the earliest established Norse trading towns. It is referred to in *The Orkneyinga Saga* as *Kirkjuvagr* – Church-bay-of-the-Vikings – indicating that the Norsemen found an Early Christian church here when they arrived. It is an ideal centre from which to explore these fascinating islands.

St Magnus Cathedral (*open Mon–Sat; only open for worship on Sun*) dominates the town, though it is not in fact as large as its clever proportions suggest. This cruciform building, founded in 1137, was built up of alternating stripes of local red sandstone and yellow stone and looks more continental than Scottish. St Magnus, who was murdered in 1116 and whose canonization may have been more political

The Ba' Game

Kirkwall has its own unique 'Ba' Game' dating from Norse times, loosely described as football. It is played on Christmas Day and New Year's Day, between the 'trsuppies' and 'trsdoonies' and often involves as many as 150 men from either end of the town. If the ball finishes up in the harbour, it is victory for the 'trsuppies'; if it reaches the goal at the old castle, then the 'trsdoonies' win. The game can last all day.

than spiritual, was the uncle of Jarl Rognvald Kilson, the founder of the cathedral. The bones of both these men were discovered during repair work in the 20th century, hidden in chests beneath the columns of the central bay of the choir. The cathedral has been carefully restored; the rose window is modern but the east window dates from 1511. Although St Magnus is still called a cathedral, the services are Church of Scotland.

The old part of the town clusters around the cathedral, with the ruin of the 12th-century **Bishop's Palace** next door (*open April–Sept daily 9.30–6.30; adm*). It was built for Bishop William the Old. It was also here that poor old King Haakon of Norway died, having struggled back this far from his defeat by Alexander III at Largs in 1263. It was rebuilt in the late 15th century and restored in the mid-16th century by Bishop Robert Reid, the founder of Edinburgh University. Further work was done by Earl Patrick Stewart who saw it as his own fortified residence.

Across the road from the Bishop's Palace is the ruin of the **Earl's Palace** (*open April–Sept daily 9.30–6.30; adm*), built by forced labour for the much-loathed tyrant, Earl Patrick Stewart at the beginning of the 17th century. The palace is L-shaped with attractive angle-turrets, once described as 'the most mature and accomplished piece of Renaissance architecture in Scotland'. The carved decorations, the oriel windows and the magnificent Great Hall are splendid, but the design was never completed. The Earl ran out of money and shortly afterwards was arrested for treason. In his capacity as Steward of Orkney and Shetland, the Earl forced the islanders to do 'all sorts of servile and painful labour without either meat, drink or hire, and his final crime was to implicate his adolescent illegitimate son instead of himself. He was executed in 1615 for his crimes against humanity, having been given a week's reprieve to learn the Lord's Prayer.

The **Orkney Museum** (*Tankerness House, Broad Street; open all year Mon–Sat 9.30–5; also May–Sept Sun 2–5; adm*) is in a well-restored 16th-century town house with an attractive courtyard and garden. Its oldest part was built in 1574 by the first Protestant priest, Archdeacon Gilbert Fulzie, as his residence. It was remodelled in 1820 by the Baikies of Tankerness, who owned it from 1641. Over 4,000 years of Orkney's history are well displayed. **Orkney Library** (*open Mon–Sat*), founded in 1683, is one of the oldest public libraries in Scotland and has an excellent Orkney Room for those wanting to go deeply into the islands' history. The **Wireless Museum**, near the harbour (*open April–Sept; adm*), gives a fascinating history of early domestic radio and wartime communications.

The **Mercat Cross** on Kirk Green by the cathedral, dates from 1621 though it was only moved here in 1762. The Cross is a replica, the original being inside the cathedral. This is where the 'Ba' is thrown up, to start the Christmas and New Year 'Ba' Games'. Public proclamations were always made from the Cross and it was also used as the town pillory. Kirk Green is the venue for the annual St Magnus Fair in August.

Stromness

Stromness, about 17 miles west of Kirkwall, is the only other proper town in Orkney and the terminal for the car ferry from Scrabster. It is a delightful place, full of charm and character, reminiscent of a Norwegian fishing village. Many of the narrow, twisting streets are cobbled and paved, tightly packed with stone houses, two and three storeys high, with gable ends to the street or harbour, many with their own landing stages. Due to wild weather, windows are small, set deep into thick walls. Many houses have been converted into shops, but retain their traditional character.

Stromness has a long history of catering for the needs of passing ships. From the 17th to the 19th centuries, Britain's various wars made the English Channel a dangerous place for trading vessels and most of them chose to take the route round the north of Scotland, despite the risk of encountering privateers. The Hudson's Bay Company did much of their recruiting in Stromness from about 1702 and appointed a Stromness merchant, David Geddes, as their local agent in 1791. By this time Orcadians comprised three-quarters of the company's workforce in Canada, and their ships used Stromness as a port for provisions and water until the early 1900s. Captain Cook, the great navigator, used the port, and his ships *Discovery* and *Resolution* called in on their return from the South Seas after their captain had been clubbed and stabbed to death in Hawaii in 1779.

From the 1770s whaling ships from Dundee and Hull, looking for young men skilled in small boats, took on crew from Stromness and engaged local merchants, establishing a link with the whaling industry until after 1900. Walter Scott immortalized John Gow, an 18th-century pirate from Stromness, in his book *The Pirate*.

The **Pier Arts Centre** (*open Tues–Sun*) occupies a well-restored 18th-century building and has an excellent collection of 20th-century paintings. **Stromness Natural History Museum** (*open daily 10–5; closed for lunch in winter; adm*) has collections of birds, fossils, shells and butterflies. There are exhibitions covering whaling, fishing, the Hudson's Bay Company, Scapa Flow and the German fleet.

Scapa Flow

Scapa Flow is a great inlet to the south of the Mainland, surrounded by protective islands. This perfect deep-water anchorage, up to 10 miles wide, was adopted as the main base of the Grand Fleet in 1912. At the end of the First World War the German Navy sailed their fleet into Scapa, having surrendered. Then, on 21 July 1919 on the order of Rear Admiral Ludwig von Reuter, whose pride balked at the shame of surrender, the whole fleet of 74 warships was scuttled. At the beginning of the Second World War a German U-boat crept through the defences and sank the *Royal Oak*, after which the Churchill Barriers were erected.

In 1916 a German U-boat managed to cross Scapa Flow, in spite of blockades, and sail north to lay mines off Birsay. One of these was hit by HMS *Hampshire*, which was carrying General Kitchener on his way to Russia at the age of 66. He was killed, together with all but 12 of the ship's company, and there is a memorial to him at Marwick Head, overlooking the place where the warship went down.

Today, sculptural wrecks break the water in violent contrast to the peaceful, lovely scenery. Most of the wrecks have been salvaged, but several remain on the bottom, giving great scope for wreck-diving.

Brough of Birsay is a tidal island reached by a causeway which is open for about two hours at low tide. There are the remains of a Viking village here and a Romanesque church, St Magnus, built in 1064 and rebuilt in 1664 and 1760, where St Magnus' body was taken after his murder in 1116, to be interred later in the cathedral. This is a good place for 'wave-watching'. Back across the causeway to the village of Birsay, there is a huge palace built by Earl Patrick Stewart, with very fine stonework. At the farmhouse close by there is a double water mill with both over- and undershot wheels, and a third which is the last water mill for meal in Orkney. There have been mills here since Viking times. Walk northeast along the footpath to **Skipi Geo**, a former fisherman's cove with a restored turf-roofed hut and two of the cleets they used for hauling up the boats in winter. (There are more of these huts at **Sand Geo** a couple of miles south of Marwick Head.) A few hundred yards beyond Skipi Geo there is a huge whalebone like a gigantic sculptured bird. A little further on, **Longaglebe Geo** is a wonderful 700ft (200m) gorge eroded by the sea. In early summer the cliffs are covered in colourful wild flowers and nesting birds.

Maeshowe and the Ring of Brodgar

Maeshowe (open April–Sept daily 9.30–6.30, last adm 6; Oct–Mar Mon–Sat 9.30–4.30, last adm 4, Sun 2–4.30; adm), 10 miles west of Kirkwall, off the main road to Stromness, is unquestionably the most outstanding Stone Age burial cairn in Britain. The passage into the cairn, made of huge single slabs of stone, is so aligned that a shaft of sunlight pierces its 36ft (11m) length into the chamber on only one day of the year, that of the winter solstice. Burial cells lead off the main chamber which has massive stone buttresses in each corner.

When Maeshowe was first excavated in 1861 the cells were found to be empty, and this fact, together with runic Viking inscriptions on the walls, misled archaeologists into thinking the tomb was Norse. Then it became obvious that the structure dates back to many centuries before that, probably to around 3500 BC. The Vikings came much later, sacking the tombs and leaving their graffiti on the walls. In fact the graffiti is just as fascinating as the much older cairn. There are references to treasure and to the Crusades, and a collection of sex slogans that are as modern as any today: 'Thorny was bedded, Helgi says so', reads one; 'Ingigerd is the best of them all', says another. Tours (timed tickets) last 45 minutes and start from the visitor centre at **Tormiston Mill**, a restored 19th-century water mill with a shop and café.

The **Ring of Brodgar** is on the narrow neck of land between Harray and Stenness Lochs, 4 miles northwest of Maeshowe. From the original 60 stones, 36 remain. They are precisely set at 6 degrees apart, with a surrounding ditch cut from bedrock, crossed by two causeways. These stones date from about 1560 BC and are believed to be some sort of lunar observatory. See these stones at dawn or dusk to get full benefit of the weird light and the shadows they cast.

The Stones of Stenness and Skara Brae

The **Stones of Stenness** date from around the 3rd millennium BC, only four stones remaining of the original circle. Excavations uncovered an almost square setting of horizontal stones, scattered with fragments of cremated bones, charcoal and shards of pottery, indicating that this must have been some sort of cremation and burial site.

The two outlying stones were probably associated with this circle, as must have been the many cists and cairns that have been unearthed in this area.

Skara Brae (*open April–Sept daily 9.30–6.30, last adm 6; Oct–Mar Mon–Sat 9.30–4.30, Sun 2–4.30; last adm 4; adm*) is 5 miles northwest of the Stones of Stenness, on the west coast and on the southern arm of the sandy sweep of the **Bay of Skaill**. This was a Stone Age settlement, hit by a massive storm that buried it in sand for about 4,000 years. Another storm then blew away some of the sand to reveal the village. It is unique, giving an insight into the whole way of life of those prehistoric tribes, rather than just revealing a burial cairn which tells only a fraction of their story. Careful excavation has uncovered about six of the original ten single-roomed houses and a workshop with covered passages from one to another, as well as a communal paved courtyard. Lack of wood meant they used stone for their furniture, and the old bed platforms, cupboards, hearths, fish tanks and tables can still be seen, as well as a fascinating collection of tools and implements. Midden (rubbish heap) excavations have revealed that the inhabitants of this earliest-known fishing village in Scotland were also farmers. A small museum gives more details of the site.

While you are at Skara Brae, you should visit nearby **Skaill House** (*open April–Sept daily 9.30–6.30; adm*), overlooking the lovely Bay of Skaill. It is one of the most complete 17th-century mansion houses in Orkney, surrounded by lawns and gardens. Built in the 1620s for Bishop George Graham, it has been added to by successive lairds ever since. Inside the beautifully restored rooms, including the Bishop's rather cosy bedroom, you can see such things as Captain Cook's dinner service.

Northeast of Skara Brae

Orkney's only surviving **Click Mill** is beyond Dounby about 8 miles northeast of Skara Brae. It is a horizontal water wheel, built in about 1800 from an earlier design and so called from the noise it makes as it turns. It is preserved in working order although the pool has been drained. A couple of miles to the south, **Corrigall Farm Museum** (*open Mar–Oct daily; adm*) is an excellent re-creation of a mid-19th-century farmstead: buildings, implements, household artefacts and the native livestock.

On the wild, windswept headland at **Gurness**, 5 miles northeast of the Click Mill, there is one of the best preserved brochs in Orkney (*open daily; adm*) dating from about the 1st century BC. A booklet describes the complicated layout of the site. Built as a broch, it was occupied by Picts and then by Vikings, who added to the original structure. It includes domestic buildings, Norse longhouses and a well.

Islands South of Mainland

Lamb Holm

Lamb Holm is linked by a mile of causeway south of the Mainland. When the Churchill Barriers were erected at the beginning of the Second World War, 1,700 men worked on them including Italian POWs. Homesick for their warm, Catholic land, these Italians created the **Italian Chapel** out of two Nissen huts on Lamb Holm in their spare time. It is a miracle of faith with its cast-concrete altar and altar rail, delicate wrought-iron tracery, and plasterboard painted to resemble bricks and marble. Domenico Chioccetti, who painted the frescoes, including a Madonna and Child behind the altar, returned in 1960 to restore his work. He died in 1999. On the 50th anniversary of the chapel's completion a group of the original Italian prisoners came back to commemorate their work, known locally as 'The Miracle of Camp 60'. **Burray**, linked to Lamb Holm by a causeway to the south, has a **Fossil Centre** (*open April–Sept; adm*) with fossilized fish over 300 million years old. There is a café at the museum.

South Ronaldsay

South Ronaldsay, joined by causeway to Burray, has a picturesque village on its north coast, **St Margaret's Hope**, the third largest in Orkney – with a poignant memory. In 1290 the seven-year-old Princess Margaret, Maid of Norway, died of seasickness in the ship bringing her from Norway to marry Prince Edward of England and unite their countries. The ship bearing the wasted body of the little princess put in to St Margaret's Hope. It is a picturesque place in a sheltered bay, with houses dating from the 17th century. In the 19th century it was a busy fishing port. The **Tomb of the Eagles**(*t (01856) 831 339, adm; call at Liddle Farm first*), on the southeast toe of South Ronaldsay, is so named because of the many sea-eagle claws found in the Stone Age chambered tomb which you can crawl into. Mr Simison, the farmer who found and excavated the tomb, will usher you along a wonderful clifftop walk to see it, and will tell you all about it. He will also show you, on a different site in the same field, an equally fascinating Stone Age house complete with oven and cooking facilities. Back in the delightfully amateur 'museum', his daughter will let you hold 5,000-year-old tools, skulls and claws.

Hoy

Hoy (Norse '*Haey*' – High Island), the largest island after Mainland, about 3 miles south of Stromness, is the only one that is not flat, and has scenery much more like Shetland. Its hills give a good backdrop to views over the rest of the islands' flat green farmland. Ward Hill rises to 1,500ft (460m).

The **Old Man of Hoy** is a familiar outline, a towering pinnacle of horizontally layered rock, sandstone on basalt, 450ft (138m) high on a promontory above the sea off the northwest coast. It is a favourite challenge to serious rock climbers; the first successful climb was in 1966, by a three-man team led by Chris Bonnington. Legend, however, tells of an elderly local who swarmed to the top for a bet, with no climbing aids, and, having left his pipe on the summit, went back to retrieve it. A marked path takes you up from Rackwick to a good vantage point, taking about 90 minutes. **Rackwick** itself is well worth seeing, with a beautiful bay surrounded by cliffs, and attractive, scattered cottages, done up in traditional style with old stone roofs.

The **Dwarfie Stane** is the only example of a rock-cut tomb in Britain, a huge rectangular red-sandstone boulder, hollowed out for a body about 5,000 years ago. It has a beautifully fitting carved block for a door and you can crawl inside. In Walter Scott's *The Pirate*, it was the favourite residence of Trold, a dwarf from Norse legend.

There is a Persian inscription among the graffiti carved in 1850 by the somewhat eccentric Major William Mouncey who had been a spy in Afghanistan and Persia and who spent several nights in this tomb in Persian dress.

St John's Head, not far north of the Old Man of Hoy, is part of a 1,140ft (350m) vertical cliff, teeming with sea birds and rare plants. Just off the main road south, clearly visible, is a white-washed gravestone – **Betty Corrigall's Grave**. Left pregnant and deserted by a visiting sailor in the 19th century, this young girl from Lyness committed suicide. By law she was not allowed to be buried in hallowed ground, and she was buried in this lonely spot on the parish boundary. **Melsetter House**, on the south coast (*not open to the public but visible from the road*), was built on to an older house in 1896 by the famous Arts and Crafts architect W. R. Lethaby. New and old have been kept distinct, but the scale and materials blend nicely into the Orkney landscape. The earlier part was looted by Jacobites in 1745.

Islands North and East of Mainland

Shapinsay

Shapinsay, to the east of the Mainland, guards the entrance to Kirkwall harbour and it was from Elwick Bay that King Haakon sailed south in 1263 to his ignominious defeat at Largs. Earlier still, in AD 84, it is said that one of Agricola's galleys was wrecked at Grucula on the west coast. **Balfour Castle** in the southwest corner was designed by David Bryce in 1848 for a Colonel Balfour and his son, who did much to improve the farming methods on the island. You get a good view of this imposing pile, with its turrets, towers and battlements, from the ferry from Kirkwall. It is now run as a private hotel (*see* p.282). There are guided tours of the castle and Victorian gardens on Sundays from mid-May to mid-September. Much of the interior is unchanged from when it was created by 30 Italian craftsmen 150 years ago. At **Burroughston** there is a reconstructed broch, with illustrated explanations of its features. Shapinsay's Lairobell Farm goat's cheese is particularly tasty, in spite of its maker's struggles with EU bureaucracy, and is worth seeking out.

Rousay

Rousay, a couple of miles northeast of Mainland, has a burial cairn at **Midhowe** on the west coast. This cairn has a chamber with 24 burial cells leading off it, in which

Washington Irving

In 1760 a family called Irving emigrated from Quholm in the northeastern corner of Shapinsay. They sided with the rebels in the American Revolution and made their fortune. Washington Irving, born in 1783, became America's first internationally renowned writer. He returned to Britain and struck up a friendship with Sir Walter Scott, who persuaded him to go back to America and write a number of best-selling essays and tales, including adaptations of *Rip Van Winkle* and *The Legend of Sleepy Hollow*. He also wrote a five-volume biography of George Washington.

the remains of 25 human bodies were found, earning it the name 'The Great Ship of Death'. Another tomb on the island, **Taversoe Tuick**, is unusual because it is two-storeyed. One tomb sits on top of the other, each with its own entrance passage. The Jacobean-style mansion, **Trumland House**, at the south end of the island, was built by David Bryce in 1876 for General Sir Frederick William Traill-Burroughs. Known locally as 'the Little General' and 'the worst landlord in Orkney', Burroughs made life impossible for his crofting tenants and caused much unrest and hatred. In contrast, in the 1930s, Walter Grant lived here and used his considerable wealth and resources to employ leading archaeologists to excavate many of the important prehistoric sites.

Wyre, a mile southeast of Rousay, has the ruin of a 12th-century stone castle, one of the oldest square keeps in Scotland, known as **Cubbie Roo's Castle** and probably the stronghold of a Norse robber baron. There is a ruined 12th-century chapel, **St Mary's**.

Egilsay

Egilsay is 2 miles east of Rousay. **St Magnus Church** marks the site of the murder of Jarl Magnus in 1116. The ruined church dominates this small, low-lying island, with a tall, tapering round tower at the west end. This design is of Irish origin, indicating close contact between Ireland and Orkney during Viking times. It was probably built in the 12th century and its walls still stand to their full height. The tower, at nearly 50ft (15m), was once taller and seems to beckon from all around. Magnus was killed on the order of his rival Earl Haakon who wanted sole power over Orkney. Egilsay has a large proportion of incomers in its small population. On **Eday**, 4 miles to the east of Egilsay, there are chambered tombs and an Iron Age dwelling that was once a roundhouse with radial divisions inside.

Westray, Papa Westray and North Ronaldsay

Westray, 7 miles north of Rousay, is one of the most Orcadian in atmosphere, having fewer resident incomers. The formidable ruin of **Noltland Castle** at its north end was built in 1560 by Gilbert Balfour, who was implicated in the murder of Cardinal Beaton and served his punishment on a French galley beside John Knox. He was later Master of the Household for Mary, Queen of Scots. Its design is Z-plan with all-round visibility and an extravagant provision of gun loops. It was burned by Covenanters in 1650.

Southwest of Noup Head, 'The Gentleman's Cave' was a refuge for a number of Orkney lairds who supported the Jacobite cause in 1745. Tradition links the cave to Noltland Castle by an underground tunnel. It is tricky to get to and you should seek local advice before trying.

Papa Westray, 2 miles off the northeast tip of Westray, is so called from the hermits who lived in the cells here. This island was part of an important Norse family estate in the 11th and 12th centuries and archaeologists discovered the remains of Neolithic settlements which have provided valuable clues to the lifestyle of those ancient inhabitants, including the earliest standing dwelling house in northwest Europe, dating from 3500 BC.

North Ronaldsay is the most northerly island of Orkney, 15 miles east of Papa Westray and 32 miles northeast of Kirkwall. It is surrounded by a sea dyke designed to keep the unique breed of sheep off the grass, so that they feed from the rich seaweed on the shore. The meat of these small, sturdy animals has a distinctive flavour as a result. **Sanday**, south of North Ronaldsay, has sandy beaches and fertile farmland dotted with large, stone 19th-century farmhouses.

Shetland

According to Tacitus, when the Romans sailed round the north coast of Scotland and found Britain was an island, they 'discovered and subdued' Orkney but they 'left Shetland alone because of the wild seas that lay between them'. He called Shetland *Ultima Thule*, that mythical island the ancients believed lay on the edge of the world.

Sixty miles north of Orkney and halfway to Norway, Shetland is extreme, dramatic and magical enough for *Ultima Thule* to seem entirely appropriate – not just one

Getting There

British Airways, t 0870 850 9850, *www.ba.com*, flies from Aberdeen (1hr), as well as from Glasgow, Edinburgh and Inverness. Flights connect with those from and to many UK and international airports. **Atlantic Airways, t** (01737) 214255, *www.flyshetland.com*, run direct flights from London Stansted in to Shetland in summer.

Sumburgh Airport is 25 miles from Lerwick and there is a connecting bus service as well as taxis. Self-drive cars can be hired at the airport.

Northlink Orkney and Shetland Ferries, t 0845 6000 449, *www.northlinkferries.co.uk*. Ferry routes between Aberdeen and Lerwick. *Check website for latest schedules.*

Smyril Line, *www.smyril-line.com*, run a summer ferry service from Shetland to Denmark, Norway, Iceland and Faroe. NorthLink have their brochures.

Getting Around

Loganair runs a regular inter-island service from Tingwall Airport, Lerwick, to the islands of Foula, Fair Isle, Papa Stour and Out Skerries. A frequent passenger and drive on/drive off **car ferry** links most of the islands with the Shetland Mainland; passenger fares are very cheap. Advance booking is recommended at peak times. Full details of schedules and fares are at Lerwick's Tourist Information Centre.

With 500 miles of roads, personal transport is the best way of exploring Shetland, either in your own car, or a hire car. **Bicycles** can also be hired.

For **coach** tours try John Leask, **t** (01595) 693 162.

For sightseeing and sea-angling trips, try **Cycharters, t** (01595) 696 598.

Tourist Information

www.visitshetland.com
Lerwick: Market Cross, Shetland ZE1 0LU, **t** 08701 999 440.
Wildlife Tours, t (01950) 422 483.

Festivals and Activities

Up-Helly-Aa is held in Lerwick on the last Tuesday in January and is a survival from Viking days. This pagan fire festival used to mark the end of Yuletide and symbolize a desire for the sun to appear again after the long winter nights. In the old days blazing barrels of tar were rolled through the streets and carried to the tops of the hills.

Fiddle music is still very popular throughout the islands. Fiddling and dancing at Islesburgh Community Centre in Lerwick provide lively entertainment (*Wed evenings in summer*), and the **Shetland Folk Festival** is a must for music-lovers (*April*), as is the **Shetland Accordion and Fiddle Festival** (*Oct*).

island but 100, of which 15 are continuously inhabited. An archipelago of outstanding beauty, the perfect place for peace and solitude. In spite of being on the same latitude as Greenland, the climate is mild because of the Gulf Stream, with plenty of summer sunshine and less rain than the Western Isles (but more than its fair share of wind). Like Orkney, Shetland has long summer nights, the 'simmer dim' twilight of midsummer. The name Shetland is derived from the Norse word *hjaltland*, meaning Highland. Locals talk about Shetland, never the Shetlands, and when they talk about the Mainland they are referring to the principal island.

Much of the terrain is peat bog and rough Highland hillside, carpeted with heather and turf and dotted with small lochs – not so green and fertile as it is in Orkney. Ronas Hill to the northwest of the Mainland is the highest point at 1,475ft (454m), and nowhere is more than 3 miles from the sea. The narrow roads deter caravans and coaches. There is wonderful cliff scenery with long winding inlets called 'voes',

Where to Stay and Eat

Burrastow House, overlooking Vaila Sound on Shetland's most westerly point, t (01595) 809 307, *burr.hs@zetnet.co.uk* (*expensive*). An 18th-century 'Haa'; small and very comfortable, with gourmet locally-produced food. The view from the Tester bed must be one of the best views in Scotland, and from the terrace you can see seals and otters. A ghillie and boat are available.

Grand Hotel, Commercial Street, Lerwick, t (01595) 692 826, *www.kgqhotels.co.uk* (*expensive*). In the town centre, with an imposing castellated tower and Shetland's only nightclub.

Kveldsro House Hotel, Lerwick, t (01595) 692 195, *www.shetlandhotels.com* (*expensive*). Luxury hotel overlooking the harbour.

Lerwick Hotel, t (01595) 692 166, *www. shetlandhotels.com* (*expensive*). 10 minutes' walk from the town centre, a comfortable modern building with a glorious view.

Queens Hotel, Commercial Street, Lerwick, t (01595) 692 826, *www.kgqhotels.co.uk* (*expensive*). Picturesque, old-fashioned and comfortable hotel right on the water.

Shetland Hotel, Holmsgarth Road, Lerwick, t (01595) 695 515, *www.shetlandhotels.com* (*expensive*). Comfortable, modern hotel, opposite the ferry terminal. Well run with friendly staff.

Busta House Hotel, Brae, overlooking Busta Voe, t (01806) 522 506, *www.bustahouse.com* (*expensive–moderate*). Large country house in a nice garden, with good food and 120 different malt whiskies.

Baltasound Hotel, Baltasound, Unst, t (01957) 711 334, *www.baltasound-hotel.shetland. co.uk* (*moderate*). Britain's most northerly hotel; log-cabin style rooms.

Buness House, Baltasound, Unst, t (01957) 711 315, *www.users.zetnet.co.uk/buness- house* (*moderate*). Wolsey Lodge in a 17th-century house, good food, glorious views.

Sumburgh Hotel, Virkie, t (01950) 460 201, *www.sumburgh-hotel.zetnet.co.uk* (*moderate*). Old manor house, next to Jarlshof, with wonderful views and a friendly atmosphere. Good value.

Alderlodge Guest House, 6 Clairmont Place, Lerwick, t (01595) 695 705 (*budget*). Sturdy, stone-built house with large, comfortable rooms and wholesome Scottish food.

Breiview Guest House, 40 Kantersted Rd, Lerwick, t (01595) 695 956, *www.breiview guesthouse.co.uk* (*budget*). Good value, modern house, 20 minutes' walk from the town centre, and there is a sandy beach within close reach.

Broch Guest House, Upper Scalloway, t (01595) 880 767, *www.brochhouse.shetland.co.uk* (*budget*). Modern no-smoking house.

Hildasay Guest House, Scalloway, t (01595) 880 822 (*budget*). Good value and will arrange trout fishing for you.

Mrs Gifford, 12 Burgh Road, Lerwick, t (01595) 693 554 (*budget*). Quiet and central.

battered into arches, fissures and jagged stacks, eroded by wind and sea into sculpture for giants. Few trees survive the gale-force winds that lash these islands.

Dairy farming and vegetable crops thrive in the south and central Mainland, and sheep-farming is important, including the black and brown Shetland sheep. The Shetland cabbage is salt resistant and grown as a fodder crop. Knitwear from the islands is world-famous. In the old days the wool was plucked, or 'roo'ed', from the sheep's neck by hand, being too fine for shears, but this is no longer common except with some show animals. A true Shetland shawl should be so fine it can be pulled through a wedding ring. The colours of the landscapes and seascapes enhanced by the extraordinary clarity of light must have had a strong influence on the natural shades used in the knitwear, particularly those in the Fair Isle designs.

Shetland ponies – not strictly wild, as they are all owned – roam over the hills and common grazings. Originally mini-draught horses on the crofts, they were then bred for work in coal mines, with 'as much strength as possible and as near the ground as can be got'. The skeleton of one found in the middle of Jarlshof Broch was smaller than the modern breed. Their tail hair was used as fishing line and it was illegal to steal hair from another man's horse. Peat cutting is still an important part of life and you will see intricately built peat stacks along the lonely roads, transported to the houses in decrepit old cars these days, instead of in pony panniers.

The old life of crofting, fishing and knitting was greatly changed when the oil boom hit Shetland, but the oil depots are well confined to the Sullom Voe area on the Mainland. They have not spoiled the rest of the islands and brought a new prosperity. In fact, it is easy to spend a holiday in Shetland and never catch a glimpse of the oil industry – the installations along Sullom Voe don't even break the skyline.

On these islands you can experience the sensation of being the only human being in a world of birds, animals and flowers, with the melody of myriad bird songs harmonizing with the ever-restless sea. For **ornithologists** there are huge colonies of birds, both northern and migrant. Among the hundreds of species to be seen is the Shetland wren – the 'stinkie' – even smaller than her more common cousin. Fair Isle, halfway to Orkney, has an observation station and is a famous staging post for migrants. With such a variety, Shetland is a twitcher's paradise.

For **botanists** the wild flowers are marvellous: there are around 500 species of plants to discover. Because much of the pasture land is untreated, many that have become rare elsewhere have survived here, including the rather hideous large Australian daisy. On Shetland, you can also find arctic flowers, the American mondey flower and the tiny blue caucasus from Asia Minor. For **naturalists** there are vast quantities of seals to watch, basking on the rocks, known locally as 'selkies' (too many of them, from the fishermen's point of view, due to culling restrictions). Otters can be seen around small rocks and skerries, too, in the more remote coastal areas. Whales, killer whales, sharks, dolphins and porpoises can all be seen off the coast.

Trout fishing is excellent in the lochs, of which there are more than 300, with brownies up to 8lbs (3½kg), and there are some salmon (including escapees from salmon farms). Sea trout can be caught, spinning from beaches or where a burn enters the sea (but not on Sundays). Char can be caught on the Loch of Girlsta. Fishing permits can be bought from the tourist office in Lerwick, where you can also get details about boats and local associations. **Sea angling** is first class and fishermen catch cod, halibut, tusk and many other white fish. Porbeagle shark of up to 450lbs (200kg) have been caught in local waters and the current European record of a 226.8lb (103kg) skate is held by Shetland. There is a staggering wealth of prehistoric remains for **archaeologists** and some of the most glorious **walking** in Scotland. Ask at the tourist office for the series of books by Peter Guy on walking in Shetland.

Mainland

Mainland is by far the biggest of the islands, its chief town being Lerwick, Britain's most northerly town, so called from the Norse *leir-vik* meaning 'muddy bay'. Looking over sheltered Bressay Sound, Lerwick has always been a refuge for seafarers, and was a stopping-off port for Norsemen; King Haakon reprovisioned his fleet here on the way to his defeat at Largs in 1263.

Lerwick

Lerwick has always been important for fishing: the home waters are productive and it lies on the edge of the valuable northern fishing fields. Dutch fishing fleets were based here in the 17th century and by the 18th century the export of salt fish was thriving. In the 17th century the town became important as a base for the British Navy. Fort Charlotte was built in 1665 to protect the Sound of Bressay from the Dutch. Today, despite its geographical isolation, Lerwick is a lot more up-to-date than some towns in the Highland region of Scotland. Sometimes the Sound is busy with vessels of all kinds and nationalities, the crews of which amble around the town adding a cosmopolitan touch with their different languages. (It is said that many Norwegians come here for bargain shopping, away from their own exorbitant prices.)

The buildings round the port are sturdy and compact, designed to withstand violent storms; some of them were the town houses of Shetland's lairds, who succeeded the Norsemen and found winter conditions rather bleak in the countryside. Now, the old houses are interspersed with a sprawl of characterless modern buildings.

The *Dim Riv* is a replica Norse longship, over 40ft (12m) long, which takes visitors on trips round the harbour in the summer. The harbour is a lively, bustling place with a picturesque waterfront and charmingly haphazard, flagstoned Commercial Street. This is the main shopping centre of the town and the steep, narrow lanes around it are said to cover a network of secret tunnels and passages used by smugglers in the past. Boat trips run from Victoria Pier and cruise round the coast in the summer. Look out for the distinctive Shetland sailing dinghy, a local design with the elegant double prow, echoing the Viking longboats, seen in most of Shetland's harbours.

Fort Charlotte (*open June–Sept daily 9am–10pm, Oct–May daily 10–4*), built by Cromwellian troops, was partly burned by the Dutch in 1673. It was repaired and restored in 1781 and garrisoned during the Napoleonic Wars. It is the only Cromwellian military building still intact in Scotland. The **Town Hall**, above

Commercial Street in Hillend, is a Victorian Gothic building, partly resembling a church. The stained-glass windows on the upper floor enclose the main hall and depict the history of Shetland, beginning with the Scandinavian conquest in 870. There are full-length figures of Norway's King Harald Harfagri, the conqueror of the islands, and Rognvald, Jarl of More, to whom Harald offered the first earldom. They also include the story of the Maid of Norway who died at sea nearby.

The **Shetland Museum** (*www.shetland-museum.org.uk; closed until autumn 2006 while a new building is constructed at Hay's Dock*) is well worth a visit. It has four galleries devoted to the history of man in Shetland. Look for the 7th-century Papil Stone, showing a procession of 'papas' or priests. Other exhibits include the history of Shetland knitting and the history of the islands' marine past. There are also replicas of the treasure found on St Ninian's Isle. **Bod of Gremista Museum** (*www.shetlandmuseum.org.uk; open June–mid-Sept Wed–Sun; adm*) has fishing displays. **Up Helly Aa Exhibition** (*open mid-May–mid-Sept Tues, Fri and Sat; adm*) has a replica galley and exhibits related to the festival.

Clickhimin Broch (*always accessible*) is on the western outskirts of the town on an island in a loch, reached by a causeway. It is 65ft (20m) in diameter, its walls 18ft (5½m) thick and 15ft (4½m) high, on a massive stone platform. Excavations on the site suggest that it may have been a late Bronze Age settlement.

A frequent car ferry crosses to the island of **Bressay** just east of Lerwick, and from here a boat crosses the 200 yards (185m) to the bird sanctuary on **Noss** (*open mid-May–Aug Tues–Sun except Thurs; adm*). Among the many birds to be seen on Noss are a colony of gannets – the great yellow-headed Solan geese. Boats run from the small Boat Harbour (*t (01950) 693 434*), in Lerwick at 1.30pm in the summer, for bird and seal spotting trips, and at various times from Victoria Pier Slipway (*t (01950) 422 483*).

Scalloway

Scalloway is Mainland's other town, in an attractive bay 7 miles west of Lerwick. It was the capital until 200 years ago and is still an important fishing port. Much older than Lerwick, it retains a quiet, old-fashioned atmosphere. There is a small local **museum** in the middle of the town which has a detailed history of the 'Shetland Bus'. During the Second World War, small Norwegian fishing boats crossed to Nazi-occupied Norway to carry out sabotage or to land secret agents and bring back refugees. 'To take the Shetland Bus' meant to escape from Norway. *The Shetland Bus* by David Howarth gives a vivid account of these brave operations. **Lunna House** in northeast Mainland, was the original headquarters of this Norwegian resistance movement before it was transferred to Scalloway.

Scalloway Castle dominates the town, a forbidding ruin built in 1600 by Earl Patrick Stewart, the notorious despot who tyrannized the Northern Isles until he was executed (*see* p.285). Built in medieval style, the roofless shell with corner turrets and gables stands on a narrow promontory by the water. The Earl is said to have hung his victims from an iron ring in one of the chimneys. The castle was, not surprisingly, left to rot after Stewart's death. Scalloway is at the southern end of the agricultural valley of **Tingwall**, so called after the site of the old Norse parliament, or 'thing', at the northern end of Tingwall Loch, reached by stepping stones. There are bridges across to the islands of **Tronda** and **Burra** just to the south.

South of Lerwick

Mousa Broch (*open daily mid-April–mid-Sept; fee for 15min ferry; booking essential*), on Mousa Island, is one of Shetland's principal archaeological treasures, accessible by boat from Sandwick, 11 miles south of Lerwick (*t (01950) 431 367, www.mousaboat trips.co.uk; 3-hour trip leaves Sandwick at 2pm daily, and 12.30 Fri and Sun; night trips at 11pm, May–July Sat and Wed, weather permitting*). Mousa Island, a mile offshore, is inhabited only by sheep and ponies (and nesting storm petrels) and its broch is the best preserved in existence. It is eerie to climb its steps and know that you are walking in the 2,000-year-old footsteps of its Pictish builders. This was one of the smaller of the brochs and probably one of the latest. Galleries honeycomb the double walls, and stairways lead to a parapet around the top. It illustrates clearly how the builders tapered the walls inwards to within about 10ft (3m) of the top and then sloped them outwards, making it impossible for invaders to climb to the top.

Mousa appears romantically in two of the old sagas. In 1150 the Norwegian Prince Erland abducted a famous beauty and held her in the broch until her son, a Jarl, unable to storm the impregnable fortress, had to consent to their marriage. Another saga tells of a young man called Bjorn, who brought Thora, whom he had seduced, to Mousa in 900, where they set up home together. Mousa is privately owned and camping is not allowed without permission.

St Ninian's Isle is 4 miles southwest of Sandwick, off the west coast of Mainland. You can walk to it along a white crescent of sand, called a 'tombolo', that forms a causeway. Here there are the foundations of a 12th-century chapel buried by sand for many hundreds of years. In 1958, Aberdeen University began excavating the site and discovered not only the foundations of the chapel but also a Bronze Age burial ground and the remains of a pre-Norse church. Under a stone slab in the chapel nave they found a hoard of 8th-century Celtic silver, which included silver bowls, delicate brooches and a Communion spoon. It is now in the Royal Museum of Scotland in Edinburgh, with a replica collection in the museum in Lerwick. It is believed that this cache was buried by the local monks, probably during a threat of Viking invasion.

Shetland Croft House Museum (*www.shetland-museum.org.uk; open May–Sept daily 10–1 and 2–5*), at Boddam, 5 miles south of Sandwick, is a restored croft house, typical of the mid-19th century, with its original driftwood furniture and all the domestic utensils. The restored **Quendale Mill** (*open mid-April–mid-Oct daily 10–5; adm*) is a 19th-century overshot water mill several miles away. The modern, clean-cut airport buildings at **Sumburgh**, on the southern tip of Mainland, present a remarkable contrast to the antiquity and character of Jarlshof, nearby.

Jarlshof (*site open daily; visitor centre open April–Sept daily 9.30–6.30; adm*) was a name invented by Sir Walter Scott in *The Pirate*. He visited the island in 1814, was impressed by the 'laird's hall', and wrote his story round it. In 1905 a violent storm revealed that the site had been occupied for over 3,000 years, by seven distinct civilizations of which the Norse Jarls were by far the most recent. Some of the artefacts dug up from the site are exhibited, with a good ground plan and helpful audiovisual interpretations.

The remains of these village settlements, from Bronze Age to Viking, are sprawled over a low green promontory by the sea. The first house dates from the early or middle part of the second millennium BC. It would be impossible to sort out the various ages and purposes of the conglomeration of stones without the excellent explanations and the guidebook. The Bronze Age huts include stalls and a metal workshop; the Iron Age settlement has two earth houses and a broch. The three 8th-century wheel-houses are thought to be family dwellings, with a central hearth. A confusion of longhouses is all that is left of the Norse occupation. It was the now-ruined medieval farmhouse that Sir Walter used as the setting for his book.

In July and August you can visit the excavations at **Old Scatness Broch**, South Mainland, one of the best Iron Age villages (*open May–Oct Sun–Thurs 10–5; guided tours; visits by arrangement at other times*). **Sumburgh Head** is a solid mass of birds (and twitchers in season). Hundreds of thousands of guillemots, puffins, gulls, razor-bills and terns crowd the cliffs and stacks below the lighthouse, despite the expansion of the airport into one of the busiest in Scotland. You get excellent views of Fair Isle from here. The **RSPB** (*t (01950) 460 800*) run free guided tours in the summer.

North of Lerwick

At **Sandness**, about 25 miles northwest of Lerwick, water mills have been restored to show something of Shetland's heritage. There is also Jamieson's traditional woollen mill. Boats run from West Burrafirth nearby to **Papa Stour**, a couple of miles off the coast (*four times a week; day trips possible on Fri and Sat*). The sea caves are said by some to be the finest in Britain and you will need to hire a boat locally to see them properly. The scent from the wild flowers on Papa Stour was said to be so strong that fishermen could fix their position from it if caught in fog out at sea.

Lunna is about 18 miles north of Lerwick as the crow flies, out on the east coast. When Lunna House was the original headquarters of the Norwegian Resistance, the barns and outhouses were used as an arsenal. The mid-18th-century **Lunna Kirk**, one of the oldest Shetland churches still in use, is a charming old building with a leper squint through which lepers could listen to the service and receive Communion without infecting the rest of the congregation. At **Brae**, about 23 miles north of Lerwick, a narrow neck of land called **Mavis Grind** prevents the northwest corner of Mainland from being an island.

Sullom Voe Oil Terminal, with its complex of buildings and jetties, occupies the peninsula of Calback Ness 7 miles northeast of Brae, joined to Mainland by reclaimed land. The terminal is discreetly tucked away, though you cannot miss the ugly buildings for the oil workers. **Firth**, nearby, was also built to house the oilmen. **Toft** is 4 miles east, and from here the car ferry crosses to **Yell**, 3 miles to the northeast.

This northern part of Mainland is dominated by **Ronas Hill**, Shetland's highest point at 1,475ft (454m) high, 10 miles north of Brae and worth climbing for the views. **Eshaness**, on the coast 15 miles northwest of Brae, has precipitous cliffs and breathtaking views of the **Drongs**, a collection of weird stacks carved by the force of the ocean, including a huge natural arch call the **Dore Holm**. **Tangwick Haa Museum**, Eshaness, North Mainland (*open May–Sept Mon–Fri 1–5, Sat and Sun 11–5*) is not to be missed: a former laird's house, renovated as a museum with the old interiors. There are microfilm census records here.

Islands Around Mainland

The island of **Yell**, to the north, is mostly peat moor. It was described by Eric Linklater as 'dull and dark and one large peat bog'. Although the second-largest of the Shetland islands, it has suffered from depopulation and can be rather depressing, but it is one of the best places in Britain to see otters. The **Old Haa** (*open late April–Sept Tues–Thurs and Sat 10–4, Sun 2–5*), at Burravoe, is an 18th-century laird's house that contains local and natural history, an art gallery, tearoom and shop – and a good atmosphere.

A minister of the kirk once said: 'Yell is Hell, but Unst – Oh! Unst!' **Unst** is Britain's most northerly island, with **Muckle Flugga** lighthouse on a rock just off its tip. The lighthouse was built by Robert Louis Stevenson's father, and while he was designing and building it, his son stayed on Unst dreaming up the story of *Treasure Island*. Unst supports a number of Shetland ponies and it has wonderful cliff scenery. **Haroldswick**, in northeast Unst, is where Harald Harfagri landed from Norway to subdue the troublesome, dispossessed Viking jarls. There is a nice little **Heritage Centre** here (*open May–Sept daily 2–5*), with island social history, geology etc. **Unst Boat Haven**, also in Haroldswick (*open May–Sept daily 2–4*), has fishing and sailing boats and maritime artefacts. **Valhalla Brewery** (*t (01957) 711 658; visitors welcome by appt*), at Baltasound, is Britain's northernmost brewery. **Hermaness Visitor Centre** (*open end April–mid-Sept daily 9–5*) is geared towards bird spotters.

Fetlar, east of Yell and much smaller, derives its name from the Norn name for 'fat land', and is the most fertile of the islands, supporting a large number of birds. Snowy owls bred on Fetlar until 1975, when the resident male died – hopeful visiting females can still sometimes be seen. Another of Fetlar's rare visitors is the red-necked phalarope which spins round on the water, stirring up insects with its long, needle-like beak. The miniature curlew-like whimbrel, usually a coastal migrant, nests on Fetlar and can be seen combing the shore for molluscs and worms.

Whalsay, a couple of miles northeast off the Mainland, is important for fishing and fish processing. On the pier there is a 17th-century Hanseatic trading booth. The Hanseatic League merchants came from northern Germany to Shetland to trade, buying fish and salting it for export, until salt tax was introduced in 1712. The traders set up booths like this one, from which they offered fine cloth, fishing tackle, exotic foods, tobacco, fruit, and gin at a farthing a pint, in exchange for fish, butter, wool and fish oil. Whalsay has two prehistoric sites: the **Standing Stones**, at Yoxie, and the **Benie Hoose**, thought to have been the dwelling for the Druid priests responsible for the ceremonies performed at the standing stones.

Foula, 27 miles west of Mainland, and still inhabited, has dramatic cliff scenery and a colony of skuas, though it is often cut off in bad weather. Norn was last spoken as a first language here in the 19th century.

Fair Isle

Only 3 miles by 1½, the 'Far Isle' of the Vikings, halfway between Orkney and Shetland, is a buffer between the North Sea and the Atlantic. It must be the most gale-battered island in Britain, presenting a tough challenge to the 60-odd people who live there. The bird population is enormous, preserved by the warden of the observatory where data is collected and analysed. Over 300 species have been recorded; as well as supporting resident colonies, it is a regular staging post for many migratory birds. Although bleak, Fair Isle is magnificent, with needle-sharp rocks pounded by ferocious seas and sheer cliffs topped by green turf and some of the 240 species of wild flowers that thrive here.

In 1588 *El Gran Grifon*, flagship of the transport squadron of the Spanish Armada, was wrecked on Fair Isle. The 17 households, already barely subsisting, took in, housed and fed the 300 survivors who stayed for six weeks. In 1984 a delegation of Spaniards in full conquistador regalia dedicated an iron cross in the island's kirkyard to the 50 men who lost their lives. Legend has it that these Spaniards taught the islanders how to knit their intricate patterns, but that is hotly denied, though it is easy to see that there could have been some Moorish influence on designs that date back to Viking times. There is an island co-operative of men and women who work machines and hand-finish 200 orders of Fair Isle jerseys, scarves, hats and gloves a year, each jersey taking seven hours to finish by hand. Hand-spinning, weaving and dyeing have also been revived in recent years, and workshops and demonstrations are organized by arrangement.

Getting There

Fair Isle is 24 miles southwest of Sumburgh and **boats** run to it from Grutness Pier near Sumburgh Airport (*2hrs – Tues, Thurs and Sat in summer; Tues in winter*). These aren't day trips: they involve a three-day stay on the island before the next boat back. For bookings, call J. Stout, **t** (01595) 760 222.

Alternatively you can fly from Tingwall, taking 25 minutes (*Mon, Wed and Fri; May–Oct also Sat*), and from Sumburgh (*May–Oct Sat only*).

Where to Stay and Eat

Mrs Coull, **t** (01595) 760 248, *kathy.coull@btinternet.com* (*budget*). Full board; friendly and excellent value.

Mrs Riddiford, Schoolton, **t** (01595) 760 250 (*budget*). B&B offering full board and all the friendly hospitality of the islands.

The Observatory, **t** (01595) 760 258, *www.fairislebirdobs.co.uk* (*moderate*). Unappealing at first glance but friendly, and warm and cosy inside. An excellent base for an outdoor summer holiday.

Clans and Families

The Gaelic *clann* means 'offspring', 'family', 'stock', 'race', derived from Latin *planta* – meaning 'sprout' or 'scion'.

When Robert the Bruce released Scotland from the English yoke in 1314, he opened the field for tremendous power struggles between the leading clans. Some became too powerful, others sank into obscurity. Many families, too weak to survive alone, sought the protection of stronger neighbours; some of these took the name of their adopted chief, others retained their own names. Thus many clans have 'septs' and dependants. Clans amalgamated for strength: the Clan Chattan Confederation consisted of a large number of clans who joined forces under Mackintosh hegemony. The chiefs of the Highland clans ruled with total disregard for the authority of the Crown, as did the powerful Border families. The final Jacobite rebellion, in 1745–46, resulted in the death of the old clan system. (*See also* 'Clans and Tartans', p.38)

Today, although all that is left is the clan name, many still live in the area traditionally associated with their clan, and there remains a pride and sense of loyalty so strong that people come from all over the world to visit the land of their ancestors. This is a list of the main clans and families, with the address (where there is one) of the clan secretary or clan centre, who can send more information. Septs, or clan branches, are not included. Anyone seriously seeking their roots should get hold of *The Clan Almanac*, by Charles Maclean (pub. Lochar), which lists, among other things, the septs and dependants of the main clans: thus, if you are called Abbot, for instance, you will find you are part of the Macnab clan. Mac and Mc mean son of, as of course does any name ending in son.

Anderson: son of Andrew, Highland version MacAndrew. From Badenoch; motto: 'Stand Sure'. Part of the Clan Chattan Confederation in the 15th century. Clan Chattan Secretary, Dyunmaglash, Westhill, Inverness-shire.

Armstrong: the original, armour-bearer to a King of Scots, saved his king, fallen in a battle, by lifting him on to his horse. He was given land as a reward and named Strong-arm. From the Borders; motto: *Invictus maneo* ('I remain unvanquished'). Clan Secretary, Brieryshaw, Langholm, Dumfriesshire.

Baird: from an old Scots word meaning 'sumptuous dress'. From Aberdeenshire; motto: *Dominus fecit* ('The Lord made').

Barclay: from the Berkeley family who came over with William the Conqueror. Settled in Aberdeenshire and Kincardineshire; motto: *Aut agere aut mori* ('Either action or death').

Blair: from Gaelic *blar* – 'field', 'battlefield'; motto: *Amo Probos* ('I love the righteous'). An ancient family, one branch having roots in Renfrew, Ayr and Wigtown; and another in Perth, Fife and Angus. The Barony of Blair, in Ayrshire, was granted by William the Lion in the 12th century. When the two branches competed for chieftainship, James VI settled the dispute by appointing the oldest man in either family to be chief. Thus the honour alternates, depending upon seniority. Clan Secretary, 15 Brompton Terrace, Perth.

Brodie: from their Norman ancestor, de Brothie. Settled in Morayshire; motto: 'Unite'. Clan Secretary, Brodie Castle, Forres, Moray.

Bruce: from the French town Brix – Adam de Brus came over with William the Conqueror. Settled in Annandale, Clackmannan and Elgin; motto: *Fuimus* ('We have been'). Robert the Bruce won independence for Scotland at the Battle of Bannockburn in

1314; Thomas Bruce, 7th Earl of Elgin and 11th Earl of Kincardine, 1766–1841, rescued the sculptures on the Parthenon from vandalism and installed them in the British Museum.

Buchanan: from Gaelic *mac-a-Chanonaich* – 'son of the canon'. Lived around Loch Lomond; motto: *Clarior hinc honos* ('Brighter hence the honour'). Clan secretary, Brechin Robb, 24 George Square, Glasgow.

Cameron: from Gaelic *cam-shron* – 'crooked nose'. Lived in Northern Argyll and Locheil; mottos (translated from Gaelic): 'Unite'; 'For King and Country'; and 'Sons of the hounds come here and get flesh'. The Cameron Highlanders, now amalgamated with the Seaforth Highlanders to become the Queen's Own Highlanders, were raised by Sir Alan Cameron in 1793. Their Clan Centre is at Aberchalder, Loch Eil, and the new Clan Cameron Museum is at Achnacarry. Clan Secretary, 78 Milton Road West, Edinburgh.

Campbell: from Gaelic *cam-beul* – 'crooked mouth'. From Argyll, Cawdor, Loudoun and Breadalbane; mottos: 'Forget not'; 'Follow me'; 'Be mindful'; 'I byde my tyme'. The Duke of Argyll is their chief and the clan centre is Inveraray Castle, Argyll.

Chisholm: means a water meadow which produces milk good for cheese-making. Lived in Roxburghshire and Berwickshire and, later, Inverness-shire; motto: *Feros ferio* ('I am fierce with the fierce'). Clan Secretary, 21 Blytheswood Square, Glasgow.

Colquhoun (pronounced *k'hoon*): the name is from the Barony, in Dunbartonshire, and they lived around Loch Lomond. Their motto, *Si je puis* ('If I can'), was said by one of their ancestors, to James I, when ordered to capture Dumbarton Castle. (He did.)

Cumming: derived from the herb cummin, which is their emblem. From Roxburghshire, Buchan, Badenoch and Altyre; motto: 'Courage'. The Comyns came to Scotland during the reign of Malcolm Canmore in the 11th century, and Sir John Comyn – 'The Red Comyn' – was murdered by Robert the Bruce in order to gain the Crown. Clan Secretary, House of Altyre, Forres.

Douglas: from Gaelic *dubh glais* – 'black water'. Lived in Lanarkshire, Galloway, Dumfriesshire and Angus and were as powerful as kings in the Middle Ages. Motto: *Jamais arrière* ('Never behind'). Sir James Douglas was

killed in 1330, while honouring his promise to take Robert the Bruce's heart to the Holy Land.

Drummond: derived from Drymen, near Stirling. Lived in Perthshire; motto: 'Gang (go) warily'.

Duncan: more properly Clan Donnachaidh – Brown Warriors. From Atholl and Lundie in Angus; motto: *Disce parti* ('Learn to suffer'). Donnaichaidh Clan Secretary, 127 Rose Street South Lane, Edinburgh.

Elliot (there are different spellings): probably derived from Old English *Aelfwald* – 'Elf Ruler', which became the Christian name Elward. One of the strongest of the Border families; mottos: *Soyez sage* ('Be wise'), and *Fortiter et Recte* ('With Strength and Right'). Clan Secretary, Redheugh, Newcastleton, Roxburghshire.

Erskine: from the Barony of Erskine in Renfrewshire; lived around Alloa; motto: *Je pense plus* ('I think more').

Farquharson: the Gaelic *fearchar* means 'dear one'. From Aberdeenshire and Invercauld; motto: *Fide et Fortitudine* ('By Fidelity and Fortitude'). They were part of the Clan Chattan Confederation. Clan Chattan Secretary, Dyunmaglash, Westhill, Inverness-shire.

Ferguson: one of the oldest clans of Scotland. Fergus founded the Scottish kingdom of Dalriada and they inhabited the lands of Argyll, Perthshire, Dumfries, Galloway and Raith. Motto: *Dulcius ex asperis* ('Sweeter after difficulties'). Clan Secretary, Pendle Cottage, Dumgoyne, Glasgow.

Forbes: from Gaelic *forba* – 'field' or 'district'. Powerful in Aberdeenshire; motto: 'Grace me guide'. Clan Secretary, Balforbes, Lonach, Donside, Aberdeenshire.

Fraser: of Norman derivation, from *fraises* – 'strawberry flowers'. Originally in East Lothian, then Aberdeenshire; motto: *Je suis prest* ('I am ready'). Clan Secretary, Balblair House, Beauly, Ross-shire.

Gordon: from Gordon in Berwickshire, where they settled in the 12th century. Powerful in the northeast in Strathbogie, Deeside and around Aberdeen; their chief was called Cock of the North. Mottos: *Animo non Astutia* ('By Courage, not Craft'); and *Bydand* ('Remaining'). Clan Secretary, Harlaw House, Harlaw Hill, Prestonpans, East Lothian.

Graham: Anglo-Saxon origin – *graeg ham*, meaning 'grey home'. William de Graham came to Scotland with David I, who gave him lands, and the family became prominent in the Wars of Independence. Their lands included those north of Glasgow, Loch Katrine, part of Perthshire, and around Dundee and Montrose. Motto: *Ne Oublie* ('Do not forget'). Clan Secretary, 23 Ardmillan Terrace, Edinburgh.

Grant: derived from the French *grand* – 'great'. Their origins are disputed: some say the first Grant was a Nottinghamshire squire married into an Inverness-shire family, some that they are descended from Kenneth Macalpine, some that they are descended from MacGregors. Lands: Strathspey, Rothiemurchus, Glen Moriston and Loch Ness; motto: 'Stand fast'. Clan Secretary, 18 Great Stuart Street, Edinburgh.

Gunn: possibly from Gunni, in the Norse sagas, or from Gaelic *guineach*, meaning 'fierce', or of Pictish descent. Lands: Caithness and Sutherland; motto: *Aut Pax Aut Bellum* ('Either Peace or War'). Clan Secretary, 22 Muirhouse Gardens, Edinburgh.

Hamilton: derived from Hameldone, meaning 'crooked hill', in England, whence came Walter Fitz-Gilbert to Renfrewshire and Arran during the Wars of Independence. Motto: 'Through'. Patrick Hamilton, 1498–1528, was the protomartyr of the Scottish Reformation. Clan Secretary, Lennoxlove, Haddington, East Lothian.

Hay: derived from La Haye, in Normandy, which stems from *haie*, or 'hedge'. Lands: Aberdeenshire and Tweeddale; motto: *Serva jugum* ('Keep the yoke'). Clan Secretary, 12 St Peter's Place, Edinburgh. Clan Centre, Delgatie Castle, Turriff, Grampian.

Henderson: in Gaelic, this clan is MacEanraig, anglicized as MacKendrick. Lands: Caithness and Glencoe; motto: *Sola Virtus nobilitat* ('Virtue alone ennobles').

Home (pronounced *Hume*): derived from Gaelic *uamh* – 'cave'. Lands: the Borders; motto: 'A Home, a Home!' Among their scions were David Hume, the great philosopher of the Scottish Enlightenment and Sir Alec Douglas-Home, Prime Minister of Britain.

Innes: meaning 'greens'. Innes was a town in Morayshire for which the family received a royal charter in the 12th century. Motto: *Be traist* ('Be faithful'). Clan Secretary, 35 East Claremont Street, Edinburgh.

Johnstone: derived from John's *toun* – 'homestead'; the Gaelic for John is Iain, giving MacIain. There are various spellings but Johnson is uncommon in Scotland. They were a powerful Border family and also had lands in Aberdeenshire. Mottos: *Numquam non paratus* ('Never unprepared') and 'Light thieves all'.

Keith: from the town of Keith in Banffshire. Their lands stretched from East Lothian to Caithness and they held the hereditary office of Great Marischal of Scotland from the 12th to the 18th centuries. Motto: *Veritas vincit* ('Truth conquers'). Clan Secretary, North Dykes, Kilbirnie, Ayrshire.

Kennedy: from Gaelic *ceann éitigh* – 'grim-headed' – or possibly from *ceann dubh* – 'black-headed'. Lands: Ayrshire, Lochaber and Skye; motto: *Avise la Fin* – 'Consider the end'. The seat of their chief, the Marquess of Ailsa, is Culzean Castle.

Kerr: pronounced either *kar* or *ker*, the name is derived from the Norse *kjarr* meaning 'brushwood'. They were an Anglo-Norman family who came to Scotland in the 12th century. Lands: Roxburghshire; motto: *Sero sed serio* ('Late but in earnest'). Legend has the Kerrs left-handed so they reversed the spiral of their staircases to allow space for the left sword-arm.

Lamont: derived from Lawman, Lawgiver; MacKeracher is the Highland version. Lands: Argyll and Cowal; motto: *Nec parcas nec spernas* ('Neither spare nor dispose'). Clan Secretary, 17 Broomhall Loan, Edinburgh.

Leslie: taken from the barony of Leslie in Aberdeenshire which they adopted in the reign of William the Lion. Motto: 'Grip fast'.

Lindsay: Lindsey means Linden (lime tree) Island. They came to Scotland with David I and became very powerful. Lands: the Borders and Angus; motto: *Endure Fort* ('Endure with Strength'). Clan Secretary, 112 Corsebar Road, Paisley.

Livingstone: from Livingstone in West Lothian where they held land, as well as in the Trossachs and Lorne. Motto: *Si je puis* ('If I can'). Clan Secretary, Bachull, Isle of Lismore, Oban, Argyll.

Logan or MacLennan: Logan is in Lothian, with MacLennan as the Highland version. Lands: Lothian, Berwickshire and Easter Ross; motto: 'The Ridge of Tears'.

MacAlister: son of Alasdair, Gaelic for Alexander, who was descended from the great Somerled. Lands: Kintyre, Arran and Bute; motto: *Fortiter* ('Boldly'). Clan Centre, Glenbarr Abbey, Kintyre, Argyll and Bute.

MacAlpin: Alpins claim descent from 9th-century King Alpin. Dunstaffnage was their traditional home, though the race had no land; motto: *Cuimhnich bàs Ailpein* ('Remember the death of Alpin').

MacArthur: the MacArthurs were the senior branch of the Campbell clan, taking their name from Arthur Campbell in the 14th century. Lands: Argyll, Cowal and Skye; mottos: *Fide et Opera* ('By Fidelity and Work') and *Eisd! O eisd!* ('Listen! O listen!'). Clan Secretary, 14 Hillpark Road, Edinburgh.

MacAulay: son of Olaf, who was King of Man and the Isles in the 13th century. Lands: Dunbartonshire, Isle of Lewis, Sutherland and Ross; motto: *Dulce Periculum* ('Danger is sweet'). Clan Secretary, Cameron Loch Lomond Ltd, Alexandria, Dumbartonshire.

MacBean: son of Beathan, or from the Gaelic *bian* – 'fair skin' – or from King Donald Ban, from whom they claim descent. Donald Ban was the son of Duncan, murdered by Macbeth. Lands: Inverness-shire; motto: 'Touch not the catt bot a targe' (without a shield). At Culloden, gallant Gillies MacBean breached a gap in a wall with his enormous body and killed 14 Hanoverians before he was himself slain.

MacBeth: derived from the Gaelic for 'Son of Life'. Lands: Morayshire and Perthshire and their most famous ancestor, King MacBeth (reigned 1040–57), was very different from Shakespeare's character: a wise, generous, pious ruler, the last of the Gaelic kings.

MacCallum: *calaman* is Gaelic for 'dove', implying a disciple of St Columba whose emblem was the Dove of Peace. Lands: Argyll; mottos: *In ardua petit* ('He has tried difficult things') and *Deus refugium nostrum* ('God is our refuge').

Macdonald: *Dòmhnall* is Gaelic for 'world ruler'. Donald of Islay was grandson of Somerled, Lord of the Isles and Ragnhildis, daughter of King Olaf of Man. Clan Donald was the largest and most powerful of the clans, with a number of branches, reigning supreme in the northwest Highlands and Islands. There are a variety of spellings, including MacDonnell. (Mac was not used in the surname until the 16th century.) It is the commonest Mac name in Scotland. The main branches were: Sleat in Skye, Clanranald in Moidart, Glengarry, Keppoch in Lochaber, and Glencoe. They were staunch Jacobites and Royalists, fiercely claiming their position on the right wing of any battle, given them by Robert the Bruce at Bannockburn and still held at Culloden. Mottos include: *Per mare per terras* ('By land and by sea'); *Fraoch eilean* ('The heathery isle'); 'My hope is constant in thee'; *Dh'aindeoin co'theireadh e* ('Gainsay who dare'); *Creag an fhitheach* ('the Raven's Rock'); and *Dia's naomh Aindrea* ('God and St Andrew'). Clan Centre, Armadale Castle, Sleat, Skye. Clan Secretary, Ceadach, 39 Redford Road, Edinburgh.

MacDougall: from the Gaelic *dubh gall*, meaning 'dark stranger'. Lands: Lorne; motto: *Buaidh no bàs* ('To conquer or die'). They fought against Robert the Bruce in the Wars of Independence, and with the Hanoverians at Culloden. Clan Secretary, Dunollie Castle, Oban, Argyll.

MacDuff: from the Gaelic *mac dubh* – 'son of the dark one'. Lands: Fife, Lothian, Strathbran and Strathbogie; motto: *Deus juvat* ('God assists'). The MacDuffs spawned a number of other clans: one MacDuff earl was known as *Mac an tòiseach* – son of the chief, which became MacIntosh. Clan Secretary, 5 Sidlaw Road, Glasgow.

MacEwan: son of Ewan, who flourished in the 13th century. Lands: Cowal, Lennox and Galloway; motto: *Reviresco* ('I grow strong').

MacFarlane: son of Partholon, whose father, Sear, took over Ireland after the Flood. Lands: around Loch Lomond, Tarbert and Arrochar; motto: *Loch Sloigh* ('Loch Sloy').

MacFie: derived from the Gaelic *Dubhsìth*, meaning 'peaceful dark one', the MacFies are a branch of the Clan Alpine. Lands: Colonsay; motto: *pro rege* ('for the king'). Clan Secretary, 120 Cockburn Crescent, Balerno, Midlothian.

MacGillivray: *gille breth* is Gaelic for 'servant of judgement' and the clan belonged to the Clan

Chattan Confederation. Lands: Mull, Lochaber and Morven, and later Inverness-shire; motto: Dunmaghlas, the name of the chief's castle. MacGillivray of Dunmaglass led the Clan Chattan at Culloden. Clan Secretary, Dunlichty, 7 Cramond Park, Edinburgh.

MacGregor: *Grioghair* is Gaelic for Gregory and they claim descent from Griogar, son of 8th-century King Alpin. Some prefer to claim Pope Gregory the Great as their forefather. Whatever the truth, they all claim royal descent. Lands: Argyll and Perthshire; motto: *S'rioghail mo drèam* ('Royal is my race'). Clan Secretary, 14 Lockharton Avenue, Edinburgh.

MacInnes: *aontaghais* is Gaelic for 'unique choice' and they were an ancient Celtic clan. Lands: Morven and Ardnamurchan; motto: *Irid Ghibht Dhe agus an Righ* ('Through the Grace of God and the King'). Clan Secretary, 35 East Claremont Street, Edinburgh.

MacIntosh: *see* Mackintosh and MacDuff.

MacIntyre: *an-t-saor* is Gaelic for 'son of a carpenter' and the clan is said to have taken this name from one who chopped off his thumb to stop a leak in a Macdonald chief's galley. Lands: Kintyre, Glenoe and Badenoch and they were part of the Clan Chattan Confederation. Motto: *Per ardua* ('Through difficulties'). Clan Chattan Secretary, Dyunmaglash, Westhill, Inverness-shire.

MacKenzie: *coinnich* is Gaelic for 'fair' or 'bright' and was a popular Celtic forename, anglicized as Kenneth. Lands: Ross and Cromarty and the Isle of Lewis; mottos: *Luceo no uro* ('I shine, not burn'); *Tulach Ard* ('The High Hillock'); and *Cuidich 'n righ* ('Save the King'). Traditionally they provided most of the men in the Seaforth Highlanders, now amalgamated with the Cameron Highlanders to form The Queen's Own Highlanders. Clan Secretary, 1b Downie Place, Musselburgh, Midlothian.

MacKinnon: Kinnon derives from 13th-century Fingan and the MacKinnons were the family of St Columba, part of the Clan Alpin. Lands: Iona and North Mull, then Skye and Arran; mottos: *Audentes fortuna iuvat* ('Fortune favours the brave') and *Cuimhnich bàs Ailpein* ('Remember the death of Alpin'). Clan Secretary, 222 Darnley Street, Pollokshields, Glasgow.

MacKintosh: *toiseach* is Gaelic for 'tribal leader' or thane, and the clan descended

from the MacDuffs, originally the leading family of the Clan Chattan Confederation. Lands: Inverness-shire; motto: 'Touch not the cat bot (without) a glove'. Brave, beautiful, Jacobite Lady Anne MacKintosh, known as Colonel Anne, masterminded the Rout of Moy, ousting 1,500 of Cumberland's troops with a mere five men. Clan Secretary, Moy Hall, Moy, Inverness-shire.

MacLachlan: Lachlan was a Celtic forename derived from *Lochlann*, the Gaelic for Norway, and the clan claims descent from Niall of the Nine Hostages, High King of Ireland, who won land in Argyllshire. They later spread to Lochaber, Perthshire and Stirlingshire. Motto: *Fortis et Fidis* ('Brave and Trusty'). Clan Secretary, Tigh-na-Croft, Enochdhu, Blairgowrie, Angus.

MacLaine: *gille Eoin* is Gaelic for 'servant of John' and they claim descent from Lachlans and MacLeans. Lands: Lochbuie; motto: *Vincere vel mori* ('Conquer or die').

MacLaren: from the Gaelic, 'son of Lawrence'. Lands: Strathearn and Balquhidder; motto: 'The Boar's Rock'. Clan Secretary, 1 Inverleith Place, Edinburgh.

Maclean: *gille Eoin* is Gaelic for 'servant of John' and they claim descent from the Kings of Dalriada. Lands: Morven, Mull, Coll and Tiree; mottos: *Bàs no Beatha* ('Death or life') and *Fear eile airson Eachainn* ('Another for Hector'). Clan Secretary, 12 Elie Street, Glasgow.

Macleod: *liotr* was old Norse for 'ugly'; *leod* was Saxon for 'prince.' They claim descent from Olaf the Black, King of Man and the Islands in the 13th century. Lands: Skye, Lewis and Harris; motto: 'Hold fast'. Clan Secretary, 38 Ravelston Gardens, Edinburgh.

MacMillan: *maoilein* means 'bald one', meaning tonsured and therefore priest, so their origins were ecclesiastical. Lands: Lochaber, Argyll and Galloway; motto: *Miseris succurrere disco* ('I learn to succour the distressed'). John MacMillan 1670–1753, founded the Reformed Presbyterian Church. Clan Centre, Finlaystone, Langbank, Renfrewshire.

MacNab: from *aba* meaning 'abbot', the MacNabs are descended from the Abbot of Glendochart, in the time of David I. Lands: Glendochart and Loch Tay; motto: *Timor* *omnis abesto* ('Let fear be far from all'). Clan Secretary, Finlarig, Killin, Perthshire.

MacNaughton/MacNachtan: *neachdainn* is Gaelic for 'pure one' and they can be traced back to Pictish royalty. Lands: Strathtay, Lewis and Argyll; motto: 'I hope in God'. The Clan Centre is at Dundarave Castle, near Inveraray. Clan Secretary, 2 Douglas Crescent, Edinburgh.

MacNeil: descended from the O'Neills who were High Kings of Ireland. Lands: Barra, Gigha, Knapdale and Colonsay; motto: *Vincere vel mori* ('To conquer or die'). Clan Secretary, 34 Craigleith Hill Avenue, Edinburgh.

MacNicol or **Nicholson:** son of Nicol, tracing their ancestry back to the dark ages. Lands: Sutherland, Skye and Argyll; motto: *Sgorra Bhreac* (Skorrybreck).

MacPherson: *phearsain* was Gaelic for 'parson'. They were part of the Clan Chattan Confederation and trace their ancestry to Ferchar, King of Lorne, who died in 697. Staunch Jacobites, they arrived too late for the Battle of Culloden. Land: Badenoch; motto: 'Touch not the cat bot (without) a glove'. Clan Secretary, 39 Swanston Avenue, Edinburgh.

MacQuarrie: *guardhre* is Gaelic for 'noble one' and they trace their roots to the Clan Alpine and Saint Columba's family. Lands: Ulva; motto: *An t-arm breac dearg* ('the red tartaned army').

MacQueen: from the Norse *sweyne*, or Gaelic *siubhne*, meaning 'good going'. They were strong members of the Clan Chattan Confederation, with close Macdonald connections. Lands: Skye, Lewis, Argyll and Lanarkshire; motto: 'Constant and faithful'. Clan Chattan Secretary, Dyunmaglash, Westhill, Inverness-shire.

MacRae: means 'son of grace', probably of ecclesiastical origin. Lands: Beauly and Kintail; motto: *Fortitudine* ('With Fortitude'). Clan Secretary, 6 Gardiners Crescent, Edinburgh.

Malcolm: followers of St Columba. Lands: Argyll, Fife, Lochore and Dumfriesshire; motto: was *Deus refugium nostrum* ('God is our refuge'), now *In ardua petit* ('He aims at difficult things'). Clan Secretary, Duntrune Castle, Kilmelfort, Lochgilphead, Argyll.

Matheson: *math-ghamhainn* is Gaelic for 'bear' and, traditionally, the Clan of the Bear

helped Kenneth Macalpine against the Picts in 843. Lands were Lochalsh and Sutherland; motto: *Fac et Spera* ('Do and hope'). Clan Secretary, Burnside, Duirnish, Kyle of Lochalsh, Ross-shire.

Maxwell: from Maxwell on the River Tweed, derived from Maccus's Wiel, they were a powerful Border family descended either from 11th-century Maccus, King of Man and the Isles, or from Norman settlers. Lands: Nithsdale; motto: *Reviresco* ('I flourish again').

Menzies (correctly pronounced *mingiz*): from Mesnières in Normandy. Lands: Atholl, Weem, Aberfeldy and Glendochart; mottos *Vil God I Zal* ('Will God I shall') and *Geal 'us dearg a suas* ('Up with the white and red'). Clan Secretary, 1 Belford Place, Edinburgh. Clan Museum, Castle Menzies, Aberfeldy, Tayside.

Moncreiffe: from Gaelic *monadh craobhe* – tree on the moor, descended from Maldred, brother of King Duncan. Lands: Perthshire. Clan Secretary, Easter Moncreiffe, Perthshire.

Montgomery: from Montgomerie, in Normandy; descended from Anglo-Norman Robert de Montgomery, who came to Scotland in the 12th century. Lands: Eglinton, Ardrossan and Kintyre; motto: *Gardez bien* ('Look well'). Clan Secretary, c/o P.O. Box 6, Saltcoats, Ayrshire.

Morrison: *gille Mhoire* is Gaelic for 'servant of Mary', presumably of ecclesiastical origin, and they trace their ancestors to the MacLeods of Dunvegan in the 13th century. Lands: Lewis, Sutherland, Skye and Harris. Clan Secretary, Ruchdi, by Loch Maddy, Isle of North Uist.

Munro: from the Gaelic *Rothach* – man from Ro, thought to be from the River Roe in Ireland. Lands: Easter Ross; motto: 'Dread God'. Their war cry, 'Castle Foulis Ablaze!', refers to the beacon that used to be lit on the chief's castle to summon the clan to arms. They were Whigs, supporting the government against the Jacobites.

Murray: from Moray, the 'settlement by the sea'. They are descended from Pictish Mormaers. Lands: Morayshire and Perthshire; motto: *Tout pret* ('All ready'). Clan Secretary, 204 Bruntsfield Place, Edinburgh.

Napier: descended from the ancient earls of Lennox; legend has it that one, having been particularly brave in battle, was ordered by his King to change his name to 'Nae peer'!

Lands: Gosford, Fife and Midlothian; mottos: *Sans tache* ('Without stain') and *To vincula frange* ('To break bones').

Ogilvie: from Brythonic *ocel fa* – 'high plain'. Ogilvie Earls of Airlie descend directly from the Earls of Angus. Lands: Angus; motto: *A fin* ('To the finish'). St John Ogilvie, 1579–1615, was a Scottish Jesuit martyr, canonized in 1976.

Ramsay: meaning 'wild-garlic island'. The family is descended from an Anglo-Norman, Simund de Ramesie, who was granted lands in Lothian by David I. Lands: Dalhousie and Perthshire; motto: *Ora et labor* ('Pray and work').

Robertson: the eponymous Robert was Robert Riabhach ('Grizzled Robert') Duncanson, 4th Chief of Clan Donnachaidh, and the Robertsons of Struan are one of the earliest known families in Scotland. Land: Struan; mottos: *Virtutis Gloria Merces* ('Glory is the reward of valour') and *Garg'n uair dhuis gear* ('Fierce when raised'). Clan Secretary, 29 Lauriston Gardens, Edinburgh.

Rose: descended from the Norman family de Rose and first recorded in Scotland in the reign of Alexander II. Lands: Strathnairn and Ross-shire; motto: 'Constant and true'. Clan Secretary, Kilravock Castle, Nairnshire.

Ross: the Gaelic *ros* means 'headland'; Brythonic *ros* means 'moor'. They are descended from Fearchar Mac-an-t-Sagairt of Applecross, created Earl of Ross in 1234. Lands: Ross-shire, Ayrshire and Renfrewshire; motto: *Spem successus alit* ('Success nourishes hope'). Clan Secretary, 57 Barnton Park View, Edinburgh.

Scott: the Scoti were the Irish tribe who gave Scotland its name. The family descend from Uchtred, *filius Scoti* – 'son of a Scot' – in the 12th century, and were one of the most powerful Border families. Lands: the Borders and Fife. One of their best-known scions is Sir Walter, the 19th-century writer.

Scrymgeour: from French *eskermisor* – sword-fencer or skirmisher. Lands: Argyll and Fife; motto: 'Dissipate'. Clan Secretary, 21 Braid Farm Road, Edinburgh.

Shaw: possibly derived from the Gaelic *seaghdha* – 'pithy' – and probably descended from 14th-century Shaw Macduff, founder of the MacIntosh clan. Principal members of the Clan Chattan Confederation. Land: Strathspey;

motto: *Fide et Fortitudine* ('By Fidelity and Fortitude'). Clan Secretary, Tordarroch House, Tordarroch, Inverness-shire.

Sinclair: from the French St Clair sur Elle, in Normandy, whence came William de Sancto Claro in the 12th century. Lands: Midlothian, Orkney and Caithness, and they were jarls of Orkney in 14th century. Motto: 'Commit thy work to God'.

Skene: from Skene in Aberdeenshire, they are descended from Robertsons of Struan. Lands: Aberdeenshire, granted by the king in the 11th century; motto: *Virtutis regia merces* ('A palace the reward of bravery').

Stewart: derived from High Steward. Walter Fitz-Allan, an Anglo-Norman, came to Scotland in the 12th century and was given land and the greatest office in the realm – Steward of Scotland. The family provided Scotland with 14 sovereigns, five of whom also reigned in England. Stuart was the French form of the name, adopted in England. Lands: Renfrewshire, Teviotdale, Lauderdale, Appin and Ardshiel; motto: *Virescit vulnere virtus* ('Courage grows strong at a wound'). Probably the best-known Stuart was the one who never got to the throne, Prince Charles Edward, 1720–88. Clan Secretary, 48 Castle Street, Edinburgh.

Sutherland: *Sudrland* was the Norse name for Sutherland, to the south of Caithness. The clan is descended from early inhabitants of Sutherland, which was granted to them in 1228. Clan Secretary, Dunrobin Castle, Golspie, Sutherland.

Urquhart: derived from Brythonic *air cairdean* – 'at the woods', the name of the district where the family originated. Lands: Ross-shire and Inverness-shire; motto: 'Mean, speak and do well'. Thomas Urquhart, 1611–60, who claimed descent from Adam, was a brilliant translator of Rabelais and is said to have died of laughter, on hearing of the Restoration. Clan Secretary, Bigram, Port of Monteith, Stirlingshire.

Wallace: derived from *Wallenses*, the medieval word for the Welsh who peopled Strathclyde, from whom the Wallaces are descended. Lands: Ayrshire and Renfrewshire; motto: *Pro Libertate* ('For Liberty'). William Wallace fought for Scottish independence, paving the way for Robert the Bruce.

Glossary

Aber mouth of: confluence of (rivers)
Advocate barrister
Aird point, promontory
Allt stream
An of the
Aros dwelling
Athole brose a delicious drink made from whisky, honey, oatmeal and cream, left to soak and squeezed through a cloth: once tasted, never forgotten
Auch a field
Auld old
Aye yes
Bairn child
Bal town; home
Ban fair
Bannock oatmeal pancake-ish scone-ish cake
Bap bread roll
Bard poet
Barr crest
Beag small
Bealach, balloch mountain pass
Bean woman
Ben, beinn mountain
Bhlair plain
Blether talk nonsense
Bogle frightening ghost
Bothy rough hut, temporary accommodation
Brae hill
Bramble blackberry
Branks bridle, halter
Braw fine
Breeks trousers
Bridie pie made with circle of pastry folded over filling of meat, onions, vegetables etc.
Brig bridge
Broch prehistoric round stone tower with hollow walls, enclosing cell-like galleries, and stairways, often built round a well, purpose only guessed at, probably dwelling for chief and refuge for clan in times of danger
Burn stream
Byre barn

Cadger pedlar
Cailleach old woman
Cairn stone monument
Callan(t) youth
Cam crooked
Canny prudent
Caolas firth
Capercaillie wood-grouse
Car curve
Ceann head
Céilidh informal social gathering among neighbours, often with spontaneous singing, music, storytelling etc.
Chanter double-reeded pipe on which bagpipe tune is played
Cil church
Clach stone
Cladach beach
Clarty dirty
Claymore sword
Cleg horsefly
Close shared entry to tenement; unroofed lane or stairway
Cnoc hillock
Collie sheepdog
Corbie crow
Corrie hollow
Crack conversation
Craig rock
Crannog small man-made island dating from Iron Age. Stones piled on wooden base with easily defended single dwelling on top, often reached by a sunken causeway.
Creel pannier-type basket, also lobster pot
Croft smallholding
Crowdie soft cheese
Cuddy donkey
Cul recess
Cutty short (cutty sark, short petticoat; cutty stool, stool of repentance)
Dal field
Dalr valley
Damph deer; steer
Daunder saunter

Ding knock, beat
Dominie schoolmaster
Doo dove
Doo'cot dovecot
Douce sweet, gentle
Dour dry, humourless
Dram officially one-eighth fluid ounce:
  commonly generous tot of whisky
Dreich dreary; boring
Drochit bridge
Dross coal dust
Drove road tracks used for herding (droving)
  cattle or sheep to market, often over long
  distances.
Druim, drum ridge
Dubh dark, black
Dun hillfort
Dux best pupil
Dyke wall of stones or turf
Dysart hermit's retreat; desert
Eaglais church
Eas waterfall; gorge
Eilean island
Esk water
Ey island
Factor land agent, usually of private estate
Fada long
Fail rock
Fank sheepfold
Fash trouble, upset, 'dinna fash yersel' – don't
  trouble yourself
Fear man
Feu feudal tenure of land with rent paid in
  kind or money
Fey susceptible to supernatural influence
Fillebeg kilt
Fionn gleaming, white
Firth wide mouth of river, estuary
Flit remove, move house
Fou full (of drink)
Fraoch heather
Gearr short
Geodha chasm
Gil ravine
Girdle iron baking tray, used over heat
Glass grey
Glen valley
Gleo mist
Gobha blacksmith
Gorm blue, green
Gowk fool
Greet cry, weep
Grieve farm manager

Harling rough-cast facing to walls
Haver talk nonsense
Heugh hillock
Hog unshorn lamb
Hogmanay New Year's Eve
Holm low ground by river; islet in river
Hope bay
How burial mound
Howe low-lying ground, hollow
Howff meeting place; refuge; burial ground
Howk dig
Ilk same, of that ilk – surname and name of
  property the same
Inch island
Inver mouth of river
Jougs iron neck collar used as instrument of
  public punishment
Kail cabbage
Kailyard cabbage patch; back yard
Keek peep
Kelpie water sprite, water horse
Ken know
Kenspeckle easily recognizable, conspicuous
Kil burial place; church
Kin head (of loch, river)
Kirk church
Knock, knowe knoll, hillock
Kye cattle
Kyle strait, narrow channel between two
  points of land
Lag, laggan hollow, dip
Laird owner of estate
Lairig, Larig, learg mountain pass
Land tenement
Larach site of ruin
Law round hill
Leac flagstone
Leana plain
Liath grey
Links dunes
Linn, linne pool
Lis garden on site of fortress
Loan lane
Loch, lochan lake, small lake
Lug ear
Lum chimney
Machair sand-peat lowland bordering
  seashore
Manse minister's house (ecclesiastical)
Maol bare headland
March boundary
Meikle large
Mhor, mor great

Mon moor
Moy plain
Muc, muic sow
Muckle large
Mull promontory
Na, nam, nan of the
Neeps turnips (bashed neeps – mashed turnips). Turnips in Scotland refer to English swedes
Ness nose
Neuk corner
Ob, oba, oban bay
Ochter high
Pit dip
Plenishing furniture, domestic equipment
Ploy activity
Poke bag
Policies grounds within an estate
Poll pool
Provost mayor
Puddock frog
Quaich shallow, two-handled drinking bowl
Rath fort
Reek smoke
Reidh smooth
Rig ridge
Ross peninsula
Roup auction
Ru, rhu, row, rubha point
Sark shift, shirt
Saugh willow
Scunner dislike
Selkie seal
Sgeir, skerry sea rock
Sgor, scuir, sgurr sharp rock
Sheiling hut for summer pasture
Sherif county court judge
Shinty form of hockey
Siccar certain
Siller silver (money)
Slochd hollow, grave

Sonsie bonnie
Soutar cobbler
Spittal hospice
Stob stake, point
Strath broad valley
Strone nose, promontory
Struan, struth stream
Swither vacillate
Syne ago
Tarbert, tarbet isthmus
Tassie cup
Thing parliament, council
Thole endure
Thrang thronged
Thrawn awkward
Tigh house
Tir land
Tobar well
Tocher dowry
Tod fox
Tom hillock
Toom empty
Torr hill
Tow rope
Tulloch, tilly, tully knoll
Uachdar upper, high
Uamh cave
Uig sheltered bay
Uisge water
Uisge beatha water of life (whisky)
Unco strange; very
Usquebaugh whisky
Vennel alley
Voe narrow bay, fiord
Wean child
Weems caves
Whaup curlew
Whinn gorse
Wick, vik bay
Wight strong
Wynd alley
Yett gate

Index

Main page references are in **bold**. Page references to maps are in *italics*.

Scotland touring atlas

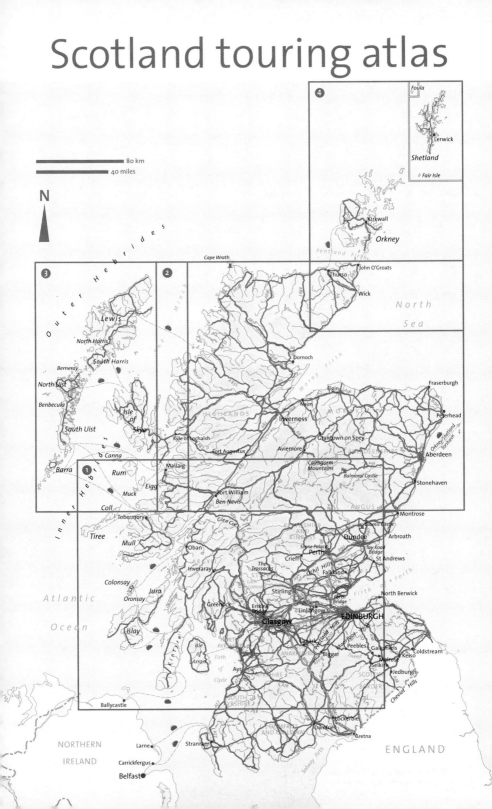

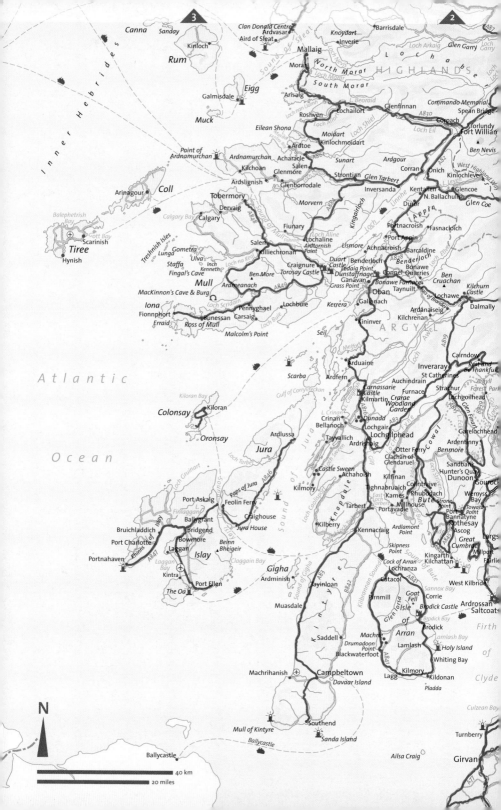

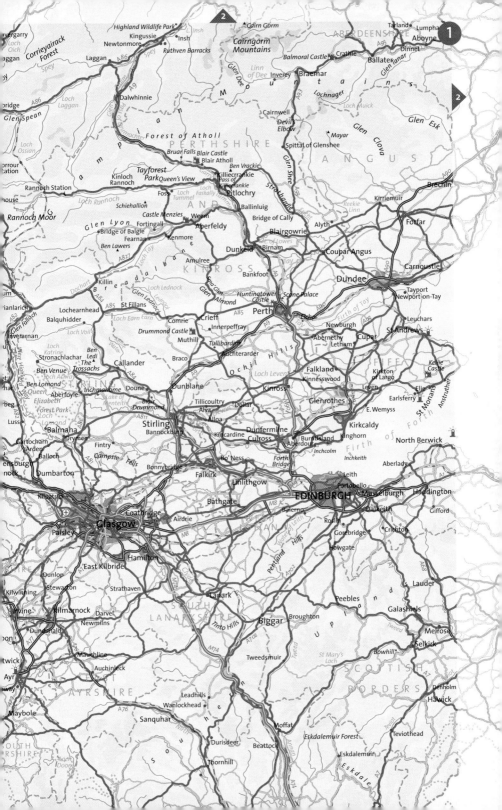

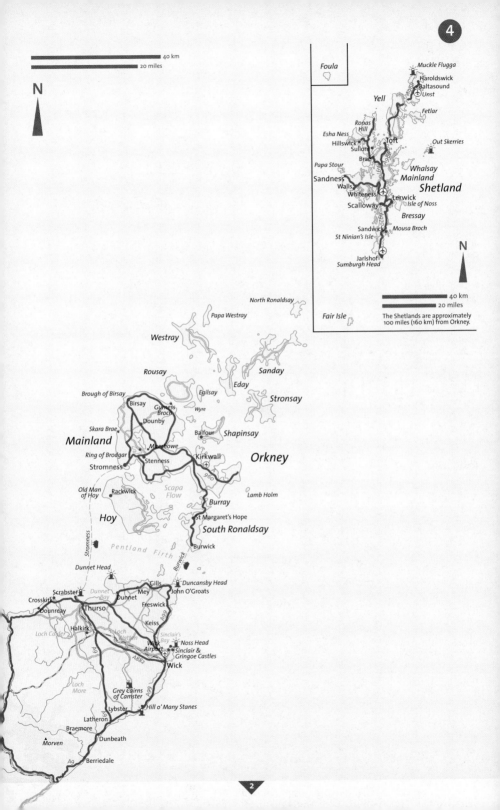

DUBLIN
Mary-Anne Gallagher

VENICE
Dana Facaros & Michael Pauls

BARCELONA
Dana Facaros & Michael Pauls

CADOGANguides

Cadogan City Guides...
the life and soul
of the city

CADOGANguides
well travelled **well read**